REA

General Crook and the
Western Frontier

GENERAL CROOK AND THE WESTERN FRONTIER

By Charles M. Robinson III

University of Oklahoma Press : Norman

ALSO BY CHARLES M. ROBINSON III

Frontier Forts of Texas (Houston, 1986)
The Frontier World of Fort Griffin: The Life and Death of a Western Town (Spokane, 1992)
Bad Hand: A Biography of General Ranald S. Mackenzie (Austin, 1993)
The Court Martial of Lieutenant Henry Flipper (El Paso, 1994)
The Buffalo Hunters (Austin, 1995)
Shark of the Confederacy: The Story of CSS Alabama (Annapolis, 1995)
A Good Year to Die: The Story of the Great Sioux War (New York, 1995; Paperback, Norman, 1996)
Hurricane of Fire: The Union Assault on Fort Fisher (Annapolis, 1998)
The Indian Trial: The Complete Story of the Warren Wagon Train Massacre and the Fall of the Kiowa Nation (Spokane, 1997)
Satanta: The Life & Death of a War Chief (Austin, 1998)
The Men Who Wear the Star: The Story of the Texas Rangers (New York, 2000)

Library of Congress Cataloging-in-Publication Data

Robinson, Charles M., 1949–
    General Crook and the western frontier / by Charles M. Robinson III.
       p.   cm.
    Includes bibliographical references (p.) and index.
    ISBN 0–8061–3358–9 (alk. paper)
       1. Crook, George, 1829–1890.   2. Indians of North America—Wars—1866–1895.
    3. Generals—United States—Biography.   I. Title.

E83.866.C94 R62 2001
973.8'092—dc21
[B]

                                                                          2001027626

1 2 3 4 5 6 7 8 9 10

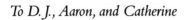

To D. J., Aaron, and Catherine

Contents

—m—

Contents

ILLUSTRATIONS

FIGURES

MAPS

PREFACE

—ⅷ—

MODERN WRITING ABOUT THE INDIAN WARS is challenging because of the changes in perception as these conflicts retreat farther into our history. It becomes all the more difficult because history cannot be broken down into the simple terms of Indian vs. government; Indians fought on both sides. For ease of identification, and for no other reason, I have chosen to refer to the Indians opposing the government as "hostile" in contrast to the "friendly" or "government" Indians, although many "friendlies" were members of the same tribal or national groups as "hostiles." This is not a matter of judgment because, indeed, the "hostiles" often had valid reasons for their hostility.

This is the story of one soldier whose duty often compelled him to fight Indians. Consequently, much of the story is told from the military perspective. I have not attempted to present an overview of the various government policies or settlers' attitudes toward Indians, but discuss them only so far as they relate to the life and career of General George Crook.

I wish to extend special appreciation to two friends, Robert M. Utley, Georgetown, Texas, and Paul Hedren, O'Neill, Nebraska, who went over the manuscript with the proverbial "fine-toothed comb." Their unsparing comments, and their advice and encouragement have created a much better book than otherwise might have been. Paul Hedren was also kind enough to provide copies of Crook's order to the Black Hills miners and Charles King's *Major-General George Crook, United States Army.*

Special thanks also go to Dr. Valerie Sherer Mathes, Sonoma, Calif., for going over the manuscript in general, and especially for her insights into Helen Hunt Jackson and the Indian rights movement.

I am indebted to the Henry E. Huntington Library and Art Gallery, San Marino, California; the Special Collections Department of Meriam Library, California State University–Cisco; the University of Oregon Library, Eugene; the Interlibrary Loan Department of South Texas Community College Library, McAllen; and Alicia Patino in the Interlibrary Loan Department of the University of Texas–Pan American Library, Edinburg.

I am also indebted to the Kansas State Historical Society at Topeka, the Nebraska State Historical Society at Lincoln, the State Historical Society of Wisconsin at Madison, and the Wyoming Historical Society at Cheyenne.

And to the Little Bighorn Battlefield National Monument, Crow Agency, Montana; United States Military Academy Library, West Point, New York, and the United States Army History Institute, Carlisle Barracks, Pennsylvania.

My appreciation also goes to Nan Card, curator of manuscripts, Rutherford B. Hayes Presidential Center, Fremont, Ohio; the American Heritage Center, University of Wyoming, Laramie; Mitchell Yockelson and staff, National Archives and Records Administration, Library of Congress, Washington, D.C.; and Thomas A. Munnerlyn, Austin, Texas.

Special thanks also go to Paul Andrew Hutton, University of New Mexico, Albuquerque, for providing prints of two early photos of Crook from the West Point Library that were used in his book *Phil Sheridan and His Army*.

I wish to acknowledge the following publishers and holding institutions for granting permission to quote from various sources: The United States Army Military History Institute, Carlisle Barracks, Pennsylvania: George Crook–Lyman W. V. Kennon Papers, Nelson A. Miles Papers, Eugene A. Carr Papers; American Heritage Center, University of Wyoming, Laramie: Thaddeus Capron Collection No. 1694; Archives Division, State Historical Society of Wisconsin, Madison: Rufus and Charles King Collection; Rutherford B. Hayes Presidential Center, Fremont, Ohio: Rutherford B. Hayes Diary and Letters and George Crook Collection; the University of Oregon Library System, Eugene: George Crook Papers (A24); The Huntington Library, San Marino, California: Charles Graham Halpine Papers, Walter Scribner Schuyler Papers, and "Major General George Crook and the Indians" by Azor Howitt Nickerson; The Newberry Library, Chicago: Richard Irving Dodge, diary of the Powder River Campaign, 1876–1877, in Everett D. Graff Collection, MS 1110, published by the University of Oklahoma Press, Norman, as *The Powder River Expedition Journals of Colonel Richard Irving Dodge,* edited by Wayne R. Kime.

The Arthur H. Clark Company, Spokane Washington: *Two Great Scouts and Their Pawnee Battalion* by George Bird Grinnell; University of North Carolina

Press, Chapel Hill: *A Virginia Yankee in the Civil War: The Diaries of David Hunter Strother* by Cecil D. Eby, copyright © 1961 by the University of North Carolina Press, renewed 1989 by Cecil D. Eby, used by permission of the publisher; Yale University Press, New Haven, Connecticut: *The Truth about Geronimo* by Britton Davis; University of Oklahoma Press, Norman: *William Tecumseh Sherman and the Settlement of the West* by Robert G. Athearn, *Indeh: An Apache Odyssey* by Eve Ball with Nora Henn and Lydia A. Sanchez, *The Exploits of Ben Arnold, Indian Fighter, Gold Miner, Cowboy, Hunter, and Indian Scout* by Lewis F. Crawford, *The Indian Reform Letters of Helen Hunt Jackson, 1879–1885* edited by Valerie Sherer Mathes, *Al Sieber, Chief of Scouts* by Dan L. Thrapp, and supplemental material by Martin F. Schmitt, editor, *General George Crook: His Autobiography*.

INTRODUCTION

GENERAL CROOK AND HISTORY

MAJOR GENERAL GEORGE CROOK'S career spanned four of the most important decades of national development. When he entered the army in the 1850s,
the frontier was little known to whites beyond the pale of civilization. He lived
into the year that the frontier officially ended, when the commissioner of census
declared it settled and therefore no longer a relevant factor. The story of his life
is also the story of an era in the history of the United States, and the changes
of his own circumstances and attitudes reflect the changes in the nation during
that time.

As a soldier serving in the last half of the nineteenth century, Crook was an
Indian fighter, and his fame is based almost entirely on his leadership during the
Indian Wars of the period. The historian Fairfax Downey, in his classic *The Indian
Fighting Army,* called Crook "one of the finest soldiers who ever served in the
Army of the United States."[1] Downey was not alone in his praise. It is an image
that Crook very carefully crafted in his lifetime, and has been handed down in
histories of the era for more than a century since his death. Oddly enough, for
a soldier so widely acclaimed as the greatest—and perhaps the most humane—
of all Indian fighters, there has not been a serious modern biography. Perhaps the
best effort was in 1946 when Martin F. Schmitt published *General George Crook:
His Autobiography.* The account is Crook's own through the Rosebud fight in
June 1876, and there it stood at the time of his death in 1890. The remaining
fourteen years of his life were filled out by Schmitt's pioneering research.[2]

Besides the reconstructed autobiography, there is *On the Border with Crook,*
written by his former aide-de-camp, Capt. John Gregory Bourke, who, despite

a subsequent falling out with the general, continued his unofficial role as Crook's press agent, a function he had assumed upon joining the general's staff in 1871.[3] Books about Crook that are not strictly biographical include J. W. Vaughn's *With Crook at the Rosebud* (1956) and Dan L. Thrapp's *General Crook and the Sierra Madre Adventure* (1972).

These efforts notwithstanding, Crook remains an enigma. Much of the problem stems from the scarcity of Crook papers, which appear to have been disbursed after his death. For many years, the whereabouts of his diaries were unknown, despite concerted efforts by the staff of the U.S. Army Military History Institute and others to locate them. Two volumes, covering the years 1885 to 1890 finally were located in the possession of Mrs. Walter S. Schuyler, wife of one of Crook's aides, who donated them to the institute in 1931. Walter Schuyler's own papers, containing much Crook correspondence, are in the Huntington Library and Art Gallery in San Marino, California. The massive correspondence between Crook and the Rutherford Hayes family, together with Crook's letter books and other papers, were donated to the Rutherford B. Hayes Presidential Center in Fremont, Ohio, by the president's son, Webb C. Hayes. The University of Oregon at Eugene possesses many important Crook letters, particularly from the closing years of his life when he and Brig. Gen. Nelson Miles were at odds over the fate of Apaches interned by the government. All these scattered resources must be gathered together and seen as a whole before a reasonably well-rounded—and hopefully accurate—picture of Crook begins to emerge. Yet even this picture is not complete; Crook's personal letters to his wife, which were reportedly in the possession of his brother-in-law, Matthew Markland, in 1905, have not been located, so any conclusions about his marital relationship must be drawn from his known diaries and the writings of others.[4]

Was Crook really as great as his image?

It must be acknowledged that his record of success was the most consistent of any general officer on the frontier. Yet there are many cases where the historical image conflicts with the man. Part of this is due to conflicts within the man himself. Part also is due to the institutional structure of the army, which, during Crook's first twenty years of service, could hardly be called a professional organization in any real sense.

In *The General,* an excellent study of command, Allan R. Millett defines the professional soldier as an educated, efficient planner, a team player who is loyal to the service, committed to its mission and goals, and loyal to his fellows within the service. By the 1860s, this sense of professionalism already had been attained by the highly disciplined armies of the German states, but the United States Army still had something of a comic opera style. The government itself distrusted a large standing army and continued to rely on the eighteenth-century minuteman concept of the citizen-soldier, even in the face of growing technology and the demands of modern war. This disdain was reflected in the U.S. officers, many of whom were drawn from civilian life, and even those trained at West Point showed a distinct amateurishness. They quarreled openly in the public press, did not hesitate to lecture their superiors, and used the privileges of staff or command positions as a convenient vehicle to pursue their various outside interests (in Crook's case, hunting, fishing, and social reform). It still was the age of "great captains" and "gifted amateurs." True professionalism did not enter military thought in this country until the generation of officers that came up after the Civil War, an event that shattered many of the old illusions of citizen-soldier and gifted amateur. By the standards of the day, Generals U. S. Grant, W. T. Sherman, and Philip H. Sheridan were great captains who achieved great results. Crook, his West Point education notwithstanding, was a gifted amateur who attained his goals almost as much by chance as by design.[5]

After Crook's death his senior aide-de-camp, Maj. Azor H. Nickerson, wrote, "Modest, unassuming and unpretentious, he held in contempt pompous pretentiousness in whatever form it was displayed, whether of pedantic egotism, or silly snobbery."[6] This is the accepted view of Crook, thanks largely to Nickerson, Bourke and others, and it has been deemed almost heretical to contradict them.[7] There is no question that Crook was stoic in the face of adversity in battle. Part of this steadiness, no doubt, was inbred; even in youth he was regarded as slow, careful, and deliberate. Part of his caution must be attributed to the uncertainties of the Indian campaigning that took up the greater part of his life. Even so, Crook could be very pretentious. Although he never held comparable rank or equivalent command, he had much in common with Douglas MacArthur of the twentieth century. Both created a distinctive image by which they could be recognized: in MacArthur's case, an oversized corncob pipe, sunglasses, and "marshal's" cap, and in Crook's, a luxuriant, forked beard, white sun helmet and canvas suit, and a mule to carry him. Both men surrounded themselves with staff officers who gave unquestioning loyalty and obedience, and who strove to present their commanders in the best possible light. And both shamelessly cultivated the press, creating an inner circle of friendly reporters and ostracizing those who were hostile.

Crook's efforts were based on his firm conviction (formed through experience) that advancement in the army was based as much on image as on merit.

Early in his career he began to believe that he was denied rightful credit for his achievements, and that other men got accolades for his efforts. Commenting on his service during one of the periodic uprisings of the Rogue River Indians in Oregon in the late 1850s, he complained that another officer arrived at the last minute "to reap the fruits of my sowing, and, strange to say, it has been ever thus through my life. I have had to do the rough work for others afterwards to get the benefits from it."[8] There was some truth to the statement because (incredible as it may seem) the nineteenth-century army was affected as much as, if not more than, today's army by politics, personalities, and the vagaries and whims of an independent news media whose priorities were not always the same as those of the soldiers. But Crook himself was not above playing the political and publicity games and, once in a position of power, made certain he received credit for achievements of his subordinates. These efforts paid off in the postwar army of the Indian frontier, when he was jumped two grades from lieutenant colonel to the active rank of brigadier general. At this time many officers with more than twenty years of service could only hope to retire as captains.

Although essentially a frontier soldier, Crook's four years as an officer in the Union Army during the Civil War were pivotal. He developed many of the personality traits that—for better or worse—would distinguish him for the rest of his life. More importantly, he came to know other Union officers, men who one day would wield power that not only advanced his own career but allowed him to champion social justice for the same Indians he so often fought.

During his Indian campaigns, Crook swung between sagacity and dullness. At times he was innovative, defying convention and achieving spectacular results. Other times, he appeared mentally lazy. All too often, he was stubborn and inflexible, pursuing a course of action long after all evidence showed it was the wrong one, refusing to recognize his own mistakes, and quick to blame others, not only for their failings but for his as well. In the end, however, his good points exceeded his bad points, making him an adequate general officer on the frontier, in a time and place where being adequate put him a cut above many of his contemporaries.[9]

Crook's frontier service was a microcosm of contradictory Indian-government relations during the second half of the nineteenth century. As a young officer fresh out of West Point, he was an unwilling participant in the vicious "pork barrel" wars of extermination waged against the small tribes of northern California and Oregon during the 1850s. As a field commander, he fought the Lakotas and Cheyennes of the northern plains and, in his most famous exploits, campaigned against the Apaches of Arizona. As he rose in rank and prestige, however, he lobbied to obtain some form of dignity and self-sufficiency for the people whose way of life he was helping to destroy.

The "Indian question" had troubled some consciences since the earliest English settlement in North America, but the organized campaign to respect the Indian as a human being grew out of the antebellum abolition movement. With the end of slavery, the former abolitionists turned their efforts toward Indian rights. Westerners wrote them off as quirky easterners who understood nothing about the realities of frontier warfare. They could not say the same about General Crook. He was a *soldier*—a man with a solid reputation as an Indian fighter—a ranking officer of the army—a friend of presidents. And while he urged firm, decisive military action to put down Indian violence, he also believed that the Indian was entitled to the same justice and dignity offered any resident of the United States. To advance the cause of the Indian as a human being, he did not hesitate to use his military position and political connections.

Crook advocated education, assimilation, and self-reliance to make the Indian into a useful and productive citizen by white standards, however devastating they might be to the Indian's own sense of self-worth. In our time, these views may appear condescending and damaging to the very people he professed to help. Crook, however, lived in the nineteenth century, and his goals were a reflection of the reformist attitudes of his era. And whatever faults these attitudes might have in retrospect, they were a major step forward from the often more popular position that the Indians either should be exterminated or reduced to permanent dependence on the government.

As an Indian fighter, Crook gained fame. As a humanitarian, he achieved greatness.

GENERAL CROOK AND THE WESTERN FRONTIER

He believed in keeping his word with an Indian as sacredly as with a white man, and in all his dealings with them he was uniformly just and kind.

—MAJOR GENERAL OLIVER O. HOWARD

He, at least, had never lied to us.

—RED CLOUD

ONE

FRONTIERSMAN

GEORGE CROOK WAS BORN on September 8, 1828, on a farm near Taylorsville, Ohio, which, at that time, was the American West. The United States extended to an ill-defined line somewhere in Utah; the regions of California, Nevada, Texas, and what became the American Southwest still belonged to Mexico. In the Pacific Northwest, the area that is now Washington and Oregon was disputed with Great Britain and, to a lesser degree, with Russia. It was appropriate that Crook would spend the bulk of his life on the frontier because he was, by birth and contemporary definition, a frontiersman.

Aside from his diaries, most of Crook's writings are service-oriented and contain little information about his early life. In preparing his autobiography for publication, however, historian Martin F. Schmitt learned that the family originated in Scotland, where the name is still common, and immigrated to the American colonies in the late seventeenth century. The name appears frequently in military records and other public and church documents of the Revolutionary War era. George Crook's father, Thomas Crook, born in Baltimore County, Maryland, is believed to have served in a local militia company defending Fort McHenry in 1813.[1]

Thomas Crook married Elizabeth Matthews, also of Maryland, on February 4, 1812. The first of their ten children, Elizabeth, was born February 18, 1813. The following year, the Crooks moved to Ohio, where Thomas became a prosperous farmer and civic leader. A contemporary account called him "a good manager, practical, industrious and well-informed. He accumulated 340 acres of excellent land, most of which he improved. He was justice of the peace for many years, and was otherwise prominent in the affairs of the township. In politics he was a Whig, and afterwards a Republican." The farm was situated on particularly fertile land and the construction of the Miami and Erie Canal through Crook property substantially increased its value.[2]

Here the other nine children, two girls and seven boys, were born. George Crook was the ninth child and sixth son, followed by a brother in 1830. In an age when large families were the norm because parents accepted that some of the children would die young, all ten Crook children survived to adulthood. The girls made good marriages, and the boys were successful in their various endeavors. The Crooks lived near Dayton, where good educational facilities were available, and three of the older brothers, Oliver, James and Thomas Crook, Jr., became business and professional men. George, however, was less of a scholar. Described as a typical farm boy, he learned slowly, but retained what he did learn. Older and larger than many of his schoolmates, he tended to protect some of the smaller boys from bullying.[3]

Living in one of the newer areas of a nation that was itself young, the people of Ohio were imbued with patriotism that was heightened by their insularity. Few people traveled. Each community was essentially self-sustaining. Social activities centered around the local churches, and patriotic holidays like the Fourth of July were community-wide celebrations where orators reminded the people of how much they had achieved in how little time.[4]

Ohio itself was only barely tamed. Indian fights were a part of living memory, and trouble with various local tribes still occasionally flared up in nearby territories. The frontier atmosphere created a certain militancy among the settlers that found its expression in war. Although Ohio was not necessarily, as one historian has suggested, an American Prussia (that distinction belonged to the South), it nevertheless gave the Union Army sixty-four generals during the Civil War, including such notables as U. S. Grant, William T. Sherman, Philip H. Sheridan—and George Crook.[5]

As Crook progressed through his teens, the militarism of the frontier was heightened by the Mexican War. Some of the older boys enlisted in local volunteer units bound for the Rio Grande and beyond, and younger ones dreamed of becoming soldiers. In that respect, Ohio was an anomaly. The war was becoming unpopular elsewhere in the North, and the soldier's profession likewise suffered in public esteem. Congressional appointments to West Point often went begging. Consequently, the Buckeye State proved fertile ground for congressmen with vacancies to fill.[6]

It is not known whether young Crook's decision to enter the army was influenced by the Mexican War. More than thirty years later, after he had become a general and a national hero, his seeming reluctance to apply to West Point was revealed by Robert C. Schenck, a former Whig congressman who sponsored his appointment. In an interview with a reporter for the *Washington Chronicle,* Schenck recalled:

> I had looked over the district to find a bright lad to nominate to West Point to fill an existing vacancy. I was unsuccessful. I finally remembered that old Squire Crook, a fine old Whig farmer, and a friend of mine, had some boys, and I sent word for him to come to town. He came in, and I enquired if he had a spare boy he'd like to send off to West Point. After studying awhile he said he didn't know but what he had. I suggested that he send him in. He did so.
>
> The boy was exceedingly non-communicative. He hadn't a stupid look, but was quiet to reticence. He didn't seem to have the slightest interest or anxiety about my proposal. I explained to him the requirements and labors of the military school, and finally asked him, "Do you think you can conquer all that?" His monosyllabic reply was, "I'll try." and so I sent him, and he came through fairly.[7]

Academically, Crook was deficient in the subjects that he needed to enter West Point, so he studied at Dayton Academy where the curriculum emphasized mathematics, natural sciences, and natural philosophy. In December 1847, the academy's superintendent, Milo G. Williams, advised Congressman Schenck that Crook had progressed enough to do well at West Point, and in March 1848, Schenck formally nominated him as a cadet from the Third Congressional District of Ohio. On June 1, Crook paid $115 on account against his expenses at West Point, and a month later officially entered the academy. He enrolled as George W. Crook, the middle initial added at the suggestion of a relative who apparently believed it might add a little extra dignity to his name. He kept the "W" during his period at West Point and during his early years as an army officer, although he had dropped it by the outbreak of the Civil War.[8]

West Point primarily was an engineering school. Strategy and tactics were taught on the lines of a conventional, European-style war. And while this curriculum served the army in good stead during the Mexican War, it did not prepare the officers for the hit-and-run warfare of the Indians in the western territories acquired during that period. Throughout the remainder of the century, soldiers would learn Indian fighting through hard, often bitter experience.

Appointments to the academy were—and to a great extent still are—political. But while politics facilitated an application to the academy, the student was on his own once he arrived. No amount of patronage could help the cadet through the entrance examinations and, once admitted, the undesirables were eliminated by the high academic standards and rigid discipline.[9]

In most of his endeavors at the academy, Crook's performance was, at best, average. Academically, he remained in the bottom half of his class throughout his entire four years, and much of that was spent at the lower end of the bottom. The one area in which he excelled was in conduct, most likely because his class work required so much effort that he did not have time to get into trouble. Only twice does he appear to have committed any serious breaches of discipline, once on May 17, 1849, when he and another cadet were under arrest in quarters "for offering compositions to their instructors as their own which were not original," and on September 7, 1849, when he was assigned two hours of extra guard duty for being absent from drill. He remained in the ranks, generally attracting neither positive nor negative notice. Of the many notable officers who were cadets at the same time as Crook, none mentioned him in their memoirs except for fellow Ohioan Philip Henry Sheridan.[10]

The son of working-class, Irish Catholic immigrants, Sheridan was odd-man-out at the patrician, largely Episcopalian academy, where even frontier cadets like Crook often came from more prosperous families. In fact, Phil Sheridan was not even certain when or where he was born. In his memoirs, and for official purposes, he stated that he was born in Albany, New York, on March 6, 1831, although at least once, early in his career, he informed the adjutant general of the army that he was "born in Ohio." Some historians believe that he might even have been born in County Cavan, Ireland, shortly before his parents emigrated. Whatever the case, he was touchy and combative, and a quarrel with a cadet sergeant over an imagined insult led to a one-year suspension so that he graduated in the class behind Crook. Nevertheless, the careers of the two men became intertwined almost from the beginning, initiating a relationship that descended over the years from friendship to hatred.[11]

Crook's cadet expense book shows him to be frugal, spending his money only on what was necessary or what was "expected" from a person in his position. In the spring of 1850, he contributed one dollar to the Washington Monument fund, and subscribed to pay the academy organist. In his third year, he allowed himself $3.50 for a subscription to the *New York Herald*. That year he also began participating financially in academy social life, contributing toward "cotillion, parties and balls." No fines or serious penalties are listed, although several times he was docked minuscule amounts for "damages to public property," specifically the mess commons, most likely for broken plates, cups or saucers.[12]

He did, however, record several visits to the dentist, one of which cost $15, a very large sum that indicates a major procedure. From this, as well as from diary entries as he grew older, it may be surmised that he suffered from chronic dental problems.[13]

Crook's personnel file maintained by the Adjutant General's Office contains virtually nothing on these formative years as a soldier. In fact, the earliest records in the file are from 1862, when he already was a lieutenant colonel of the volunteers. Consequently, the record of his advancement must be gathered from other sources, such as his autobiography, recollections of those who served with him, and the records of the various jurisdictions to which he was assigned.[14]

Graduating thirty-eighth in a class of forty-three in 1852, Crook was promoted to brevet second lieutenant of the Fourth Infantry, and temporarily attached to garrison duty at Fort Columbus, New York. In November, he was assigned to Benicia Barracks, California, sailing from New York with three classmates, John Mullan, August V. "Dutch" Kautz, and John Nugen. Kautz was a fellow Ohioan and lifelong friend whose career as an officer on the western frontier often paralleled Crook's. Even before entering West Point, he had gained some military experience, having served as an Ohio volunteer during the Mexican War. Like Crook, he had been posted to the Fourth Infantry.[15]

The journey to California would take the young officers from New York to Nicaragua, which they would cross by using the local rivers and the country's great inland lake. Crook recalled that he was so seasick during the voyage that he did not care whether his ship sank. Upon arriving on Nicaragua's Caribbean coast, they transferred to steamers that took them up the San Juan River while they marveled at the great rain forest and the diversity of tropical wildlife. One night, a storm struck, and in the flashes of lightning they could see the rainwater pouring down from the canopy of the jungle. Years later, Crook wrote, "It presented one of the wildest and most weird scenes I have ever witnessed before or since."

At Castilla Rapids, they paid a dollar to throw their blankets on the floor of a hotel barroom for the night, and the next day boarded steamers above the rapids and traveled on to Lake Nicaragua. From there to San Juan del Sur on the Pacific, they traveled overland and were so covered with mud that they waded into the ocean to wash it off their clothes. That night, they set sail for San Francisco and, although the Pacific was smoother than the Atlantic, Crook once again was seasick.[16]

San Francisco was then in the throes of the Gold Rush. Crook remembered the city of that period was

> a conglomeration of frame buildings, streets deep in sand; wharf facilities were very limited. . . . there was mud and marsh which was overflowed by the tides. Everything was excitement and bustle, prices were exorbitant, common laborers received much higher wages than officers of the Army, although at that time, by special act of Congress, we were allowed extra pay [an additional two dollars a day for officers in California and Oregon].[17]

Nor was he happy with army life on the West Coast. The isolation of the military posts—far removed from regular association with other soldiers and the supervision of the army command—frequently created an unpleasant atmosphere that undermined the morale even among the officers, particularly those freshly arrived from the East. Here the post commander reigned supreme, with little restraint on either his official or private doings. Low pay (a second lieutenant like Crook received $25 a month) and a hopelessly slow promotion system frequently drove the most competent officers to resign, leaving the army with aging mediocrities who often descended into alcoholism from the sheer monotony of their duties. In fact, Crook's first duty upon arrival was to serve as file closer supervising the enlisted escort for the funeral of Maj. Albert S. Miller, Second Infantry, who had died of excessive drinking.[18]

Describing West Coast service during the 1850s in his autobiography, Crook wrote:

> Most of the customs and habits that I witnessed were not calculated to impress one's morals or usefulness. Most of the commanding officers were petty tyrants, styled by some Martinets. They lost no opportunities to snub those under them, and prided themselves in saying disagreeable things. Most of them had been in command of small posts so long that their habits and minds had narrowed down to their surroundings, and woe be unto the young officers if his ideas should get above their level and wish to expand. Generally they were the quintessence of selfishness. Everything within their reach was made subservient to their comforts, and should there be more of anything than they wanted, then the rest might have it.[19]

On January 20, 1853, Crook's unit, Company F of the Fourth Infantry, together with Company B, was ordered north to Humboldt Bay, to establish a post that ultimately would become Fort Humboldt. The detachment departed

San Francisco on the steamer *Goliah* [*sic*], on January 27, and arrived at Humboldt Bay three days later. The change did nothing to enhance Crook's opinion of the local military. The commanding officer, Bvt. Lt. Col. R. C. Buchanan, selected a site for the post near the little town of Bucksport, where he not only tyrannized his own officers but alienated the local civilian population as well. To avoid dealing with him, Crook began spending as much time as possible hunting the myriad of game in the surrounding countryside. Although he later said he had always been interested in hunting, this appears to have been his first serious effort, and he confessed his excitement and inexperience.

He also saw his first Indians, the Wiyots, who eked out a meager existence along the bay. "They were poor, harmless, scrofuletic, and miserable creatures who lived principally on fish," he wrote. "Many of them were deformed, and the most loathsome looking human beings that I have ever seen." On the other hand, he seemed to respect the Athapaskans who lived in the surrounding hills, and who were not adverse to killing whites and committing other depredations.[20]

In the spring of 1853, Crook took a squad of infantry to hunt down and arrest a lone Indian for raids on the stock of local ranches. The suspect was brought in and placed in the guardhouse at Fort Humboldt, as much for his own safety against the vengeance of the stockmen as for any other reason. The prisoner, however, escaped, and Buchanan organized the first full field expedition from Fort Humboldt. The detachment, under command of Lt. John C. Bonnycastle, Fourth Infantry, included Crook and fourteen infantrymen. They were to contact the Indians along the Trinity River and impress on them the reprisals they could expect if depredations continued. Although the attacks were largely nuisance raids by only a handful of Indians, Buchanan was concerned that local citizen-volunteers would retaliate against any Indians they encountered, guilty or not.

The expedition left Fort Humboldt in May. Unfamiliar with the country, the troops were slowed by rough terrain and exhausted their rations before they were even close to their goal. The few Indians they saw were wary, apparently believing the soldiers would shoot them on sight. Although Crook later noted the expedition was "without result," innocent Indians were, in fact, massacred in "one of the most fiendish acts that has ever disgraced civilization."[21]

The following October, Crook was promoted to active second lieutenant of Company E, Fourth Infantry, and ordered to join the company at the recently established post of Fort Jones.[22] This fort was located on Scotts River fifteen miles from Yreka, and some 224 miles north of San Francisco via wagon road. During Crook's tenure, the post was visited by Col. J. K. F. Mansfield, inspector general of the army, who reported, "This is an important post from its vicinity to the Trinity and Klamath rivers, and the number of Indians on and about them, and should be maintained till the population becomes sufficient to protect themselves beyond doubt and be secure against massacre. The Indians within 30 miles number about 100 warriors, and are armed with good rifles and guns; and this post, in conjunction with Fort Lane [84 miles away] on the Rogue River, exercises a constraining influence over say 1,000 warriors within 250 miles." The white population within a thirty-mile radius was estimated at two thousand, primarily miners, traders, and farmers, and widely scattered. On the other hand, the report stated the valley in which the fort was situated was "fast filling up" with farmers.[23]

Despite its importance, Fort Jones was all too typical of western posts in the under-strength army. The garrison of Company E was authorized three officers, eight non-commissioned officers, and seventy-four privates. In reality, the company rolls listed only thirty-four officers and men, and often many of these were unavailable for duty because of detached service elsewhere, illness, or various other reasons.[24]

Concerning his inspection, Col. Mansfield noted:

> The quartermaster's duty is performed by Lieutenant Crook. There are no citizens in his employ. His expenditures for the quarter ending 30h June [1854] were 1,346 97/100 dollars, and he had on hand at date 886 81/100 dollars, kept in his quarters. Barley is had here at 6 ½ cents, and hay at 20 dollars the ton, and grazing and wood abundant. . . .
>
> The commissary duty is also performed by Lieutenant Crook. Beef costs here, as required daily, 17 cents the pound; other supplies are brought from San Francisco via Fort Reading and are all good. But a good flouring mill is now probably in operation in this valley, and undoubtedly flour will be had here soon and at a much less cost. The transportation, now being on pack mules and over mountains, is expensive—12 cents the pound from this [post] to Fort Lane. Lieutenant Crook expended in the second quarter of 1854, 553 33/100 dollars and had on hand at date 2,364 33/100 dollars which is kept in his quarters.[25]

Once again, Crook passed his free time in his newly discovered fondness for hunting. "I soon became familiar with all the country within reach of the post. I also used to go hunting with the Indians, and in this way learned something of their habits, as well as those of game." His passion for the outdoors remained with him for the rest of his life, and as he rose in rank, it almost seemed as though he used his army assignments as a means of having free time to hunt or fish.[26]

At this time, he probably either had already developed, or was beginning to develop, other personality traits that would distinguish him. He had no particular aversion to alcohol and enjoyed a drink now and then, but was not known to drink regularly or excessively. He did not use tobacco in any form. He did, however, have a lifelong fascination with card games and played whenever he could, although he was vehemently opposed to any form of gambling. Whenever possible, he rode a mule in preference to a horse, another lifelong trait that perhaps stemmed from his childhood on a farm. His demeanor seemed to reflect his surroundings. When the atmosphere was depressing, he became somber and almost sullen. But in a relaxed situation, he enjoyed laughing and joking.[27]

In January 1854, Capt. Henry M. Judah, Fourth Infantry, arrived to assume command of both Company E and Fort Jones. A West Point graduate with a distinguished record in the Mexican War, Judah nevertheless suffered from severe alcoholism. Almost immediately after his arrival, miners and Indians exchanged gunfire on the upper Klamath. A courier from Yreka appeared at the fort with a petition from the mining camp at Cottonwood, calling for military protection. According to the courier, a hundred Indians hidden in a cave overlooking the river had surrounded and killed some settlers who were trying to recover stolen livestock.

Judah left Fort Jones under command of a noncommissioned officer and, on January 16, took Lieutenants Bonnycastle and Crook, Assistant Surgeon Francis Sorrel, and about twenty soldiers to investigate. At Yreka and at Cottonwood, they were joined by a ragtag group of volunteers, about twenty in all. Judah organized the command into an advance guard, commanded by Crook, the main body under Bonnycastle, and the volunteers in the rear.

The expedition was ferried across the Klamath about noon, and began marching up the bank. Snowfall, although intermittent, was so heavy that Crook later recalled that he sometimes could not see the main body of troops. About dark, the troops halted and waited for Captain Judah and the rear guard, but none appeared. Finally, about 10 P.M., the command started backtracking and encountered part of the rear guard staggering drunk along the trail. About an hour later, Judah straggled in with several more.

"Judah was so drunk that he had to be lifted from his horse," Crook noted. "It seemed that the rear guard had gotten some whisky, and were all drunk and scattered for at least ten miles back." It took another day for the remainder of the rear guard and all the equipment to get assembled in camp. Judah, mean-while, was suffering from the after-effects of his drinking spree.[28]

After a day to reassemble supplies, equipment, and men, and to give the commanding officer and volunteers time to recover, the expedition moved up to falls in the river, where they found the corpses of the slain whites, frozen and partially scavenged by animals. The Indians were barricaded in a cave at the top of a steep slope about a hundred feet below the bluffs. The soldiers, volunteers, and Indians exchanged gunfire, and one volunteer who attempted to peer into the cave was killed. Judah, who was barely in command of his senses, ordered a charge, but Bonnycastle and Crook convinced him that it would be suicidal.

The following morning Crook and Dr. Sorrel were sent to Fort Lane, about two days' ride, to procure a howitzer. The post commander, Capt. A. J. Smith, accompanied them back to the Klamath with the gun and an officer and fifteen men of the First Dragoons. Deciding that the cave was too steep for effective artillery fire, Smith had the presence of mind to determine the cause of the conflict. The Indians, it seemed, initially had been attacked by a party of miners who were attempting to steal their ponies and women. Seven had been killed and the remainder had withdrawn into the cave. When the miners attacked a second time, the Indians returned fire, which accounted for the corpses at the base of the slope. Securing a promise from the Indians to discuss the problem when warm weather came, Smith dismissed the expedition and returned with his men to Fort Lane. Judah took his troops back to Fort Jones where, to avoid charges of drunkenness by Bonnycastle, he took an extended leave. When spring came, the Indians came down from the cave and were escorted to their homes by Bonnycastle, although sporadic killings continued.[29]

During Judah's absence, Bonnycastle commanded the post. The only other officers were Crook, who would distinguish himself in the Union Army in the coming Civil War, Bvt. Second Lt. John Bell Hood, later a famous Confederate general, and Dr. Sorrel, who likewise would serve the Confederacy.[30]

In the 1850s, the government began seriously to consider a transcontinental railroad. Because the army had engineers available, the War Department was charged with military and geographical surveys of the country west of the Mississippi. Among the requirements was a general investigation of the Pacific Northwest, including terrain, geology, fauna and flora. On May 1, 1855, Secretary of War Jefferson Davis ordered Lt. R. S. Williamson of Topographical Engineers to make a two-stage survey. The first would determine the feasibility of a railroad connecting the Sacramento Valley in California with the Columbia River in Oregon, and the second would examine the practicality of a route through the Sierra Nevada between San Francisco and Salt Lake City. William-son would be assisted by Lt. Henry L. Abbot, who served as second in command.[31]

Williamson himself was an experienced soldier, having already spent several years on the West Coast attached to the staff of the commanding general. During that time, he had made several reconnaissances in California, and several of the routes that the expedition would use were based on his earlier findings.[32]

The expedition of officers and civilian engineers, surveyors, and scientists left its depot near Fort Benicia, California, July 10, 1855, arriving at Fort Reading eleven days later. Here Williamson picked up the packtrain and a military escort commanded by Lt. Horatio Gates Gibson, Third Artillery. Lieutenant Hood, now assigned to the Second Cavalry, was placed in charge of mounted detail, and Crook served as commissary and quartermaster. There were a hundred men in all, twenty of whom were dragoons and the rest being artillerymen from Gibson's regiment and soldiers of the Fourth Infantry brought by Crook from Fort Jones.

As the detachment prepared to leave, Gibson became ill and, to avoid delay, sent Crook ahead on July 26 with the infantry and packtrain to establish an advance camp. It did little good, however, because there were not enough mules to handle all the supplies and equipment. Some animals were loaded with as much as three hundred pounds, causing further delays. Although Crook had no comment on the situation, it no doubt was at least partly responsible for the care and attention he would give to the pack trains in later years.[33]

Abbot departed Fort Reading with the rest of the expedition two days later, got lost, and after spending a cold, miserable night, finally located Crook the next morning. Soon afterward, Gibson was able to join the party. Crossing the western chain of the Sierra Nevada near Lassen Peak, the soldiers and civilians descended through the lava fields toward the Pit River. They investigated passes among the mountains, prepared maps, and sent out scouting parties to exam-ine potential railroad routes. The work was hampered by the Indians who set fire to the wood, and the smoke, mixed with the dust raised by the expedition's animals, made the air almost unendurable. They saw no Indians, but smoke signals from the surrounding hills showed their progress was being watched. On August 1, they encountered a hungry warrior whom they took into their camp and fed. He returned the following day with about twenty companions. After giving them food, the whites departed, leaving them to collect the scraps about the campsite.[34]

Two days later, Crook's old roommate, Phil Sheridan, caught up with the expedition as it camped on the Pit River. Now assigned as a lieutenant of the Fourth Infantry, he had been sent to replace Hood, who had been ordered back east to rejoin his regiment. Crook had little to say in his memoirs except that the change occurred. No doubt he was glad to see Sheridan, but sorry that Hood was leaving. They had become close friends and hunted together. They also were partners in a ranching venture. Crook commented that, upon being transferred out, Hood sold his share "while I held on and lost money." He never saw Hood again.[35]

As quartermaster and commissary officer, Crook spent most of his time around the depot camp, while Abbot and Williamson explored the region. With the myriad of wildlife in the surrounding country, he had ample opportunity to indulge his enthusiasm for hunting and fishing. He also studied the animals he hunted, and Abbot called him "a thorough sportsman and a careful and accurate observer."[36] As the expedition explored the Cascade Range, Crook hunted and fished in the mountains, bagging trout, loons, otter, and elk, among other animals. Once he took a couple of soldiers to the summit. "It was one of the grandest and most picturesque countries I had ever seen. The summit must have been from twenty to forty miles in breadth, covered with lakes and parks scattered amongst a heavy growth of pine and spruce timber. From one prominence I counted eleven of these lakes, some of which were six or seven miles in length, and almost as wide. Around some of the shores there were beautiful meadows of luxuriant grass."[37]

Crook's hunting interests corresponded with the scientific needs of the expedition in an era when zoology was based on large numbers of dead animals collected for study and classification. In a detailed listing of all the animals observed on the expedition, Abbot noted that many of his specimens were killed by the officers. Crook provided "a beautiful white gull" (listed in the report with the equivocal designation of "larus eburneus??"), which Abbot thought particularly remarkable because it was taken "two hundred miles from the ocean, and not nearer than about one hundred miles to any considerable body of water."[38]

In early September, Williamson was exploring the mountains while Abbot went up to Fort Dalles. Williamson sent Sheridan to draw more supplies, but Crook had moved the depot camp. Striking his trail, Sheridan followed it until he arrived in the camp where he spent the night. "We had a grand time together talking over what we had seen, etc. etc.," Crook later remembered. "Soon after he left, I killed a magnificent elk and returned to camp, the meat of which was a godsend to all in camp."[39]

In his memoirs, Sheridan said virtually nothing about hunting and fishing, preferring to dwell on various Indian scares. The Indians, however, proved more of a help than a threat, showing the best routes and fords, and providing information on conditions ahead. Abbot's report frequently mentions visits to Indian camps, and contains considerable information on the soon-to-vanish native life and customs of the Pacific slope. Crook added to the knowledge by helping Williamson compile a partial vocabulary of the Klamath language from Indians who wandered into camp.[40]

Williamson took the main party to Oregon City on the Willamette. Here he discharged Gibson's men, allowing them to return to Fort Jones and Fort Reading, but kept Sheridan's cavalry escort. His own health was failing, and he wanted to prepare for the second phase of the expedition—into the Sierra Nevada—the following spring. So he left Crook in charge to await Abbot, while he took the steamer back to San Francisco.

Abbot rejoined the group on October 19, in time for an Indian outbreak along the Rogue River. Sheridan's cavalry was detached over Abbot's protests and ordered to join an expedition against the Indians. Abbot took the remnants of the expedition and started back south toward Fort Reading. En route, they saw signs of the war—a wagon with dead oxen in their yokes and a blood-stained seat, ruined crops in the fields, and dead swine and other domestic animals. The Indians had burned the grass, and the expedition's animals began to get hungry. Nevertheless, they reached Fort Lane without difficulty. Continuing south toward Fort Jones, they encountered a detachment headed for the war zone under Captain Judah, now returned from his extended leave. The captain ordered Crook to remain at Jones and resume his duties there. The survey expedition reached the fort on November 8 and spent the next two days settling accounts, after which Abbot continued on to Fort Reading.[41]

In their separate scouting parties, Abbot and Williamson filled in many of the voids on the map of northern California and Oregon, both discovering practical railroad routes north from San Francisco. The survey ultimately would assure San Francisco's place as the western terminus for a future transcontinental line.[42]

It also drew attention to Crook as a competent, reliable officer. In his letter transmitting the official report to Secretary Davis, Abbot gave a general summary of expedition personnel, then wrote, "Of those who accompanied me when detached from the main command, I feel at liberty to speak in less general terms. Lieutenant Crook, who was the only officer with me, officially and personally contributed, in a high degree, to the success and harmony of the expedition."[43]

The survey of the Sierra Nevada never materialized. Before he could get it organized, Williamson was ordered back to Washington, and ultimately the project was canceled.[44]

TWO

Indian Fighter

The sporadic fighting in the Pacific Northwest gave Crook his first experience in the so-called Indian question, which, more than anything else, would define him both as a soldier and a man. Because so much of his life would be spent dealing with the situation, it deserves some examination.

Racism and greed certainly were motivating factors in nineteenth-century white attitudes, but the animosity was far more deeply ingrained in the white psyche. It began with Columbus's first voyage when he encountered the previously unknown, indigenous, Western Hemispheric people that Europeans would call "Indian." This discovery traumatized the Europeans, themselves only just emerging from the Middle Ages, because it went against all their historic knowledge of the world. Unable to explain or even comprehend the existence of the American Indian through contemporary learning, Europeans turned to religion. God, they reasoned, had created the human race in His own image, yet these people were different in both appearance and custom from anyone in their previous experience. They knew, however, that God had placed a mark on Cain as punishment for the murder of his brother, casting him out to live in the wilderness. They also knew that Noah had cursed his dark-skinned son, Ham, and his heirs to an eternity of servitude, and that the sons of Noah had been dispersed over the face of the earth. The American Indian, therefore, must be part of that accursed, debased race, unworthy of any esteem. The Indian's person, therefore, was undeserving of respect, and any rights of property or prior occupancy did not need particular consideration. By the nineteenth century, the notion that the Indians were an inferior race had become a convenient rationale for seizing their lands and killing them. Nevertheless, the religious aspect of Indian-white relations remained so strong that even the clergy of the period (with the admirable exception of the Roman Catholics) saw no incongruity in calling for the extermination of American Indians, as well as the exclusion of blacks, Asians, and Mexicans of mixed or Indian heritage from the mainstream of American life.[1]

The antebellum army in which Crook served was caught in the middle of the brutal white-Indian conflict, created to a large extent by the whites who were aided and abetted by the civil governments of the recently admitted state of California and the territory of Oregon. The unruly mining communities especially wanted the Indians exterminated, and California, through a series of deliberate legal lapses and loopholes, was ready to encourage it. Many miners and settlers had learned to hate Indians as a race from dealings with the tribes of the plains during their westward trek and, upon arrival, transferred that hatred to the generally inoffensive local tribes. Even those who did not consciously hate Indians at least feared them and were willing to keep silent while they were massacred. For the later arrivals of the mid-1850s, it was all the more easy, because the local Indians were already being debased by contact with those who had come earlier. The white people of the mining districts in California or Oregon needed little excuse or justification; they simply murdered Indians when it was convenient. And because most California and Pacific Northwest tribes were small, often speaking mutually unintelligible languages, and beset with various local jealousies, there was little opportunity to organize or resist as did the tribes in the East or on the plains.[2] As the great Western historian Hubert Howe Bancroft pointed out later in the century, "The savages [*sic*] were in the way; the miners and settlers were arrogant and impatient; there were no missionaries or others present with even the poor pretense of soul-saving or civilizing. It was one of the last human hunts of civilization, and the basest and most brutal of them all."[3]

Bancroft might have noted, as did historian Robert Utley a hundred years later, that the military's position was particularly unenviable. Many of the soldiers sympathized with the Indians, but were forced to fight them anyway; their duty was to protect the citizenry from Indian outbreaks, almost invariably provoked by the citizens themselves.[4] Crook was among those who believed the Indians had just grievances. Pointing to the plight of the nearby Shastas, he wrote they were "generally well disposed, but more frequently forced to take the warpath or sink all self respect, by the outrages of the whites perpetrated upon them." Crook continued: "It was of no unfrequent ocurrence for an

Indian to be shot down in cold blood, or a squaw raped by some brute. Such a thing as a white man being punished for outranging an Indian was unheard of. It was the fable of the wolf and lamb every time. The consequence was that there was scarcely ever a time that there was not one or more wars with the Indians somewhere on the Pacific Coast."

He blamed much of the problem on greed by the white settlers and indifference by the federal government. More and more, he became convinced that the Indian was the victim as often as not. As he rose in rank, his concern over Indian rights and grievances increasingly would occupy his thoughts and efforts even as he carried out the government's policies of Indian suppression.[5]

Interestingly enough, the greed of white settlers was not a key factor in the Rogue River War that had disrupted the survey expedition to which Crook belonged; the tribes of Oregon's Rogue River Valley had already lost most of their land in treaties that followed an earlier uprising in 1853. On the other hand, white intolerance—the belief that all Indians were inherently savage—and white abuse were key factors, as was an unrelated political dispute between the Democratic Party and the Know-Nothings, an anti-Catholic, anti-foreign, white supremacist faction that challenged the Democrats' dominance of territorial politics. This dispute ultimately spilled over into the reservation set aside for the Rogue River tribes, undermining the authority of the government officials responsible for its administration. Sporadic clashes erupted between Indians and whites.

Besides these factors, the area was beset by a drought that dried up the watercourses essential to mining operations in the area. Mining was the lynchpin of the region's economy, and the large number of unemployed miners needed some other source of revenue. By midsummer, many whites began to see an Indian war as the answer to the area's economic problems; the unemployed miners could serve for pay as volunteer troops, and the amount of provisions required by an Indian campaign would bring a badly needed boost to local merchants. Sporadic fighting erupted between Indians and whites, culminating in a pitched battle on October 8, when whites attacked an Indian camp. By the end of the following day, retaliatory raids by Indian warriors had left a trail of devastation along the roads and farms of the Rogue River Valley.[6]

Crook saw very little action during the first months of the Rogue River War. The closest he came was during the return trip with Abbot to Fort Jones at the end of October 1855. Expedition members had gone into camp at a wayside inn known as the Six-Bits House, where they learned that a detachment of regulars and volunteers from Fort Lane under Captain Smith had been badly mauled in a fight with Indians the day before. That afternoon a company of the Second Oregon Mounted Volunteers also pitched camp at the Six-Bits House. Their nominal commander was Capt. Laban Buoy, but Crook noted his orders were generally met with shouts of "Go to hell!" and similar insubordination.

"A motlier crew has never been seen since old Falstaff's time," Crook noted. "They were mounted on horses and mules of all sizes and degrees, some wore plug hats, and others caps; all were mostly armed with old-fashioned squirrel rifles."[7]

Arriving at Fort Jones, Crook as the senior officer present assumed command of the post until December 10, when Judah returned from the field. After an uneventful winter, Crook was ordered, in March 1856, to take Company E up to Fort Lane. Upon arriving, Captain Smith told him to escort two friendly bands of Rogue River Indians to a reservation where they would be out of harm's way. He performed the task and was preparing to return to Lane when a group of whites concealed in the brush opened fire and killed one of the Indians. Crook followed their trail for several miles before losing it.

Back at the post, he developed rheumatism in his left shoulder and an abscess in his left arm, and was unable to lead his company when it left for the field several days later. Although he recovered, his arm was weak and stiff for a year. He also seems to have suffered a mild case of addiction to the morphine he was administered as a pain killer because he noted, "It was some time before I could sleep well without it."[8]

On March 11, 1856, Crook was promoted to first lieutenant of Company D, Fourth Infantry. Near the end of the month, he was ordered back to Fort Jones, which was then under command of Bvt. Maj. F. O. Wyse, Third Artillery. Two months later, Crook was sent down the Rogue River with a company of Third Artillery to join an expedition under Captain Smith, during which he would assume command of Company E. Uncertain of Smith's whereabouts, Crook had to search for him. In the meantime, on May 27 and 28, Smith and about eighty men had engaged a large band of Indians, losing about a third of his command in killed and wounded before a relief column arrived under command of Capt. Christopher C. Augur.

Crook, meanwhile, was moving down the river on foot through rough terrain. While hunting, he encountered a group of Indian women and children, who told him that they had become separated from the main band, but that most of their people had been rounded up by the soldiers. Reaching the confluence of the Rogue and the Illinois, Crook noted "everything pointed to the fact that both troops and Indians had moved down the river at some time previous, together," which, as far as he was concerned, corroborated the statements of the women. Backtracking to Fort Lane, Crook learned the Indians had surrendered and were being sent to reservations along the coast of Oregon. The captured women were sent to join them.[9]

The Rogue River War ended in the summer of 1856, in part because of military action and in part because the heavy influx of whites drove the Indians away and cut them off from their food sources. The effect was devastating. Between fighting and starvation, they had lost about eighty percent of their population, and approximately eight thousand square miles of territory. The survivors were rounded up, loaded on steamers, and transported down the Columbia River for concentration on the coastal reservations.[10]

For the time being, the region was quiet. In February 1857, however, the Indians on the Pit River, some hundred miles east of Yreka, destroyed Lockhart's Ferry on the river, killed five settlers, and slaughtered livestock. The region was separated from Yreka and Fort Jones by a high mountain range and the passes were snowbound. Consequently, Captain Judah, once again in command at Jones, secured agreement from departmental headquarters to wait until the weather cleared before sending a detachment to police the area. While the army waited, the settlers took matters into their own hands, forming a volunteer unit that killed more than fifty Indians and took sixteen children captive.

On May 18, Judah mounted his two infantry companies, D and E, on mules and led them over the mountains to the Pit River. After five days through still-heavy snow, they reached the river, which his men crossed on a log raft, losing one mule in the process. Verifying the story of the attack, Judah spent the next several days marching around the area. Several times they sighted Indians but were unable to come close enough to have any effect. Determining any further effort was futile, he decided to return to Fort Jones with the bulk of his men, leaving Crook with twenty-five soldiers on the Pit "for the purpose of protecting travel upon the wagon road between Shasta and Yreka, as well as the ferry at this point."[11]

Crook was not enthusiastic. "I fully realized the situation, and knew that there were plenty of Indians, and that my only show was to find where the Indians were, without their knowledge, and to attack them by surprise. I furthermore was satisfied that they watched our movements all the time, and kept out of our way."

On the plus side, he speculated that with Judah taking most of the troops back to Fort Jones, the Indians might become less cautious. Accordingly, he took two men and scouted the area southeast of the ferry to see if he could locate the Indian camps. On the second day, they ran across a camp and the Indians, seeing them, signaled for a parley. Not allowing them to approach, Crook explained that he and his men were heading toward Yreka, a statement the Indians seemed to accept. Then he rode back to the ferry to gather up the remainder of his men.

After a night march, they relocated the Indian camp, then lay concealed all day, hoping to surround the Indians at daylight the following morning. By some mix-up, however, the troops became scattered and it took the remainder of the night and part of the morning to reassemble. By the third morning, the Indians had abandoned the camp.

Finding the Indian trail, the troops followed until they saw Indians scattering in front of them. Crook was excited and grew careless. He chased down one warrior and shot him, but suddenly found himself surrounded by warriors, their arrows flying. Wheeling about, he spurred his horse back to find his men, and returned to the scene. By now, the Indians had scattered again, and the soldiers found only an Indian woman tending the body of the man Crook had killed. "This was my first Indian," he noted.[12]

Crook realized the Indians in the district would be wary, and so returned to his camp at Lockhart's Ferry. On June 7, however, marauders stole three horses from settlers at the head of the valley and, two days later, he took five men north, hoping to head them off. The next morning, Crook's party followed the river into a nine-mile stretch of canyon.[13] "It afforded good protection to the Indians," Crook wrote. "The old emigrant road passed near the place, and it was always considered very dangerous."

Riding along the bluff, they rounded a bend and spotted an Indian camp by the river. The Indians saw them at the same time; some dove into the river while others took refuge in the rocks. Dismounting, Crook led his men down the slope, and shot one warrior who was trying to swim the river with his bow and arrows and wolf robe over his head. "He sank, and the robe and weapons floated down the stream," he recalled.

Crook was reloading his muzzle-loader when his guide shouted, "Look out for the arrows!" Almost simultaneously, he felt one strike his thigh and penetrate three or four inches. He jerked out the shaft, but the flint point stayed in his leg. He began pulling himself up the slope, but by the time he reached the top, he was covered with sweat and "deathly sick."

The fighting broke off, and Crook managed to mount his horse. By the time the soldiers reached their camp by the ferry, however, his groin was "all green." For two days, Crook suffered. He did not want to notify Captain Judah at Fort

Jones because he knew he would be ordered back to post and, given the animosity between the two men, he preferred to remain in the field. By June 12, however, he could no longer bear the pain and sent his guide back with a report of the fight. Even so, he tried to downplay the incident, telling Judah, "I wish you would have the kindness to send out someone to extract the flint. I feel confident that if it was out I would be able to ride in 3 or 4 days & attend to my duty."

The garrison at Fort Jones sprang into action. Judah ordered Lieutenant Hiram Dryer, Fourth Infantry, to take twenty-five men and a surgeon to Crook's camp and assume command. Dryer was to "use all the means at his disposal for the punishment of the Indians recently engaged with the force under Lieut. Crook. . . ." With his men mounted on mules, Dryer managed to cover the 110 miles in sixty-nine hours. The surgeon, Dr. C. C. Keeney, examined Crook's wound and speculated that the arrow shaft had been tainted by running it through a piece of fresh liver permeated with rattlesnake venom. Under the circumstances, he believed it was best to leave the arrow point in the wound and let the infection run its course. In 1886, on the twenty-ninth anniversary of the fight, Crook noted in his diary, "still have arrowpoint in my leg." It was never removed.[14]

During his stay, Dryer found many of Crook's animals without shoes and therefore too lame to be of any use. He managed to have enough horses reshod so that, together with his own mules, he could mount twenty-five men for a three-day scout up the east branch of the Pit River, which failed to locate any major Indian activity. Returning to the ferry, he learned that during his absence, Crook ordered all the useless animals shot. Even so, grass for the mules at the ferry was not adequate, and that circumstance, together with "whisky shops (over which I have no control) becoming too numerous near Camp," prompted Dryer to move the detachment ten miles up the west branch of the river, where there was good water and grass.

Crook, meanwhile, was healing rapidly and, only twelve days after the fight, Dryer was able to report: "Mr. Crook is very nearly recovered. There being no sickness among the men[,] the detachment being larger than is required for service in the Valley, and the number of Rations for the command becoming very much reduced, I deem it my duty to relieve Dr. Keeney from duty with this detachment and send him with a detachment of Thirteen men to Fort Jones tomorrow."

Shortly after sending this report, Dryer led another three-day expedition, which struck a trail. Following it, his party encountered an Indian couple with a child. "The Man we killed," he noted. "The Woman and Child were not molested." He did not say whether the man had tried to fight.[15]

On June 26, Crook was well enough to assume an active role in the camp and, on learning that twenty head of cattle had been stolen by the Indians the previous night, Dryer detailed him with twelve men to accompany the owners in search of the stock. The trail led into a rough, broken field of lava where, despite the large number of cattle, it became hard to follow. "No one but an Indian could have driven those cattle through this country," Crook wrote, "for in addition to the rough character of these rocks, there was a thick undergrowth of brush growing out of the crevices in the rock where a sufficient amount of earth had collected to support them."

They found an ox that had become wedged in a fissure, where it was slaughtered by the Indians. Farther on, they came onto soft ground where the trail was more visible. Soon, they discovered the remains of a large temporary camp with ample evidence that the cattle had been slaughtered, and the unconsumed beef packed for future use. Crook determined the main Indian camp could be found in the vicinity, and so returned to his own camp. Dryer, having received orders from Captain Judah to return to Fort Jones, departed the following day, taking only two men and leaving the rest behind. This gave Crook a total of thirty-three soldiers. Almost immediately, he took the bulk of the command back out after the Indians.

Reaching the temporary Indian camp he had found two days earlier, Crook could see no fresh sign and so, that night, he took one man up the side of a mountain where they looked over the lava beds and surrounding countryside for campfires. Seeing nothing, he returned to his own camp and, the next morning, marched his men north along the base of the mountain to give the impression that he was leaving the area. Then he doubled back to parallel his original trail. Two Indians were killed along the way, but Crook did not bother to record the circumstances. Finally, just before dark, the soldiers spotted smoke from campfires about three or four miles away, out in the lava beds.

The brush in the lava beds being too thick for them to see ahead, they had to wait until daylight for a sense of direction. Leaving two men to guard the mules and the camp, Crook led the rest toward the Indian camp. Eventually, they spotted a lone Indian who was preoccupied with "making something" and didn't notice the soldiers in the brush. The camp was a quarter of a mile away. Crook divided them into three squads, two of which would circle around either side while he took the main group straight in.

One man was left to shoot the Indian sentry as soon as he heard gunfire from the camp. The sentry, however, had seen one of the flanking parties and tried to slip up on them, but was overtaken by the soldier. The Indian attempted to surrender and Crook sent a second soldier with orders not to shoot. About that time, however, shooting erupted between the Indians in the camp and the other flanking party, and the first soldier, not getting the change in orders, killed the Indian. Crook led his group into the middle of the camp. "A worse pandemonium I never saw before or since," he wrote. "We met them face to face, so close that we could see the whites of each other's eyes. The yelling and screeching and all taken together made my hair fairly stand on end."

A clichéd description, perhaps, but both sides were fighting for their lives. Many of the warriors were killed outright, and the rest took cover in the brush. Skirmishers were deployed to flush them out. About eighteen were killed and a like number wounded, most of them mortally. Inspecting the camp, they found it full of beef, leaving no doubt in Crook's mind that this was the band that had stolen the cattle. The women and children were rounded up, given something to eat, and then turned loose.

Scouting the area for several more days, Crook was satisfied that his movements had prompted most of the Indians in the district to scatter and so he ordered a return to camp. The march through the lava beds had taken a toll on equipment and some of the men came into camp barefoot, their shoes having been ripped to pieces by the sharp rocks.[16]

Even as Crook scouted for Indians, the government was pondering various solutions to the trouble in the Pit River country. Two tribes, the Achumawi and Atsugewi, lived along the upper part of the river, and among the creeks and marshes that fed it. They harassed travelers between the Sacramento Valley and Oregon, prompting both the War and Interior Departments to take action. Indian Superintendent Thomas J. Henley decided to send an agent to negotiate with the tribes along the Pit River. Meanwhile, Brig. Gen. N. S. Clarke, newly appointed commander of the Department of the Pacific, opted to garrison the district.

On July 1, a company of First Dragoons under Capt. John William Tudor Gardiner arrived at Crook's camp with orders to establish a post where he could protect the crossings of the Pit River as well as travelers on the road between the Sacramento River and Oregon. As the senior officer with orders to take command in the district, Gardiner became Crook's immediate superior. Crook's own detachment was to return to Fort Jones as soon as Gardiner could "dispense with his services." Crook duly reported the matter to Captain Judah, adding, however, that Gardiner would recommend stationing an additional company at the new post. "I feel quite confident I will be stationed here if they get your recommendation to that effect, at H'd. Qtrs,." he added.

Judah, however, did not appreciate what he apparently considered an infringement on his prerogatives as Crook's company and post commander, nor did he care for Crook's "expressed desire" to remain with his company under Gardiner's command. He dispatched a letter to Gardiner, pointing out that as a matter of courtesy Gardiner should have advised him of any orders affecting troops under Judah's command, adding that he was aware of the need to protect residents of the Pit River Valley and travelers on the road. He also said that, if called on, he would prove to headquarters that a detachment "of from twelve to twenty men" from Fort Jones was adequate for the job, implying that Gardiner's troops were unnecessary.

That said, Judah turned his anger against Crook, pointing out that he had sent Crook to the Pit River Valley on orders from headquarters and, thus far, those orders had not been countermanded. If Gardiner intended to take over responsibility for the Pit River Valley, Judah was prepared to let him. That being the case, however, Crook was ordered to report back immediately to Fort Jones with his troops or face court-martial for insubordination. Eventually, however, Judah calmed down and allowed Crook to stay.[17]

No doubt Crook's desire to remain with Gardiner stemmed not only from his animosity toward Judah but from Gardiner's almost unheard-of decision to name the new post Fort Crook because of the lieutenant's efforts in subduing the Indians in the district.[18]

Even while Fort Crook was under construction, the new garrison was busy with expeditions to pacify the area. In early August, Crook led a scouting expedition consisting of Company D, Fourth Infantry, and Company A, First Dragoons, the first of several such forays for the remainder of the summer, tracking the Indians to their camps and harassing them. His only casualty during the campaign was one infantryman, who recovered from a shot in the chest with an arrow. Operations were suspended on orders from departmental headquarters, where the authorities worried that the continuing military movements might hinder the efforts of the Indian agent, Edward R. Stevenson, who had been sent to deal with the Pit River tribes.

Accompanied by Lieutenant Crook, Stevenson left Fort Crook to try to meet with the Indians. After several false starts, a large group of Pit River Indians came in and camped by the fort. Happy with the outcome, Stevenson next made contact with the Modocs, who also came in. Stevenson recommended that a reservation be established.

If the Pit River district now was peaceful, the Klamath River area around Fort Humboldt simmered, and the Indians on the Klamath reservation itself were growing restless. Indian Superintendent Henley asked General Clarke for troops on the Klamath Reservation. Initially, Clarke said he had none to spare. Then, remembering Crook's success on the Pit as well as his strained relations with Captain Judah at Fort Jones, Clarke ordered him to take his company to the Klamath to protect the agent and determine the source of the problem. In transmitting the orders, Departmental Adjutant William W. Mackall wrote: "Firmness united with prudence is here required, and Brigadier General Clarke hopes to find these qualities, as conspicuous on this new field as were your energy, perseverance and activity on that from which you are now removed." He was to establish a temporary post, drawing on the agency for whatever specialized labor he might need, and was to maintain good relations with the agent.[19]

Crook arrived at the Klamath Reservation on October 13, and began look- ing for a site that was protected, one close enough to the agency to protect the agent but far enough removed to avoid friction between soldiers and Indians. He settled on a grassy flat across the river, against a stand of redwoods. The Indians called the flat "Ter-waw," which Crook took to mean "beautiful place," and so he named the post Fort Ter-waw.[20]

Investigating the problems on the reservation, Crook found the local Indians peaceful. The problem lay with a Smith River tribe, the Tolowas. Although they had been given to understand they would have a reservation in their home territory, they had been uprooted and moved to the Klamath at the urging of citizens of Crescent City. There was not enough food at the Klamath Reser- vation for the six hundred Tolowas, they were congregated with the local Indians whose language they did not understand, and Crescent City residents sought to use them as cheap labor.

Despite the new military post, the Tolowas continued to simmer until, by November, the Klamath Indians reported that the Tolowas were conspiring to murder Crook, Klamath Agent H. P. Heintzelman, and his employees, and return to their homeland. They apparently were under the impression that, with Crook dead, the soldiers could not react. Crook put Fort Ter-waw on alert, but tried to avoid anything that would give the impression he was aware of the plot.

By November 14, agency employees found it was unsafe to venture out of sight of their offices. Three days later, the Indians asked Heintzelman to come tend a sick person. Heintzelman and an employee went but, upon arriving at the Indian houses, were jumped "from all sides with knives, bows and arrows." Heintzelman and the employee managed to hold off their attackers for half an hour until Crook arrived with troops. The Indians fled into the brush and the soldiers fired after them, killing about ten and wounding several others. The rest scattered. About twenty-six warriors returned, along with some women and children. The rest, including about a hundred warriors, returned to their homeland on the Smith River, from which they sent word that they were prepared to fight to the death.

In San Francisco, General Clarke sent word for the troops to remain close to the agency until Clarke could consult with Superintendent Henley and Crook about the Tolowas on the Smith River. There was a risk that the disaffected Indians would spread discontent to other tribes and provoke a general war. Crook and Heintzelman, however, had their own ideas about the source of the trouble. In a letter to departmental headquarters, Crook was blunt.

> There is a party of low, unprincipled whites about Crescent City and vicinity who have been living with squaws, and subsisting off the Indians, and who with a few head men of the Smith River tribe, have been at the bottom of all this trouble. . . . It is these men now, who pretend to sympathize with the Indians and say that they were starved and ill-treated on the Reservation, when to my positive knowledge there has been no just cause given them here, for dissatisfaction since my arrival! And it will be these very same men, if the Indians are let remain amongst them, who will cause a war, and at the close of which, bring in a large claim . . . for services, never performed.

The most serious problem facing the Tolowas on the Smith River was that they did not have time to lay up a winter food supply, and therefore would be forced to steal or starve. Consequently, Crook and Heintzelman believed the Indians should be compelled to return to the reservation. If this led to fighting, Crook was confident it would be confined to the Smith River area, because the reservation Indians were content. Superintendent Henley, on the other hand, was less certain and ultimately decided to leave them on the Smith River, leaving Crook with little to do but protect the agency. Meanwhile, despite Crook's misgivings, the Smith River area remained reasonably quiet.[21]

For the next three years, Crook continued with mundane assignments in the stagnated officer corps of the antebellum army. At various times his duties in the Department of the Pacific took him from the Mexican to the Canadian border. He rose more rapidly than many other officers of the period, attaining the rank of captain on May 14, 1861, after only nine years of service. Even so, there was little opportunity to go higher. In the East, however, the nation was rapidly plunging toward a civil war that would propel Crook up through the grades and set his life in a new direction.[22]

THREE

VOLUNTEER OFFICER

—॰॰॰—

CROOK SAID NOTHING ABOUT the outbreak of the Civil War, but his feelings must have been similar to those of Sheridan, also isolated on the West Coast, who wrote: "Most of the time we were in the depth of ignorance as to the true condition of affairs, and this tended to increase our anxiety. . . . At this time California was much agitated on the question of secession, and the secession element was so strong that considerable apprehension was felt by the Union people lest the State might be carried into the Confederacy. As a consequence great distrust existed in all quarters."[1]

On August 1, 1861, Crook and ten other officers departed San Francisco for New York on the Panama steamer. During a stopover in Acapulco, they got partial details of the first battle of Manassas, and were led to believe the North had won. Arriving in Panama, however, they heard a full account of the fight, and, according to Crook, "a bluer set of people could not well have been found."

Sea traffic from California to New York involved steamer to Panama, where the passengers debarked for the overland journey across the isthmus to Aspinwall (now Colón). There, they boarded one of the giant Vanderbilt "California steamers" for New York. These ships made monthly runs between Panama and New York, carrying the West Coast gold on which so much of the United States' economic well-being depended. Consequently, they were a potential target for Confederate commerce raiders. Although the Confederate high seas fleet was still in its embryonic stage, rumors abounded that commerce raiders were lying in wait for the California steamers, and Crook and his companions found the idea unsettling.[2]

The officers reached New York without incident, and Crook accepted an appointment as captain of the Fourteenth Infantry. His acceptance was returned, however, with a note that he could remain in the Fourth Infantry, and because the Fourth was still in California, it would increase his chances of getting into the Volunteers. Volunteer service in a state regiment was more attractive because the government had frozen regular officers in their positions. State units, on the other hand, were subject to the governors of those states, who jealously guarded their right to appoint the regimental colonels; state officers below colonel were elected.

The concept of volunteer army versus regular army was a carry-over from the citizen-soldier of the Revolutionary War, and the traditional American view that a large, professional army was undemocratic. Contemporary wisdom held that a small standing army would be augmented during an emergency by volunteers drawn from the citizenry. Sometimes entire regiments were organized from a particular city or county, and troops identified with their homes and their states. Regional considerations predominated to such an extent that, as the war progressed, the majority of incoming troop levies were formed into entirely new and often unnecessary regiments, rather than used to build up existing units, and thus the size of the Regular Army diminished, and its regiments fell woefully understrength, while the number of Volunteers grew. In keeping with notions of Jacksonian democracy, officer commissions were based on political patronage and popularity among the troops, which did little to facilitate training or discipline. Nevertheless, the same system offered promise of rapid advancement to an officer like Crook who, at the outset, appeared to be frozen in place if he remained with the regular service.[3]

Having determined that his best course would be to join the volunteers, Crook's next step was to obtain a leave of absence from the Regular Army. He went to Washington to enlist the aid of the man who had appointed him to West Point, Robert Cummings Schenck, who was now a brigadier general of Volunteers. The next day, Crook and Schenck presented the case to Abraham Lincoln. The president advised them that the cabinet had agreed to allow a hundred regular officers to transfer to the Volunteers, but added he would not personally intervene on Crook's behalf because he tried to avoid interfering with the various branches of government.

Next they went to the War Department, to discuss the matter with Adjutant General Lorenzo Thomas. The adjutant general acknowledged the cabinet action, but added that if he had his way no officer of the Regular Army could transfer to the Volunteers. Schenck, who had a running feud with Thomas, "told him that thank the Lord he didn't have his own way, and talked very sharp to him." As a career soldier, Crook was startled at Schenck's attitude toward the adjutant general of the army, but added, "I since have learned that he is little more than a clerk, and what influence he has is generally assumed."[4]

Thomas relented and told Crook it would be necessary "for the governor of some state" to apply for his release from the regular service in order to fill a slot in the Volunteers. Crook then telegraphed Governor William Dennison, Jr., of Ohio that he was free to command a state regiment if there was an opening. The timing worked in Crook's favor because the position of colonel of the Thirty-sixth Ohio Volunteer Infantry was available. The Thirty-sixth Ohio, posted in Summersville, West Virginia, was in a demoralized condition.[5] Although the regiment was only a month old, having been organized in August 1861, there already had been several failed efforts to secure a competent regular officer to command. By the time Crook arrived in mid-September, the regiment was totally undisciplined, on the verge of mutiny, and suspicious of any colonel from the regular army.

In his autobiography, Crook indicated the men had not yet been issued uniforms, and their civilian clothing was already worn out. Many of them were barefoot. Neither the officers nor enlisted men understood the need for drill. Meeting with the officers, he told them he "would not expect too much of them," but that certain basic standards would apply, and he alone would be the judge of those standards. Anyone who failed to perform his duty would be replaced. "I must say that I never saw a more willing set of men in my life," he wrote.

The first few months were a learning process. The men had to be conditioned to camp life, as well as endure the camp diseases, such as typhoid, that claimed so many lives during the Civil War. A large shed was constructed so the men could drill regardless of weather. Additionally, the district was notorious for bandits and was an operating ground for Confederate partisans (Crook lumped both groups together under the single term "bushwhackers"). Pickets had to be impressed with the importance of keeping an eye out for partisan groups. Here, Crook's western experience helped, because the partisans used essentially the same hit-and-run tactics preferred by the Indians. Scouting expeditions were sent to hunt them down, and many were rounded up for internment. Soon, however, the partisans were released and back in operation so that eventually, Crook's scouts adopted a policy of taking no prisoners.[6]

In the spring of 1862, the Thirty-sixth was combined with the Forty-fourth Ohio Infantry and the Second West Virginia Cavalry as a provisional brigade under Crook's command. The brigade was sent to Lewisburg, West Virginia, to act as an advanced observation post for a Union push against the Shenandoah, a 150-mile valley that runs northward through west-central Virginia, bounded on the east by the Blue Ridge Mountains and on the west by the Alleghenies. Lewisburg's location made it the obvious route for any Confederate invasion of the North, and posed a direct threat to the city of Washington. The Confederate units defending the valley were, by and large, mediocre, but this lack was offset by their commander, Maj. Gen. Thomas J. "Stonewall" Jackson, one of the South's most gifted and imaginative officers. Soon after assuming command in November 1861, Jackson determined to offset his disadvantages by going on the offensive. In the months since, Federals and Confederates had slashed away at each other and, although Jackson was giving ground, the Union was unable to exploit the gains and occupy the valley.

By May, Jackson's eighteen-thousand-man army faced two superior Union forces, the Department of the Shenandoah, commanded by Maj. Gen. Nathaniel P. Banks, and the Mountain Department under Maj. Gen. John C. Frémont. Banks was a political appointee who had risen from poverty to success in the civilian world, but was an inept field commander. Frémont, in whose department Crook's brigade served, was a national hero known as the "Pathfinder" because of his western explorations. Yet he was not a particularly impressive combat officer, and his situation was made worse by the organization and layout of his department.

Brig. Gen. Jacob D. Cox, who served under Frémont in the campaign, later wrote, "There was a little too much sentiment and too little practical war in the construction of a department out of five hundred miles of mountain ranges, and the appointment of the 'path-finder' to command it was consistent with the romantic character of the whole." Although the mountain barrier allowed relatively small numbers of Union troops to protect the Ohio Valley behind them, a forward movement across the Alleghenies was hindered by wilderness that made supply virtually impossible.[7]

Frémont's plan, to crowd Jackson from the north in the upper Shenandoah Valley while Banks pushed up from the lower valley, was doomed to failure because of the Union's supply problems, and because the railroad lines in the upper valley were situated in a way that gave the Confederates much greater mobility. The Shenandoah Campaign of 1862 therefore centered around the much larger struggle between Jackson and Banks. Consequently, Frémont's operations had little significance, and are of interest here primarily because of Crook's involvement.[8]

Crook's brigade remained camped on the west side of Lewisburg, where it covered the local turnpike. The town had about eight hundred residents and was situated in a hollow near the Greenbrier River. On the night of May 22, Confederate forces under Brig. Gen. Henry Heth crossed the Greenbrier in an effort to take the town and dislodge Crook. Early the following morning, they occupied the eastern crest overlooking Lewisburg and opened artillery fire on the Union camp.

Reacting immediately, Crook sent his hospital and baggage to the rear, and marched the two infantry regiments into town, where he formed them into line of battle on either side of the main street. The Confederates charged, but Crook's attention to drill and discipline paid off when the Union troops counterattacked, driving the Southerners out of the town and back over the crest in disarray. Crook's men seized four artillery pieces and turned them against the fleeing Confederates. Besides the guns, Heth lost sixty killed and 175 captured. Union losses were seven killed, forty-four wounded, and five captured.

Crook was hit in the foot by a spent ball, "which gave me no particular trouble until the battle was over, when my foot became very painful." Over the next few weeks, his troops had several minor skirmishes but no major battles. Even so, his success in the Lewisburg fight gained him a brevet promotion to major in the regular army "for gallant and meritorious services."[9]

Elsewhere, the tide was turning in favor of the Confederates. Banks was in retreat, forcing Frémont to abandon his plans. On June 26, the Pathfinder was relieved at his own request, and the Mountain District, having served very little purpose, was abolished. In August, Crook's provisional brigade was disbanded, and portions of it were combined with General Cox's brigade to form the Kanawha Division, with orders to join Maj. Gen. John Pope's army in Virginia.[10]

Crook viewed the reorganization with misgivings because he was uncertain how it would affect his own Thirty-sixth Ohio. Having nursed the regiment from its uneasy beginnings in Summersville to a first-class fighting force at Lewisburg, it was, he wrote, "the pride of my heart. I knew every man in it, and had spent so much hard work on it, that I regarded it as one of my own family. I feared that we would be attached to some brigade that would take no interest in it, and feared being sacrificed."

He managed to get the regiment detailed as bodyguard for General Pope. Pope's headquarters was in Centerville, Virginia, and Crook established his camp on a ridge behind the town. From that vantage point, he witnessed the humiliating Union defeat in the Second Battle of Manassas on August 28–30. On the final afternoon, as the Union lines crumbled under an unexpected assault by Maj. Gen. James Longstreet's Confederate division (Pope had not even been aware that Longstreet was in the area), Crook was told to draw his men into line and round up fleeing troops who had been separated from their units. He gathered about "ten or fifteen thousand" stragglers, together with some Confederate prisoners, and herded them back to his camp behind Centerville.

Crook was appalled. "It was my first introduction to a demoralized army," he wrote. "No one can fully appreciate what a demoralized army means unless they can witness it as I did." He saw officers who had thrown away their shoulder straps and swords so they would not be recognized.

A light rain began to fall the next morning, and Crook wandered down to General Pope's headquarters, just as Brig. Gen. Samuel Sturgis arrived from Alexandria.

"Too late, Sammy, too late," Pope remarked.

"Damn it," Sturgis replied in frustration, "didn't I tell you that all that was necessary for you to hang yourself was to give you plenty of rope!"[11]

Crook also formed an impression of Maj. Gen. Franz Sigel, one of the many political appointees that permeated the Union officer corps. That night, as the Union troops withdrew through the rain and mud, he saw evidence of the general belief among the soldiers that Sigel was most adept at retreat. "All was pandemonium," he wrote. "All were rushing to the rear, apparently regardless of each other. The road was one jam of wagons. Every few moments someone would call out, 'Halt! Whose wagon is this!' The reply would almost invariably come back, 'General Sigel's headquarters train,' 'General Sigel's headquarters ordnance train,' or 'General Sigel's headquarters supply train.' Most every wagon or ambulance seemed to belong to General Sigel."[12]

With the retreating Union army jamming the roads to Washington, the Confederate commander, General Robert E. Lee, decided the time had come for the Confederacy to go on the offensive with an invasion of Maryland. Besides relieving Union pressure on Richmond, a thrust into Maryland would draw attention away from northern Virginia, giving the area time to recover from a year of fighting. As it was, northern Virginia's agricultural resources had been stripped bare, and the area was no longer able to support an army, while Maryland anticipated a good autumn harvest. Lee also hoped the arrival of Southern troops would encourage a general rising in Maryland, where discontent with the federal government was widespread. The Confederates crossed the Potomac into Maryland on September 4. On the Union side, Maj. Gen. George McClellan, who assumed command in the wake of Pope's fiasco, was reorganizing the federal Army of the Potomac. After arranging for the defenses around Washington, he moved northwest to intercept Lee.[13]

Crook's regiment, meanwhile, had been relieved from bodyguard duty and now formed a brigade with two other Ohio volunteer infantry regiments, the Eleventh and Twenty-eighth, all under command of Col. Augustus Moor of the Twenty-eighth.[14] This brigade, together with one commanded by Col. Eliakim P. Scammon, Twenty-third Ohio, formed General Cox's Kanawha Division. Each brigade had about fifteen hundred men, and the division also included two batteries of artillery and a squadron of cavalry.

The Kanawha Division itself was attached to Maj. Gen. Jesse Reno's IX Corps which, together with Maj. Gen. Joseph Hooker's I Corps, formed part of the right wing of the army under Maj. Gen. Ambrose Burnside. McClellan sent the right wing on two different routes to Frederick, Maryland, which Burnside's vanguard captured with little resistance on September 12. The only Union casualties were two men killed and seven captured, but among the latter was Colonel Moor, who had rushed ahead with his staff in the excitement. With Moor a prisoner, command of his brigade devolved on Crook.[15]

The following day, the main bodies of McClellan's right and center came through Frederick, and Union cavalry cleared the way to the base of the South Mountain Range, a ridge that runs some forty miles across the Maryland panhandle from the Potomac to Pennsylvania. Here McClellan obtained a copy of Lee's plans, showing he had divided his army, sending part of it against Harper's Ferry and Martinsburg. Reacting with uncharacteristic determination, McClellan decided to force a passage across South Mountain to Boonsborough and Rohrersville, relieve the Union garrison at Harper's Ferry and come up against Lee from behind. Two passes were favorable—Turner's Gap, through which the National Road crossed the mountains and which the right and center would use, and Crampton's Pass, five or six miles below. Although not the most direct route to Harper's Ferry (despite McClellan's subsequent claim), Crampton's Gap would have to be forced by the left wing in order to flank the Confederates. Here McClellan made his first great mistake of the campaign—had he made a forced march that night, he would have beaten the Confederates to Crampton's Gap and been able to relieve the Harper's Ferry garrison with minimal resistance. But, because he did not expect a fight at South Mountain, he opted to wait until morning on September 14, by which time the Confederates had reached the passes and were prepared to defend them.[16]

At 6 A.M., Colonel Scammon's brigade marched from Middleton to support a reconnaissance of Turner's Gap by Brig. Gen. Alfred Pleasanton, while Crook remained in camp. Colonel Scammon's brigade, accompanied by Cox, moved ahead and to the left of the main road to feel out the Confederates and determine the potential resistance on that side of the pass. En route, they encountered Colonel Moor, who had been paroled the night before, and was on his way back to Union lines. As a paroled prisoner of war, Moor was not permitted to give detailed information about the Confederates, but said just enough to convince Cox that a large Southern force covered the gap. Cox dashed back to camp and ordered Crook to turn out and support Scammon. Pleasanton and Cox agreed that the gap was too strongly held for a direct assault, so Pleasanton would make a demonstration on the main road with cavalry and artillery. Meanwhile, the Kanawha Division—Scammon and Crook—would follow the Old Sharpsburg Road through another pass, Fox's Gap, about a mile to the south, flank the Confederates and force the summit. Cox notified Reno, who replied that the column would be supported by the entire corps [17]

Starting toward Fox's Gap along the Old Sharpsburg Road, Crook's brigade moved across a field and up a hill surmounted by a stone wall with timber beyond. Unsure of exactly where the Confederates were, Crook formed his men into line of battle just below the crest of the hill and had them lie down. "Some of our men amused themselves by sticking their hats on their ramrods, and raising them high enough to meet the enemy's vision," he wrote. "A dozen bullet holes were made through them." He now knew that the Confederates held the wall and were formed up in the timber beyond.[18]

About half a mile from the summit, Confederate artillery opened up on Scammon with case shot. He turned off the road and into the timber where his soldiers formed in line, while Crook closed up the rear. The Union men fixed bayonets and charged, the Confederates responding with musket fire and shrapnel. Soon they were over the wall and had broken the Southern line.

"A great many of their men were killed," Crook wrote. "Some of them were bayoneted behind the stone fence. Many more were killed farther down in the woods, near an old well or sunken road."

The Confederates then attempted to flank the division from a high ridge to the left, and Crook sent the Eleventh Ohio to throw them back and drive them from the ridge. On Cox's orders, he moved the Thirty-sixth Ohio to the right. With both flanks covered and Scammon in the middle, the entire Union line pushed forward. Elsewhere, Union troops were forcing their way through Turner's Gap. Fighting continued throughout the day and into the evening and, by next morning, the Confederates had retreated, giving McClellan Turner's Gap, Fox's Gap, and Crampton's Gap. Among the Union dead was General

Reno, so Cox moved up to command the IX Corps, while Scammon succeeded to command of the Kanawha Division.[19]

In his report, Cox commended Crook's "gallantry and efficiency." Crook, however, was less cheerful. Although he considered his losses "comparatively light," he qualified that by saying: "I cannot help but shedding tears over some of my regiment who were killed, and one pretty boy not over 16 or 17 years of age, a nice mother's boy, who lay mortally wounded, whose pleading face looked so pitiable. I had seen so much of them for the last year, knew them all, and felt as though they were my own family." Later Crook's own family informed him that his mother had been born and reared on a farm adjacent to the battlefield.[20]

In pausing the night of September 14 to lick his wounds from South Mountain, McClellan lost the initiative for the last time in his career. With a large Confederate contingent under Jackson preoccupied with Harper's Ferry, Lee's force would have been unable to hold off pursuing federals, had McClellan chosen to pursue. He did not, and the following morning he realized the Confederates had withdrawn from South Mountain and crossed Antietam Creek and were forming up on either side of the Boonsborough Road north of Sharpsburg. About noon, he learned that Jackson had taken Harper's Ferry and was now moving to join Lee. McClellan, then, would face the main Confederate army.[21]

While Lee was deploying behind Antietam Creek, Hooker's I Corps was temporarily detached to move through Boonsborough, while Burnside took the remainder of his command, including the Kanawha Division towards Sharpsburg. Crook's brigade marched past the sunken road where the previous day's Confederate dead still lay unburied.[22]

On arriving opposite the Confederates that afternoon, McClellan found only two divisions in position, with the rest halted "some distance in the rear." Now, displaying his old lethargy, he decided it was too late for attack and, the following day, noticed the Confederates had slightly redeployed, and so spent the day rearranging his own troops as they came into place.[23] "Antietam Creek," McClellan noted, "was crossed by four stone bridges, the upper one on the Keedysville and Williamsport road; the second on the Keedysville and Sharpsburg turnpike, some two and a half miles below; the third about a mile below the second, on the Rohrersville and Sharpsburg road; and the fourth near the mouth of Antietam creek, on the road leading from Harper's Ferry to Sharpsburg, some three miles below the third. The stream is sluggish, with few and difficult fords."[24]

That last statement showed McClellan's total ignorance of the terrain, which he admitted he gave only "a rapid examination." There were, in fact, many places where infantry could ford the stream, albeit in some cases they might have to hold their rifles above their heads. Why the engineers failed to do a more thorough reconnaissance and why the corps and division commanders accepted a cursory examination of the creek at face value have never been explained, but this oversight would be critical to the conduct of the battle.[25]

Confederate artillery harassed the Union troops throughout September 16. Crook wrote that they fired case shot that exploded over their heads and rained "old, round musket balls" on them with little ill effect. That afternoon, McClellan and Burnside looked over the terrain, and decided Burnside would cover the lower bridge. The Kanawha Division was to be divided, with Scammon's brigade supporting Brig. Gen. Isaac P. Rodman's division at a ford where the creek curved deeply into the Confederate side, and Crook going with General Sturgis's division astride the road leading to the bridge. "Crook," Cox wrote, "was ordered to take the advance in crossing the bridge, in case we should be ordered to attack. This selection was made by Burnside himself, as a compliment to the division for the vigor of its assault at South Mountain."[26]

As the battle got underway the following morning, McClellan ordered Burnside to ready his men to assault the bridge and await further orders. Crook's brigade remained in place, although he could hear the sound of firing to the right and to the front. At 10 A.M., he received orders to take the bridge by assault, covered by skirmishers from the Eleventh Connecticut from Rodman's Division and supported by Sturgis's Division. "Crook's position was somewhat above the bridge," Cox wrote, "but it was thought that by advancing part of Sturgis's men to the brow of the hill they could cover the advance of Crook, and that the latter could make a straight dash down the hill to our end of the bridge." Crook, however, missed the bridge, reaching the creek some distance above, where his brigade was brought to a standstill by heavy Confederate infantry and artillery fire.[27] Years later, perhaps in an effort to explain the error, he contended that he was completely in the dark as to what he was supposed to do: "About ten a.m., Capt. Christ on Gen. Cox' [sic] staff came to see me, and said, 'The General wishes you to take the bridge.' I asked him what bridge. He said he didn't know. I asked him where the stream was, but he didn't know. I made some remarks not complimentary to such a way of doing business, but he went off, not caring a cent. Probably he had done the correct thing."[28]

This may have been the case, but as an excuse, it appears thin. In his own recollections, Cox wrote that Burnside and McClellan had set up the dispositions for the battle on the previous afternoon. This is largely borne out by McClellan, whose version of the afternoon meeting is virtually identical in detail. The "Capt. Christ" mentioned by Crook was in fact Col. B. C. Christ, who commanded the First Brigade, First Division, IX Corps, and therefore would have had little, if anything, to do with Crook. In his own report, Christ does not even mention Crook, stating only that at 10 A.M. he was ordered "to support some batteries covering our advance near the stone bridge across Antietam Creek."[29]

Perhaps all these plans and dispositions were devised without anyone telling a brigade commander, but it seems terribly farfetched, even allowing for the haphazard organization of the Army of the Potomac under McClellan, and Crook's version is at odds with everyone else's. Whatever the case, Crook's immediate problem was to get his men under cover and return fire. He called for artillery fire that pinned the Confederates down on the opposite bluffs. Still, the Union assault bogged down, and Crook finally had to pull back. For more than two hours, about six hundred Confederates held down four Union divisions, largely due to the Union command's ignorance of the terrain around the bridge. Finally, under pressure from McClellan, Burnside ordered Cox to take the bridge regardless of cost. Meanwhile, troops from the Twenty-eighth Ohio of Crook's brigade found a ford about 250 yards upstream from the bridge, and five companies crossed in knee-deep water. A second ford was located about four hundred yards downstream, and Scammon's men began crossing there. Cox gave the task of forcing the bridge to General Sturgis, who detailed the Fifty-first New York and Fifty-first Pennsylvania. To clear the way, Crook located a light howitzer amid the heavy Parrott guns of the artillery batteries, and placed it in line with the bridge to fire point-blank into the Confederates at the opposite end. Double charges of canister tore into the Confederates as the New Yorkers and Pennsylvanians dashed across the bridge, followed by Sturgis's division and those of Crook's brigade who had not crossed by the ford. Against heavy Confederate resistance, the Union troops pushed up to the heights overlooking the Antietam. By 3 P.M., most of Burnside's force was across, relieving the exhausted troops of Crook and Sturgis, replenishing ammunition, and placing light artillery. Elsewhere, the battle of Antietam, the bloodiest single day of fighting in the history of the United States, was drawing to a close. As Crook later remembered, "We had our hands so full that we knew but little of what was going on elsewhere, but of course knew that a big battle was going on."[30]

At the end of the day, Crook's brigade withdrew back across the creek to the top of the bluffs where it had begun the advance that morning. "It was heartrending to hear the wails of the wounded and dying in our front all night," he wrote. "Our men alleviated all [of] this suffering they could, but we had to keep ourselves intact for fear of an attack." Although Crook later complained that he had "a good many men killed" when he was stopped at the creek, his losses were comparatively light—two officers and six enlisted men killed, fifty-eight officers and enlisted men wounded, and seven missing. The dead officers, however, were both senior: Lt. Col. A. H. Coleman, Eleventh Ohio, who had personally captured Confederate colors at South Mountain, and Lt. Col. Melvin Clarke, Thirty-sixth Ohio.[31]

Crook was breveted to lieutenant colonel of the Regular Army for his actions at Antietam and, on September 7, was appointed brigadier general of Volunteers. On October 1, he was given command of the Kanawha Division, which spent the autumn reoccupying and securing its namesake Kanawha Valley.[32]

The Kanawha River begins in North Carolina and flows northward through Dublin, Virginia, below the Shenandoah Valley, and up through West Virginia near Charleston, finally emptying into the Ohio River on the West Virginia–Ohio line. Troops occupying the Kanawha theoretically were poised to thrust southwest into Tennessee or due south into Virginia and North Carolina, or to move northeast, around the Alleghenies and into the Shenandoah. As a result, Crook was well situated when he was ordered to join Maj. Gen. William S. Rosecrans's Army of the Cumberland for a push into southeastern Tennessee to take Chattanooga.

Located on the east bank of the Tennessee River, only a few miles from the juncture of Tennessee, Georgia and Alabama, Chattanooga was the hub of four major railroad lines that could supply Confederate troops from several directions. Rosecrans encountered Confederate Gen. Braxton Bragg's Army of the Tennessee at Murfreesboro, eighty-five miles northeast of Chattanooga, on December 31 and, during a three-day battle known variously as Murfreesboro and Stones River, had barely defeated it. Now, as Bragg reorganized his badly mauled army, Rosecrans, who was decisive in battle but otherwise lethargic, settled down and waited for spring while, in Washington, the furious general-in-chief of the army, Maj. Gen. Henry W. Halleck, urged him to move on and take Chattanooga.[33]

Among other things, Rosecrans wanted to build up his army for the push to Chattanooga. In January, Crook was ordered to move the Kanawha Division to Tennessee. The troops took steamers from Charleston, arriving in Nashville January 25, 1863. Here they were augmented by two Kentucky regiments, and again embarked on steamers up the Cumberland River to Carthage, Tennessee, to guard Rosecrans's flank. He emplaced himself on a high eminence that gave a good view of the surrounding countryside, protected by water on the left and rear, and strengthened by earthworks and artillery. "With a force of 6,000," he noted, "this will be a most impregnable position."[34] Two gunboats were assigned to him, but were delayed in coming. In the meantime, he began constructing a gunboat by protecting a steamer with baled hay and cotton, although arming the boat took guns from his artillery. His most serious problem, however, was a shortage of cavalry. "The enemy," he complained to Rosecrans, "has been scouting all around us, and we can do nothing with these small parties without cavalry."[35]

He also had trouble with some of the new troops who had been sent to him. "I found that I had been assigned some 'mauvaise sauvages,' and that I was expected to discipline them," he recalled. "We had no more than landed at Carthage before these men took the town, desecrated the churches by stealing what valuables they had, raided hen houses, etc."

The arrival of six horse companies from Tennessee to alleviate the cavalry shortage only aggravated the discipline problem. "These were the worst yet, perfectly lawless, and with little or no discipline." Rosecrans, he suspected, had sent them to him to rid himself of a nuisance. One regiment, the Fifth Tennessee, was composed largely of loyalists from the immediate region. Their Union sympathies had brought them serious trouble under the Confederates, and now they were out to settle scores. "I had my hands full, what with looking out for the enemy and restraining the lawlessness of our own people." When he tried to discipline them, they accused him of disloyalty, but fortunately Rosecrans upheld him.[36]

Besides shortages, discipline problems with his own people, spies, and skirmishes with the Confederates, Crook also had to deal with runaway or liberated slaves, called contrabands, who flocked to the Union lines. "Contraband women are coming in in such numbers that I cannot afford to feed them," he complained to Brig. Gen. James A. Garfield, Rosecrans's chief of staff. "What can I do with them?"

In the midst of all these aggravations, he was ill, having developed what he called "serious liver troubles," although he did not specify the problem. Because Crook was not known as an excessive drinker, the ailment may have been caused by bad food or water, and the generally unsanitary conditions of an army camp.[37]

On June 2, the Army of the Cumberland finally began to move, and Rosecrans wanted Crook to accompany it as part of Maj. Gen. George H. Thomas's

XIV Corps. General Burnside, now commanding the Department of Ohio, was ordered to relieve Crook at Carthage.[38] Two days later, Crook notified General Garfield from Carthage: "A scouting party, composed of the Thirty-sixth Ohio Regiment, sent to Trousdale Ferry, on Caney Fork, succeeded in capturing 16 prisoners and 32 horses. . . . We are now crossing the river. Have been ferrying all day yesterday and all last night. Will be at Liberty to-morrow."[39]

The command bivouacked in Liberty, where it was augmented by units of Brig. Gen. John B. Turchin's Second Cavalry Division. On June 26, Lt. Col. John D. Wilder's Seventeenth Indiana Volunteers got into a heavy fight with Confederates at Hoover's Gap, and Crook was ordered to relieve him. The weather, so far, had been hot and humid, and most of the men had thrown away their heavy gear, including blankets. The cavalrymen had been ordered to leave their tents behind when they went to Liberty. Now, however, heavy rain set in, and the wet, miserable troops marched through the afternoon, arriving at Hoover's Gap that evening, and digging into the mud.

The Union soldiers were behind a fence on one side of a rise while the Confederates were on the other. Sporadic firing continued all night. "The rain still continued to pour in torrents," Crook wrote. "The troops had trod up the mud into a thin mush of two or three inches deep. I ordered the men to stack arms, and to cook supper if they had any. But they were tired, stacked their arms, and flopped down in the mud and went sound asleep, many of them without blankets."

Crook hunched up under a tree with a "gum coat" or rubberized poncho over his legs and knees, trying to keep dry. The rain continued into the next day, and the wet, hungry men huddled in camp with Confederate bullets hitting the trees all around them. After another night of misery, Thomas's forces advanced and the Confederates retreated across the river.[40]

In July, Crook and General Turchin were ordered to exchange commands. Crook took charge of the Second Cavalry Division, while Turchin assumed the Kanawha Division. Before leaving, Crook sent a special message of gratitude to the Kanawha men, expressing his pride in them and his sorrow at leaving. He praised "their superiority in drill and discipline, their ready obedience to the will of their Commander, their promptness, energy, lofty patriotism, and fidelity to the cause of their country."

The feeling in the Kanawha Division was not mutual in every case. One officer of the Twenty-first Indiana Battery wrote his sister, "I am not dissatisfied with the change—not on account of General Crook, but because he had a staff by no means agreeable."[41]

The Second Cavalry Division was part of Rosecrans's Cavalry Corps, under Maj. Gen. David S. Stanley, whose headquarters was across Lookout Mountain from Alpine, on the Alabama side of the Georgia line and about forty miles south-southeast of Chattanooga. Crook's new command consisted of two mounted units, Col. Robert H. G. Minty's First Brigade, and Col. Eli Long's Second Brigade. There was also an artillery battery under Capt. James H. Stokes. From July through the first part of September, the division was almost always in the field scouting or raiding in Tennessee, Alabama, and Georgia. During one reconnaissance, Crook crossed the Tennessee River and found the Confederates had evacuated an "almost impregnable position." Believing it was a ruse to draw the Union forces across the river, he reported it to Rosecrans, who replied that his information was the Confederates were preparing to retreat. Crook was unconvinced, but said nothing, and continued his forays that resulted in "picking up many stragglers and deserters."[42]

Rosecrans's estimate proved more accurate, for on September 6, Stanley had secured information that Bragg was in fact preparing to retreat. He passed it on up the chain of command to Rosecrans "for what it is worth," adding, "we will try and prevent this, blocking the descent from the mountains." As it turned out, the information was worth a great deal because, over the next two days, the Confederates evacuated Chattanooga, which Union forces occupied on September 9.

The same day, Stanley began a push northward across Lookout Mountain and into Broomtown Valley, toward La Fayette, some twenty miles away. Crook's division was in the lead, he already knew the area, having scouted it and skirmished with the Confederates a few days earlier. Nearing Henderson's Gap, which leads into the valley, he drove back Confederate pickets and found the narrow pass obstructed with logs and boulders. After spending about an hour clearing it out, Crook was able to move into the valley, where he encountered Confederate cavalry and infantry firing from heavy timber adjacent to open fields. Reenforced by Col. Edward M. McCook's First Division, he was able to shove them back, driving them to within ten miles of La Fayette, where he determined Bragg's entire cavalry force was concentrating. He returned with about twenty prisoners.

Stanley, however, was unable to continue his push. He was sick, and his report stated that the "marching had been very heavy, and our horses are very much jaded." On September 13, he sent Crook on another reconnaissance into Broomtown Valley. He struck the Confederate pickets about ten miles from La Fayette and drove them within three and a half miles of town, where he encountered the main force. The Ninth Pennsylvania charged in and snapped up the Confederate pickets, stirring up so much dust that the Southerners in the line of battle could not find a target. The Pennsylvanians returned with seventeen prisoners, having lost three wounded and two missing.

Despite the information on Confederate strength and the harassment, Rosecrans was not satisfied. As far as he was concerned, Stanley was procrastinating and he said so in a blistering letter. Still ill, Stanley asked to be relieved. He was replaced as commander of the Cavalry Corps by Brig. Gen. Robert B. Mitchell. Crook, meanwhile, moved to Dougherty's Gap, remaining there until September 19.[43]

The cavalry concentration reported by Crook apparently was part of a Confederate effort to reenforce Bragg. Rosecrans's position at Chattanooga was vulnerable because his troops were scattered along a forty-mile line in two states, and on September 17, he slowly began concentrating them south of Chattanooga, where they faced Bragg's newly strengthened Confederates along Chickamauga Creek. The following day, Bragg set his own troops into motion, crossing Chickamauga and attempting to drive a wedge into the Army of the Cumberland that would isolate and destroy a third of Rosecrans's forces and cut the rest off from Chattanooga. The Confederates moved with incredible slowness, and Rosecrans prepared to counter them.

The two-day battle of Chickamauga began about 8 A.M., September 19, when two opposing cavalry units on reconnaissance collided and started fighting. The main bodies of both armies rushed in to support. Crook was ordered to reenforce the Cavalry Corps on the front at Crawfish Spring, arriving about 10 A.M., September 20.

The line had been held by a brigade of Brig. Gen. Jefferson C. Davis's First Division, XX Corps, which had an artillery battery lying in a field in front and to the west of a juniper thicket. General Mitchell ordered Crook to take his artillery, relieve that brigade, and "take post at once in front of the fords of the Chickamauga and hold that point at all hazards." The road ran two and a half miles around the thicket. Crook objected to the artillery, but on Mitchell's insistence took two guns.[44] In a near repetition of the scene at Antietam, Crook wrote: "When I reached the 1st Division I found it posted in a woods in front of the thicket, which had considerable underbrush. I asked the officer in command where Chickamauga Creek was. He said he'd be damned if he knew. I told him what my orders were, and he said that the woods in his immediate front were full of the enemy. He knew nothing about the creek."[45]

The Confederates, he learned, had already crossed the creek, and were in a strong position. Crook formed two skirmish lines, dismounted in front, and mounted in the rear, and ordered his artillery to open up "on a certain clump of timber in my front." Confederate infantry and cavalry came charging out. Fighting was heavy and close, and Crook later wrote that once or twice he thought he would be captured. Sustaining heavy losses, he fell back about two hundred yards, where he managed to hold. On orders from Mitchell, however, he eventually withdrew to the corps' hospital, one and a half miles to the rear. At the hospital, Crook placed his men on a wooded ridge behind an open field that the Confederates would have to cross to get to them. This slowed the Southern advance but, by late afternoon, the Union troops were forced to fall back. The fight had cost Crook seventeen enlisted men killed, six officers and seventy-four enlisted men wounded, and three officers and thirty-six enlisted men missing.

That night, Crook's battered troops acted as rear guard to the retreating Union forces. "The whole country was lit up by burning fences, so we had no difficulty in marching," he wrote. "My fear was that they would attract the enemy's attention, and that a flank attack would be made upon us, as we feared that our main army had been badly worsted."[46]

Although Rosecrans had been driven back at Chickamauga, General Bragg descended into one of the periods of indecision for which he was famous, and the Confederates lost the initiative. Nevertheless, anticipating a prolonged siege in Chattanooga, the Federal forces began throwing up defensive works which, Crook commented, "were finished after all danger was over." Soon afterwards, Maj. Gen. U. S. Grant, whom Crook had known as a captain at Fort Jones, California, assumed command of the Departments of the Tennessee, Cumberland, and Ohio, and upon his recommendation, Rosecrans was replaced in command of the Army of the Cumberland by Maj. Gen. George H. Thomas, who managed to hold Chattanooga against Bragg. One of the key elements was the successful Union defense of the railroads into the city, which General Halleck noted was partly due to the near destruction of the Confederate cavalry in separate actions by Crook, Colonel McCook, and General Mitchell. Crook spent much of the remainder of the year in northern Alabama, where he was ordered to "break up a band of cut-throats, bushwhackers, and thieves, and besides to break up an illicit traffic that was being carried on between Nashville and the South."[47]

In February 1864, Crook was named to command the First Infantry Division and the District of the Kanawha in the Department of West Virginia, partly in response to political pressure from Ohio, and partly because Grant, now appointed lieutenant general and named to succeed Halleck as general-in-chief of the United States Army, wanted him available nearer to the Virginia front. Although the transfer undoubtedly represented a step up from a cavalry division in the Army of the Cumberland, Crook commented, "I regretted quitting that army just then, for I stood a good show to have been put in command of all the cavalry of the Army of the Cumberland."

The top spot in the First Infantry Division was available because Crook's predecessor, General Eliakim P. Scammon, had been captured and was being held in Richmond to await exchange. Scammon had gone to Point Pleasant and had taken a river steamer back up the Kanawha River to Charleston. The steamer tied up for the night at Red House Shoals, where it was boarded by Confederate irregulars who made prisoners of all on board. Unfortunately, General Scammon's capture under such embarrassing circumstances was viewed almost as amusing by at least some of the regimental commanders of the division and, as events ultimately would prove, neither they nor Crook profited from the example.[48]

FOUR

The Shenandoah Campaign

In the spring of 1864, General Grant turned his attention to the Shenandoah Valley. He was preparing an offensive against Richmond, and believed a Union move through the valley would prevent the Confederates from using all their resources to defend their capital. The Shenandoah was under the jurisdiction of Franz Sigel's Department of West Virginia. A native of Baden, Sigel had trained as a soldier, but was forced to flee Germany after taking part in the revolutionary movements of 1848. He ultimately arrived in New York, and taught school in various places while holding a commission as a major in the New York Militia. When the war broke out, the federal government embarked on a policy of trying to attract immigrants into the armed services, and Sigel's prominence in the German community led to his appointment first as brigadier general and subsequently as major general. In combat, he proved to be a mediocre commander, but nevertheless served his purpose by rallying the Germans to the federal cause, and for that reason he was allowed to hold responsible positions throughout the war, despite his many shortcomings.[1]

From a military standpoint, the most critical feature of the Shenandoah was not natural but man-made—its railroads. In the Union-held territory, the Baltimore & Ohio cut across the northern part of the valley, providing the main communication between Washington and the Western Theater, and was vital for the almost incessant transfer of troops and equipment. The main line ran directly through Maryland to Washington, while feeder rails opened the back door to Pennsylvania. At the opposite end of the valley, the Virginia and Tennessee Railroad served the same purpose for the Confederacy. Emerging from Tennessee, it ran to Saltville, just inside the Virginia line, then across the southern part of Virginia to Wythesville, Dublin, and Lynchburg before reaching Richmond. Besides being the capital, Richmond was the hub of a network of rails serving Virginia and eastern North Carolina. One of these, the Virginia Central, ran from Richmond up through Hanover Junction and Charlottesville, crossed the Blue Ridge into the central part of the Shenandoah Valley at Rockfish Gap, and continued on to Waynesboro and Staunton before terminating in the Allegheny foothills near the West Virginia line. Thus, the South had two lines in the Valley, both leading to the capital, and both essential to Confederate supply.

A large portion of Sigel's troops was assigned to Crook in the Kanawha region, with the remainder along the Potomac line and in the lower part of the valley. Their primary function was defensive—to protect the North from invasion through the Shenandoah, and to cover the critical Union rails. Their secondary mission was to damage the Confederate supply system by harassing the Southern lines.[2]

As part of his offensive preparations against Richmond, Grant reversed the priorities, giving precedence to the campaign of harassment. "Little expeditions could not so well be sent out [as] to destroy a bridge or tear up a few miles of railroad track, burn a storehouse or inflict other little annoyances," Grant explained in his memoirs. "Accordingly, I arranged for a simultaneous movement all along the line."

Grant assigned Maj. Gen. E. O. C. Ord to destroy the East Tennessee and Virginia Railroad "so that it can be of no further use to the enemy during the rebellion." Crook was directed to destroy the Virginia and Tennessee bridge at New River, then move along the railroad, destroying it en route and, if feasible, continuing on to Saltville, and destroying the salt works there. Sigel himself would lead a secondary column to draw attention away from Crook by threatening the Virginia Central and occupying Staunton. At Staunton, the two columns were expected to meet and move together against Lynchburg. The movements were timed to coincide with Grant's advance against Richmond from Culpeper. "Either the enemy would have to keep a large force to protect their communications, or see them destroyed and a large amount of forage and provision, which they so much needed, fall into our hands," Grant remarked.[3]

Crook, who had very little confidence in Sigel's discretion, told Ord he would prefer that Sigel get only the minimal amount of information necessary to conduct his own operation, and nothing of Crook's proposed route. Otherwise, he said, Sigel was "sure to blow," alerting the Confederates and endangering the entire operation. Ord agreed and passed Crook's misgivings on to Grant. The general-in-chief, however, pointed out that Sigel was commander of the department, and entitled to the confidence of his officers.[4]

Because the withdrawal of so many troops from his base in the Kanawha Valley would leave his right flank exposed, Crook divided his forces. A cavalry column of about two thousand men under Brig. Gen. William W. Averell would cover his right, hitting the railroad in the vicinity of Saltville. If the town could be taken, Crook told Averell to "destroy all the saltworks both public and private, bearing in mind at the same time to collect such supplies & material, as you can transport, that will be useful to our command." From Saltville, Averell was ordered to march up the railroad, "destroying the road as thoroughly as possible under the circumstances." Crook, meanwhile, would take the main force, consisting of eleven infantry regiments, two battalions of artillery and four hundred cavalry troopers—altogether, 6,155 men—and destroy the New River Bridge. Once Averell had complete his mission, he was to join Crook's force.[5]

Among Crook's officers was fellow-Ohioan Rutherford B. Hayes, colonel of the Twenty-third Ohio Volunteer Regiment. Hayes's letters show a passionate attachment to his wife, Lucy, who frequently visited him in camp, often accompanied by their sons, Rutherford, Jr., Webb, and Birchard. Crook, at this point in his life, was a bachelor, and would always be childless, and the family included him in their activities.

No doubt Crook looked forward to the visits. Despite a grim, taciturn image, he loved children, who seemed to provide a welcome break from the formality of the army. An aide once observed, "Twenty minutes after leaving his office where he seemed to be coldly distant and dignified, I have seen him rolling on the floor of his parlor with a pair of chubby, childish hands alternately pulling his hair and whiskers, while a favorite dog was tugging away at the tails of his army blouse; and it would have been difficult to decide which was enjoying the romp more, the man, the child, or the dog."

He was particularly attached to Webb Hayes, becoming almost a second father, a relationship that continued as long as Crook lived. When the family was back in Ohio, the letters Hayes received from home sometimes included a special greeting from Webb to Crook. Hayes's own feelings toward the general amounted almost to hero worship, and one begins to see the loyalty that Crook as commander would inspire in subordinate officers throughout the remainder of his career.[6]

The Twenty-third Ohio was one of the infantry units in Crook's column. The First Brigade, also commanded by Hayes, included his own regiment as well as the Thirty-fourth and Thirty-sixth Ohio (Crook's old regiment); the Second Brigade, led by Col. C. B. White, was composed of Twelfth and Ninety-first Ohio, and Ninth and Fourteenth Virginia (Union); and the Third Brigade, under Col. Horatio G. Sickel, combined Third and Fourth Pennsylvania, and Eleventh and Fifteenth Virginia (Union).[7]

Hayes had confidence in both his men and his commander. "We are under the immediate command of General Crook," he told his mother. "We all feel great confidence in his skill and good judgement." To his uncle, Sardis Birchard, he added, "We expect to see some of the severe fighting. The Rebel troops in our front are as good as any, and we shall attempt to push them away. My Brigade is three large Regiments of infantry, containing a good many new recruits. They have been too much scattered (at ten or twelve places) to be properly drilled and disciplined. Still we have some of the best men in service. . . . I have no misgivings on my own account."[8]

Crook moved out on May 2, heading toward Fayetteville and Princeton. As a decoy, he sent one infantry regiment and a detachment of scouts up the Lewisburg road. The plan worked so well that the Confederates pulled out of Princeton and marched to defend Lewisburg. Not until the Union forces neared Princeton did they actually meet any resistance, and that was merely a skirmish with a small company of Southern cavalry. Entering Princeton, Crook remarked, "So little did they expect us on this route they had left their tents standing, and the tools they had been erecting fortifications with in their barracks, all of which were destroyed."[9]

Hayes noted that the Confederates had called their earthworks Fort Breckenridge after their commanding officer, Maj. Gen. John C. Breckenridge, but added, "Our boys changed it to Fort Crook."[10]

By the evening of May 8, Crook was at Shannon's Bridge on the northwest slope of Cloyd's Mountain, only seven miles from his objective, the Virginia and Tennessee Railroad at Dublin. The Confederates, however, had recovered from the initial surprise and were two miles ahead on the summit. At daylight, Crook rode toward the enemy lines and studied them through his binoculars. The Confederates had thrown up defense works on the opposite ridge, about three quarters of a mile away. The two armies were separated by brushy ridges and gullies to Crook's left, and by a meadow directly in front. "The enemy is in force, and in strong positions," he observed. "He may whip us, but I guess not."

In fact, the Confederate forces were in disarray. General Breckenridge was in the Shenandoah proper to oppose Sigel, and had left Brig. Gen. Albert G. Jenkins to deal with Crook. Jenkins had held hasty conferences with his officers and local citizens familiar with the terrain, and chosen his ground accordingly. His line, though formidable in appearance, included militia and home guards.

Crook took advantage of the thick timber on his ridge to cover his troop deployments. The Second Brigade was sent to the left, and after struggling across the ridges and gullies, came into position. Then Crook started the rest of his troops across the meadow into a hail of musket and artillery fire.[11]

"The ranks wavered a little in spots," Crook reported, "but the general line moved steadily on until near the enemy's formidable breast-works on the crest of the ridge, a species of cheval-de-frise made of rails inverted, when the men rushed forward with a yell, the enemy remaining behind their works until battered away by our men."[12]

Describing the fight to Sardis Birchard, Hayes wrote: "We charged a rebel battery entrenched in a wooded hill across an open level meadow 300 yards wide & a deep ditch wetting me to the waist & carried it without a particle of wavering or even check, losing however many officers & men killed & wounded. It being the vital point Gen Crook charged with us in person."[13]

Finally, the Confederates broke and fled, pursued as hard as the exhausted condition of the Union soldiers would allow. Two miles out of Dublin, they encountered Confederate reenforcements sent by railroad from Saltville by Brig. Gen. John Morgan. Their train had arrived too late for the main fight, and they tried to cover the Confederate retreat. For a few moments, they held the Union in check, but soon they, too, were overwhelmed and forced to retreat.

"Colonel [John H.] Oley with his cavalry was ordered up, but his men were the odds and ends of several regiments, many with broken down horses, and were not in a condition for the service that was required of them," Crook wrote, adding, "Had I but 1,000 effective cavalry none of the enemy could have escaped."

As it was, Crook entered Dublin unopposed, having lost 107 killed, 508 wounded, and 28 missing. The Union troops buried over 200 Confederate dead, and captured 230 unwounded prisoners. Estimates of total Confederate wounded ranged between eight hundred and one thousand, including General Jenkins, who subsequently died of his injuries. The Confederate forces, meanwhile, had fled toward New River Bridge.[14]

In Dublin, Crook found dispatches from Richmond stating that Grant's drive toward the capital had been had been repulsed and his army was now in retreat. No longer preoccupied with Union forces in the East, General Lee was now free to detach part of his forces and cut off Crook's retreat. Crook decided to conclude his mission as soon as possible, and fall back across the Alleghenies.

There, he not only would be covered but also would be in a better position to link up with Sigel. He destroyed abandoned Confederate military stores in Dublin, and prepared to move out.

The following morning Crook moved up the railroad to the bridge, where he found the Confederates had evacuated their defenses and retreated across the river. They were now formed in line on the other side. The First Kentucky Battery was ordered up on the heights facing the southern troops and opened fire. After a two-hour artillery duel, in which the Union forces lost only one man killed and ten wounded, the Confederates were driven off. Crook took the bridge and burned it. [15]

On May 19, Crook reached Union, where he rendezvoused with General Averell. Averell had not attacked Saltville, determining it was too strong, and instead had moved against the lead works in Wythesville. Here he was repulsed by Morgan's forces, and so had retreated up the railroad, destroying track, as well as the depot and repair shops in Christianburg, before linking with Crook.

The expedition was a success. The New River Bridge was gone, along with eighteen miles of track, depots, shops, and stores. "Altogether this is our finest experience in the War & Gen Crook is the best General we have ever served under not excepting Rosecrans," Hayes wrote in unabashed admiration. [16]

On May 15, while Crook was marching back toward Union, Sigel was defeated by Breckenridge at New Market. As a result, Grant replaced him with Maj. Gen. David Hunter, who took command on May 21. His orders were "to push on if possible to Charlottesville and Lynchburg and destroy railroads and canal beyond possibility of repair for weeks, then either return to your original base or join Grant via Gordonsville." [17]

Hunter intended to move immediately up the Shenandoah and rendezvous with Crook and Averell at Staunton, then take the combined force to Charlottesville and Lynchburg, following more or less Sigel's original plan. "We are to advance without baggage and to cut loose entirely from our base of operations and live on the country," his kinsman and chief of staff, Col. David Hunter Strother, noted in his diary. To effect the rendezvous, the general telegraphed Crook to advance immediately on Staunton and, to be doubly sure the message was received, sent the order by courier as well. [18]

Crook, meanwhile, had shifted his forces to Meadow Bluffs, near Lewisburg. He began the six-day march to Staunton on May 31, hampered by woefully inadequate transportation. "We can get plenty of fresh beef in this country, but the other necessary supplies cannot be obtained in this country, even if every pound was taken from the people," he complained to Hunter. "I shall, however, drain the country of all supplies as I pass through." His forces lacked even the barest essentials necessary for an army in the field—horseshoes, horseshoe nails, hats, socks, canteens, trousers, shorts, blouses, boots, shoes and other basic essentials. Many of his troops were barefoot. "I shall insist on having on investigation of this matter, so as to have guilty parties punished," Crook wrote.[19]

During the march, Crook destroyed the Virginia Central Bridge over the Calf Pasture River and tore up several miles of track. Averell skirmished with Confederate cavalry who, Crook noted, "annoyed us some by occupying the gaps and passes, but did not detain us." The Confederates did not attempt a serious stand because they already knew what Crook would soon learn—that Hunter had smashed a sizeable Confederate force at Piedmont, clearing the way to meet Crook at Staunton.

The two forces linked at Staunton on June 8. Together with his own infantry and Averell's cavalry, Crook had about ten thousand men and two batteries of artillery, giving Hunter a total of about eighteen thousand men and thirty guns. In the city, Crook was able to requisition shoes for his and Averell's barefoot men. Hunter, meanwhile, destroyed factories, and stores and equipment, besides wrecking the Virginia Central's tracks, repair shops, warehouses, depots, culverts, and trestles for several miles around. Brig. Gen. John D. Imboden, the Confederate commander in the district, later wrote, "Hunter remained two or three days at Staunton resting his troops and burning both public and private property, especially the latter."[20]

The destruction around Staunton inaugurated a scorched-earth policy that Hunter would follow during his tenure as the federal commander in the area, and he was determined to carry the campaign to Lynchburg. Crook was less enthusiastic, realizing a move against Lynchburg would threaten Lee's rear and his bases of supply, and prompt him to send a large Confederate force into the valley. Discussing the situation with Colonel Strother, the chief of staff, Crook said he believed Hunter might be able to take the city with the forces available, "but, depend upon it, Lee would not permit us to hold it long, nor could we do so for want of supplies. If we expected to take Lynchburg at all we must move upon it immediately and rapidly."[21]

On June 10, Hunter began the push toward Lynchburg, moving up four almost parallel roads. The first thirty-six miles between Staunton and Lexington were covered in two steady marches. On the right, Crook pushed Brig. Gen. John C. McCausland's Confederates ahead of him, and as McCausland retreated, he burned the bridge over the North River. The structure fell into the river, but enough remained for the soldiers to use as a crossing. McCausland, however, had posted an artillery battery at the edge of town, and had positioned sharp-shooters in the heavy cedar thicket on the Lexington bank and among the adjacent buildings of Virginia Military Institute. These opened up on the Union column, and several men were killed and wounded. Hunter sent Averell's cavalry to ford the river above town and flank it while the Union artillery distracted the Confederates by throwing a few shells into the buildings of the institute. Because Averell moved too slowly, the Confederates saw him and retreated.

The Union forces entered Lexington from the west, and found locals already plundering the town. Hunter ordered the Virginia Military Institute burned, along with the home of former Virginia Gov. John Letcher, who had issued what Hunter called "a violent and inflammatory proclamation . . . inciting the population of the country to rise and wage a guerilla warfare on my troops."

Crook saw no point in Hunter's order. "I did all my power to dissuade him, but all to no purpose," he later wrote. He was particularly upset over the burning of Letcher's home; the former governor's wife and daughters had been turned out on ten minutes' notice. Hunter's motive for burning Virginia Military Institute seems to have been based on the martial nature of the school; Lexington's other great institution of learning, Washington College (now Washington and Lee University), was spared, although the West Virginia troops were allowed to take the school's statue of Washington as a trophy. The burning of the Letcher home, however, caused grumbling among the Union officers, who didn't care to be associated with depredations against civilians.[22]

After destroying property, transportation, and stores, Hunter continued on toward Lynchburg. He sent Brig. Gen. Alfred N. Duffié ahead with cavalry to reconnoiter, but Duffié was late in returning; Crook later contended that Duffié had spent more time plundering the countryside than looking for the Confederates. Whatever the reason, the delay threw Hunter seriously behind schedule. Nevertheless, he pushed onward, with Crook working his way up the railroad, burning ties and bending rails to render them useless. At 10 A.M., June 17, Crook was eight miles out of Lynchburg and, learning the Confederates had retreated toward the city, halted and waited for support from Brig. Gen. Jeremiah Sullivan's First Division. By 4 P.M., Sullivan had not arrived. Ahead, however, General Imboden's exhausted Confederates had taken position behind a fence line near a Quaker meeting house just outside of town, and managed to bring Averell to a complete halt. Crook sent one brigade to assist, and the Confederate line broke. Meanwhile, Lt. Gen. Jubal A. Early had arrived in Lynchburg with fresh troops and, riding out to the front, saw that Imboden could not hold. As the Union troops pushed Imboden ahead of them, they were met by fresh

Confederate brigades. Crook later contended that nightfall and lack of famil-
iarity with the terrain prompted him to halt and go into camp outside of town
but, in fact, it was a determined Confederate infantry charge led by Early himself
that blocked the Union forces.

Early's arrival proved Crook's prediction that Lee would not allow Lynchburg to fall. Nevertheless, Early's position was weak. As he awaited the arrival
of more troops, he had those on hand run an empty train up and down the
tracks and make as much noise as they could. Throughout the night, Union
soldiers heard what they thought were troop trains rolling in, and cheers and
shouts of presumably newly arriving Confederate units. Prisoners reported that
Lynchburg was now defended by thirty thousand men. The ruse worked.
Hunter failed to realize that, as late as noon the next day, he still had a considerably larger force. At that point, a fresh Confederate assault caught the Union
soldiers completely unawares. Hunter consulted his commanders, who were
unanimous that they should withdraw. "Crook was cool and matter of fact,"
Strother wrote in his diary. "Averell was excited and angry."[23]

As Hunter saw it, Duffié's delay had diminished his chances of taking
Lynchburg, and Sullivan's failure to arrive in time to support Crook during the
fight at the Quaker meeting house had made the objective impossible. "Gen.
Hunter had no confidence in the rest of the command, and I shared this opinion with him," Crook wrote in his autobiography. So far, Crook had been his
most successful and dependable commander, and Hunter "had gotten so now
that he would do nothing without first consulting me. . . . We decided that the
command, excepting my division, would commence falling back about three
or four o'clock [June 19] by the shortest route to the Kanawha Valley, and that
I would commence falling back soon after dark, leaving our picket fires burning after we left. All this time, a brisk [gun] fire was going on, which was kept
up until dark."[24]

The retreat took ten exhausting days. The soldiers had been constantly
moving for almost two months. In his report, Crook remarked, "The division
became a little straitened for provisions, but came in in good shape." This was
overly cheerful. On June 22, three days into the march, Strother wrote in his
diary, "Worn out with fatigue, without support in a country producing little at
best and already wasted by war, the troops are beginning to show symptoms of
demoralization, and short of ammunition we will hardly save our army [if the
Confederates tried to cut off it off and attack]."[25]

Crook's autobiography states: "The men were dodging out of ranks so they
could hide away and go to sleep. I stayed in the rear so as to look out for these

things. I knew that the enemy's cavalry would be along early in the morning and gobble up all stragglers. But even the knowledge of that fact had no terrors for the poor, worn-out wretches. I had to be very cross and make myself exceedingly disagreeable, but all that failed to prevent many from falling out."[26]

When Lee sent General Early to Lynchburg, his orders were to strike Hunter and, if possible, destroy his forces, then move down the Shenandoah, cross the Potomac into Maryland, and threaten Washington. Early initially had planned to attack Hunter immediately but, upon discovering the Union forces in retreat, instead launched a pursuit, harassing them from the rear. In three days, his men chased Hunter sixty miles before he decided to rest them. Lee, meanwhile, determined that Early should continue down the valley, forcing Hunter to follow him. Early would then strike Pope and knock him out, then turn and finish Hunter. Early, however, was prepared to go one better. Although Lee believed an actual attack on Washington was impossible, Early was convinced it could be done. After the destruction of Confederate offensive capability at Gettysburg, it is remarkable that Early should have even contemplated such a move. What is all the more remarkable is that it very nearly succeeded. As one Union officer later said, Early's offensive was "the only period during the civil war when the Capital was in real danger and the only time the District of Columbia was actually invaded by the enemy."[27]

Early resumed his march on June 23, reaching Staunton in advance of his troops three days later. Moving rapidly, he pushed on deep into the Shenandoah, defeating the Union defenders at Monocacy and, on July 11, was at the outskirts of Washington, sweeping down on the city from the north. Only a frantic redeployment, a calling up of reserves, and timely arrival of troops being transferred from the West saved the capital. Faced with unexpectedly heavy resistance, Early withdrew.[28]

In response to the threat, General Grant assigned Maj. Gen. Horatio G. Wright as supreme commander of all troops "moving out and against the enemy. He should get outside of the trenches with all the force he possibly can, and should push [Early] to the last moment."[29] Wright, in command of VI Corps, marched out of Washington and into Maryland, and within five days was beyond Leesburg. Meanwhile, on July 16, Crook's scouts encountered Early's rear guard at Snicker's Gap, a deep gorge in the mountains leading to the Shenandoah River, attacked his train and captured part of it. Before he could move up his infantry, however, the Confederates had made good their retreat. The next morning, he learned they had crossed the Shenandoah at Snicker's Ferry and were holding the ford.

On July 18, Crook and Wright arrived at Snicker's Gap. "The enemy was across the Shenandoah River," Crook wrote, "but we could not tell whether they were in force or not." Wright ordered him to send troops across the river, but no sooner had they made the crossing than the Confederates turned out in force to meet them. Crook asked permission to pull them back, but Wright said he would send Brig. Gen. James B. Ricketts across to support his troops. Ricketts, however, felt the Confederates were too strong, and declined to take his men over. Consequently, Crook later wrote, "I lost some valuable men here, murdered by incompetency or worse." He ordered his troops to fall back across the river and reported the matter to Wright, who took no action. Crook got some consolation in the thought that his badly mauled soldiers had managed to inflict enough punishment on the Confederates that they did not attempt to follow them to the river. He might have received additional satisfaction from the knowledge that on the same day he was brevetted to major general of Volunteers.[30]

Early continued his withdrawal up the Shenandoah Valley and, with the threat to Washington removed, VI Corps returned to the capital. Crook, meanwhile, shifted his men to Winchester to give them a rest. Like most Union officers at this point, he believed that Early's retirement meant he was leaving the valley and returning to the vicinity of Richmond. Lulled into a false sense of security, he miscalculated the position of the Confederates, who were not very far ahead. On learning that Crook's troops were in Winchester, the Confederates turned on him and, on July 24, appeared at his front. Crook moved his men to Kernstown, a short distance out from Winchester, and formed them into line. He hoped to hold the Confederates as long as possible until his supplies could be moved out of danger of capture.

Early, however, saw that Crook had left his left flank exposed, and hit him there with one division, while three more moved against the right and center. The Union line fell apart. Crook later wrote that his command at that time consisted of "so many odds and ends . . . picked up from different places." He complained that a large number were "professional bummers"—stragglers, looters and hangers-on. Whatever the case, he admitted in his report that "the greater portion of my dismounted cavalry, along with some infantry, the whole numbering some 3,000 or 4,000, broke to the rear the first fire, and all efforts to stop them proved to no avail."

He managed to break off the fight and retreat twelve miles to Bunker Hill, the Confederates going into camp some ten miles away. The following morning, harassed by Southern cavalry and unable to ascertain the whereabouts of their infantry, he fell back to Martinsburg.[31]

Overlooking his own complascency, Crook placed much of the blame for the defeat on his cavalry. Duffié's reports were totally contradictory and unreliable, and Averell, he later wrote, "was accused of getting drunk during the fight." Some of the "stampeded cavalry" even burned a few of their own wagons. Hayes's judgment was less severe, but nevertheless he wrote Lucy, "The real difficulty was our cavalry was so inefficient in its efforts to discover the strength of the enemy that General Crook and all the rest of us were deceived until it was too late."[32]

General Hunter thought there was enough blame to go around. In a private letter to his adjutant, Col. Charles G. Halpine, he wrote:

> Our Cavalry and some of our Infantry behaved in a most disgraceful manner in the recent fight of Crook's near Winchester—the officers in many instances leading off their men to the rear, stampeding the trains, and starting all kinds of lying reports with regard to disaster, defeat, &c. &c. In fact, the little army was only saved from utter annihilation by the steadiness and bravery of the Infantry we brought [from a raid elsewhere]. . . . I have dismissed some thirty officers for cowardice, drunkenness, basely deserting their commands, and spreading lying reports.[33]

FIVE

SHERIDAN TAKES COMMAND

THE EVENTS OF THE SUMMER OF 1864 convinced General Grant that Hunter had to go. His choice for a replacement was Crook's old comrade, Phil Sheridan, now a major general and commander of the cavalry of the Army of the Potomac.

The Shenandoah, as Sheridan biographer Paul Andrew Hutton noted, had already ruined five Union generals, the most recent being Sigel and Hunter. Now, the thirty-three-year-old Sheridan would have his chance. Lincoln and Secretary of War Edwin Stanton had misgivings because of his age, but Grant insisted.[1]

The new commander was not a complete stranger to the valley. During Hunter's initial thrust in June, Sheridan had moved to link up with him but the expedition had been aborted by Hunter's withdrawal before Lynchburg. This time, Grant intended that there would be no slip-ups. The Shenandoah Valley was vital to the Confederates because its crops provided the subsistence for their armies around Richmond. Although Grant initially had believed that Early would rejoin Lee, his subsequent movements indicated that he intended to remain in the valley. Here he had no problems with subsistence, and remained in a position to threaten Washington. Grant and Sheridan now realized that the Confederate government intended to hold the valley, at least until after the crops had been harvested and sent to the depots at Lynchburg and Richmond, and would not give it up without a desperate struggle.[2]

Grant's instructions were explicit. Scorch the earth. Feed the Union soldiers from the countryside, and leave nothing behind.[3] To expedite the assignment, the War Department created a new geographical command, the Middle Military Division, which consolidated the old Middle Department, Department of Washington, Department of the Susquehanna, and Department of West Virginia. Troop assignments were also restructured, with Wright continuing in charge of VI Corps; Brig. Gen. William H. Emory, XIX Corps; and Crook in command of VIII Corps as well as the Department of West Virginia. Crook's corps was the smallest in the command, being composed of two small divisions under Cols. Joseph Thoburn and Isaac H. Duval; in fact VIII Corps, or "Army of Western Virginia" as it was called, was actually no larger than a medium-size regular division. On the other hand, the bulk of the troops were West Virginia mountaineers, known for their tenacity, their ability to march, and their confidence in their commander.[4]

For the next several weeks, the two forces—Early's Army of the Valley and Sheridan's Army of the Shenandoah—maneuvered around each other, skirmishing, but never engaging in full battle. At times, it almost seemed that Sheridan was in retreat as Hunter and Sigel had been, but he maneuvered so that Early was not able to exploit the advantage. In reality, Sheridan was buying time. At this point, he did not know the country, and his numerical superiority did him little good because many of his troops were tied up covering trains and protecting Maryland and Pennsylvania. With the presidential election nearing, he did not believe the government could stand another defeat in the Shenandoah, and wanted to familiarize himself with his surroundings and avoid battle until he could decisively smash Early.[5]

Sheridan also had the political headaches that did so much to impede command during the Civil War. In one instance, Bvt. Maj. Gen. Benjamin F. Kelley retained several Ohio regiments beyond their enlistments, "creating great dissatisfaction in Ohio." The complaints reached General Halleck, who remained in Washington as chief of staff after Grant's elevation to general-in-chief, and Halleck passed them on to Sheridan. Because Kelley was assigned to the Department of West Virginia, the problem was referred to Crook with instructions to "order all regiments whose terms of service has [sic] expired to their place of rendezvous to be mustered out. . . ."[6]

In late August, Sheridan got a reprieve. Earlier in the summer, General Lee had dispatched reenforcements to the Shenandoah Valley under the command of Lt. Gen. Richard Anderson. Now, however, the Army of the Potomac's assault on Confederate defenses near Petersburg forced Lee to recall Anderson to bolster his own forces. Leaving his cavalry with Early, Anderson departed for Richmond with Maj. Gen. Joseph B. Kershaw's infantry division, and Sheridan took advantage of the withdrawal to occupy the line between Clifton and Berryville. Crook's VIII Corps was assigned to Berryville, which, by chance, lay on Anderson's route through the Blue Ridge to Richmond. Just before nightfall, September 3, the Confederates stumbled onto the Union troops who were going into camp. Both sides quickly recovered from their surprise and a brutal fight ensued, much of it in darkness. A Confederate charge routed several of Thoburn's regiments, and Crook had to send in Duval to force back the Southerners and retake the position. Anderson finally retreated, leaving behind fifty-nine of his men as prisoners. Crook counted 23 men killed, 124 wounded, and 19 missing after the night fight.

Unaware that Sheridan had reestablished the Clifton-Berryville line, and believing he faced only one corps, Early rushed to assist Anderson only to find himself facing the bulk of the Union Army. Realizing that Sheridan was now moving against him, he countermanded Lee's orders to Anderson, deciding instead that he would have to remain in the valley with his troops for the time being. After another skirmish at Berryville, he withdrew his army beyond Opequon Creek toward Winchester.

Even with Early in retreat, Sheridan was reluctant to attack him behind the Opequon; its banks were steep and the fords were deep. He spent the next ten days redeploying, with occasional skirmishes, while waiting for things to move his way. As part of the shift, Crook was ordered to fall back northward to Clifton, and in the process his ambulance train was "attacked and badly stampeded" by six of Col. John S. Mosby's partisans.[7]

Sheridan's greatest problem was lack of information, a particularly serious problem in view of Early's extensive intelligence system of partisan rangers and a friendly populace. To deal with the situation, he organized a detachment of scouts under Maj. H. K. Young, which soon located an elderly black man who carried a Confederate travel permit to go into Winchester three days a week and sell vegetables. Discreet inquiries determined the man was loyal and willing to act as a Union messenger. Because Crook was acquainted with Union sympathizers in Winchester, Sheridan asked if he knew of "some reliable person who would be willing to cooperate and correspond with me." Crook recommended Miss Rebecca Wright, a young Quaker who taught at a private school. But he cautioned that she was also under constant surveillance because of her well-known Union sympathies.

Sheridan hesitated but decided to give it a try. The old vegetable seller, who knew Miss Wright, agreed to carry a message to her on his next trip into town. Miss Wright's reply went beyond Sheridan's expectations: Kershaw's division, along with twelve guns and men from the artillery, all commanded by General Anderson, had finally left the valley and, because of the situation around Richmond, no further Confederate reenforcements were expected. Although she was unable to give precise information on troop dispositions, Miss Wright was certain that the remaining Confederate strength in the valley was "much smaller than represented."[8]

This was the information Sheridan needed. The time had come to go on the offensive and bring the valley campaign to an end. He was determined that once Early was driven from the Shenandoah, no Confederate force would ever return. After a conference with Grant at Charlestown, he returned to his headquarters to find that Early was taking two divisions of infantry to Martinsburg. With the Confederates now split, he determined to attack immediately those remaining at Winchester.

Winchester was the key to the Shenandoah Valley, and is said to have changed hands more than seventy times during the four years of conflict. Situated midway between the Blue Ridge on the east and North Mountain to the west, it is on the Valley Pike, twenty-two miles south of Martinsburg, and about the same distance in a direct line from Harper's Ferry. Opequon Creek is four miles to the east, and is fed by two tributary streams, Red Bud Creek on the north and Abraham's Creek on the south. All these waterways would have to be negotiated by the Union troops attacking Early.

At 2 A.M., September 19, Sheridan's forces began moving. The cavalry would move in first to neutralize the Confederate cavalry, followed by VI Corps, which would form up west of the Opequon facing Winchester. The XIX Corps would form on the Opequon itself and move in to support VI Corps, while Crook's two divisions, being among the farthest from the front, were assigned to follow VI and XIX Corps to the Opequon, and remain in reserve until needed.[9]

The cavalry opened the attack, and the infantry from VI Corps moved in to support. But XIX Corps, blocked by the artillery and trains of VI Corps, took several hours to get into line, and it was not until late morning that all the units were deployed according to plan. Early was quick to exploit the situation. His artillery opened up with canister and counterattacked, hitting the barely organized lines of XIX Corps. The first part of the battle of Winchester (sometimes called "Opequon" to distinguish it from various other battles of Winchester) was turning into a Union fiasco, and Crook blamed Sheridan for opening the attack before the infantry was completely deployed.[10]

Crook later claimed that, with XIX Corps repulsed and the right flank of VI Corps battered, he asked Sheridan to give him a cavalry division and he could "turn the enemy's right and cut off his retreat up the valley while the remainder attacked the enemy in the front."[11] Sheridan, however, did nothing, admitting in his memoirs that he was advised to bring Crook in, but delayed. His original intention was to keep Crook in reserve until the battle was winding down, then send him down to take over the Valley Pike and cut off the Confederates from the rear. Finally, though, he realized the fight was not going according to plan, and he ordered Crook's two divisions to bolster XIX Corps on the right.[12]

Describing the scene as his men moved into battle, Crook wrote: "The road from Opequon Creek up to the battlefield was one jam of ambulances, ammunition wagons, etc., so the troops could not march on the road. About one division marched on either side of the road, and met with more or less delay. They met the fugitives from the two corps engaged seeking safety to the rear, spreading the most doleful and alarming reports of our disaster at the front. There seemed to me to be as many fugitives as there were men in my command."[13]

After about an hour pushing through the crowd of men, animals, and vehicles, Crook's troops came into line, turning the Confederate left, after which, Sheridan later wrote, "Crook pressed forward without even a halt." Early was forced to retire through Winchester and up the valley with Crook's troops at his heels, Sheridan riding along to watch the show.[14]

Entering the town, Crook and Sheridan met three excited young women. Pro-Union, they had watched the fight from the rooftops throughout the day, and the sight of the two Union generals riding up the main street assured them of victory. Crook, who already knew them, cautioned them not to be overly exuberant in their celebration, because Winchester had changed hands too many times to be completely secure. The girls replied that Early's army had retreated broken and demoralized, and they were certain they now were permanently under federal jurisdiction. After calming the girls, Crook took Sheridan to meet Rebecca Wright, the informant who, according to Sheridan, "had contributed so much to our success." He used a desk in her schoolroom to write a telegram informing General Grant of the victory.[15]

Enthusiastic women aside, the victory left Crook bitter. He complained that this troops had taken over a thousand prisoners, but the cavalry took them over and turned them in, getting credit for the capture.

> I complained of this to Gen. Sheridan, who asked me to say nothing about it in my report, but that he saw the whole affair and would give me credit for it . . . instead of giving me the credit I deserved, he treated the subject something in

this wise: that I was placed in a fortunate position where I could turn the enemy's flank, giving the impression that my turning the enemy's flank was part of his plan, whereas so far as I know the idea of turning the enemy's flank never occurred to him, but I took the responsibility on my own shoulders.[16]

Crook never forgave Sheridan for usurping credit for taking prisoners and out-maneuvering the enemy. Regardless of whose idea it was to turn Early's flank, it was the beginning of a breach between the two old friends and roommates that ultimately degenerated into pure hatred.

Early had been beaten but, recognizing his impending defeat as the battle progressed, he had saved his train and stores and kept the bulk of his army intact. Still full of fight, he retreated twenty miles south of Winchester to Fisher's Hill, a height overlooking Strasburg, where a spur of the mountains contracts the Shenandoah Valley from twenty miles wide to four. It was an excellent defensive position, and here the Confederates dug in and waited until the Union cavalry discovered them on September 20. At first, Sheridan believed the only way to dislodge Early would be by direct assault, but as he assembled his troops, he realized the Confederate position was too strong and decided to use Crook to turn Early's flank as he had done at Winchester. The following day, Sheridan sent General Wright to fight his way up the heights overlooking Tumbling Run, a creek fronting the Confederate position. Then, after dark, he concealed Crook in the timber north of Cedar Creek. From there, Crook's westerners could use the woods to cover their movements when the fight began.[17]

During Crook's deployment, there was a brief flurry of excitement when the mass movement of troops flushed out a fox that ran between two of the divisions. "The men set up such a yell that poor Reynard was paralyzed with fear and lost all his cunning, jumped around in a circle, and allowed himself to be captured," Crook wrote.[18]

The next morning, September 22, Crook began his semicircular swing northwest from Cedar Creek, completely around the Union rear, and then southwest toward Little North Mountain facing the Confederate left. Meanwhile, VI Corps and XIX Corps moved on Early's front, concealing Crook's movements while easing over to link up with him and sweep the Confederate flank. Crook personally led his troops, following a series of ravines and making the color bearers trail their flags, hoping they would not be spotted by a Confederate signal station on the heights. The movement took the better part of the day and, on reaching the timber on Little North Mountain, "I halted and brought up my rear division alongside of the first, and in this way marched the two by flank, so that when I faced [the Confederates] I would have two lines of battle parallel to each other."

Meanwhile, Early already had concluded that the advance of VI and XIX Corps was more than he could handle, and had given orders to withdraw after dark. He was more correct about the outcome than he could possibly have imagined. Preoccupied with the Union line to the front, he had neglected his vulnerable left flank, and was unaware of Crook's movement in that direction. About sunset, the westerners rushed out of the woods and charged the Confederate line. "Had the heavens opened and we been seen descending from the clouds, no greater consternation would have been created," one Union officer recalled.

At about two hundred yards, Crook's men hit the Confederate skirmishers. Southern artillery opened fire, but it was too late to train the guns well and they had little effect on the Union troops. Their blood stirred by the exploding shells, the westerners gave a massive yell and rushed the trenches. "Unless you heard my fellows yell once," Crook wrote, "you can form no conception of it. It beggars all description." Now VI and XIX Corps came up to link with Crook and the Confederates were overrun and routed.[19]

Even in the midst of battle, Crook found time for a quarrel. The Confederate infantry rallied behind some stone fences at the top of the ridge, temporarily blocking the westerners. His immediate support was the division commanded by Ricketts, who had left him stranded at Snicker's Ferry during Hunter's campaign. Although Ricketts had drawn Confederate attention while Crook slipped into the woods on Little North Mountain, now his division momentarily halted, and Crook suspected he was about to be stranded again. Soon, however, Ricketts began working across the ridge. Nevertheless, Crook was ready for an argument and when he saw about fifty men pulling captured artillery from a Confederate position, "I pitched into them for not being at the front, thinking they were some of my men. They replied that they were pulling them by order of their general, Gen. Ricketts. Just then Gen. Ricketts, who looked as though he was stealing sheep, said he wanted to turn them in as his captures. I told him that my men had been over there some time previous, and that all able-bodied men were needed at the front."[20]

His own crankiness notwithstanding, Crook's two divisions had performed spectacularly. Not only had they penetrated the Confederate left, they had broken and scattered the entire army. By the time complete darkness set in, the battle of Fisher's Hill was over and Early was retreating in confusion. Sheridan pursued all night but eventually gave up the chase; his cavalry had been deployed to swing around from the south, and failed to arrive in time to be of any use.

The cavalry was Averell's responsibility, and Sheridan considered this the last straw in a long line of problems he had experienced with Averell almost since his arrival in the Shenandoah. Averell was relieved of duty.[21]

The Crook-Sheridan squabble gained momentum at Fisher's Hill. In his memoirs, Sheridan indicated it was his idea for Crook to turn Early's left flank, and Bvt. Maj. Gen. Wesley Merritt, who commanded one of the cavalry divisions, essentially agreed in an article for the Century Company, a New York publishing firm. On the other hand, Crook and his adherents, including Rutherford Hayes, always contended that Sheridan initially wanted to put him against the Confederate right. Crook, however, claimed that such a deployment was "folly" and convinced Sheridan to allow him to move against the Confederate left.

Crook and his immediate circle of loyal officers were not alone. The entire VIII Corps was affronted by the praise heaped on Sheridan. It was a small corps, accustomed to operating more or less independently in a secondary theater. Now, it was fighting alongside VI and XIX Corps, veterans of the great campaigns of the East, and even though the westerners were largely responsible for the victory at Fisher's Hill, the two larger corps viewed them with contempt and they repaid in kind. For the time being, Crook kept his feelings to himself, preferring to express his rancor against Sheridan in various petty ways over the ensuing decades, but Hayes was vehement, particularly about press coverage. Almost all the units composing VI and XIX Corps were from the metropolitan areas of the Northeast, and naturally the correspondents of the large newspapers were assigned to cover them rather than the westerners. Hayes, however, almost suspected a deliberate conspiracy to boost them at the expense of the smaller VIII Corps, and particularly at the expense of General Crook. "Gen Crook has nobody to write him or his Command up," he told Sardis Birchard. "They are of course lost sight of."

The importance of press coverage was not lost on Crook, particularly after the war's end when he saw that career officers with the better notices received higher promotions in the reorganizing regular army. "I learned too late that it was not what a person did, but it was what he got the credit of doing that gave him a reputation and at the close of the war gave him promotion," he observed. Henceforth, whenever he was in a position to control the news, he made certain that correspondents were always present and always friendly. Ultimately, he would be accompanied by more correspondents than any other general of his era. In this manner Crook began a campaign of image manipulation that would last a century beyond his own lifetime.[22]

Hayes, meanwhile, did his part to boost his general's image. On October 5, he learned that six days earlier Lucy had given birth to another son, weighing ten pounds. He decided the boy should be named George Crook Hayes "after our favorite Corps commander."[23]

After his defeat at Fisher's Hill, Early withdrew to the east with the remnant of his army, and as far as Sheridan was concerned the Shenandoah Campaign had effectively ended. On October 1, he wrote General Grant, "The rebels have given up the Valley, except Waynesboro. . . . I think that the best policy will be to let the burning of the crops of the Valley . . . be the end of this campaign, and let some of the army go somewhere else." Sheridan himself was ready to leave the Shenandoah. He believed that Crook could hold the valley and VI and XIX Corps could be transferred to the Union forces around Richmond.

He now began a program of devastation, sending his cavalry across the valley "burning, destroying, or taking away everything of value, or likely to become of value, to the enemy," according to General Merritt. Sheridan sent the infantry ahead of the cavalry, recalling that "as we marched long[,] the many columns of smoke from burning stacks, and [from] mills filled with grain, indicated that the adjacent country was fast losing the features which hitherto had made it a great magazine of stores for the Confederate armies."[24]

Sheridan was backtracking down the valley toward Winchester, and now that he was withdrawing, Early did the unexpected—he reentered the Shenandoah in force, sending his cavalry ahead to harass the Union columns from the rear. Although Sheridan apparently did not realize the Confederate cavalry was the vanguard of a much larger army, he nevertheless was determined to put a stop to the almost daily skirmishes. On October 9, he turned on the Confederates with his own cavalry, smashing them, driving them twenty-six miles, and capturing virtually all their equipment. Fought at Tom's Brook, this battle fatally weakened Early's cavalry.

The following day Sheridan occupied the heights around Cedar Creek, just above the junction with the Shenandoah opposite Fisher's Hill. The XIX Corps was in the center, Crook on the left, and VI corps in reserve. At this point, Early showed his hand and on October 13 reoccupied his old position on Fisher's Hill. The situation was almost the same as it had been three weeks earlier except that now the advantage was with the Confederates. Cedar Creek was an exposed position, and the line of wooded ravines leading down from Fisher's Hill worked for Early. Union pickets who normally would be the first warning of enemy movement could not venture too far out from camp without being captured.

Crook was not happy with his position, which was over a mile from the other two corps. His losses for Winchester and Fisher's Hill came to 105 killed, 840 wounded, and 8 missing, for total casualties of 953. Together with men detailed for what he called "guards of different kinds," this left him with less than three thousand effective combat troops divided into two divisions. Colonel Thoburn's First Division was on the extreme left, while Second Division was in reserve under Hayes, who had assumed command after Colonel Duval was wounded at Winchester. Crook felt the line was too strung out and too isolated.

Sheridan was less concerned. The Union devastation of the valley meant that Early would have to bring supplies and forage by wagon from Staunton. Eventually, he would have to attack or retreat and when, after two days, he did nothing, Sheridan believed he was not strong enough to pose a serious threat. Sheridan had been summoned to Washington to confer with Secretary of War Stanton, and decided to wait and handle the Confederates on his return—assuming that the Confederates were still in the valley by then. Departing on October 15, he took the cavalry as an escort as far as the railroad at Rectorville. This removed the cavalry pickets from several fords on Cedar Creek near Crook's line. Crook complained to General Wright, in charge during Sheridan's absence, who promised to remedy the situation when the cavalry returned.

Over the next three days, Early kept his men quiet, so that Union patrols reported little or no Confederate movement. On October 18, Crook sent out a reconnaissance brigade under Col. Thomas M. Harris, which went as far as Early's first encampment on Hupp's Hill. Finding nothing, and not realizing that Early had moved, he presumed the Confederates had abandoned the area. At 9 P.M., Crook advised Wright that Early "had doubtless retreated up the Valley." Nevertheless, Wright ordered two more reconnaissances to get started as soon as the foggy, misty weather cleared the next morning. He also placed almost all his cavalry on his right, which he considered his weakest point, and the fords by Crook's position remained unprotected. He doubted the Confederates would try to attack the front, where XIX Corps held strong entrenchments, and the rugged terrain and entrenchments to the left would cover Crook. About 10 P.M., some soldiers from a New York unit saw lights flashing from the Confederate signal station on Three Top Mountain. No one bothered to report it.[25]

In fact, Early was making his move. He was running low on provisions and, as Sheridan had anticipated, he was forced to choose between retreat and attack. He opted for attack. His own reconnaissance expeditions had given him accurate information on the layout of the Union forces, and he decided to hit the line where least expected—on the left and front—then drive up the Valley Pike. Soldiers were told to leave canteens and sabers in camp to make as little noise as possible, and to begin moving at 5 A.M.[26]

In the Union camp, no one suspected anything. Crook himself was complacent. Colonel Harris's report led him to the same conclusion that everyone else had—that Early had retreated. Crook apparently was unaware that his officer of the day failed to return from his nocturnal rounds, having been captured while checking on pickets outside the line.[27]

An early morning fog hung over the ground, hiding the mass of butternut-clad soldiers as they moved toward the Union lines. The men of Thoburn's division were roused by musket fire. Stumbling half-asleep from their tents, they found General Kershaw's infantry rushing out of the fog, over the parapets, and into the camp. The Union soldiers were completely routed. Many were trying to dress as they fled.

Crook had two batteries totaling twelve guns placed between Thoburn's division and XIX Corps. A few of his troops had the presence of mind to hitch up and rescue five guns, but seven were captured and turned against them, firing in conjunction with Early's own artillery. The Confederates continued their sweep with more troops coming around from the rear, hitting Hayes's division, and plunging into XIX Corps. Hayes had a little more time to organize his men, but before he could establish any real semblance of order, his horse was shot from under him and the fall momentarily knocked him senseless. Seeing their colonel go down, the men of Second Division broke and ran. Emory was forced to pull back his XIX Corps to prevent complete disaster and wholesale capture. Seeing that any effort to resist would be futile until the shattered army was consolidated, Wright ordered a withdrawal in order to get the men concentrated. Finally, about 10 A.M., he regained control and formed them into line of battle.[28]

Despite the initial rout of Union forces, Early accomplished very little. The federal cavalry, at the far end of the line from the point of attack, had gotten saddled and was threatening Kershaw. Early was feeling the heavy losses his own cavalry had taken at Tom's Brook, and the situation was further aggravated when his infantry lost the momentum of their attack by stopping to plunder the captured Union camps. He was faced with actually having to halt some of his advancing units to prevent their being cut to pieces by the Union cavalry.[29]

Sheridan, meanwhile, had spent the night in Winchester. About 6 A.M., the picket officer woke him up with a report of artillery fire in the direction of Cedar Creek. On determining that it was sporadic, rather than sustained,

Sheridan assumed it was a skirmish of reconnaissance details, and tried to go back to sleep. He was uneasy, however, and when the officer returned to say the firing was still going on, he decided to go to the front himself. At Mill Creek, he rode ahead of his escort and, reaching the top of a rise beyond the creek, saw his panic-stricken troops fleeing from the battle. Plunging into the crowd of retreating soldiers, he ran into Maj. William McKinley, General Crook's adjutant, who spread the word that Sheridan had arrived. Gaining confidence, the men began to collect themselves.

Sheridan's appearance at the height of the battle is considered one of the most dramatic incidents of the war. He came up to a point where Brig. Gen. George Getty of VI Corps had managed to combine with Hayes's division and form a line to hold the pike. Sheridan described the scene: "I then turned back to the rear of Getty's division, and as I came behind it, a line of regimental flags rose up out of the ground, as it seemed, to welcome me. They were mostly the colors of Crook's troops, who had been stampeded and scattered in the surprise of the morning. The color-bearers, having withstood the panic, had formed behind the troops of Getty."

The Confederates were suffering as much of a battering as the Union men. The see-sawing back and forth along the pike, loss of momentum, and the thrusts of Union cavalry had left the Southern lines jagged and broken. Sheridan strengthened the Union right, which moved forward and threw back the Confederates on that quarter. Realizing he had played out his hand, Early had no option but to withdraw. The battle of Cedar Creek was over.[30]

That night, as they sat around the campfire, Sheridan said, "Crook, I am going to get much more credit for this than I deserve, for, had I been here in the morning the same thing would have taken place, and had I not returned today, the same thing would have taken place."

Crook contended that he gave the comment little thought at the time, but years later, he wrote:

> Myself and division have never had justice done us in this affair, for we had always been spoken of as the Eighth Corps, giving the impression that we had enough men to constitute a corps. We were assigned to duties that required a corps to perform, and then were not properly supported, and have been held responsible for the surprise that does not belong to us, for had the cavalry pickets been where we had every reason to expect them, the surprise never could have happened, and without the surprise the enemy would never have dare to have gotten so near us with their small force.[31]

He remained bitter about this for the rest of his life. Even in 1890, with Sheridan already dead, he still tried to vindicate himself for that day. In his memoirs, he also stated that the Shenandoah Campaign rightfully should have ended a month earlier after the battle at Opequon Creek, indicating that Sheridan (whom he did not mention by name) had failed to take advantage of his tactical position in the valley and of his overwhelming numerical superiority.[32]

With Cedar Creek, the Shenandoah Campaign was finished and the Confederates were expelled from the valley forever. As General Merritt noted, "The victory was a fitting sequel to Winchester, a glorious prelude to Five Forks and Appomattox."[33]

For Rutherford Hayes, the close of the campaign had special significance. He had distinguished himself throughout, and Crook was determined that his efforts (and no doubt his unquestioning loyalty) be recognized. As early as October 2, he had recommended that Hayes be promoted "for gallant and meritorious services during the battles of Winchester & Fishers Hill."[34] When the battle of Cedar Creek ended, he went over Hayes's record during the campaign with Sheridan, who decided the colonel deserved promotion for Cedar Creek as well. On the cold afternoon of December 9, Crook went to Hayes's headquarters, and informed him he been appointed brigadier general of volunteers. Writing to Lucy that night, Hayes said:

> Gen. Crook gave me a very agreeable present this afternoon—a pair of his old Brigadier General straps. The Stars are somewhat dimmed with hard service but will correspond pretty well with my rusty old blouse. Of course I am very much gratified by the promotion. I know perfectly well that the rank has been conferred on all sorts of small people and so cheapened shamefully, but I can't help feeling that getting it at the close of a most bloody campaign on the recommendation of fighting generals like Crook and Sheridan is a different thing, from the same rank conferred—well, as it has been in some instances.[35]

SIX

THE CLOSING BATTLES

—m—

WITH THE END OF THE Shenandoah Campaign, Crook returned to his head-quarters at Cumberland, Maryland, in an area where Confederate partisans were still active. Perhaps the most famous was the Forty-third Battalion of Virginia Cavalry, better known as Mosby's Rangers, after their commanding officer, Col. John S. Mosby. To counter the Confederate partisans, and specifically to "clean out Mosby's gang," Crook established a counterguerilla company composed largely of West Virginians and Ohioans under Capt. Richard Blazer. He hardly could have chosen better; even the Confederates grudgingly acknowledged that Blazer was not only a brave and tenacious fighter but also humane. His attitude was in stark contrast to that of the usual ruthless Union counterguerrilla leaders and won him widespread support among the citizens. As one Confederate partisan commented, Blazer "so disarmed our citizens that instead of fleeing on his approach and notifying all soldiers, thus giving them a chance to escape, but little notice was taken of him. Consequently many of our men were 'gobbled up' before they were aware of his presence." Blazer made substantial headway against Mosby, but ultimately he was superseded by a counterguerrilla unit organized by General Sheridan to serve throughout the entire Middle Division.[1]

The Army of Western Virginia, meanwhile, had been reorganized into three divisions. The First Division under Brig. Gen. Isaac H. Duval and the Second under Bvt. Maj. Gen. Benjamin F. Kelley were assigned to the Cumberland area, while Brig. Gen. John D. Stevenson's Third Division was at Harper's Ferry.[2] On February 17, 1865, Crook, his staff, and the officers of the first two divisions hosted a hop at the Revere House, his hotel and headquarters in Cumberland. Crook himself headed the Committee of Invitation, with Kelley and Brig. Gen. J. A. J. Lightburn in charge of arrangements, and Duval and Rutherford Hayes heading the Committee on Floor. Headquarters often held such social events, inviting the young ladies of the town. Crook enjoyed the company of beautiful women; they were his weakness—albeit never a serious weakness— and his staff realized that a woman might be able to sway him toward some course of action when logic failed. At these headquarters-sponsored affairs Crook probably met and courted Mary Dailey, whose father owned the Revere House, and whom he married later in the year. They may already have been engaged at the time of the February 17 hop.[3]

Ironically, Mary's brother, James Dailey, belonged to a local company of Confederate irregulars known as McNeill's Rangers after their first commander, Capt. John H. McNeill. McNeill himself was dead, having been mortally wounded and captured during a fight at Mount Jackson, Virginia, on October 3, 1864, but command had passed to his twenty-two-year-old son, Jesse. As a family, the McNeills had a grudge against General Kelley, dating from a wound the elder McNeill had received in Missouri during the summer of 1862. He had been invalided back to his home in Virginia to recuperate, and his wife had made the trip by way of Ohio to see friends. When she tried to get through the lines to Virginia, however, Kelley refused to give her a pass. After McNeill's death in 1864, the hot-tempered Jesse not only inherited command of his father's company but the grievance against Kelley as well.[4]

Most of McNeill's Rangers were from the Cumberland area and, according to Crook, "had relatives and sympathizers all through that country who kept them posted on everything that transpired within our lines." Two Rangers, John B. Fay, a native of Cumberland, and C. Ritchie Hallar from Missouri, went in and scouted the town, obtaining detailed information on the federal camp, where the generals were staying, roads and escape routes. After hearing their report, Jesse sent them back to Cumberland one more time to double-check.[5]

About 3 A.M., February 21, 1865, Jesse led some thirty of his Rangers across the Potomac about four miles above Cumberland. They wore blue overcoats and the sentinel who challenged them presumed they were federal cavalry. According to one of the sentinels, a Confederate leaned over as if to whisper the countersign but, instead, put his revolver against the sentinel's head and forced him to surrender. The Rangers slipped into town.[6]

Whether Jesse McNeill was gunning specifically for Kelley is a matter of conjecture. Nevertheless, the two scouts had ample information, and the

Confederates seemed to know exactly for whom they were looking. About six or eight went to the Revere House for Crook, while another group went to the St. Nicholas, where Kelley was staying. No effort was made to take Lew Wallace or Hayes. The guards at the Revere were overpowered, and four Confederates went inside where a porter, thinking them Union soldiers, led them to Crook's room, where they woke him, ordered him to dress, and took him out to a waiting horse. Others returned with General Kelley, and Capt. Thayer Melvin, Kelley's adjutant. They also took three "fine" horses belonging to Kelley, and four or five other mounts. Besides the officers and horses, the Confederates captured two privates—apparently the pickets or guards—and the headquarters flag.

While the generals were rounded up, the main party of guerillas broke into the telegraph office and destroyed the equipment. Then they rode off and crossed the Potomac below town in the direction of Romney. The whole thing happened so quickly that they were gone by the time an officer in the room across from Crook's, stirred by the noise, could fully awaken and investigate.[7]

The porter gave the alarm, and a party of cavalry began pursuit immediately. It took about an hour before telegraph service could be restored, and messages were sent to federal troops at New Creek, and to General Sheridan at Winchester. McNeill's men, however, knew the country and scattered, while the Union cavalry horses bogged down in the snow and quickly gave out. The Confederates made good their escape, riding a hundred miles in twenty-four hours.[8]

Jubal Early learned about the capture when a young officer sent by McNeill came to his room at Staunton "and with a great flourish begged leave to present Maj. Gen. Crook and Maj. Gen. Kelley of the Federal Army." Early laughed at that, as he recalled later. Even so, he respected Crook, and used the opportunity to meet with him and discuss the Shenandoah Campaign. When Early commented that "Sheridan ought to have been cashiered for the Winchester fight," Crook "smiled, and said nothing."[9]

Early was not the only one who enjoyed the situation. A Confederate topographical officer who happened to be present chortled in his diary, "Major-Generals Kelley and Crook were brought here by McNeill's men, boldly captured from their beds at Cumberland last Tuesday morning, from the very midst of an army of 5,000 men."[10]

On the Union side, no one saw the humor. The loss of Crook and Kelley was unpleasantly reminiscent of the Confederate capture of Crook's predecessor, General Scammon, a year and two weeks earlier. At the time, Hayes thought Scammon's capture was "the greatest joke of the war." Now, however, Crook and Kelley had been removed from their hotel rooms right under the noses of the federals. "It is a very mortifying thing to all of us," he wrote to Lucy.

Hayes did not consider anyone culpable, remarking to Lucy, "The picket post was not blameable I think—at least not flagrantly so." Crook, on the other hand, later complained that the Confederates used threats to make "the ignorant Dutchman who happened to be on picket give them the countersign."[11]

Taken to Richmond, Crook remained in Confederate hands less than three weeks. On March 10, he, Kelley, and Captain Melvin were sent north together with several hundred soldiers paroled from Libby Prison. Although Crook was free, as a parolee he officially remained a Confederate prisoner of war, under Union supervision but still subject to Confederate jurisdiction until a formal prisoner exchange could be negotiated. The arrangements took time, and Crook was indiscreet enough to comment publicly that the War Department was dragging its heels. This was a direct slap at Secretary Stanton, who had to approve all exchanges. Stanton had never cared for Crook, and already was fuming over the humiliating circumstances of the general's capture. Infuriated by Crook's comments, Stanton decided to block the exchange and let him stew for awhile in the enforced idleness of a prisoner. Grant, however, wanted Crook back in action, and pressured Stanton to approve the formalities.[12]

Now a new complication arose. Upon Crook's capture, Sheridan temporarily assumed direct command of the Department of West Virginia in addition to his duties as division commander. A few days later, however, Sheridan returned to his cavalry command under General Grant, and General Winfield Scott Hancock was ordered to take over the Middle Division. Hancock, in turn, assigned General William H. Emory to take charge of Crook's department. But on March 21, exactly one month after his capture, Crook returned to Cumberland without consulting Hancock or Emory.

Actually, Crook's presence was only temporary; Grant intended to place him in command of the cavalry of the Army of the Potomac. Nevertheless, he wanted one day back in charge of his old department to show that he was not in official disfavor. His appearance, however, offended Hancock who, as commander, was responsible for the assignments in the Middle Division and who had already given the Department of West Virginia to Emory. As far as Hancock was concerned, Crook had committed a serious breach of discipline by getting General Grant's approval for the one-day resumption of command without first clearing it through divisional headquarters. There was speculation in the division that Crook would resume command in defiance of Hancock and, if he did, Hancock would have him arrested.

Determined that Crook have a show of support from the troops, Hayes organized a demonstration by his brigade. He wrote to Lucy, "You would have boiled over with enjoyment if you had been here today.... Both bands were out and *all* men. We had about forty rousing cheers; a speech from Chaplain Collier, a good talk from the General, a little one from me, and lots of fun." An old man "hard looking and generally full of liquor" who delivered wood and built fires in the camp remarked, "I was glad to see Uncle George." Like so many things in Crook's life, the celebration appeared spontaneous but was carefully contrived.[13]

By mid-March it was obvious to all that the great Confederate stronghold of Petersburg was no longer tenable, and when it fell, the Confederates would be forced to abandon their capital in Richmond. In an odd sort of way, this would actually assist General Lee, who no longer would be preoccupied with defending the capital. Lee still had a railroad at his disposal, and the Confederate army could travel more lightly and move more rapidly than the Union army. Consequently, General Grant was anxious to make one last, decisive thrust against Lee and crush him. Otherwise, he feared the Confederate general would move his army south, link up with Lt. Gen. Joseph E. Johnston's Confederate forces in North Carolina, and prolong the war another year. Grant proposed, instead, to drive a wedge between the two Confederate armies and smash Lee, while Maj. Gen. W. T. Sherman, who was cutting a swath of destruction through the Carolinas, would cut off Johnston.[14]

To prepare for the coming campaign, Grant reorganized his forces, placing Sheridan in command of all the cavalry. This force would include two mounted divisions of the Army of the Shenandoah under General Merritt and the Second Division of the Army of the Potomac under Crook. Crook's division consisted of three brigades, the First under Brig. Gen. Henry Davies with a battery of artillery; the Second under Col. J. Irvin Gregg, with two batteries; and the Third commanded by Col. Charles H. Smith. Grant planned to send II and V Corps toward Dinwiddie Court House on March 29. Sheridan's cavalry would move up by the left of V Corps, circling around Lee's right and coming up from behind to force him out of his trenches in front of Petersburg. Then the Confederates would be exposed to Grant's main assault.

"I understood ... that if the assault was successful, all right," Crook wrote, "and in case of a repulse, the cavalry was to turn the enemy's right, and raid down to Sherman's army, while the Army of the Potomac was to return to their trenches. The country was to be given to understand that the object of this demonstration was to let out our cavalry."[15]

Early on the morning of March 29, Sheridan started his forces toward Dinwiddie. The roads were a thick clay crust over quicksand, and the spring thaw, together with rain that began soon after the march began, turned them into a quagmire. The first couple of companies of cavalry could pass over them, but then the ground, weakened by the damp and the horses, would give, and the horses from the units following would break through the crust and become mired in the quicksand. The more they struggled, the deeper they sank until some were in up to their chests and had to be abandoned. The only incident was a series of skirmishes between Gregg's brigade in advance, and bands of Confederate cavalry. Crook's division, and Brig. Gen. Thomas C. Devin's First Division from the Army of the Shenandoah camped near Dinwiddie Court House, where they could cover the Vaughan, Flatfoot, Five Forks, and Boydton Plank Roads and guard the rear of V Corps.

At daylight the next morning, Sheridan began moving toward Five Forks, which was held by the Confederates under Maj. Gen. Fitzhugh Lee. Crook was ordered to send Gregg's Brigade to hold the Stony Creek crossing on the Boydton Plank Road, while Davies supported Devin, and Smith was held in reserve near Dinwiddie. About 11 A.M., however, the Confederates attacked Smith who, because of the thick undergrowth, was forced to dismount his men and fight on foot. Although this attack was thrown back, Fitz Lee apparently had anticipated the Union movement against Five Forks and thrown in his infantry around Davies on both sides, cutting him off from Smith. Crook sent in Gregg's brigade, which forced the Confederates up the creek. Davies was forced to fall back, and fight his way back through the Confederate ranks until nightfall, when he rejoined the division on the Vaughan Road. Elsewhere, however, the Southern troops hit Smith a second time with artillery and cavalry, although his men held their ground until nightfall when, ammunition exhausted, they were forced to fall back. Gregg's brigade had also run low on ammunition, and fell back toward Dinwiddie in the face of the advancing Confederate infantry. Lee's troops halted at the junction of the Boydton Plank and Vaughan Roads, and Crook's badly mauled division went into camp on the latter road, some three miles from Dinwiddie.[16]

Crook later estimated that he lost about one-third of his troops in casualties during the fight on the roads, and his division spent the next few days on guard duty, missing the fight at Five Forks on April 1. By April 3, the Union forces had broken the Confederate lines, Richmond was evacuated, and Lee was in retreat. "We all felt that the end of the war was near at hand, and that the Confederate army was in its last throes," Crook wrote in his autobiography.

General Grant was pushing Lee west toward the Appomattox River. The cavalry was hard on the heels of the scattering Confederates, and at 3 A.M., April 4, Crook was ordered to move his division up toward Jetersville on the road to Danville, where he learned that morning that Lee expected rations for his starving army. Sheridan split the cavalry into two groups. Merritt moved toward Amelia Court House, approaching Jetersville from the northwest. Crook was sent to take the railroad between Amelia Court House and Burkeville, then follow the line into Jetersville. The V Corps entered Jetersville late that afternoon, with Crook and Merritt following shortly thereafter.

The next morning Sheridan had Crook send Davies out on a reconnaissance of the Confederate rear. Davies overtook the headquarters trains of both Robert E. Lee and Fitzhugh Lee, and returned to Jetersville with 5 guns, 11 flags, 320 white prisoners, "an equal number" of black teamsters, and over 400 draft animals. He burned two hundred ammunition and headquarters wagons, caissons, and ambulances. Crook took Smith and Gregg to assist, and repulsed an attack on the road. The Confederates then attacked the advance guard with the prisoners, and Smith and Davies threw them back, and the entire division with prisoners managed to reach camp. "The fighting continued all along my front until near nightfall, when the enemy desisted," Crook wrote in his report.

On April 6, Crook's division continued up the road and attempted to cut the Confederate train, but it was too strongly guarded. Crook then moved across the country to Merritt's left as the two Union cavalry commands followed the disorganized Confederates of Lt. Gen. Richard Ewell's II Corps toward the forks of Sayler's Creek, a tributary of the Appomattox. Ewell formed his men behind hastily thrown up breastworks at the fork known as Little Sayler's Creek. Crossing the creek, Crook and Merritt moved in from the south. Crook ordered Gregg's and Smith's brigades dismounted, with Gregg moving to the left and taking possession of the road, while Smith moved to the right adjacent to Merritt's troops. Davies's mounted troops attacked from the front. Gregg's men went over the Confederate works, and Davies made what Crook called "one of the finest charges of the war, riding over and capturing their works and its defenders." The fighting gave Sheridan time to send in Horatio Wright's VI Corps, which bombarded Ewell's position, then attacked across the creek from the northeast. The desperate Confederates fought hard, even clubbing and biting their Union opponents, but to no avail. Cut off from support, the Confederate line collapsed and over eight thousand men, one-fourth of Lee's army, were killed or captured. Among the eight generals taken were Ewell and Kershaw.

The next day, Crook crossed the Appomattox to attack a Confederate position at Farmville. Gregg's troops were in the lead and, for some unaccountable reason, "became stampeded" by the appearance of a small detachment of Southern cavalry. Gregg was captured, and command of his brigade devolved on Col. S. B. M. Young, Fourth Pennsylvania Cavalry. When Crook reached Farmville, he found the Confederate provision trains had managed to reach that point, but his arrival prevented their being unloaded. The trains, however, managed to pull out before the Union forces could capture them.[17]

On April 8, Crook's and Merritt's forces consolidated, although each appears to have retained independent command. A division under Bvt. Brig. Gen. Ranald Mackenzie was attached to Crook's command, and the combined Union cavalry began moving toward Appomattox Station. This apparently was the first time Crook met Mackenzie, whom he would come to know well during the subsequent Indian wars. A member of a prominent naval family, who had broken tradition by joining the army, the twenty-four-year-old Mackenzie was one of the "boy generals" who attained prominence in the Union army during the war. Already, he had been badly wounded several times and, from a military standpoint, was almost an invalid, unable to ride or walk any distance without considerable pain. He had lost part of his right hand from a shell fragment at Petersburg, and was showing early signs of emotional instability that would plague him throughout his life. Nevertheless, he was a brilliant and tenacious fighter, and General Grant went so far as to call him "the most promising young officer in the army."[18]

Union scouts once again located the Confederate trains chugging aimlessly several miles west of Appomattox depot, their engineers uncertain where Lee's forces were. Sheridan sent word to Crook to push ahead of the trains and cut the tracks. Brevet Major General George Armstrong Custer, with his troops in advance, was able to seize the station and drive back a Confederate advance guard, while two of his regiments swung around and headed off the trains, destroying the tracks and preventing their escape. Just before dark, Devin arrived and was put on Custer's right, and one of Crook's brigades was placed on the left with the others in reserve. The Confederates were forced back along the Appomattox Road and the two opposing armies finally went into camp in the vicinity of Appomattox Court House. The trains were turned over to soldiers who, in civilian life, had been railroad engineers and who, in Sheridan's words "were delighted evidently to get back at their old calling. They amused

themselves by running the trains to and fro, creating much confusion, and keeping up such an unearthly screeching with the whistles that I was on the point
of ordering the cars burned. They finally wearied of their fun, however, and ran
the trains off to the east toward General Ord's column."[19]

Shortly after midnight, Crook sent Smith's brigade to hold the road leading
from Appomattox Court House to Lynchburg. Smith found a slight ridge near
the courthouse, and had his men build barricades across the road, placing two
guns, and sending his horses to the rear. The night passed quietly, and Sheridan
was certain that if the Union infantry could catch up with the cavalry at
Appomattox Court House by the next morning, the war would be over.
"Merritt, Crook, Custer, and Devin were present [at Sheridan's headquarters]
at frequent intervals during the night," Sheridan wrote, "and everybody was
overjoyed at the prospect that our weary work was about to end so happily."

Just before daylight, General Ord's troops arrived, having marched all night.
Although this might seem to have ended it, the Confederates still had enough
determination to make one last push. At 9 A.M., Maj. Gen. Bryan Grimes's
troops slammed into Smith's in an effort to break through toward Lynchburg.
Smith was able to hold until Mackenzie arrived, but the cheering Confederates
smashed through in such overwhelming numbers that both Smith's and
Mackenzie's lines were broken. Confederate cavalry, meanwhile, came around
from the rear and forced the Union troops to withdraw. The arrival of Union
infantry, pushing its way through the fleeing cavalrymen, slowed down the
Southern advance, and Crook was organizing a counterattack when word of a
truce reached both sides. All fighting stopped and, at 3 o'clock that afternoon,
Lee and Grant agreed to terms by which Lee would surrender the Army of
Northern Virginia.[20]

A letter to Hayes, written three days later, showed how much Crook appre-
ciated the history he witnessed, and how the inconvenience of his capture
earlier in the year had, in the long run, put him in a better position. It also
showed that, despite strain and fatigue, he was capable of humor. "Thanks to
the *Gorillas* [*sic*] for my capture or now I would in all likelihood be quietly [in]
command of the Mid. Mil. Division in Hancock's place. I would have missed
this campaign & of being in at the death."[21]

On April 14 General Sherman, negotiating with General Johnston in North
Carolina, proposed surrender terms along President Lincoln's line of forgive-
ness and reconciliation. The same night, however, Lincoln was assassinated, and
the Radicals in Congress used the tragedy to stir up public feelings of vengeance against the South. Sheridan's troops, Crook included, were ordered to

North Carolina to back Sherman in case Johnston's army resisted. Within a few days, however, new terms had been offered and accepted, and Sheridan returned to Petersburg. During that march, they learned of Lincoln's death which Crook, in his memoirs (written after more than a decade in the postwar West), called a "massacre."[22]

In the wake of the assassination, the Radicals saw plots at every hand, but Crook realized the South had had enough. "The rebels," he wrote Hayes from Petersburg, "seem to be very dicile & peacebly disposed & all regard the rebellion as a failure & that there [is] no possible hope left for it & have given up their former much vaunted threats of the guerilla warfare that they were going to annoy us with, & I think they will be sensible & come back & resume their old relations with the government, much wiser & better than they were before."[23]

The Civil War, as historian Paul L. Hedren has observed, was a proving ground for men who would serve on the frontier. If, like Crook, they already had some frontier experience, the war prepared them for command. It was also a place where the future frontier officer made friends, assessed potential competitors, and acquired enemies. In Crook's case, his association with Grant one day would advance his career, while the friendship with Hayes would allow him to pursue his own agenda. As a frontier officer, he would command Mackenzie and Merritt, and again would serve under Sheridan.[24]

Overall, Crook's performance during the war was no better or worse than that of many other Union generals. He made mistakes. At Kernstown, Cedar Creek, and Appomattox, his complacency allowed the Confederates to break his line, and at Antietam, he was not even where he was supposed to be. In each case, however, he managed to recover sufficiently to avert disaster and, in some cases, even improve the situation. Although he inspired devotion from some of his immediate subordinates, there is no indication that this loyalty was shared by the rank and file.

Perhaps Crook's greatest blunder was allowing his security to become so lax that he could be taken prisoner from his bed in his own headquarters. This ridiculous scenario was a display of overconfidence that frequently manifested itself throughout his career, and generally when he least could afford it.

General Early later said Crook was one of the most capable Union generals, and gave him much of the credit for the federal victory in the Shenandoah. It is understandable that Early might want to acknowledge someone besides Sheridan. Defeated generals rarely love those who have defeated them, and quite possibly Early was trying to remove some of the sting of his loss by assigning the victory to Sheridan's subordinates.

Crook, of course, accepted Early's views because they reenforced his own notion that his efforts in the valley were unappreciated. He may even have come to see himself as the real hero of the Shenandoah, whose glory was stolen by Sheridan. Few, however, will dispute that Sheridan, not Crook, was the true architect of the Union success in the valley.[25]

With the national crisis largely resolved, Crook took his troops to Fairfax Court House, then went to Ohio on leave. Returning to Virginia, he was formally relieved of command of the Cavalry Corps of the Army of the Potomac on June 27, 1865.[26] Once the Union Army was demobilized, he would be mustered out of the Volunteers and revert back to captain in the Regular Army, the rank he had held at the outbreak four years earlier. He already had accepted an appointment as captain in the Fourth Infantry when he relinquished his cavalry command. Even so, the brevet held certain advantages. Although it had been cheapened by indiscriminate promotion of desk soldiers at the end of the war, a high brevet rank still could be interpreted as qualification for command. In fact, in the years immediately following the war, brevets frequently were invoked to give officers responsibilities far greater than their actual rank normally would allow. In Crook's case, and despite the appointment to the Fourth Infantry, his brevet rank in the Volunteers continued in effect for another six months as the reorganizing army shifted its priorities to Southern Reconstruction. He commanded the military district around Wilmington, North Carolina, until January 22, 1866, when he finally was mustered out of the Volunteers and reincorporated into the regular service, a captain once again, but entitled to the courtesy address of "general."[27]

Rutherford Hayes, likewise, was mustered out of the Volunteers, and returned to Ohio, where he was preparing to go into politics. He and Crook maintained their close bond of friendship, which continued for the remainder of Crook's life. There was a tinge of sadness to the relationship. George Crook Hayes, whom the family sometimes called "the little General" or "the little soldier," died of scarlet fever on May 24, 1866. He was five days short of being twenty months old. "He was a very handsome child," the grieving father wrote, "abundant, waving light hair—very large blue eyes, a broad full forehead. . . . The brothers called him 'the King' because he had his own way."[28]

There can be little doubt that the death affected Crook, but if he wrote about it the letter is not on file, even though the extensive Crook-Hayes correspondence preserves many short notes congratulating Hayes on his accomplishments and consoling him in other bereavements. The loss probably strengthened Crook's already strong bond with Webb Hayes.

On July 18, 1866, Crook was promoted to major and posted to the Third Infantry. He was soon to be promoted again, however, because of a general reorganization of the army, which had demobilized too rapidly following the end of the Civil War. The bulk of the Union army consisted of volunteer forces, and their return to civilian life left only a small cadre of regular troops to meet the demands of frontier defense and Reconstruction of the South. By the summer of 1866, the manpower shortage was such that Congress considered an act to expand the infantry from nineteen to forty-five regiments, and cavalry from six to ten regiments. The act was approved on July 28 and, the same day, Crook was advanced to lieutenant colonel of one of the new regiments, the Twenty-third Infantry. Despite a jump of two grades in less than two weeks, Crook felt he deserved better, particularly because two of his brigade commanders had received appointments as full colonels. This confirmed in his own mind that advancement in the army depended on actions for which an officer received credit rather than on actual achievement.

On the other hand, he had the satisfaction of belated recognition for his efforts at Opequon because, on Sheridan's recommendation, he was appointed brevet major general of the Regular Army, retroactive to September 19, 1864. In presenting Crook's case to Secretary Stanton, Sheridan wrote, "His services in the East, in West Virginia, then in the West, then again in the East, give him a better record than many of those recommended by the Army Board of which I was an absent member." There is no indication, however, that this recommendation altered Crook's deteriorating opinion of his former commander.[29]

Before joining his new regiment, Crook made a major change in his personal life. On August 22, 1866, the long-time bachelor married Mary Dailey of Cumberland, whose father owned the Revere House, where Crook had been captured.[30] Crook made little mention of Mary in his autobiography, which is largely the self-promoting professional memoir of an army officer and is not overly concerned with his private life. His diaries, however, contain many entries—things they did together, travel, entertainments, their wedding anniversaries, her friends, and the state of her health.

SEVEN

"I GOT INTERESTED. . . ."

THE TWENTY-THIRD INFANTRY WAS CREATED by severing a battalion from the existing Fourteenth Infantry, and strengthening that battalion by two additional companies. By the time the changes formally took effect on September 21, 1866, the battalion-turned-regiment was already on station in the Northwest under Maj. Louis H. Marshall. The appointment as lieutenant colonel made Crook de facto commanding officer of the Twenty-third because the regimental commander, Col. Jefferson C. Davis, was on detached duty much of the time—duty that included heading the Military District of Alaska after its purchase from Russia in 1867. Crook was to supersede Major Marshall not only in the regiment but as commanding officer of the District of Boise, in Idaho Territory.[1]

Leaving Mary in Baltimore, Crook departed New York on the Panama steamer *Ocean Queen* on November 5, 1866. The day was cold, a wind was blowing, and the deck was empty except for Crook and a young officer who was out in the open air in an effort to stave off seasickness. At first, they did not speak, but simply walked up and down the deck until, finally, it was impossible to stay out without some sort of acknowledgment. In the ensuing conversation, Crook learned the man was Lt. Azor H. Nickerson from Elyria, Ohio, a Union army veteran on his way to join the Fourteenth Infantry in Arizona.[2]

Years later, Nickerson recalled his first impressions of Crook:

> I should have believed from his looks, that he was fully forty and perhaps forty-
> five years of age, though in point of fact, he had barely passed his thirty-sixth

birthday [Crook was thirty-eight]. His hair, beard and moustache were exceedingly light color, so light, indeed that they appeared to be absolutely white, giving a somewhat grizzled look to his countenance and adding several years in appearance to his age. His head was set squarely upon his broad shoulders by a neck short and thick; the jaw was heavy and, together with a full-sized mouth, gave indication of great firmness of character;—a positiveness which I afterward learned often approached stubbornness. The cheek bones were very high and prominent. The eyes which were bluish-gray in color and rather small, when not animated in conversation, or by some pleasant thought, were cold and stern in their expression. The nose was a pronounced Roman with a decided inclination to be hooked at the extremity. He looked to be about six feet in height, and weighed probably about one hundred and sixty-five or seventy pounds. Though not what is called a "natty" looking soldier, he nevertheless at this time, bore the unmistakable marks of the training he had received at the West Point Military Academy. . . . He was plainly but neatly dressed in a suit of blue cloth, or serge, a coat of which was a semi-military sack with no distinguishing mark of the military service about it, the buttons themselves being of the same texture and color as the coat. He wore one article of dress, however, which would indicate to the most casual observer that he either was or had been in the military service—a black slouch hat of the pattern worn by officers of the Union Army of almost every grade, at the close of the Civil War and in the Army of the Potomac, pretty generally known as the Burnside hat.[3]

For his part Crook took to this young officer, as he did to any Ohioan who had served in the Union army. He later wrote Hayes that Nickerson "served through the war in the 8th Ohio, was wounded four times and in the battles of Antietam and Gettysburg was left for dead, and his recovery was regarded as almost a miracle. He has now a hole in his chest which you can nearly stick your fist in, and in consequence his health is delicate and at times he suffers terribly from this wound. Notwithstanding this, his ambition and zeal to do his duty has been so great, that he has been constantly on duty ever since the war."[4]

Crook would come to know about Nickerson's "ambition and zeal," because, on learning that Nickerson's orders did not designate a specific battalion of the Fourteenth Infantry, and knowing that one battalion of the regiment was on duty in Idaho, he invited the younger man to become his adjutant. Arriving in San Francisco, Crook called on General Halleck, now commander of the Military Division of the Pacific, and asked him as a personal favor to send Nickerson to Boise instead of Arizona. Halleck not only agreed but promised that when permanent assignments of lieutenants were made, he would transfer Nickerson to the Twenty-third Infantry, Crook's own regiment, to facilitate his appointment as adjutant.[5] In Nickerson's words, "My chance meeting with General Crook on the deck of the Ocean Queen on that November day decided, not only the regiment to which I should go, but, also all the important events of my subsequent military career."[6] He would serve Crook loyally for ten years, and would do much to enhance his image after his death.

On the first leg of their journey from San Francisco to Boise, Crook and Nickerson took the Central Pacific Railway, covering much of the same ground that Crook had helped explore as a young lieutenant during the Williamson-Abbot survey eleven years earlier. The rails terminated at Cisco in the Sierra Nevada and from here the men took the Overland stage across the mountains and into the Truckee Valley of Nevada. At this point they had to leave the well-built Concord coaches of the Overland for the "dead-axle" or celerity wagons of the Idaho Stage Company that, according to Nickerson, "possessed neither springs nor any other convenience for the comfort of the traveler. It was all one could do to cling to his seat when he was wide awake and in the full possession of all his strength and faculties; but when tired out, exhausted and sleepy, it was next to an impossibility."

The trip took six days and nights, the passengers pausing only to change horses or to have meals of bread, bacon, and tea at erratic hours. Much of the area was desert, and alkali dust coated the travelers, clinging to their beards and hair, and working its way into their eyes and ears. By now Nickerson was well enough acquainted with Crook to know that he was fastidiously clean, so he was surprised to see that he did not bother to wash. When Nickerson asked why, Crook explained the water was also impregnated with alkali. If he washed his face, the alkali water mixing with the alkali dust would "constitute a powerful lye" that would burn his eyes and take the skin off his face. From then on, Nickerson followed Crook's example of wiping his face with a dry cloth.[7]

The District of Boise was a subdivision of the Department of the Columbia, under command of Maj. Gen. Frederick Steele. The department, in turn, was a subordinate branch of General Halleck's Military Division of the Pacific, one of three such divisions into which the United States was divided for military administrative purposes.[8] The Military Division of the Pacific included the Pacific Coast states and territories and those immediately adjacent; the Military Division of the Missouri, the central two-thirds of the United States; and the Division of the Atlantic, from Ohio to the Northeast. Additionally, there were several departments and military districts to administer the postwar South, which were abolished and incorporated into the Divisions of the Missouri and the Atlantic as Reconstruction ended.

As described by General Halleck, the Division of the Pacific included the states of Oregon, California, and Nevada, and the territories of Washington, Idaho, and Arizona. Alaska was added following its acquisition from the Russians, bringing the total to about 1,218,000 square miles, with about 12,750 statute miles of seacoast, including offshore islands. Halleck estimated the white population at about 70,000, and Indians at about 130,000. This enormous area was policed by two regiments of cavalry, one regiment of artillery, and four of infantry. At the time of Crook's arrival, the division was separated into two departments: the Columbia, which included Washington, Oregon and Idaho, and the Department of California, which covered the remainder. Alaska formed a third department beginning in 1867.⁹

Crook's appearance in Boise, on December 11, was greeted with enthusiasm. The district was rife with Indian troubles and lawlessness. Conditions were so bad, and the army so ineffectual, that local citizens had organized a volunteer company to deal with Indians, and vigilantes had lynched some sixty supposed lawbreakers, including Boise Sheriff Dave Opdyke, who was hanged as a highwayman by three employees of the Overland Stage company.

The real crisis, however, was with the Indians. First Major Marshall, and then Crook, inherited an ongoing conflict with the Paiutes under their chief, Paulina. The latest outbreak resulted from the government's attempts in 1865 to locate the mutually antagonistic Paiutes and Klamaths on the same reservation, and was aggravated by starvation the following winter when government rations failed to arrive. Most of the Paiutes abandoned the reservation and were kept from returning in the spring by their warrior faction. On April 22, 1866, Paulina himself left the reservation and began leading the warriors against stagecoaches and trains of prospectors bound for Idaho. Paiute depredations extended as far south as Nevada.

Several companies of federal and Oregon state troops had been requisitioned by Marshall, but were concentrated in only a few areas, leaving much of the countryside unprotected. The road between Boise and The Dalles was guarded by only two companies, and raiding was so rife that the express company refused to carry valuable cargo along the route. Marshall himself led an expedition against Indians toward the headwaters of the Owyhee River, but had been badly mauled and forced to abandon a howitzer, ammunition, and provisions. Indians attacked a party of Chinese miners, killing at least fifty, and raided horse and cattle ranches.¹⁰

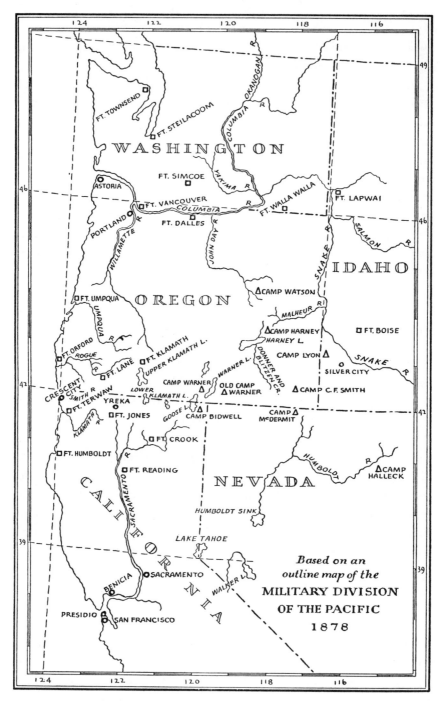

Military Division of the Pacific.

"The feeling against [Marshall] and many of his officers was very bitter," Crook wrote. "They were accused of all manner of things. One thing was certain: they had not, nor were they, making headway against the hostile Indians. There was much dissipation amongst many good officers, and there seemed to be a general apathy amongst them, and an indifference to the proper discharge of duty."[11]

Crook was determined to restore discipline and combat efficiency, and to subdue the hostile Indians in the region. He had the advantage of the season because the Indians would not be expecting any military activity during winter. They were accustomed to raiding with impunity this time of year because the onset of bad weather normally sent soldiers into winter quarters, and campaigning was suspended until spring. A few days after Crook's arrival in Boise, however, he decided to go after a band of Shoshones that was marauding along the Boise River about twenty miles south of town.

The expedition consisted of one company of First Cavalry under Capt. David Perry, ten Indian scouts from the Warm Springs Reservation, and two civilian guides. In his autobiography, Crook wrote that he took "one change of underclothes, toothbrush, etc. . . . intending to be gone a week. But I got interested after the Indians and did not return [to Boise] again for over two years."

The Indian scouts accompanying the expedition were typical of Crook's campaigns. Although they became almost his hallmark, and he their strongest advocate, he did not originate the concept. Indians had participated in various military actions in the Northwest for more than a decade, and the Army Bill of 1866 provided for attaching Indian scouts to regular forces. Two companies had been recruited at the Warm Springs Reservation from Indian groups traditionally hostile to the Paiutes and Shoshones. These companies were formed on the orders of Oregon Governor George L. Woods, who secured congressional authorization over the objections of Steele and Halleck. Company commanders were Dr. William McKay and John Darragh, who were officially designated "interpreters," although they drew officers' pay and had command responsibilities. Even before Crook's arrival, these government Indians had distinguished themselves with their ruthless determination to seek out and destroy all hostiles regardless of age or sex.[12]

Besides the Warm Springs scouts, Crook raised a company of friendly Paiutes, an example of his preference for scouts who were closely related to those he was fighting, and therefore more able to comprehend the enemy. The Paiutes were led by Archie McIntosh, a thirty-two-year-old native of Fort William, Ontario. The son of a Scotsman employed by Hudson's Bay Company and a

Chippewa woman, McIntosh had attended school in Vancouver and Edinburgh. Returning to Canada, he followed his father into Hudson's Bay Company, serving briefly as a clerk. He began scouting for the U.S. Army in 1855, and by the time he met Crook, he had a well-deserved reputation as a competent leader of Indians. Although many who represented themselves as scouts were charlatans, the regimen of Hudson's Bay Company, where success depended on knowledge of Indians and their country, had thoroughly prepared McIntosh for his responsibilities. He was prone to heavy drinking, but Crook had unlimited faith in him.[13]

With his troops and scouts, Crook followed the trail of the Shoshones up the Owyhee River. "Much of this march was made in a violent snow storm," Nickerson wrote, "men and officers alike being without tents and with only a meagre supply of blankets to keep us from freezing."

About daylight, December 18, they located the Shoshone camp on the Owyhee. Leaving ten men to guard his own camp, Crook took the remainder and attacked. The camp contained about eighty warriors who, despite the surprise of a winter attack, put up a hard fight. After a struggle lasting several hours, Crook took the camp, capturing several women and children, and some thirty horses. About twenty-five or thirty of the hostile Indians had been killed, against the loss of one sergeant.[14]

Rather than returning to his headquarters, Crook remained in the field. In January 1867, the Indian scouts discovered a hostile camp on the California road about fifteen miles from Owyhee Ferry in what was then Baker County, Oregon. The troops attacked at daylight, killing sixty, and taking thirty prisoners and a large number of horses. A civilian with the expedition was killed, a second civilian wounded, and three soldiers wounded. A short time later, they attacked a smaller camp, killing five warriors and capturing the survivors. One of the prisoners was recognized as a warrior who previously had been captured and paroled on condition of abandoning war against the whites. He was shot for violating parole.

McKay, meanwhile, was operating separately with his Warm Springs scouts in the Malheur Lake area, and on January 6 they attacked a Paiute camp, killing three warriors and capturing some horses and ammunition. Soon afterward, he discovered the main camp of the Paiute chief, Paulina, at the top of a rocky, two-thousand-foot height. The Warm Springs Indians began scaling the height, but a day-long fight among the rocks ended in a draw. That night, however, McKay's scouts attacked yet another camp, killing twelve Paiute warriors and taking prisoners. By now, the heavy snow and the strain of the long campaign on their horses forced the Warm Springs Indians to break off their operations.

Elsewhere, Crook had moved down to the Snake River, sending back to Boise for supplies and additional Indian scouts. When they arrived, he marched up the Malheur River into the area where McKay had been operating. He located a hostile camp, but the Indians fled upriver until they joined a second band that was protected by a series of sloughs covered with tangles of willows and wild rose bushes. The troops tried to move through the brush, but it proved impenetrable. They were in the open, and the Indians, concealed and invisible only a few feet away, took potshots at them. "In all my experience in campaigns against Indians, this was the only time I could have used artillery to advantage," Crook remarked.

At dark, Crook called a halt and the Indians began a parley, saying they wanted peace. Their haughty attitude, and the fact that they had recently been raiding, convinced him they were lying. Nevertheless, soldiers and warriors drifted back and forth between the two camps, talking and trading. Although the troopers left their rifles in their own camp, they kept their sidearms, and eventually enough were in the Indian camp to control it. "When the Indians saw this," Crook noted, "their whole demeanor changed at once, and they got ready to go with us." Examining their camp, he realized it was virtually impregnable, and was relieved that the encounter had ended peacefully.

Crook next decided to march up to Camp Lyon, located on a tributary of the Owyhee, near the mining town of Silver City, Idaho, fifty miles southwest of Boise. This meant crossing the plateau that divided the valley of the Malheur from the valley of the Owyhee. As the troops marched over the heights, a blizzard struck, blowing so hard that the men found it hard to keep their seat in the saddles, and with snow so fine that it soaked through their clothing. Fortunately, Archie McIntosh was able to keep them on the trail and managed to get them into the warm, sheltered Owyhee valley and to Camp Lyon with no hardship other than the general misery of the storm.[15]

Crook remained at Camp Lyon just long enough to take a dim view of the post. "From appearance and information the normal condition of the officers there was drunkenness," he wrote. "They didn't seem to do much else but get drunk and lie around doing nothing." The post was under command of Capt. J. C. Hunt, First Infantry, who Crook apparently decided needed some time in the field. After sending Captain Perry's company back to Boise, he took Hunt's company, along with twelve Indians and four white scouts, out to reexamine the Owyhee, where hostile bands once again were reportedly active. The column traveled mostly by night, with the scouts well in advance. On January 20, they reported a hostile camp near the eastern slope of Steen's Mountain in southern Oregon. Crook timed his moves to reach the spot before dawn.

At daylight, the command was formed into line of battle about two hundred yards from the camp, whose inhabitants appeared oblivious to any danger. Crook sent the scouts around to some foothills behind the camp, to cut off any that might try to escape. He ordered his men to hold their fire until they actually were in the camp. Then he gave the signal to charge, and everything went wrong.

Crook had intended to remain behind so he could get a good view of the attack and see how the troops performed. But as the charge began, his horse bolted and took the lead. About that time the troopers, ignoring his instructions, opened fire. "The balls whistled by me, and I was in much more danger from the rear than I was from the front. My horse ran through the village, and I could not stop him until he reached some distance beyond, most of the men following me."

Despite the problems, the attack was a success. Sixty warriors were reported killed, and the soldiers took twenty-seven prisoners. One civilian accompanying the expedition was killed, and another wounded, and three soldiers were wounded. The prisoners initially were taken to Camp C. F. Smith, in southeastern Oregon, and from there sent to Boise.[16]

Crook augmented his current force with a company of cavalry from Camp C. F. Smith, and started for Camp Warner in south-central Oregon. The trek was uneventful except for giving him time to evaluate Archie McIntosh. He learned to respect McIntosh's advice and opinions, which almost invariably were correct. He also became accustomed to the scout's drinking binges, for which he developed an amused tolerance, irritating though they sometimes were. Once, McIntosh went out on a foray and was gone so long that Crook worried abut his safety. When he finally returned, "he made some cock and bull report, but I was satisfied that he was drunk the greater part of the time, and the hostiles he saw and slayed were mostly in his mind."[17]

Throughout the spring and early summer, pressure against the Paiutes continued, not only from soldiers and Indian scouts but from the growing number of farmers and ranchers moving into the area. From March onward, troops and Indian scouts patrolled the road between Boise and Canyon City, Oregon, keeping it clear of marauders and following the trails of any that might venture into the area. In late April, they were joined by irate farmers and ranchers, after Paulina led a small band of Paiutes on a cattle-stealing expedition among the farms and ranches around Canyon City. In the ensuing fight, Paulina was killed by a rancher and his place of leadership was taken by two men, Weahwewa and Ocheo.

Since his arrival in the Northwest, Crook had been evaluating the fighting power of his adversaries. He realized that they consistently were well supplied with ammunition and, unlike most tribal peoples dependent on a very limited number of warriors, they did not appear to be particularly damaged or demoralized by the heavy losses they sustained in the constant fighting. Thus he concluded that the Oregon Indians were getting help from the California tribes, who would slip out of their reservations and ride up to Oregon for horse-stealing raids. The stolen horses would be driven back to the reservations in California, where they would be traded for arms and ammunition. These, in turn, would be traded back to the Oregon tribes for more livestock.

"By this means," the contemporary San Francisco historian Hubert Howe Bancroft noted, "a never-failing supply of men, arms, and ammunition was pouring into Oregon, furnished by the reservation Indians of California. Such, at all events, was the conviction of Crook, and he determined to act upon it by organizing a sufficient force of cavalry in his district to check the illicit trade being carried on over the border."[18]

His efforts were facilitated by divisional headquarters in San Francisco which, since the beginning of 1867, had been restructuring districts within the Department of the Columbia. Crook's initial command, the District of Boise, had been abolished in January, and replaced by an expanded jurisdiction designated the District of Owyhee. This included Fort Boise and Camps Lyon, Winthrop, C. F. Smith, and Warner. On August 16, Crook was reassigned to command the District of the Lakes in southern Oregon and northern California, comprising Fort Klamath, and Camps Watson and Logan. Camps Warner and Bidwell remained under his command.[19]

Even before being officially posted to the Lakes, Crook was preparing for his California expedition. He had hoped to get underway by July 1, but delays in mounting his infantry and arranging for his troops to be supplied in the field forced postponement for almost two months. In the meantime, he assembled his troops at Camp C. F. Smith and in late July began moving them toward Camp Warner. On July 27, he was scouting between the two posts with three companies of cavalry and two companies of Warm Springs, Columbia River, and Boise Shoshones when he came across a large Paiute camp in the Pueblo Mountains of southern Oregon. The scouts, eager to distinguish themselves, were allowed to attack while the troops were held in reserve. The government

Indians completely surrounded the camp and moved in, taking thirty scalps as trophies.[20]

About the same time, Darragh's scouts returned to Camp C. F. Smith from an expedition into The Dalles. Joseph Wasson, co-owner and correspondent of Silver City's *Owyhee Avalanche,* reported: "They had a little fight somewhere on the way, killing four and getting one [of their own] killed. They made a display of scalps and parade on their advent here. Their war songs may be music to them. Together with the Boise Indians, they made camp howl last night."[21]

Wasson himself had joined Crook at Camp C. F. Smith as one of the nation's first western war correspondents. Previously, newspaper accounts of Indian fighting were largely imaginary, often written by editorial staffers who never left their desks in the eastern cities. Crook, remembering the effect of publicity on advancement and prestige in the Union army, was willing for Wasson to accompany him and get the story firsthand. The correspondent was no greenhorn. At twenty-six, he had already been in the West for seven years. A native of Wooster, Ohio, at the age of nineteen he had joined a company of prospectors. During that journey, they were attacked by Indians, which act instilled in him a lifelong hatred toward them. In 1865, he and his brother, John, drifted into Silver City, where they established the *Owyhee Avalanche.* Wasson served as correspondent for, besides his own paper, the *San Francisco Evening Bulletin,* assuring Crook of exposure in the metropolitan West as well. Ultimately, he accompanied Crook not only in the Northwest but in his later campaign against the Lakotas and Cheyennes. He also supported Crook's efforts in Arizona. With Wasson in his entourage, Crook could be certain of friendly coverage.

The relationship worked two ways. Wasson quickly learned that news correspondents who wrote favorably were elevated to an "insider" status. For while Crook may have kept his plans to himself where his officers were concerned, he made certain that friendly correspondents were fully briefed. Officers often were frustrated by the fact that they knew less of their commander's plans than the newspaper representatives.[22]

As he prepared for his expedition, Crook had to select a new site for Camp Warner because the existing location, some five thousand feet above sea level, was unsuitable for winter campaigns. Indeed, during the unusually severe winter of 1866–67, the garrison had barely avoided freezing to death. On July 29, he took a detachment of troops and Indian scouts to find a better site. Two days later they selected a spot on the eastern boundary of California that was five hundred feet lower and accessible year round. On their return trip, they found fresh trails leading into California, confirming Crook's suspicions about the involvement of Indians from that state in the Oregon raids. "Many side scouts were made, with numbers of small parties of Indians being killed and captured," Crook wrote. On August 3, he set out to establish another winter post, which was located at the south end of the Blue Mountains of Oregon and designated Camp Harney.[23]

Joe Wasson accompanied Crook on all these treks, and within a few weeks had seen enough of him to form an opinion that he passed on to his readers: "The success of the Command so far, and upon success alone is everything judged in this practical world, implies that Gen. Crook's plan is as good as any; and I believe he has the Indian character a little nearer down to a scratch than any man in the regular service. By having sufficient men to surround and whip any band liable to be met, and good scouts with a change of horses, he can sweep a wide belt of country and keep it up continually."[24]

Finally, all was ready for the California expedition. The troops were in good condition, and Crook ordered an extra month's rations so that they could remain out, if necessary, until October 20. One of the officers of the Twenty-third Infantry, Lt. W. R. Parnell, observed that four years of Civil War had left them "full of fight and capable of enduring any amount of fatigue and hardship." Wasson noted frontier experience as well. "I find a goodly number of the old Regular Army here," he wrote, "men who can tell of nearly every expedition on this Coast. It is a noticeable feature that the Cavalry is composed of Americans, while the Infantry, on the other hand, is mostly made up of foreigners."[25]

Archie McIntosh took eighteen Indians and scouted south into the Goose Lake Valley in advance of the main force, and got the worst of a running fight with a band of warriors armed with modern weapons. McIntosh's failure was largely because the scouts had been issued obsolete, Mexican War–vintage muskets. Consequently, when a group of supply wagons arrived from Boise with new firearms, Crook saw to it that the scouts were issued new Sharps rifles. Lieutenant Parnell's company drew Spencer repeating carbines.

The command finally moved out on August 30. It included two companies of Twenty-third Infantry, who were mounted, and two companies of First Cavalry, a total of 360 men, of which 280 were soldiers, and the rest Indian scouts and mule packers. Marches were made at night, and the distance varied from one day to the next so that no pattern would be established that Indians might rely on for an ambush. They moved across the Goose Lake Valley and into the mountains, sometimes halting for a day or two to graze the animals and give the Indians a chance to scout the country ahead. Crook spent his free time fly fishing and hunting. No hostile Indians were encountered during the first two weeks, but on September 11, fresh signs were discovered. Two days later, Crook divided the command, sending Perry north with two companies of cavalry, and Darragh's and McKay's scouts to the north to investigate the area from Summer and Silver Lakes to the headwaters of the Deschutes River, while he continued southward with the two companies of mounted infantry and McIntosh's scouts.

On September 22, Crook crossed the state line into California, and Indian sign became plentiful. That night, his men saw campfires in the west, and he sent two parties of scouts under McIntosh and a civilian known as "Dad" Wilson to investigate. If they located the Indian camps, they were to move in as close as possible, try to estimate the numbers, and report back. Then Crook would make a night march and catch them at dawn. He was uneasy about Wilson, and rarely gave him any sort of responsibility, because the man boasted too much about Indian fights he probably never had. At this point, however, Crook apparently felt he had no choice.

Wilson blundered almost immediately by building a large fire visible for miles around. To compound the error, early the next morning his group discovered a large camp but, instead of reporting back to Crook, he opened fire and then fled for his life. About noon, he came rushing into camp to report what he had found, but by now every Indian in the vicinity was thoroughly alarmed and signal fires could be seen in every direction. When McIntosh's scouts returned, bearing the scalp and rifle of a warrior they had killed, they reported seeing runners spreading warnings of the troops. Crook immediately discharged Wilson, and some of the infantrymen were preparing to lynch him for cowardice and incompetence when an officer intervened.

Over the next several days, a sense of gloom settled in as the troops marched farther into California. They had traveled almost four hundred miles without seeing any serious action, and were exhausted and foot-sore. At one camp, Wasson saw Crook sitting under a pine tree roasting the seeds in their cones, and whittling and whistling. He was trying to put on a cheerful face, but, as the correspondent observed, the general "considered the campaign 'all up.'" McIntosh's horses were worn out, and most of the animals were sick. The hostiles, meanwhile, had scattered.[26]

On September 26, the command moved eastward into the Pit River Valley, where McIntosh reported a large band of warriors dug in on the same lava beds where Crook had fought as a young lieutenant. The Indians had set themselves up on a high bluff that actually was the rim of an extinct crater. The crater rim itself formed a natural fortification, but the Indians had improved it. Two parallel promontories about thirty feet apart ran into the southeastern rim. Each was about 150 feet long and thirty feet high, and the area in between was a ravine that formed a sort of moat. The Indians had fortified these promontories with breastworks built of lava rock piled up chest-high, with small openings for rifle loops. Holes and cracks in the ground gave access to fissures and caves below. The position was defended by about seventy-five Paiutes, thirty Pit River Indians, and a few Modocs.

Crook sent McIntosh and his scouts to a bluff that overlooked the hostile position from about four hundred yards, then ordered Lieutenant Parnell to dismount half his men and form a line south of the promontories. Lieutenant John Madigan was ordered to do the same on the north side, with the two lines coming together on the east. Lieutenant Isaac Eskridge was placed in charge of horses, packers, and supplies. By 1 P.M., the troops were in formation, and Crook ordered Parnell to move up the ravine. The Paiutes and their allies opened fire, but Parnell rushed his men ahead to shelter under the rim of the ravine. The angle was so steep that the hostile Indians had to lean over their breastworks to get a shot, and so they ceased firing. Parnell's men then began reconnoitering up the ravine, but had a hard time finding their footing on the steep slope that was covered with boulders and loose rocks. Just ahead, a group of warriors concealed among the rocks let loose a shower of arrows, killing Pvt. James Lyons, mortally wounding Sgt. Charles Barchet, and wounding two privates.

The arrows gave away the Indian position, and the soldiers on the slopes moved in. The ground was so rocky, however, that the warriors were practically invisible, and the troops had to get within twenty yards of them before they found a target. Crook ordered Lieutenant Eskridge to go into camp and prepare to receive wounded. Then he sent a squad of Parnell's men to join Archie McIntosh and his Indian scouts on the bluff and pour a steady fire into the Paiute position. Meanwhile, he reconnoitered breastworks from every angle.

As night fell, an electrical storm moved in and lasted until midnight. The lightning flashes illuminating the broken lava rock added a weirdness to the scene. Crook ordered all the men to get full rations, and stationed pickets around the hostile position to make sure the Paiutes did not try to escape. McIntosh's Indian scouts came down from the bluff and worked their way up the slope among the rocks until they were within a hundred feet of the easternmost breastworks. The troops were also moving into a better position. From above, Crook's men could hear the sounds of moving rocks as the Paiutes and their Pit River allies strengthened their breastworks; their voices echoed from the caverns inside the promontory. Sporadic fighting continued all night. The hostile Indians shot arrows and threw stones at random, to keep the troops and Indian scouts from coming too close. The soldiers occasionally opened up with a cross-fire in the darkness, and a shot from Parnell's line accidentally killed one of Madigan's men.[27]

Shortly before daybreak, Crook came up from the camp, and told Parnell and Madigan to form their men up under the crest on the east side. McIntosh and the scouts were ordered around to the opposite side. Eager to get in on the action, Joe Wasson and a civilian named Lawrence Traynor volunteered to go with the troops, and were placed with Madigan's squad. Then Crook spoke to them. Wasson told his readers, "The General talked to the men 'like a father'— told them that at the word 'Forward,' they should rise up quick, go with a yell and keep yelling and never think of stopping until they had crossed the ditch, scaled the wall and broke through the breastworks, and the faster the better."[28]

About daylight, the troops began moving up the slope. They had gone twenty feet when the Indians opened up with rifles and arrows, killing Madigan and wounding seven others, including the civilian Traynor. The rest charged ahead until they came over the crest overlooking the Indians' eastern breast-works. Sergeant Michael Meara shouted, "Come on boys, we've got 'em," then fell over with a fatal bullet in his head. The other troops poured over the breast-works, but the Indians threw down their rifles, clambered over the works, and disappeared among the rocks of the ravine. A shower of arrows and bullets flew over from the works on the western promontory, but soon Parnell's men secured the defenses.

Now in control of the Paiute works, Crook began to think they were "the 'White Elephant' prize." In the early morning light, the troops were silhouet-ted against the sky while the hostiles were among the rocks in the darkness of the ravine. "I never wanted dynamite so bad as I did when we first took the fort and heard the diabolical and defiant yells from down in the rocks."

The troops held the breastworks all day, ducking bullets and arrows from below. That night, the Paiutes and their allies slipped away to Crook's great relief. Seven men were killed, and ten soldiers and the civilian Traynor were wounded. The dead, with the exception of Lieutenant Madigan, were buried side-by-side in separate graves on a flat by the river. The excess dirt was removed, and horses were herded over to obliterate any sign of the burial, so that the Indians would not dig up the bodies. It apparently served no purpose because when a burial detail returned to the site to recover the bodies, they could not be found.

Crook was upset at the loss of Madigan, of whom he later remarked, "a braver officer never lived." As a special tribute, the lieutenant's body was taken a day's march downstream, and buried with as much honor as could be mustered under the circumstances. Ironically, when the command returned to Camp Warner with the wounded on October 4, the mail contained a letter of promotion for Madigan.[29]

The fight in the lava field came to be known as the Battle of Infernal Caverns. Wasson's account of the fight and of the campaign as a whole was favorable. Crook, he said, "set about whipping the Indians and learning their haunts, with an energy unparalleled."[30]

Not everyone was impressed. In his history of Oregon, Bancroft, who normally was a Crook partisan, or at least neutral, acidly commented:

> That General Crook sacrificed his men in the affair of Pit River [Infernal Caverns] in his endeavor to achieve what the public expected of him is evident, notwithstanding the laudatory and apologetic accounts of the correspondents of the expedition. Had he let his Indian scouts do the fighting in Indian fashion, while he held his troops ready to succor them if overpowered, the result might have been different. One thing, indeed, he was able to prove, that the foe was well supplied with ammunition, which must have been obtained by the sale of property stolen in marauding expeditions to the north.[31]

A month after the fight, the *Sacramento Union* also published a critical account, calling the fight a "defeat" and "retreat," apparently because of the number of soldiers killed and wounded. An editorialist in the *Owyhee Avalanche* (probably Wasson) responded by writing, "Altogether, Crook's Campaign south of Goose Lake is the most important affair that has occurred in the way of settling the Piutes and their allies. . . . There is a queer notion that—if men get killed in an Indian fight—the victory must be on the side of the Indians, no matter what the Indians may have suffered. It is Crook's style to save his men, but where the point can't be made without somebody getting hurt, 'war to the knife' is the word; and Indian is the meanest of all warfare at best."[32]

With the campaign concluded, Crook went to Camp Harney. His wife, Mary, whom he had not seen in a year, had recently come from the East, and was spending time in San Francisco and Portland while she waited for him to finish in the field. She arrived at Harney about October 20, and he took her back to Camp Warner, where he maintained his headquarters. The camp was still unfinished, and in his autobiography, he wrote that they spent that winter "in a log hut, with the cracks plastered with mud, no windows, and a tent fly for a covering. Our only light by day was through the roof."

The winter of 1867–68 was another especially severe season. The food at Camp Warner was poor and in short supply. Crook supplemented his own supply by hunting. By spring, many in the garrison had scurvy, which was relieved by digging up the wild onions that grew in the vicinity. But the harsh winter had positive effects as far as the government was concerned; it forced the Indians down from the mountains and into the valleys, where they were continually harassed by the troops. Some portion of Crook's command was almost always in the field, marching as much as twenty miles a day through fields of heavy snow. On March 17, 1868, Crook led his troops through a blinding snowstorm to fight the Paiutes on Donner and Blitzen Creek south of Malheur Lake, killing and capturing fourteen. A month later, several Paiutes were also killed in a fight near Steen's Mountain.[33]

On April 1, Crook was assigned to temporary command of the Department of the Columbia, and went to departmental headquarters in Portland to assume command and familiarize himself with his responsibilities. While he was away, the expeditions continued and, as Parnell later wrote, "so demoralized the Indians, by destroying their provisions and lodges, capturing their women and children, and killing many of their chiefs and braves, that nothing was left for them but to surrender and beg for clemency."

A message was sent to Crook, who summoned the chiefs and various bands to a council at Camp Harney. Crook and his staff arrived at Harney on June 29, and the council was held the following day. Among the leading chiefs were Weahwewa, who had taken over leadership of the Paiutes following the death of Paulina, and E-ah-gant and Big Head. In Crook's view, the normal diplomacy of government peace commissioners was flawed in two respects: it flattered the chiefs and made them feel they were in a position to dictate terms, and it deluded them with promises that the government almost certainly would not honor. Consequently, he went to the council determined to impress Weahwewa with the hopelessness of more fighting, while dealing with him fairly and honestly as one human being to another.

When, Weahwewa started to shake hands, Crook ignored the gesture. "Tell him," he told the interpreter, "that I did not come here to shake hands with him. He has been too bad an Indian; murdered too many people. I came to hear what he has to say for himself."

Startled, Weahwewa said his people could take no more fighting. "Your great white people are like the grass," he said, "the more you cut it down the more it grows and the more numerous its blades. We kill your white soldiers, and ten more come for every one that is killed; but when you kill one of our warriors, or one of our people, no more come to replace them. We are very weak and cannot recuperate." They wanted peace, he continued, even to the point of abandoning their time-honored tradition of horse stealing.

Crook replied that his soldiers were there to fight, and as long as the Paiutes continued their depredations, the troops would harass them until the last Indian was dead. On the other hand, if they maintained peace, the soldiers would be their friends and protectors. As a gesture of good will, he asked Weahwewa for ten warriors to serve as scouts against the Pit River Indians. Ten of the best warriors immediately volunteered.[34]

The final terms of the treaty took time to arrange, but the council between Crook and the chiefs at Camp Harney signaled the beginning of ten years of peace in Oregon, and Crook was invited to Salem to receive the thanks of the legislature.[35] In his annual report on the condition of the division for 1868, General Halleck wrote:

> The Indian war which has been waged for many years in southern Oregon and Idaho, and the northern parts of California and Nevada, has been conducted with great energy and success by General Crook since he took command in that section of the country. On the 22d of August he reported that about eight hundred hostile Indians had surrendered, and that the war was virtually closed. Since that time no new depredations have been committed. . . .
>
> Too much praise cannot be given to General Crook for the energy and skill with which he has conducted this war, enduring without complaint the hard- ships, privations, and dangers of its numerous marches, scouts, and battles.[36]

Crook's success in the Northwest convinced many leading citizens and public officials that he deserved advancement. When Brig. Gen. Joseph Hooker's retirement was announced in the fall of 1868, they banded together to campaign for Crook's appointment to the vacancy. Letters advocating Crook came from notables such as Gov. H. H. Haight of California, several U.S. senators, former Gov. Addison C. Gibbs of Oregon, and *Portland Oregonian* editor H. W. Scott. Nor was it limited to the West. Rutherford Hayes used his influence as governor of Ohio, and Gov. Arthur Ingram Boreman of West Virginia also wrote a letter of support. Crook was passed over for the appointment, however, no doubt in part because it would have been a jump of two grades and the army had a large number of full colonels ahead of him on the promotion list.[37]

In the midst of his responsibilities in the Northwest, Crook found time to keep in touch with Hayes. He sent Hayes three pairs of elk antlers, two for his sons, Conly and Kennedy (Webb was in Europe at the time), and one for Hayes himself. Hayes was delighted. "They are indeed magnificent," he wrote. "I shall prize my pair exceedingly. You find your portrait in my library [illegible] under a pair of bucks horns of unusual size. But the poor little bucks head is [illegible] by the side of Mr. Elk." In return, he sent Crook a portrait of his daughter "to show you how she is growing."

Like her husband, Mary Crook enjoyed the friendship with Rutherford and Lucy Hayes, and doted on their children. Frequently, when traveling between her husband's assignments in the West and her home and family in Maryland, she would stop in Ohio and spend a few days with the Hayeses.[38]

The year 1869 brought changes to the army. General Grant was inaugurated as president, and Sherman succeeded him as general-in-chief. Grant appointed Phil Sheridan to lieutenant general and commander of the Military Division of the Missouri, even though Halleck and George Meade both outranked him. Sheridan's advancement over senior officers was an example of Grant's penchant for cronyism that would help Crook in the future.[39]

Grant's inauguration also brought a shift in the federal Indian policy. This in itself was nothing new. Political indecision had long been a hallmark of government-Indian relations, and was created, in part, by rivalries in Washington that dated back two decades. Indian affairs had been the responsibility of the War Department until 1849, when jurisdiction was transferred to the newly established Department of the Interior. Nevertheless, the government continued to call on soldiers to suppress outbreaks, and in doing so convinced the army command that the Department of the Interior was incapable of administering Indians. Both the War and Interior Departments lobbied their cases with Congress, which itself was divided. The Senate's constitutional power to ratify treaties extended to pacts with the Indians, and a jealous House of Representatives sought to extend its influence by including Indian legislation in its own bills. The result was a tangle of contradictory positions leaving military commanders on the frontier to sort things out as best they could.[40]

Jurisdictional disputes aside, both the Interior Department and the civilian arm of the War Department were corrupted to such a degree that public imagination institutionalized this corruption and gave it a name—the Indian Ring. A loosely knit cadre of politicians, bureaucrats, and contractors, the ring administered Indian programs through a system of graft that reached from the highest levels down to the individual agencies. Large sums were made by Indian agents who padded the numbers of Indians enrolled at their agencies, and by contractors who provided substandard food and equipment to Indians at the agencies as well as to soldiers at military posts. The situation was so lucrative that officials of the War and Interior Departments responsible for appointing agents and granting contracts often expected large payoffs in exchange for their patronage.

Upon taking office, President Grant implemented what became known as the Peace Policy. First, the president placed the Indian agencies under the jurisdiction of various religious denominations. While this did much to clean up corruption, the good intentions of many of the agents were not enough to deal with the realities of their responsibilities. Second, in an attempt to improve the public perception of the Department of Interior's Indian Bureau, Congress created the nine-member Board of Indian Commissioners to serve as unpaid advisors to the president and secretary of the Interior Department. This only aggravated the problem. Although the board had no executive power, the act establishing it gave the impression that it had some legal authority, thereby prompting a jurisdictional dispute between the board and the Department of the Interior. William Welsh of Philadelphia, first chairman of the board and a man who would remain active in the Indian rights movement, resigned when the board failed to obtain control over the government's Indian expenditures. Even so, with Grant's support, the board continued to exercise a powerful influence over policy on the frontier.[41]

There is no indication that Crook was particularly concerned with the Peace Policy during the remainder of his tenure in the Columbia, but it would become a critical issue in his next assignment.

EIGHT

ARIZONA
—⚏—

"A Sharp Active Campaign"

Now that the Northwest was peaceful, Maj. Gen. George Thomas, who had succeeded Halleck as division commander, offered Crook a new jurisdiction then being organized within the Division of the Pacific. Designated the Department of Arizona, it would encompass the Territory of Arizona as well as southern California and parts of Nevada. Currently, the area was managed directly from division headquarters in San Francisco, but Arizona, Nevada, and southeastern California were so remote that communication with headquarters took weeks. The problem was particularly acute in Arizona itself. For centuries few outsiders had expressed any particular interest in the territory, which was considered largely a wasteland. But the discovery of its abundant underground resources brought hundreds of people, and towns and mining camps sprang up in the mountains north of the Gila River. Development brought conflict with the native Apaches, who raided ranches and camps and waylaid travelers. The establishment of a separate department for Arizona was expected to allow local command and streamline military operations.

Crook was not enthusiastic about the general's offer. "I told him I was tired of the Indian work," he wrote, "that it only entailed hard work without any corresponding benefits. Besides, the climate of Arizona had such a bad reputation that I feared for my health." Arizona's extremes of bitter heat and cold were notorious. Thomas assured him he could remain in the Columbia, and when the Department of Arizona was formally established on April 5, 1870, Col. George Stoneman was designated commander. Eight days earlier, however, General Thomas had suffered a fatal stroke in his office in San Francisco, and his successor, Maj. Gen. John Schofield, arrived with a new set of priorities. In August, Brig. Gen. Edward R. S. Canby was named to relieve Crook in the Department of the Columbia.

While he awaited reassignment, Crook served on a retiring and reduction board in San Francisco. Known as "Benzine Boards" because they "cleaned up" the army (benzine was a popular cleaning fluid of the day), the retiring and reduction boards were created under the Army Appropriations Bill of 1869, which required drastic cuts in military personnel. A board in Washington decided which field officers were to be discharged or retained, and departmental boards made the selections among the junior officers.[1]

Meanwhile, Apache raids in the Southwest convinced many in Arizona that Crook should command their newly established department, regardless of his own feelings. The territory was then in the throes of a long and bloody conflict known as the Cochise War, named for a Chiricahua Apache chief whose depredations in the southwestern U.S. and northwestern Mexico were so extensive that he was blamed for virtually every incident, whether or not he actually was involved. Although not the only hostile Apache leader at the time, Cochise certainly was one of the most tenacious and gifted and, as a general rule, almost all his warriors were armed with modern weapons. The war was fought on two fronts, with the Apaches facing U.S. federal troops in Arizona and Sonoran state troops in Mexico, the latter motivated by a bounty on Apache scalps.[2]

With the Cochise War entering its second decade and no end in sight, Colonel Stoneman attempted to implement President Grant's Peace Policy in Arizona, and in doing so, placed himself in a no-win position. He alienated the eastern supporters of the Peace Policy by continuing military pressure against Apaches who remained hostile. Ironically, these efforts were largely demonstrations to satisfy the Arizona public's demand for some sort of action; any effort to mount a major Indian campaign was hindered by the same congressional cutbacks that had created the "Benzine Boards." Even as he pursued hostiles, however, Stoneman also established a series of "feeding stations" throughout the territory to provide Apaches a place to settle and draw rations if they agreed to remain passive. As he anticipated, the plan encouraged many bands to come in and settle down. Nevertheless, the feeding stations alienated local citizens, who feared that the peace would only be temporary, just long enough for the army to suspend operations entirely and reduce the number of troops in Arizona. That, in turn, would lead to an even bigger Apache uprising once the troops were gone. Their fears appeared justified when Stoneman recommended closing five military posts, despite ongoing depredations by some Apache bands. Citizens of Tucson decided the time had come for decisive action.

Tucson was within easy striking distance of Camp Grant, which served a nearby feeding station for some three hundred Aravaipa Apaches under Chief Eskiminzin. During the first three months of 1871, Camp Grant was commanded by Lt. Royal Emerson Whitman, Third Cavalry, whose even-handed policy toward the Apaches earned him the enmity not only of the area's Anglo-Saxon community but also of the Hispanic population, and of Indians from tribes hostile to the Apaches. On April 1, Capt. Frank Stanwood assumed command, but had enough confidence in the lieutenant to take the bulk of garrison out on a scouting expedition.

Stanwood and his troops left Camp Grant on April 24, leaving Whitman in charge of the post with only fifty soldiers. This presented the locals with an opportunity to clean out the Apaches and discredit Whitman. At daybreak, April 30, about forty Anglo and Hispanic vigilantes from Tucson, aided by about a hundred Apache-hating Papago Indians, attacked Eskiminzin's rancheria and slaughtered the sleeping Apaches. Estimates of the dead ranged from a low of twenty-one to a high of 144, but probably were in the neighborhood of about eighty-five. Several of the women were raped before they were killed. Almost thirty children were taken by the Papagos to Sonora and sold into slavery.[3]

The Camp Grant Massacre, as it soon became known, horrified easterners, and President Grant threatened to put Arizona under martial law unless the perpetrators were tried. In Tucson, Territorial Gov. Anson P. K. Safford demanded Stoneman's removal, blaming the massacre on his policy of feeding the Apaches. As a replacement, Safford wanted Crook, who now had an established reputation as an Indian fighter. When General Schofield approached him about it, however, Crook gave him essentially the same reply that he earlier had given Thomas. Safford himself visited San Francisco to discuss the matter personally with Crook and, on being told that he remained uninterested, promised not to push the matter.

Despite this assurance, Safford went to Washington, where he and Republican Sen. William R. Stewart of Nevada urged Grant to send Crook to Arizona. The proposal drew objections from Secretary of War W. W. Belknap and General Sherman, both of whom cited Crook's low active rank of lieutenant colonel. Departmental command was the responsibility of senior officers. Crook's position in the Columbia had been a fluke, and was possible largely because the army was in the process of reorganizing in the wake of the Civil War. Now, however, the reorganization was essentially completed, and command of the

Department of Arizona rightfully belonged to a brigadier general or to any one of the forty full colonels who outranked Crook.[4] Intervening personally, Grant overrode them and, on May 1, 1871, Adjutant General E. D. Townsend telegraphed Secretary Belknap, who was in Cincinnati: "The President directs me to inform you of his desire that Lieut. Colo. George Crook be assigned on his brevet rank to relieve Colonel Stoneman in command of the Dept. of Arizona until a new arrangement next fall."[5]

Crook was not happy about the appointment. He was particularly irritated when General Townsend pointedly advised him the assignment was only temporary, and a new department commander would be appointed in the fall. Nevertheless, after winding up his affairs in Portland and San Francisco, he departed the latter city by steamer for San Diego on June 3, accompanied by Andrew Peisen, his "striker" or military valet, Archie McIntosh, and Azor Nickerson, who would serve him as aide-de-camp and acting assistant adjutant general. "Archie was drunk and had to be taken aboard the ship under guard," Crook remembered. He stayed drunk throughout most of the journey from San Francisco to Tucson.

The following day, the steamer stopped for several hours at the little seacoast town of Wilmington, near Los Angeles, where Colonel Stoneman maintained his departmental headquarters at Drum Barracks. Here Crook formally assumed command and accepted a courtesy invitation to dinner with the Stonemans. It was not a pleasant meeting; through all the politeness, Crook could sense a strong feeling of resentment, particularly from Mrs. Stoneman. Part of this, no doubt, was because Stoneman had been relieved by an officer of lower rank.

Crook left Nickerson at Drum Barracks to handle administrative details, and rejoined McIntosh and Peisen on board the steamer for the remainder of the trip to San Diego. They took the stage to Yuma, and from there a military ambulance to Tucson. Crook was struck by the barrenness of the country and the intense heat. Even the nights were so hot that sleep was difficult, and he woke up almost as tired as when he went to bed.[6]

Upon arriving in Tucson, then the territorial capital, Crook had lunch with Governor Safford, who used the opportunity to defend the local vigilantes who had taken part in the Camp Grant Massacre and to vilify Lieutenant Whitman as the source of much of the trouble. Although Crook did not necessarily condone the massacre, he believed the citizens had provocation. He also was already developing a dislike for Whitman, although the reasons are obscure because there is no record that the two as yet had ever met. This dislike soon would turn to hatred.[7]

Crook also had a dim view of Eskiminzin, whom he called "Old Skimmy." The chief and his people had attempted to return to Camp Grant a few weeks after the massacre, but were attacked by a column of troops from Camp Apache. Convinced now that the whites could not be trusted, and perhaps also trying to restore his own prestige because his trust had brought his people so much suffering, Eskiminzin stopped by the ranch of a white friend, Charles McKinney, shared his supper, and then murdered him. A short time later, he attacked an army train between Fort Bowie and Tucson, although concealed riflemen drove him off with a loss of thirteen of his warriors. Thus, between Cochise and Eskiminzin, Crook had arrived to find southern Arizona in the midst of a general uprising.[8]

Now that he had reached his new command, Crook set about reorganizing it with his usual thoroughness. In establishing his headquarters at Drum Barracks on the coast of southern California rather than in Arizona proper, Stoneman had virtually defeated the purpose of maintaining the territory as a separate department. However much he disliked the Arizona climate, Crook believed the headquarters should be where it was most useful, and he transferred it to Whipple Barracks at Prescott. In another action, he ordered that Indians would no longer be fed at military posts unless they were confined as prisoners of war. He also summoned every officer in southern Arizona to report as soon as possible for a personal interview. One officer later recalled:

> From each he soon extracted all he knew about the country, the lines of travel, the trails across the various mountains, the fords where any were required for the streams, the nature of the soil, especially its products, such as grasses, character of the climate, the condition of the pack-mules, and all pertaining to them, and every other item of interest a commander could possibly want to have determined. But in reply not one word, not one glance, not one hint, as to what he was going to do or what he would like to do.

This was the point in Crook's character that made the strongest impression upon every one coming in contact with him—his ability to learn all that his informant had to supply, without yielding in return the slightest suggestion of his own plans or purposes.[9]

The interviews also allowed him to assess his officers so that he could make adjustments to his staff. Two of these men, Lt. William J. Ross, Twenty-first Infantry, a tough, hard-drinking Scotsman, and Lt. John Gregory Bourke, Third Cavalry, the scholarly son of well-to-do Irish immigrants, were appointed aides-de-camp, allowing Nickerson to concentrate on his administrative duties as adjutant.[10] The choice of Bourke could not have been better, given the conditions in the Regular Army at the time. The "Benzine Boards" had reduced the size of the service to such an extent that normally promotions occurred only when an officer died or left the service, thereby creating a vacancy. Competition for these vacancies was fierce, and officers routinely advanced their own cases and denigrated potential rivals in the newspapers. Bourke, who was shrewd, intelligent, and highly literate, became a press agent who advanced Crook's cause, both during his lifetime and after his death. His frequent articles on Crook's campaigns culminated in a book, *On the Border with Crook,* published a year after Crook died. Historians generally agree that much of Crook's modern reputation is based on Bourke's efforts.[11]

John Gregory Bourke was born in Philadelphia, on June 23, 1846. His early education in a parochial school was augmented by a Jesuit tutor who taught him Gaelic, Greek, and Latin. His upper-level education was interrupted in 1862 when, caught up in the patriotic frenzy of the Civil War, he lied about his age and enlisted in the Fifteenth Pennsylvania Volunteer Cavalry. Bourke served gallantly, winning the Medal of Honor at Stones River. When the war ended, he entered West Point, graduated in 1869, and was assigned to various posts in New Mexico and Arizona. When he was not fighting Indians, he studied their lives and cultures, ultimately establishing a reputation not only as a soldier but also as a highly respected anthropologist. Even so, he appeared destined for the oblivion of a career soldier at isolated frontier posts when Crook appeared, took him under wing, and thus assured both their futures.[12]

Recording his impressions of Gen. Crook for posterity, Bourke wrote:

> He reminded me more of Daniel Boone than any other character, with this difference, that Crook, as might be expected, had the advantages of the better education of his day and generation. But he certainly recalled Boone in many particulars; there was the same perfect indifference to peril of any kind, the same coolness, and equal fertility of resources, the same inner knowledge of the wiles and tricks of the enemy, the same modesty and disinclination to parade as the hero or a great military genius, or to obtrude upon public notice the deeds performed in obedience to the promptings of duty.[13]

Not everyone who served with Crook or under him would agree with Bourke's view.

As in the northwest, Crook saw no point in sitting idle when the war could be carried to the Indians. He was determined to use the limited forces at his disposal to convince the Apaches that their survival depended on submission to the government. On July 11, he left Camp Lowell near Tucson with five companies of Third Cavalry—a total of 204 men—for a reconnaissance of Apache country between Lowell and Camp Bowie. Scouts had been sent ahead to "scour" the country south of the road between the two posts, They arrived at Bowie a day after Crook and the main column without having found any sign of Indians.

Conscious that the Apaches might be watching him, Crook remained at Bowie for only a few hours, departing after dark to conceal his movements and marching along the west side of the Dos Cabezas Mountains. At daybreak, some of the packers ran across a small group of Apaches herding stolen livestock from Mexico. The Indians saw the whites first and fled. Continuing onward, the troops saw "a couple of Indians," who escaped into the mountains. Indian signs became more plentiful as Crook reached the foot of Graham Mountain. A scouting party sent to the summit ran into a raiding party, but the Indians dashed down the other side before the troops could react. "I saw it was useless running down the horses and men trying to catch them," Crook commented.[14]

Approaching Sulphur Springs Valley, the column saw a cloud of dust that Crook surmised was made by a large raiding party returning from Mexico. He sent a pursuit detail under Capt. Alexander Moore, Third Cavalry, to head them off at a spring, while he stationed other detachments at various points where the Apaches might try to escape. Instead of going to the spring, however, Moore moved across an open plain, and the Indians spotted him and fled.

"We thus lost one of the prettiest chances of giving the enemy a severe blow," Crook complained in his autobiography. "I was then satisfied that Capt. Moore lacked one of the most essential qualities of a soldier. . . . " Crook's assessment was more correct than perhaps he realized at the time. Three years later, in Montana and again under Crook, Moore would commit an even greater blunder.[15]

Approaching the vicinity of Camp Grant and Camp Apache, Crook made no effort to go after Indians for fear of accidentally attacking friendly bands. About thirty miles out from Camp Apache, he found several large bands maintaining cornfields. He had several long visits with their leaders, Miguel, Pedro, and Capitan Chiquito. "Their evidence of sincerity in their profession of friendship were as satisfying as they were gratifying," he reported, "and I regard it as really the entering wedge in the solution of this Apache question."

Experience had taught Crook that he would need Indian scouts—preferably Apaches themselves—who were at home in the region and knew its every feature. "I have not only always found Indians used in this way of invaluable service to the troops," he wrote to army headquarters, "but that the treatment would go further to convince them of the benefit arising from their being our friends, than all the blankets and promises government could heap upon them."

Recruitment was not difficult. Apaches were known for squabbling among themselves, and members of one group saw nothing wrong in aiding the enemies of another group. Even within a particular group, members of that group returning from captivity tended to arouse suspicions that they might have gone over to the enemy during detention, and so were outcasts in any case. As early as the eighteenth century, the Spaniards had recognized this trait, and used members of one Chiricahua group against other Chiricahuas. There were incentives as well. As the government bound more Apaches to the reservations, scouting for the army meant freedom from the monotonous life there. And it gave the warrior what he prized most after freedom—a rifle and ammunition. Even before Crook arrived, Apaches were scouting for the U.S. Army in Arizona. Now he arranged for the Indians to enroll as scouts at Camp Apache, where they would get identification papers, and assured the chiefs they would be soldiers with the appropriate pay and allowances.[16]

To coordinate the Apaches, he needed officers and civilians familiar with Indians who could gain their respect and confidence. He already had Archie McIntosh and, although his experience was with northwestern Indians, he could be counted on to learn the ways of the desert. Crook also hired Albert Sieber, a twenty-six-year-old Rhinelander brought to the United States as a child, who had served in the Union Army and moved to Arizona after the war. Sieber was a tough, straightforward man, and he knew the territory and the Apaches. He and Archie McIntosh disliked each other on sight. Nevertheless, each respected the other's abilities as a frontiersman, and despite their personal feelings, they generally worked well together. Captain Guy V. Henry, Third Cavalry, was placed in charge of the company.[17]

During the stay at Camp Apache, a party of Mexicans and Apaches rode in with a letter from Agent O. F. Piper of the Cañada Alamosa reservation in New Mexico. According to Piper, their mission was to find Cochise and persuade him to surrender. Crook didn't trust them, commenting, "[T]wo of this party were recognized by several as being Cochise's worst men. . . . I felt very suspicious that they were there in the capacity of spies." His own impression was that Cochise was playing on the reservation system, allowing some 130 noncombatants, mainly children and old people, to go into Cañada Alamosa, where government rations relieved the stress on his own resources. In a letter to army headquarters, he said, "I earnestly recommend that the attention of the proper authorities be called to this matter, and that Cocheis [*sic*] with his band be either compelled to go on that reservation and live, or that these 130 noncombatants be compelled to follow his fortunes in the mountains."[18]

Cochise, in fact, was looking for a way to end the conflict, at least on the U.S. side of the border. His people were exhausted from ten years of fighting. He understood the implications of the stepped-up military operations in Arizona, and he was sophisticated enough to realize that the resources of the United States were far greater than his own. Already he had discussed the problem with Thomas J. Jeffords, a sometime mail contractor, prospector, and Indian trader, and the only white he trusted. Now, as Jeffords began sounding out the authorities, Cochise remained deep in his mountain refuge in southern Arizona and, except for a few scattered skirmishes, managed to avoid any clash that would set the army after him.[19]

Crook organized an expedition under Captain Henry, consisting of three companies of Third Cavalry, several Mexican scouts, and some of the newly recruited Indian scouts, sending it from Camp Apache in the direction of Camp McDowell, east of Prescott, while he continued on toward Camp Verde to organize additional expeditions. Henry's expedition was a success. He told Crook "that the combination of the Indian with the soldier [exceeded] his most sanguine expectations; that the Indians were invaluable and that they enabled him to kill 7 warriors and take 11 women prisoners, under the most unfavorable circumstances." He was less enthusiastic about the Mexicans, whom he had included primarily at the instigation of Governor Safford. Carried away by their ancient hatred for Apaches, they tended to kill indiscriminately, without bothering to distinguish between warriors and noncombatants, and taking all the scalps they could in order to collect the bounty.

Crook himself left Camp Verde on August 15, following a trail along the ridges of the Mogollon Mountains where it became broken and hard to follow. His only guide was Archie McIntosh, whom Bourke described as "totally unacquainted with Arizona, but a wonderful man in any country." Even so, Archie's unfamiliarity with the country was obvious, and despite his best efforts, together with those of Tom Moore, chief packer of the mule train, the trail did not improve. The vagaries of Arizona weather soon were apparent. They were beginning to experience a critical water shortage when the hot desert sun became obscured by dark clouds. "In a short time the rain came down in torrents, and shortly we had all the water we wanted, for both man and beast," Crook observed.

Coming out of the Mogollons, they entered the Tonto Basin, a rugged area surrounded by the Mogollons, Mazatzals, and Sierra Ancha. The well-watered basin had grasslands and forest, and offered a variety of useful and edible plants to sustain bands of Indians. The column was passing through a pine forest—Crook, Tom Moore, and some of the officers riding a little ahead of the cavalry—when a small group of Tonto Apaches began shooting arrows at them. The trees obstructed their aim, and they were already fleeing when the cavalry rode up. Two of the Indians were cut off, but fled down a rock face. Crook managed to shoot one in the arm, but both escaped. The command reached Camp Verde without further incident.[20]

Crook had established to his own satisfaction that with proper support, war could be carried to the Apaches. In his report to Army headquarters he wrote: "The number of troops in this Dept. would be ample, provided all the Cavalry here were mounted, but at least one third of it will be dismounted; (even after the arrival of the 400 horses now enroute) with a great many of the horses now in use unserviceable; and should be condemned and sold."[21]

Pleased with the results so far, Crook was organizing new expeditions when his efforts were interrupted by politics. Already that year there had been a fundamental change in government–Indian relations more far-reaching even than the Peace Policy. Partly in response to the House of Representatives' jealousy of the Senate's treaty-making authority, the government abandoned the long-standing position that Indian tribes were independent states with the power to make treaties. Henceforth, all Indians would be regarded as wards of the government, whose fate would be decided by both houses of Congress. To further complicate the situation, the Board of Indian Commissioners had gained new influence after the Camp Grant Massacre, which convinced much of the public that a purely military solution—at least to the Apache conflict—had failed. Consequently, the government agreed that Board Secretary Vincent Colyer should visit the Southwest and examine the situation firsthand. Among other things, he would monitor $70,000 that Congress had appropriated to establish the Apaches on reservations and provide them with subsistence.[22]

The local population of Arizona was outraged at the notion of an easterner offering peace to Indians who had left so much death and destruction in their wake. Bourke went so far as to privately call him "that spawn of hell, *Vincent Colyer.*" Some newspaper editors even hinted that Colyer's assassination would not be unwelcome. The public mood was such that Governor Safford had to issue orders for the commissioner's protection. For his part, Crook bristled at what he felt was useless meddling in his jurisdiction. In a letter to army headquarters, he complained:

> These Indians have been at war with the Mexicans for over a century; and at war with us since we have known them; therefore it is not reasonable to expect they will keep their promises of peace with us now, when they have violated the same promises made under similar circumstances, [many] times before; nor is it reasonable to expect them to make a sincere peace with a people for whom they express their contempt by calling us cowards and fools. . . . if this entire Indian question be left to me, with my present arrangements and knowledge, I have not the slightest doubt of my ability to conquer a lasting peace with this Apache race in a comparatively short space of time, and a peace which will not only save the Treasury millions of dollars, but will save the lives of a good many innocent whites and Indians.

Although he privately agreed with the idea of church administration and outside oversight of the Indian Bureau, he mistrusted those who were implementing the policies. He erroneously believed that Colyer (whom he called "Vincent the Good") was a pawn of the Indian Ring, and saw the visit as an attempt to interfere with his campaign and prolong the conflict so that members of the Ring could line their pockets with government contracts. Nevertheless, when Colyer arrived in September, he suspended his preparations to give the commissioner an opportunity to deal with the Indians.[23]

Crook restricted his opinions to a few close associates, and Colyer appears not to have detected any animosity. His report stated that Crook received him "quite cordially," and offered his own quarters to the commissioner for his stay. "The general and I differed somewhat in opinion as to the best policy to be pursued toward the Apaches, but as these differences were honestly entertained and kindly expressed, it did not lesson the cordiality of our intercourse."[24]

Contrary to local belief, Colyer was not a complete amateur, having previously conferred with Apache chiefs at Fort Defiance, Arizona, in 1869. And despite Crook's misgivings, the mission was partly successful. Colyer established temporary reservations at various military posts where bands of Apaches and Yavapais began to congregate under the watchful eyes of the troops. Additionally, Colyer and other members of the board exposed enough corruption to force the resignation of Commissioner of Indian Affairs Ely Parker.

Despite this success, Colyer saw only part of the situation. Prone to generalized assumptions, he believed all Apaches desired peace and, if left alone, would come on the reservations and settle. The problem, as he saw it, was the rapacious whites, who should either leave Arizona or remain with the knowledge that they were the cause of all the bloodshed and grief. Consequently, he took evidence only from the Apaches, commenting in his report that "my official duties were wholly with the Indians." He declined an invitation to address a citizens' meeting in Prescott on grounds that he would require an armed guard, and refused to consider anything that might conflict with his own views. He was particularly impressed with Eskiminzin, who (according to Crook) announced that Colyer "could not come of mortal parents, for no man so good as he was could be so born."

There is no question that many Apaches were, in fact, innocent of depredations, just as many whites were innocent of indiscriminate killing of Apaches. Even so, other Apaches were just as adept as the worst settlers at unprovoked murder, plunder, and rape. Colyer's failure to consider this side of the issue resulted in a prolonged suspension of Crook's operations, encouraging the marauding bands to continue their depredations. In fact, in the year following Colyer's visit, they made fifty-four raids, killing forty-one settlers in Crook's jurisdiction. Crook's only satisfaction from the visit came when Interior Secretary Columbus Delano, angered by Parker's forced resignation, used his control of the Indian budget as leverage to oust Colyer from the Board of Indian Commissioners. Applauding this as a positive step, Crook nevertheless understood that much of the problem lay not only in misplaced idealism but in corruption within the system. "The fact is," he wrote Rutherford Hayes, "there is too much money in this Indian business, for these people to die without a hard struggle, and I am particularly anxious that the honest and good people of the country should understand what a gigantic fraud this Indian ring is."[25]

In the meantime, a grand jury had convened in Tucson at the insistence of U.S. Attorney C. W. C. Rowell, to consider the Camp Grant Massacre. When it refused to take action, Rowell hinted that the suspects might be tried by court martial, which would virtually assure conviction. The grand jurors returned indictments against 108 men for murder, but also indicted Eskiminzin for the murder of Charles McKinney. The indictments in the Camp Grant case created so much outrage that Rowell and his clerk were burned in effigy, and in subsequent proceedings troops were scattered among the crowd at the courthouse to protect them. The trial itself was a mere formality, and the jury acquitted the Camp Grant defendants after nineteen minutes of deliberation. Eskiminzin never came to trial for the McKinney case.[26]

Crook resumed preparations for his campaign, insofar as the constraints imposed by Colyer's visit allowed. Privately, his sympathy for the Indians was beginning to reemerge, although he believed that a lasting peace could not be achieved without decisive military action to convince the Apaches that they had no other alternative. Discussing his position in a letter to Adjutant General Townsend, he repeated some of his earlier assertions.

"I think the Apache is painted in darker colors than he really deserves, and that his villanies arise more from a [false] conception of facts than from his being worse than other Indians," he wrote, adding, "Living in a country the natural products of which will not support him, he has either to cultivate the soil or steal, and as our vacillating policy satisfies him we are afraid of him, he chooses the latter, also as requiring less labor, and being more congenial to his natural instincts[.] I am satisfied that a sharp active campaign against him, would not only make him one of the best Indians in the country, but would save millions of dollars to the Treasury and the lives of many whites and Indians."[27]

Already, the time had passed when a permanent department commander for Arizona should have been named, but none was announced. It was becoming increasingly obvious that, as in the Columbia, Crook's temporary assignment would become long-term. In November, General Schofield authorized him to enforce strict supervision of the reservation Apaches, and to attack all those who refused to come in and submit to the authority of the government. In response, Crook issued General Orders No. 10, requiring all Indians to report immediately to the reservations or "be regarded as hostile and punished accordingly." The problem in attacking the hostile bands was that they could move freely between Arizona and New Mexico, whereas Crook could not because New Mexico was attached to the Military Division of the Missouri, beyond either Crook's or Schofield's jurisdiction. Cochise appeared still to be hanging about the reservation at Cañada Alamosa on the New Mexico side of the line, but individual bands under his chieftaincy ranged back and forth across the line.

"I wish," Crook advised departmental headquarters, "that this Indian, Cocheis [sic] either return to this side of the line where he belongs, and come upon some Reservation to be designated, or that he be required to show the sincerity of his professions of peace, by joining such troops as may be designated in New Mexico or Arizona, for the purpose of following and punishing those bands formerly under him who still refuse to be peaceable."[28]

To avoid allegations that he was overly eager, Crook gave the Apaches until mid-February to come into the reservations and make peace. Otherwise, he would go after them. Against the latter possibility, he gave special attention to the packtrains that would carry ammunition and provisions for his troops in the field. One of Crook's greatest innovations during these early Arizona campaigns was his overhaul of the military packtrain system. He did not invent the concept; mule trains had been the standard method of moving supplies and equipment since Spanish times. He did, however, improve on it until it became one of the most efficient methods for military campaigns until the advent of motorized vehicles.

Crook found the existing system was contracted by the army, and run purely as a profit-making venture. The result was an assortment of ill-suited men and animals, hired at the beginning of a campaign and discharged at its conclusion. Crook's first act was to contract trains under the most experienced packmasters, getting rid of packers who were cruel to the animals, drank too much, or were otherwise unsuited. He also selected mules that had good, strong overall conformation, were healthy, and had sound hooves. He likewise scrapped the ill-fitting government-issue *aparejos,* or pack cushions, in favor of cushions stuffed with straw and designed to distribute evenly the weight along the animals' backs and sides. Mules were first given a *suadera,* or sweat-cloth, which then was covered with two or three saddle blankets. The aparejo was placed over that, followed by the pack saddle, *corona* or saddle cover, and finally the load.

"Every article used in these pack-trains had to be of the best materials," Bourke wrote, "for the very excellent reason that while out on a scout, it was impossible to replace anything broken, and a column might be embarrassed by the failure of a train to arrive with ammunition or rations."[29]

Meanwhile, the situation continued to deteriorate, with large bands of Apaches marauding throughout the countryside. On November 5, a stagecoach was attacked eight miles west of Wickenburg. Six people were killed outright, and a seventh later died of wounds. Among the dead were three members of a surveying party, including Frederick W. Loring, whom Bancroft called "a young man of literary and scientific attainments . . . whose fate made a sensation in the east, doing much to call attention to the real state of affairs." Shortly before departing for Arizona, Loring had visited with Bancroft in San Francisco and, pointing to his closely cropped hair, told the historian the Apaches would find it hard to take his scalp.

Yet there was some question as to whether Indians alone were responsible for the massacre, because it showed as much evidence of bandits as Indians; the horses, blankets, and curtains of the stage were found at the scene, and Indian looters almost invariably carried these off. Some citizens believed the purpose was to rob the passengers of the substantial amount of gold they were supposed to have been carrying. On the other hand, soldiers investigating the attack found sign of Indian involvement as well, indicating that if they were not the sole perpetrators, they at least had been active participants.

In January, Crook learned that some of the Indians at the Date Creek Reservation, sixty-two miles southwest of Prescott, may have been mixed up in the affair. Soon afterwards, he got more conclusive information from Dan O'Leary, one of the region's leading scouts. O'Leary had raised an orphaned Yavapai boy, who told him that a group of Yavapais had summoned the boy and asked him the value of paper money they had stolen in the raid. The Yavapais then used the money for a drinking binge, boasting about the raid and generally making nuisances of themselves. The Mohave chief, Iretaba, took a party of warriors to Whipple Barracks and informed Crook.[30]

Crook now had two objectives—the hostile Apaches as a whole, and the Yavapais involved in the Wickenburg massacre. Based on the information from O'Leary and Iretaba, he was satisfied that the Indians involved in the Wickenburg affair were at Date Creek, but wanted to be certain that he got only those who were guilty. Most of the Date Creek Indians minded their own business and did not create any problems, and he did not want them to become innocent casualties. On February 7, 1872, he served notice that the Apaches had nine more days to come in to the reservations. Any still out after that would be considered hostile, and would be received only as prisoners of war.[31]

Once again, however, Crook's efforts were frustrated by the government. President Grant, aware of Colyer's shortcomings, sent Brig. Gen. Oliver Otis Howard to investigate the situation in Arizona and try to arrive at an equitable solution for both Indians and whites. This annoyed Crook even more than the Colyer visit; Howard outranked him by two grades and had the authority to supersede him if he saw fit. The general had to be accommodated. Crook would have to wait before taking any action against the Indians involved in the Wickenburg massacre. Against the day he could, however, he kept quiet to avoid arousing any suspicion among the guilty parties.[32]

Howard was known as the "praying general" for his strong religious convictions, although Crook preferred to think of him as a self-righteous Bible-thumper. Born in 1830, he was educated at Bowdoin College and at West Point. After graduating from the academy, he served in the Seminole Wars in Florida. Given his beliefs and the limited opportunities of the antebellum army, he was considering resigning and going into the ministry when the outbreak of the Civil War altered his plans. He distinguished himself as a volunteer officer and, despite the loss of his right arm at Seven Pines on June 1, 1862, by the end of the year he had risen to major general of the Volunteers.

After the war, Howard was appointed to head the Bureau of Freedmen, Refugees and Abandoned Lands—the notorious Freedmen's Bureau—created by Congress to help the recently emancipated slaves become established in a free society. It was a post he still held at the time of his visit, prompting Crook to remark sarcastically "that he thought the Creator had placed him on earth to be the Moses to the Negro. Having accomplished that mission, he felt satisfied his next mission was with the Indians." Given the overall disrepute of the Freedmen's Bureau at the time, Crook added, "I was at a loss to make out whether it was his vanity or his cheek that enabled him to hold up his head in this lofty manner."[33]

Whatever Crook's opinions, Howard's account of the visit indicates little rancor between the two men. Upon his arrival in April 1872, he was invited to stay in Crook's home in Prescott. Crook, Howard recalled, "had that art which some men possess of saying very little to you in conversation, being at the same time such an attentive listener that one was unconsciously drawn out in discourse. The time passed pleasantly and swiftly. It was a delight to a fellow-officer to find himself at his table, particularly when his genial wife presided at the head of it."

As for Crook's relations with the Indians, Howard noted: "He was indeed a favorite with the Indians, and though terrible in his severity when they broke out and made war, and perhaps at all times distrustful of them, yet he believed in keeping his word with an Indian as sacredly as with a white man, and in all his dealings with them he was uniformly just and kind."[34]

Even so, Howard almost immediately exasperated Crook by intervening on behalf of Lieutenant Whitman, the officer in charge of Camp Grant at the time of the massacre. Whitman's continuing influence and prestige among the Apaches prompted Crook to write that he "had deserted his colors and gone over to the 'Indian Ring' bag and baggage, and had behaved himself in such a manner that I had preferred charges against him."

The charges had nothing to do with the Camp Grant Massacre or anything involving the Apaches. The first, a catch-all charge of "conduct unbecoming of an officer and a gentleman," had several specifications involving drunkenness and disorderly conduct over a ten-month period from November 1870 to September 1871. The second was "conduct to the prejudice of good order and military discipline," with the specification that Whitman had been betting in a card game while serving as disbursing officer. Either or both of these charges

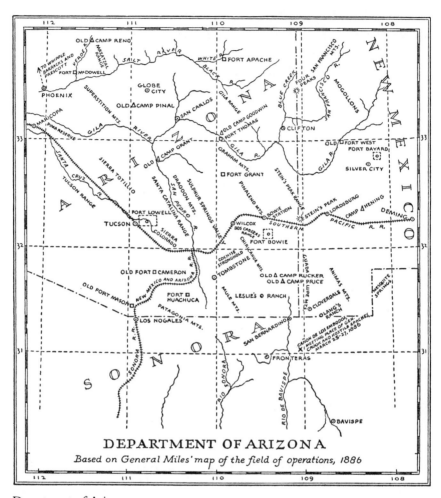

Department of Arizona.

could have been leveled at the vast majority of officers in the frontier service at the time, particularly in a desolate assignment like Arizona.

On December 4, 1871, a court-martial board had thrown the charges out, accepting Whitman's contention that he was, at least in part, the victim of a smear campaign by William S. Oury, a prominent local citizen who had helped organize the Camp Grant Massacre, and by the Indian-hating Wasson brothers, Joe and John, who had made their way from Idaho to Tucson and now ran the

Arizona Citizen. Crook refused to approve the board's finding, and when it was allowed to stand, he continued working to discredit Whitman. On March 12, 1871, the unfortunate lieutenant again was arrested, this time on charges of disobedience initiated on the orders of General Schofield, although there is no doubt that Crook was behind it. Whitman's detention at Fort Crittenden upset the Apaches at Camp Grant, and General Howard ordered him released so he could go to Grant and quiet them down.

Even when one considers that the nineteenth-century army offered very few disciplinary alternatives to court-martial, the Whitman case borders on the absurd. The campaign against him was largely political, orchestrated by prominent locals including Oury and Governor Safford, and encouraged by Joe Wasson in the editorial pages of the *Arizona Citizen.* Crook had allowed himself to be drawn into the fray, and now that he was in it he saw no way to extricate himself. He was particularly infuriated by Howard's attitude.

"One of the first things General Howard did after his arrival [at Camp Grant] was to parade up and down the garrison, arm in arm with Whitman," he complained. He apparently did not realize, or at least did not choose to acknowledge, that despite the difference in rank, Howard and Whitman were long-time friends, close to the same age, with common interests, and distantly related by marriage. There was an additional motive for Howard's interest. Whitman had written at length to the Indian Bureau on the mistreatment of the Camp Grant Apaches, and the general was obligated to investigate.[35]

Howard called a council across the San Pedro River from Camp Grant on May 21, 1872. Most of the various Apache bands of the region were represented, as were the Pimas and Papagos. Crook recalled that the Apaches "had assembled in quite large numbers, and a more saucy, impudent lot of cut-throats I had never seen before. Many of them were armed with lances and guns. . . . I must confess I was afraid of them, and kept close to camp for fear some of them would want to be a hero at my expense."

Howard and Crook spread their blankets on the bank of the San Pedro which, at that point, was a narrow stream some ten or fifteen feet wide, and waited. Governor Safford, U.S. District Attorney James E. McCaffrey, and several citizens from Tucson and the surrounding area joined the group. Howard also had convinced some of the Mexicans to come and bring the Apache children they held captive. Lieutenant Whitman was present because he was virtually the only white that many of the Apaches trusted.

Before opening the council, Howard dropped to his knees and began to pray loudly. Not knowing what the general was doing, the Apaches panicked and scattered. Eskiminzin, who hid behind a building, motioned to Whitman for an explanation. On being told this was how Howard began any undertaking, the Apaches were reassured and began drifting back. Howard observed that Eskiminzin "was not at all prepossessing; he stammered in his speech, and was inordinately proud, though he exercised a fierce leadership over his tribe."

Over the next two days, Howard listened while both sides presented their grievances. The Aravaipa Apaches were particularly touchy on the matter of the children, whom they wanted returned. The Mexicans, on the other hand, were equally adamant about keeping them. Many claimed they had come to view the children almost as their own, and were rearing them accordingly. Governor Safford and District Attorney McCaffrey backed their position.

To Howard, the critical issue was whether the Apache children's parents were still alive. When he asked Eskiminzin, the chief replied, "Of course not, they were killed by the citizens." Nevertheless, the chief insisted on their return. Howard was inclined to agree, but Crook and Safford doubted the wisdom returning them, and McCaffrey vehemently objected. This led to an exchange in which McCaffrey accused Howard of deceiving the people into bringing children to the council by not telling them the children might be taken from them. Howard countered by threatening to have McCaffrey removed from his federal appointment. Finally, Howard agreed to defer the decision until the next day.

That night, Howard discussed the problem with C. H. Cook, a missionary who lived with the Pimas. When Cook advised returning the children, Howard replied, "Few of their parents are living and the Mexicans seem to have taken good care of them."

"I know that," Cook answered, "but they use them as servants—as slaves—and the children have relatives among the Aravipas [sic]. They were carried off by force, some of them badly wounded. It is right to give them back and I would do it."

The next day, Howard returned, still uncertain about what to do. McCaffrey apparently offered the solution by demanding the matter be referred to federal authorities in Washington. Howard jumped at the idea, and said the decision would be made by President Grant alone. In the meantime, he said the children would remain at the agency in the care of "a good Catholic woman" who would allow visits by both the Apache relatives and the Mexican foster parents.

McCaffrey, however, wanted the children to remain with the Mexicans, and offered a bond pending the president's decision. "No bonds are necessary," Howard replied, "General Crook, with his army and authority, will see to it that everything is carried out to the letter as I have decided." Ultimately, President Grant decided the children would be returned to their relatives.[36]

Crook was unhappy with events so far. In his autobiography, he claimed that after the council, he confronted Howard, telling him:

> General Howard, many of these people have lost their friends, relatives, and property by these Indians. They carry their lives constantly in their hands, not knowing what moment is to be their last. Now, if, instead of affording relief, you not only fail to give it to them but outrage their feelings besides, you must not expect your position to shield you from hearing plain words. These people have suffered too much to have any false ideas of sentiment. Besides, you have come here under the garb of religion, and have been prostituting my command by holding out inducements of eastern stations if certain officers would do so and so.

Then Crook came to what, for him, probably was the real issue, "When I had Lt. Whitman under guard for gross misbehavior, you walked publicly, arm in arm with him, thereby showing that you espoused his cause as against myself."

It is debatable whether Howard actually tried to undermine Crook's officers with "inducements of eastern stations" or whether Crook simply used that as an excuse to air his resentment about Whitman. Whatever the case, Crook's charges upset Howard so much that "he could not go to sleep until he found relief in prayer about three o'clock in the morning."[37]

However Crook might have felt, Bancroft astutely observed that Howard "was a very different man [from Vincent Colyer], his peace theories being strongly tinged with common sense." To Crook's ultimate satisfaction, Howard endorsed military action against hostile Apaches, as well as the use of Apache scouts. On the other hand, Howard's visit reassured the friendly Apaches, and he managed to arrange a peace between them and their hereditary foes, the Pimas and the Papagos. To reduce the chance of clashes with settlers, he relocated the Camp Grant reserve northward from the San Pedro River to the Gila, and on a second visit in late summer, he abolished Colyer's reservations at Camp McDowell, Date Creek, and Beale Spring, permitting the Indians to chose among the more remote reservations. As a result of Howard's efforts, President Grant organized two vast reservations, designating the Gila River tract as the San Carlos Reservation, and the second to be known as the White Mountain or Fort Apache Reservation.[38]

NINE

THE GRAND OFFENSIVE

THROUGHOUT HIS TIME IN ARIZONA, Crook's official family grew. The immediate household now included Mary's brother, James Dailey, the former McNeill Ranger who probably was involved in Crook's capture almost seven years earlier. Bourke described Dailey as a "volunteer" on his Apache expeditions; such nepotism was no doubt similar to that practiced by George Armstrong Custer, who always managed to find places for relatives in his own command.

Besides Nickerson, Ross, and Bourke, the military family soon included two young lieutenants of the Fifth Cavalry, Charles King and Walter S. Schuyler. The latter two officers would serve Crook in various capacities over the ensuing years, and were known among the Indian agents in Arizona as "Crook's bloodhounds," from their tenacity in seeking out hostiles. King, whose service career spanned seven decades, and who wore campaign medals of every U.S. conflict from the Civil War through the First World War, has also been called "America's Kipling" because of his short stories, novels, articles, and memoirs of army life that made him famous in his own time. Many of his fictional characters were based on people he knew in the service, not the least being Mary Crook, whom he portrayed as a inveterate matchmaker for unmarried officers.[1]

As the wife of the departmental commander, Mary handled Crook's social responsibilities, organizing parties, hops, and receptions that her husband now seemed to tolerate more than enjoy. Becoming increasingly withdrawn from society as time passed, he often would gather the men into another room for cards while she visited with the women. Crook's behavior indicates he had not been exaggerating when he said he was "tired of this Indian business." Burdened with the responsibility of command in a region where settlers and Indians fought with equal savagery, he became aloof and taciturn, and would remain so until the approaching end of the Indian Wars and the vagaries of army politics finally relieved him of that responsibility. Even his wife sometimes was thrown off-balance by Crook's seemingly erratic behavior. During one of his absences in the field, Mary greeted the wife of a newly arrived officer, saying, "I am truly sorry the General is away; I should like for him to meet you; you are just the sort of woman he likes." When the young woman did meet Crook, she found him courteous but otherwise indifferent, prompting her to observe "that women are often mistaken judges of their husband's tastes."[2]

Now that the political interference had abated for the time being, Crook once again planned to move against the Apaches. "Having in view the great and earnest desire of the government to find a peaceable solution of this problem," he wrote in his annual report, "I have earnestly and honestly supported the agents sent out for this work, and the long and bloody lists of murders and robberies committed during the year by the very Indians, who at one time or another have been fed at the public expense[,] is a ghastly commentary upon the result."[3]

Although he had been in Arizona little more than a year, Crook had learned much about the people he was preparing to fight. They had modern weapons which, combined with their endurance and their knowledge of the country, made them formidable enemies. They could live off the land indefinitely. Their few worldly possessions could be carried on their backs, giving them rapid mobility.

"The Apache," he later wrote, "can endure fatigue and fasting and can live without water for periods that would kill the hardiest mountaineer. Every thing he has ever received from the white man is a luxury which he can do without as he had done from time immemorial. . . . The Apaches only fight with regular soldiers when they choose and when the advantages are all on their side."[4]

Crook intended to open the campaign by going to the Date Creek reservation, which had not yet been closed, and arresting the Yavapais responsible for the Wickenburg massacre. Before his arrival, however, Hualapai Indian scouts warned him that the Yavapais planned to strike the first blow. The plan was to call Crook to Date Creek for a council. After a few minutes of cordiality their chief, Ochocama, would roll and light a cigarette. When he took the first puff the man next to him would kill Crook, and the others would open fire on any whites who happened to be present.

The plan went awry because of the unexpected death, on August 29, of Capt. Philip Dwyer, Fifth Cavalry, military commander at Date Creek. Sending Bourke ahead to assume command, Crook then went in person to force the issue with the Yavapais, arranging for Iretaba and his Mohaves to meet him there and identify those responsible for the Wickenburg affair. Upon arriving, he found that about two-thirds of the Indians assigned to the agency were absent. Those who remained were "uneasy and suspicious, and in very bad temper, appearing with their arms and war paint."

Crook informed the Indians he would meet with them the following day, September 8, 1872. Soldiers were scattered among the Indians, and there were a dozen or so mule packers who, Bourke noted, "had been engaged in all kinds of melees since the days of early California mining." Each packer had his revolver at full cock and his knife loose and ready.

The Indians were uneasy and Ochocama appeared nervous. After some hesitation, he took some tobacco and rolled a cigarette. Meanwhile, the Mohaves were in the process of identifying those involved at Wickenburg, and as the soldiers moved in to make the arrests one trooper was stabbed by an Indian immediately behind him. A shot rang out, possibly from the soldier's carbine. Ochocama's companion leveled his carbine at Crook, but Lieutenant Ross, waiting for the move, kicked it out of the way so that the bullet went wild and killed one of the Indians.

Both sides began shooting, and about seven Indians were killed or wounded. Three packers grabbed Ochocama, but the chief broke free and was about to escape when Dan O'Leary grabbed his hair and twisted it, forcing him to the ground. Carried to the guardhouse, he continued struggling furiously, and managed to break loose and escape. Packer Hank Hewitt grabbed another ring-leader and smashed his head into a rock, fatally injuring him. Most of the Indians managed to fight their way out and escape into the surrounding hills before Crook could stop the shooting.[5]

Crook returned to Prescott, but a few days later was back at Date Creek after some of the Indians came in to ask for amnesty. He agreed to pardon all who were involved in the assassination attempt except the ringleaders. Although he had one in the guardhouse, and some of the others had been killed in the fight, most were still on the loose. Runners were sent out into the hills to spread the word, and several came in to accept the amnesty but the majority refused. Many on and off the reservation blamed Iretaba and the Mohaves for the fight, and there was talk of a vengeance raid against them. Crook managed to calm the Yavapais on the reservation, but held off from any action against those who had fled, hoping to give them enough time to become complacent.

On September 20, Hualapai scouts reported that several hundred hostiles were assembled in the vicinity of a spot called Muchos Cañones, where five canyons merged to form the Santa Maria. According to the scouts, Ochocama and the other chiefs were planning to raid along the different roads, as well as move up to the Colorado River to settle scores with the Mohaves. Crook dispatched Capt. Julius W. Mason, a tough, experienced officer, with three companies of Fifth Cavalry and about eighty Hualapais, who tracked them to a large encampment where they were in a position to hit the Colorado Agency. The troops and scouts attacked at dawn September 25, killing forty and capturing a large number of women and children.[6]

Pleased with the results, Crook inaugurated what Apache wars historian Dan Thrapp called his "grand offensive." His first step was to resurrect the long dormant General Orders No. 10, requiring all Indians to report immediately to their agencies or be regarded as hostile. He sent Capt. W. H. Brown, acting assistant inspector general of the department, to Camp Apache and Camp Grant to implement the orders there. Brown was not to interfere with the routine duties of the agents, but Crook was determined that "the military was to see to their control, and make a daily count of the Indians." Meanwhile Crook began organizing expeditions against all those who failed to comply. On November 16, he sent out three columns from Camp Hualpai, each composed of one company of cavalry and thirty to forty Indian scouts. They were to operate in the vicinity of the San Francisco Mountains and along the headwaters of the Rio Verde. Two expeditions were also organized out of Date Creek. His plan was essentially to encircle the hostile tribes, battering the outlying areas and driving them inward toward the Tonto Basin. The basin itself would then be criss-crossed by mobile units until the last resistance was smashed.[7]

Crook's instructions to the troops, as recorded by Bourke, were simple and straightforward:

> Indians should be induced to surrender in all cases where possible; where they preferred to fight, they were to get all the fighting they wanted, and in one good dose instead of a number of petty engagements, but in either case were to be hunted down until the last one in hostility had been killed or captured. Every effort should be made to avoid the killing of women and children. Prisoners of either sex should be guarded from ill-treatment of any kind. When prisoners could be induced to enlist as scouts, they should be so enlisted, because the

wilder the Apache was, the more he was likely to know the wiles and stratagems of those still out in the mountains, their hiding-places and intentions. No excuse was to be accepted for leaving a trail; if horses played out, the enemy must be followed on foot, and no sacrifice should be left untried to make the campaign short, sharp, and decisive.[8]

Bourke, meanwhile, had acquired a small notebook for a record of the campaign. When it was concluded, he labeled the front page in large, neat letters:

> Field Notes,
> Scouts in
> Arizona Territory
> Bvt. Maj. Genl. George Crook
> Commanding.
> From Nov 18th 1872
> to April 8th 1873.
> John G. Bourke,
> 2nd Lieut., 3rd Cav.
> A.D.C.[9]

This was the beginning of the Bourke Diary, which ultimately would fill 124 volumes and become perhaps the most complete personal record of the Indian Wars from within the command structure, as well as a great source of information on the various Indian tribes themselves in their last days of independence. Besides Bourke's own observations, the volumes include copies of such official correspondence as he deemed important, orders, rosters, newspaper clippings, and photographs.

On November 18, Crook left for Camp Apache and Camp Grant to personally organize expeditions from those posts. The march to Camp Apache was routine, allowing Crook to indulge in some hunting. On November 27, Bourke noted in his diary, "Gen. Crook killed (38) thirty eight wild ducks and Lt. Ross and Mr. McCoy [Mason McCoy, a scout from Crook's Oregon days] killed a back-tailed deer which dressed about 175 o[r] 200 lbs."[10]

Arriving at Camp Apache two days later, Crook found the conditions of General Orders No. 10 were functioning smoothly, and the situation was under control. In his official report, he wrote: "The Indians were a little peevish and afraid [of the consequences for all] if the bad ones left but after I explained the intention and benefit of the order, and the alternative in case of their non obeyance, they came up to all of its requirements with alacrity, and when I asked them to help me punish the bad ones who were out, more volunteered than I wanted."[11]

Privately, however, he observed: "I found the Indian people [at Camp Apache] very indignant at me, and hinting around that I would soon have my comb cut for transcending my authority, that I had been reported to the Secretary of the Interior, Mr. [Columbus] Delano, for outraging their service by unwarranted assumptions, and that they were daily expecting a reply."[12]

Believing that the authorities in Washington would uphold the Indians, Crook decided to disobey any order he might receive that went against his plan, confident that if his campaign was successful, the disobedience would be overlooked. Either way, he felt he had nothing to lose. Already, he had twice been interrupted by politicians, and believed if he were interrupted a third time he would, in any case, become the scapegoat for a failed peace policy.

Before leaving Apache for Camp Grant, he organized the troops into commands consisting of white soldiers and Indian scouts, with a separate packtrain for each command, allowing it to function independently of the others. He intended that each command would be large enough to fight its way out of a tight spot, but small enough to move through rough country without attracting attention. Ever mindful of potential political interference, he instructed each commanding officer not to obey any orders, "even from the President of the United States," unless he first cleared them.

Interestingly enough, none of the effort would be directed at Cochise. During Howard's second visit, he had met with the Chiricahua chief and, in October, they had negotiated a truce, although Crook and many others were skeptical of Cochise's sincerity, particularly since his band continued to raid into Mexico. Crook was particularly unhappy that a reservation had been set aside for Cochise's people in the Dragoon Mountains near the Mexican border, and believed they should be required to congregate on the other reserves with the rest of Arizona's Indians. As it was, the Dragoon reservation provided Cochise with "great facilities for his outrages. In my opinion," he wrote to divisional headquarters, "there will be constant trouble so long as he is allowed to occupy it." Nevertheless, in deference to General Howard's efforts, he was prepared to postpone action against Cochise until the present campaign was finished.[13]

Crook left Camp Apache on December 3, and arrived at Camp Grant four days later. He held a council with Indians, similar to that held at Camp Apache. Among those present was Eskiminzin, who promised to aid in hunting down the hostiles. Crook detested the idea of dealing with "Old Skimmy"; nevertheless, thirty-one Apaches enlisted as scouts. A day later, ten more signed up.

At both Apache and Grant, he found the civilian agents had issued rations to the Indians far in excess to the numbers enrolled at the agencies, although the military command had done much to rectify the situation. He also noted large numbers of cattle, horses, and mules stolen from the surrounding areas were being brought to the agencies for disposal.[14]

There remained the question of Cochise and his Chiricahuas. Crook resented the fact that their reservation in the Dragoons was exempt from his jurisdiction, and he seriously questioned that any hostile Apache chief would willingly seek peace, Howard's assurances notwithstanding. For his part, although Cochise was never able fully to end depredations in Arizona by some of the more rambunctious warriors, he and most of his followers scrupulously observed the peace—in the United States. Mexico was a totally different matter, and the raids into Sonora continued. The U.S. government, however, was obligated to prevent Indian raids into Mexico from U.S. territory, and Crook considered that legitimate reason to go after Cochise. His resolve was strengthened on December 10, when someone whom Bourke described as "an escaped captive" reported that Cochise intended to break out in the early spring. Crook decided to impose General Orders No. 10, which would put the Chiricahuas under his authority, thereby controlling the chief and at the same time undermining General Howard.

Cochise's friend Thomas Jeffords, who was now the agent for his band, and Fred Hughes, the reservation clerk, warned that the Chiricahuas would never submit to the daily roll call required under the orders, and any attempt at enforcement would provoke a war. Hughes suspected that Crook hoped to start trouble by imposing the order on Cochise and, in fact, the general appears to have been planning around that probability. On January 9, 1873, he advised Gov. Ignacio Pesqueira of Sonora that if the Chiricahuas refused to assemble for roll call, he would move against them. Because they would probably head for the mountains of Sonora, he suggested that Pesqueira station troops along his side of the border and head them off. Then he began preparation by moving thirteen companies of cavalry and a hundred Indian scouts to points within striking distance of Cochise's camps.[15]

As he drew closer to a showdown, Crook apparently had second thoughts. Part of his frustration was due to ignorance. Despite his responsibility for the security of Arizona, no one had bothered to advise him of the terms of the agreement Howard had reached with Cochise. Consequently, he was unsure of his position and, in late January, he decided to send a mission to meet with Cochise. The group would be headed by Captain Brown, the departmental inspector general, and would include Jeffords as interpreter, George H. Stevens, acting agent for San Carlos, Bourke, and Lt. C. H. Rockwell, Fifth Cavalry. Archie McIntosh went along to form some idea of the terrain in case it was necessary to move against the Chiricahuas.[16]

The council was held on February 3. Meeting Cochise, Bourke was convinced of "his determination to leave the war-path for good, and to eat the bread of peace." The chief himself was "a tall, stately, finely built Indian, who seemed to be rather past middle life, but still full of power and vigor, both physical and mental. He received us urbanely, and showed us every attention possible." Perhaps the only person who was not impressed was the younger of his two wives because, when the officers noted a fresh injury to his right hand, Cochise acknowledged she had bitten him in a jealous rage.[17]

Brown opened the conference by stating that Crook was aware that Cochise desired peace, and was prepared to cooperate. However, he had not yet received a copy of the agreement between Cochise and Howard and, in the interest of expediency, believed it better to send a delegation to meet with Cochise. Crook was particularly concerned about movement of troops in the reservation and asked whether there had been any understanding about raids into Mexico.

Cochise replied that troops were free to use the roads across the reservation, but they could not establish posts, nor could settlers move in. He attempted to evade the question of Mexico, but when Brown persisted he answered:

> The Mexicans are on one side in the matter and the Americans on another. There are many young people here whose parents and relatives have been killed by the Mexicans, and now these young people are liable to go down, from time to time and do a little damage to the Mexicans. I don't want to lie about this thing; they go, but I don't send them.
>
> I made peace with the Americans, but the Mexicans did not come to ask peace from me as the Americans have done. I don't myself want to go down to Mexico and will not go, but my boys may go there. I consider that I myself am at peace with Mexico, but my young men, like those at all the other Reservations, are liable to occasionally make raids.

Brown reiterated that the raids would have to stop, and Cochise once again assured him of his own good intentions, after which the council ended amicably.[18]

Crook had mixed emotions about Brown's report of the council. On the one hand, he seemed to feel that Cochise might be making a good-faith effort to maintain the peace, at least where the Americans were concerned. "He did not understand he was violating his peace by raiding on Mexico, he made no secret that his people were raiding on Sonora," he wrote to departmental headquarters. On the other hand, he was chagrined by the fact that Cochise continued to occupy his own territory, more or less on his own terms. This, Crook believed, in the long run would make him more defiant of the government and would encourage new depredations in U.S. territory. There was also the diplomatic problem because, if the U.S. could not control Indian raids into Sonora, Mexico would not necessarily feel compelled to control bandit raids into the United States.

Nevertheless, because of Cochise's overall attitude, and especially in view of General Howard's agreement that soldiers could only pass through the reservation, he decided that any effort to enforce General Orders No. 10 on the Chiricahuas "would be an act of bad faith on our part." The troops assembled for the Cochise expedition were redeployed back to the Tonto Basin, and Crook notified Governor Pesqueira that plans for a campaign were postponed indefinitely. It was just as well. Until his death in 1874, Cochise maintained the peace he had made with General Howard.[19]

Elsewhere, Crook's offensive was showing results. For the first time, the various military operations were coordinated under a single policy. Columns of troops from virtually every post in southern and central Arizona struck the outlying hostile camps, destroying rancherias and supplies and pressuring the Indians into an increasingly smaller area in the Tonto Basin. Those who did not surrender or who were not killed were forced to keep moving, unable to rest or lay in supplies for the winter. The troops, meanwhile, returned to Camp Verde for reprovisioning, then once again took to the field. By mid-December 1872, Crook had nine expeditions on the move.

The key to Crook's success, as he well realized, was his Indian scouts. The best of all were the Apaches. "The longer we knew the Apache scouts, the better we liked them," Bourke wrote. "They were wilder and more suspicious than the Pimas and Maricopas, but far more reliable, and endowed with a greater amount of courage and daring." Ultimately, Crook relied almost exclusively on Apaches.[20]

One of the strongest expeditions consisted of two companies of Fifth Cavalry and thirty Apaches out of Camp Grant, under command of Captain Brown. Rationed for thirty days, it was instructed to scout the Mescal, Pinal, Superstition, and Mazatzal Mountains, and link up with an expedition out of Camp McDowell under Capt. James Burns, also of the Fifth Cavalry. Their instructions called for a special effort to hunt down Delshay and Chunz, two of the most notorious Apache leaders.

Brown's march was arduous, taking the troops from the warm valleys into the hip-deep snow of the mountains. Bourke, who accompanied the column, remembered that the pine was so wet from snow and rain that it would not burn, and unless the men could find cedar they could not build fires. The scouts, led by Archie McIntosh, Joe Felmer, and Antonio Besias, were kept twelve to twenty-four hours in advance of the troops. Enjoying war, they were hard to control and looked for any opportunity for a fight, sometimes getting into scraps that would better have been avoided. In one instance, they came up on Chunz's rancheria, but were discovered by a hostile woman before they attacked. All of Chunz's people escaped, but the scouts destroyed the rancheria and his winter stores. Whatever minimal effect these skirmishes might have had, they nevertheless demonstrated the willingness and ability of the Apaches to assist the troops against their own people.

The two columns linked in the Superstitions on Christmas Day. Burns had been slightly more successful, attacking a rancheria in the Mazatzals, killing several, and capturing a woman and a boy. Two days later, the joint command bivoucked in a canyon near the base of Four Peaks in the Mazatzals. The combined strength was 220 soldiers, along with Brown's Apaches, and about a hundred Pimas who were scouting for Burns. Here Brown learned that Delshay was camped in an formidable position among the bluffs of the Salt River. The information was erroneous, for Delshay did not operate in that particular area, but was correct about the largeness of the rancheria. One of the scouts, Nantje, had been a member of this particular band, and once night fell he could locate the stronghold by the position of a particular star.

To avoid giving away his own presence, Brown ordered complete silence, although, as the sky became overcast and the air grew cold, he allowed the Indians to stew a mule that had died during the day. Meanwhile, each man checked his weapons, filled his cartridge belt, drew enough rations for a couple of days, and stripped himself of anything not absolutely essential. At 8 P.M., the Apaches moved out, followed by Burns's company, then Brown's companies, with the Pimas bringing up the rear. After several miles, they began following a trail up the side of a steep mountain, reaching the summit shortly after midnight. Here they waited for almost an hour while the Apaches scouted ahead. They returned to report that they had spotted fires in the canyon below.

The troops waited in the cold until dawn, but could see nothing. Felmer took some scouts down the trail toward the Salt, and had gone only a few hundred yards when he found a recently abandoned rancheria. Pushing on, they came to a small herd of ponies and mules. Ahead, they spotted an almost impregnable rancheria at the mouth of a cave. "This handful of our comrades, with a gallantry that cannot be too highly extolled at once charged the Indians, killing (6) six and driving the remainder into the cave," Bourke recorded in his diary.

Soon, Brown arrived with the rest of the men to find that the terrain had created a temporary stand-off. The cave was screened by a natural rampart of sandstone about ten feet high, giving the hostile Apaches ample cover. The soldiers and scouts, however, were protected by large boulders scattered in front of the cave, and had freedom of movement while the hostiles were penned inside. "Orders were given to make no charge upon the works, to pick off every Indian showing his head, to spare every woman & child, but to kill every man," Bourke wrote.

Twice Brown called on them to surrender, promising their lives would be spared, and each time he was met with defiant shouts. Finally, he ordered his men to pour heavy fire into the cave. Several times, groups tried to escape, but were cut down. "For (3) three minutes, every man in the command opened and closed the breech-block of his carbine as rapidly as his hands could move. Never have I seen such a hellish spot as was the narrow little space in which the hostile Indians were now crowded," Bourke recorded. Meanwhile, Burns's company managed to work its way overhead and began tumbling large rocks down the cliff, crushing and mangling those concealed behind the sandstone rampart. Finally, Brown ordered a charge. "Upon entering the enclosure a horrible spectacle was disclosed to view—in one corner (11) eleven dead bodies were huddled, in another four and in different crevices they were piled to the extent of the little cave and to the total number of (57) fifty-seven and (20) women and children were taken prisoners." Most of the prisoners were wounded. The government's loss was one Pima scout killed.[21]

The band in the cave belonged to Nanni-chaddi, whose raids had devastated the area along the Gila and Salt Rivers. His body was found among the dead. The Battle of the Cave, or the Salt River Cave Battle, as it was then called, completely ended those depredations by annihilating that band. It also demonstrated Crook's tenacity. Nevertheless, because Apache society was fragmented, it failed to break resistance, and troops were forced to continue hunting each band down, destroying its rancherias and supplies, and killing or capturing as many as possible.[22]

The climax came on March 11, 1873, when a band of Indians killed three men—John McDonald, George W. Taylor, and Gus Swain. Taylor was taken alive and tortured to death. Nickerson, who arrived at the scene immediately afterwards, wrote:

> They [took Taylor] up to a sheltered spot among the rocks, stripped him of his clothing, tied his hands behind him, fastened his feet together, and commenced to torture him by shooting arrows into his naked body, taking care not to strike a vital spot . . . .
>
> The ground where the victim had laid, was all matted down as he rolled over and over in his awful agony, breaking off the arrows as he rolled until over one hundred and fifty of these cruel missles [sic] had been broken off in his body. And then, when by reason of the loss of blood, he could move no more, they finished him in a manner so excruciating and beastly that I could not, if I would, shock my readers with a hint of the method of his final taking off.[23]

These killings made Crook all the more determined to break the Apaches once and for all. Columns of troops combed the countryside, forcing the hostiles into increasingly harsh country and following them to their rancherias. Within two weeks, field reports coming back to headquarters at Whipple Barracks showed heavy hostile casualties.

Near the end of the month, an expedition of Twenty-third Infantry under Capt. George M. Randall pushed northward toward the forks of the Verde. Near the forks the troops encountered fresh signs of Indians, and Randall began precautionary measures, moving only at night. The country was rugged, making it hard to keep track of all the mules in the train, and some wandered away, falling into the hands of the Apaches. They sent up smoke signals, and Randall, understanding the significance, became even more careful. Working ahead, one of the Indian scouts captured a woman and returned her to camp where, after what Crook called "intimidation," she agreed to guide the soldiers to her rancheria, which was nearby.

The troops wrapped their feet in gunnysacks to deaden the sound of their shoes and, led by the woman, started out after dark. The trail followed the banks of the Verde, then went up a forty-five-degree incline of broken lava to a palisade at the base of Turret Mountain. Here a portion of the palisade had collapsed, creating a narrow, rugged notch. At one point the soldiers had to crawl on their stomachs before they finally reached the summit where the hostiles were camped.

At dawn, the soldiers fired into the camp and charged with a yell. The Apaches had felt so secure that they panicked, running in all directions. Some ran right past the rocks that the soldiers were using for cover, and were cut down. Others disappeared over the edge, some perhaps jumping off a sheer escarpment on one side and smashing themselves on the rocks below, and others probably tumbling down the slopes on the other side and hiding in the brush. No men were taken alive, but most of the women and children were captured. From the prisoners, the soldiers learned that members of this band had been involved in the killings of McDonald, Taylor, and Swain. "So retributive justice had soon overtaken these brutes," Crook noted with grim satisfaction.[24]

Randall's fight at Turret Mountain broke Apache resistance. By April 12, Crook was able to write divisional headquarters that he had just returned to Prescott from Camp Verde, where "I had the satisfaction of meeting large bodies of the Indians, against whom I have been operating, who followed the troops in with most abject pleas for peace. Being satisfied that their professions were sincere I have agreed to allow them to come in, in fact have concluded a peace with them that I believe will be lasting. Although I do not anticipate but there may be acts of violence from straggling bands still at large, yet I believed the war is virtually at an end, so far as all the tribes in this Territory are concerned, except perhaps for Cochise's Band."[25]

As far as Crook was concerned, the campaign actually had ended five days earlier on April 7, when the last of the major hostile bands had surrendered. "Had it not been for their barbarities," he wrote, "one would have been moved to pity by their appearance. They were emaciated, clothes torn in tatters, some of their legs not thicker than my arm."

One of their most prominent chiefs, Cha-lipun, told him, "You see, we're are [sic] nearly dead from want of food and exposure—the copper cartridge has done the business for us. I am glad of the opportunity to surrender, but I do it not because I love you, but because I am afraid of General."[26]

Besides the army's seemingly endless supply of ammunition, Cha-lipun also cited the Apache scouts and the tenacity of the troops. No matter where they hid or how rugged the country, the scouts hunted them down, and the soldiers followed. As one officer of the Twenty-third Infantry later wrote, "The Apaches found, for the first time, that they were overmatched by skillful, daring and untiring American soldiers, who swept them from the Salt River Cañon and the summits of Turrent [sic] Mountains and Diamond Butte." The government recognized the efforts of both soldiers and scouts—twenty-two medals of honor were awarded for this campaign, ten of which went to Apaches.[27]

Now that the Grand Offensive was concluded, Crook was determined to make certain the peace would be effective. In a general order, he stated that the

Indians were required to end their depredations, remain on their reservations, and comply with government regulations issued through their agents. In exchange, they would have "all their rights under the law." He would allow "a sufficient time" to communicate the terms to any bands still on the loose, after which they would be hunted down and "forced to surrender or be destroyed."[28]

A second general order established procedures for troop commanders at the various agencies, including the establishment of civil government, Indian police, and maintenance of order. "While [the Indians] should not be judged harshly for acts which in civil codes would constitute minor offense," the order cautioned, "care should also be taken that they do not succeed in deceiving their agents and the officers, in matters of great import, being careful to treat them as children in *ignorance* not in *innocence*."[29] In other words, officers should not overreact, but should always be on their guard against Apache attempts to manipulate them.

To divert the Indians from thoughts of war, Crook set them to developing their reservation, which was established eighteen miles from Camp Verde. Captain Mason and Lieutenant Schuyler were put in charge of the program, which centered around establishing farms. The various bands, each under its own chief, were set to work digging an irrigation canal, and when it was ready, a water wheel was constructed. By summer, fifty-seven acres had been planted with melons and turnips, and preparations were underway for barley and corn. At Camp Apache, the Indians raised some 500,000 pounds of corn and 30,000 pounds of beans alone and were becoming, in Crook's words, "more or less interested" in agriculture. He was pleased with the result. "Everything goes well, so far as I am now advised throughout the Dep't. as far as the Indians are concerned," he wrote to Schuyler on July 24.[30]

Once again, Crook's success raised the possibility of advancement, particularly as the impending retirement of Brig. Gen. Philip St. George Cooke had created another vacancy. This time, the push was too strong to be ignored. On October 29, 1873, Secretary Belknap, acting on instructions from President Grant, issued the order jumping Crook two grades to brigadier general, adding in a postscript, "Genl. Crook will retain his present command." The appointment coincided with completion of the new telegraph line from Yuma to Prescott, and the construction superintendent, R. R. Haines, sent the first message, informing him of the completion and congratulating him on the promotion. Eleven days later, from Camp Apache, Crook wrote his acceptance.[31]

Crook's appointment over senior officers created hard feelings within the military establishment. Among the officers passed over was Colonel Nelson

Miles of the Fifth Infantry, who was especially resentful. This was the beginning of a quarrel that would turn into mutual hatred as the two men came to know each other on the frontier.[32]

Whatever might have been the feelings within the army, the people of the West who depended on him were elated. On January 12, 1874, the California Legislature approved a resolution urging the U.S. Senate to confirm Crook's appointment, citing his "great services rendered . . . to the settlers on the frontier in protecting life & property from destruction by hostile Indians & giving security to both." Given the large amount of support, confirmation was a foregone conclusion. Crook had his general's star.[33]

Not all was as quiet as it seemed, and by the time of this accolade, Crook once again had been compelled to field more expeditions. Major Apache troubles had begun anew only weeks after the surrender the previous spring. On May 27, 1873, Lt. Jacob Almy, Fifth Cavalry, was killed trying to break up a disturbance between rival factions at San Carlos. Terrified by the act, both peaceful and hostile Indians fled the reservation. Many of the peaceful ones returned, but others began raiding and murdering settlers in the San Pedro Valley. Crook was determined that none of the hostiles would be allowed to surrender unless they brought in—dead or alive—three chiefs he especially wanted—Chunz, Cochinay, and Chan-deisi.

At the Verde reservation, meanwhile, Schuyler was beginning to have trouble with Delshay, who had surrendered to Randall on April 25. He became the center of some of the most incorrigible Apache leaders and, as summer progressed, Schuyler told Crook that he feared trouble.

"By all means arrest Delche [sic] & send him with a strong guard to Camp Verde so there will be no chance of his escaping," Crook replied. "Get sufficient men from the post so as to prevent a collision & do your utmost to prevent one, but should one unavoidably occur, have your men so posted that they can kill all the ring leaders who support Delche in his opposition. As soon as you make the arrest tell Delche that if his people make any attempt to rescue him that he will be the first one you will kill & that he must prevent them from committing any overt act, also that the length of his confinement will depend on the conduct of his people whom he leaves behind him, &c. &c."[34]

Schuyler intended to make the arrest during a routine roll call on the agency parade ground. Delshay, however, was one jump ahead. Several Indians kept him informed of the soldiers' plans and one, an interpreter named Antone, managed to unload Schuyler's rifle just before he went to the parade ground to meet the Apaches. When they gathered, Schuyler informed Delshay he was under arrest, but the chief laughed. Schuyler tried to lever a shell into the chamber of his Winchester, only to find the rifle empty. The Indians, meanwhile, pulled pistols and rifles from under their blankets and surrounded Schuyler and the small squad of soldiers with him. Only the quick intervention of Mohave scouts prevented a massacre, and Delshay bolted the reservation with eighteen warriors and twenty-four women. Now four of the most ruthless chiefs—Chunz, Cochinay, Chan-deisi, and Delshay—were all on the loose.[35]

Crook's new campaign was organized along the lines of his grand offensive, and was equally effective. Over the next several months various columns hammered away at the Apache strongholds. Chunz, Cochinay, and Chan-deisi managed to escape, but several casualties undercut their following. Delshay was lying low, although Crook and Schuyler had a personal interest in finding him. "I have requested Maj. Randall to try & have Delche's head," Crook told Schuyler, "but if he has a strong party with him it is doubtful whether Maj. Randall's scouts will succeed."

Crook's comment about Delshay's head was more than just a figure of speech. To impress the Apaches with his determination, and demonstrate that he could be as ruthless as they, he had issued a savage ultimatum to the hostiles who had begun drifting back to the reservations—he would overlook their depredations if they would bring in the heads of their leaders. Delshay's head was particularly important because it carried a bounty.

The ultimatum, which raised a furor among the eastern humanitarians, illustrates the complicated nature of Indian fighting. Soldiers like Crook dealt with Indians on a regular basis, and learned to view them as human beings with just grievances. Even so, these same soldiers were all too familiar with Indian warfare. They knew that plunder, torture, murder, and rape were the honors of a warrior, and compassion for the enemy was seen as weakness. As members of that warrior culture, the Apaches understood Crook's order perfectly and hastened to comply.

The first head was that of Cochinay, which was displayed at San Carlos after he was caught by a small band of scouts within three miles of Tucson.[36] A month later, on June 23, Crook wrote Schuyler, "Recent telegram from Babcock [Lt. John B. Babcock, Fifth Cavalry] says that John Daisy's [Chan-deisi] head was brought into Camp Apache the other day, which leaves now only Chunz's head on his shoulders. . . . Start your killers as soon as possible after the head of DelChe & Co. The more prompt these heads are brought in, the less liable other Indians, in the future, will be to jeopardize their heads."[37]

Chunz's head was delivered to San Carlos on July 25, by a group of Apaches under a warrior named Desalin. They brought it together with six other heads, and lined them all up on the parade ground. Delshay's turn came just a few days later, but because of the bounty for him, some Apaches became overly zealous. Three of Schuyler's Tonto scouts from Camp Verde returned with a scalp and ears that they claimed belonged to Delshay. Then, Desalin returned to San Carlos with a head that was more generally agreed to be Delshay's. Crook settled the disagreement by paying for both.[38]

Once again, Arizona was peaceful, and this time there were few incidents. The Apaches had been effectively broken. Now, however, the government intervened. In 1874 it transferred control of the Indians from the War Department to the Indian Bureau. The following year, it began implementing General Howard's plan to abolish the outlying reservations by removing the Camp Apache and Camp Verde Indians to San Carlos.

Bourke and Crook blamed Tucson contractors and businessmen with connections to the Indian Ring, who wanted to profit from the proximity of the large reservation. Bancroft, likewise, speculated that the transfer benefitted whites who wanted the lands of reservations scheduled for closure. Crook believed that, aside from undermining his efforts to make them self-sufficient, the removal of the Camp Apache bands, who were mountain Indians, to the wastes of San Carlos would undermine their health.

While profiteering at the expense of the Indians may have been a partial motive, the move nevertheless followed the general policy of the federal government of removal and concentration of the Indians into large reservations where they could be more effectively controlled. Crook's protests notwithstanding, the removals and concentrations continued for the remainder of his administration and after his transfer elsewhere.[39]

Despite the shortsighted government policies, and Crook's own failure to grasp the significance of Howard's truce with Cochise (he always mistrusted anything and anyone he did not control), Crook's administration in Arizona was a success. In only four years, he had managed to bring peace to the territory, something that the various efforts of Spain, Mexico, and the United States had failed to do over the preceding two centuries. His success was due to his ability to grasp the reality of Indian fighting, and plan accordingly. As Nickerson observed: "The campaigns in Arizona did not owe their ultimate success to any particular Waterloo-like victory, as much as they did to the covering of a great deal of ground by a comparatively small number of men, permitting the Indians no rest, and rendering any and every hiding place insecure."[40]

Much of the credit, however, belonged to General Howard for negotiating the truce with Cochise. Although Crook always suspected Cochise of aiding hostiles from the San Carlos and White Mountain reservations, Howard's truce kept a major portion of the Apaches quiet while Crook concentrated on the remainder. Bancroft probably understood better than most that both men deserved credit, each in his own way. "Howard," he wrote, "had offered the olive branch, and Crook, with the sword, was enforcing its acceptance."[41]

But perhaps the greatest tribute of all came from the Indians themselves. Referring to the color of Crook's eyes, along with the ability of his troops to track them down to their most remote strongholds, they called him "Gray Fox."[42]

Perhaps the earliest known photograph of Crook (left) shows him as a brevet second lieutenant fresh out of West Point, together with Philip H. Sheridan (center), and Bvt. Second Lt. John Nugen. Initially, Crook, Nugen, and Sheridan were classmates, but Sheridan fell a year behind after being suspended for fighting. All three were from Ohio and were assigned to the West Coast prior to the Civil War.

A Mathew Brady photograph taken at the close of the Civil War shows Maj. Gen. Philip H. Sheridan with four of his generals: (from left) Wesley Merritt, Sheridan, Crook, John W. Forsyth, and George Armstrong Custer.

Crook and his wife, Mary.
The photo appears to
have been taken about
1876 or 1877. They were
married at the end of the
Civil War.

Rutherford B. Hayes, as a
congressman in the years
immediately following the
Civil War. Crook developed a
lifelong friendship with the
Hayes family when Hayes
served under him as a volunteer officer in the Civil War.
Hayes became his staunch
admirer, even naming one of
his sons after Crook. More
than a decade later, as president of the United States,
Hayes turned to Crook for
advice in Indian affairs.

Lucy Webb Hayes.

Babes Ascending, an allegorical paint-
ing in the Hayes home in Fremont,
Ohio, represents the ascension into
heaven of George Crook Hayes and
Joseph Hayes, both of whom died in
infancy.

Webb Cook Hayes
became a surrogate son for
the childless Crook.
R. B. HAYES PRESIDENTIAL
CENTER, FREMONT, OHIO

The George Crook Oak (right) towers above Spiegel Grove, the Hayes mansion in
Fremont, Ohio, where Crook was a frequent guest.
AUTHOR'S PHOTO

Azor H. Nickerson.

Lt. Col. George Crook
wears the civilian attire he
preferred over uniforms in
this tintype taken about
1870.

John Gregory Bourke.
LITTLE BIGHORN BATTLEFIELD
NATIONAL MONUMENT

Oliver O. Howard.
U.S. ARMY MILITARY HISTORY
INSTITUTE

Walter S. Schuyler (seated, left) poses with several other officers during Crook's 1873
campaign in Arizona. The casual civilian dress reflects Crook's attitude of campaigning in clothing that was practical for the terrain, rather than the prescribed military
uniform.

Philip H. Sheridan.
KANSAS STATE HISTORICAL
SOCIETY

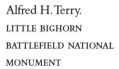

Alfred H. Terry.
LITTLE BIGHORN
BATTLEFIELD NATIONAL
MONUMENT

Crook's vast camp overlooks the North Platte River in Wyoming in 1876. Fort Fetterman is on the bluff at the top right.

As Crook's starving, exhausted troops neared the Black Hills settlements, they were met by relief trains carrying provisions. One of the trains was accompanied by photographer Stanley J. Morrow, who got soldiers to reenact scenes of the march for his camera. Here soldiers demonstrate how the wounded were transported from the fight at Slim Buttes.

Troops butcher a worn-out horse that has been shot for meat. Crook's soldiers were reduced to living on horse meat during the final weeks, giving the march its name.
PHOTO BY STANLEY J. MORROW, U.S. MILITARY ACADEMY LIBRARY

Their long ordeal almost ended, exhausted soldiers rest in a camp of wickiups at Bear Butte, near what is now Sturgis, South Dakota.
PHOTO BY STANLEY J. MORROW, U.S. MILITARY ACADEMY LIBRARY

Red Cloud.
U.S. MILITARY ACADEMY
LIBRARY

Government officials and Indians gather as Crook commissions Spotted Tail head chief of the Lakotas at the Spotted Tail Agency on October 24, 1876.
U.S. MILITARY ACADEMY LIBRARY

Ranald S. Mackenzie.
AUTHOR'S COLLECTION

Nelson A. Miles.
LITTLE BIGHORN
BATTLEFIELD NATIONAL
MONUMENT

Standing Bear.
NEBRASKA STAATE
HISTORICAL SOCIETY

Chato is shown here in
1885, when he was
sergeant-major of Britton
Davis's Indian Company
"A" during the Geronimo
campaign.
NATIONAL ARCHIVES PHOTO
NO. 111-SC-87761

Geronimo in 1887.

Seated in front of the center tent with his trademark white sun helmet, Crook poses with interpreters, scouts, and packers in 1886.

Geronimo (second from left), and other Chiricahua leaders and warriors confer with Crook (second from right) in camp in Mexico in March 1886. The Chiricahuas surrendered, but Geronimo and several others subsequently reneged.

Second Lt. Lyman
W.V. Kennon.
U.S. ARMY MILITARY
HISTORY INSTITUTE

Crook breaks his usual
habit of civilian clothing by
appearing in dress uniform
in this 1888 photo. By now,
his field service had ended,
and he divided his time
between military duties and
campaigning for Indian
rights.
U.S. ARMY MILITARY HISTORY
INSTITUTE

TEN

THE GREAT SIOUX WAR

W<small>HILE</small> C<small>ROOK BUSIED HIMSELF</small> in Arizona, the great Indian nations of the northern plains were seething with discontent. The trouble had its roots in the Fort Laramie Treaty of 1868, designed to clear the way for national development, and prepare the Indians for assimilation into the mainstream of American society. One of the key articles of the treaty established a reservation comprising all of what is now South Dakota west of the Missouri River, along with a small portion of the present state of North Dakota. It stipulated that, except for those authorized under the treaty, which is to say representatives of the civil government and the military, no persons would be allowed "to pass over, settle upon, or reside in the territory" without the permission of the Indians and the consent of the government. It obligated the government to evict anyone who entered the reservation without permission, by military force, if necessary. Besides establishing the reservation, the treaty recognized large portions of southeastern Montana and northeastern Wyoming as "unceded Indian territory," again off limits to outsiders, but where the Indians could roam, live, and hunt at will.

The most powerful of the Indian nations in the region were the Lakota, or Western Sioux. Their population and territory were so extensive that they were divided into three great tribes—Oglala, Brule, and Hunkpapa—and four lesser tribes—Sans Arcs, Blackfeet, Two Kettles, and Miniconjous. The Lakotas were most capable of resisting, and indeed, the treaty and reservation were largely directed toward them. The Great Sioux Reservation, as it was called, included the Black Hills of western South Dakota. To the Lakotas, the Black Hills had multiple functions. Not only were they regarded as sacred—perhaps the homes of spirits—but they also had utilitarian uses. The vast stands of lodgepole pine were a seemingly inexhaustible source of tipi poles, and the abundant wildlife was a ready source of food in times of need. Consequently, the Lakotas placed a high value on the region, and considered it virtually inviolate for anyone besides themselves and their ancient allies, the Northern Cheyennes.

In the 1870s, the Lakotas and Cheyennes had been allied for more than a century. In their push westward from their early homeland in the western Great Lakes region, they had earned the enmity of many of the midwestern and western tribes, among them the Pawnees, Shoshones, and Utes. They were especially despised by the Arikaras (also known as Rees) and the Crows, whom the Lakotas and Cheyennes had forced out of their territories. Most, if not all, of these other tribes were ready to ally themselves with anyone—including the government—who took the field against the Lakotas and Cheyennes.[1]

The area occupied by the Lakotas and Cheyennes was in the Military Division of the Missouri, commanded by Sheridan, whose headquarters were in Chicago. Like the Military Division of the Pacific, the Division of the Missouri was divided into departments, in this case four: the Department of Texas, under Brig. Gen. Christopher C. Augur in San Antonio; Department of the Missouri, under Brig. Gen. John Pope in Fort Leavenworth, Kansas; Department of the Platte, under Brig. Gen. E. O. C. Ord in Omaha, Nebraska; and the Department of Dakota, under Brig. Gen. Alfred H. Terry in St. Paul, Minnesota. The Great Sioux Reservation was in the Department of Dakota, but the traditional range of the Lakotas and Cheyennes also extended into most of the Platte, and even into Pope's Department of the Missouri.

Although the Fort Laramie Treaty was designed to build harmony in the region, it was unworkable because of the divergent Indian and white interests, and its failure was virtually assured by the Panic of 1873, an economic depression of unprecedented proportions. To many in the East, a $1.25 million annual annuity payment guaranteed to the Indians under the treaty appeared to be a luxury the government could ill afford, and the Great Sioux Reservation itself, together with the unceded lands, seemed prime real estate for dispossessed easterners looking for a fresh start. More importantly, the Black Hills and the unceded lands had long been rumored to contain gold deposits, and a fresh infusion of gold seemed the ideal stimulant for a badly depressed economy. By early 1874, whites began pushing into the region in blatant violation of the treaty. Within a few months, fighting erupted.

The situation grew worse in June, when Lt. Col. George Armstrong Custer, Seventh Cavalry, was ordered to lead a survey expedition into the Black Hills.

The expedition established the existence of gold in the hills, and prospectors began flocking into the area in such numbers that General Terry believed it would be impossible to keep them out. Consequently, the government began preparations to arrange what President Grant called "the extinguishment of the Indian title" to the hills by whatever means necessary. In March 1875, as a clash loomed between treaty ideals on the one hand and political and economic realities on the other, Crook was ordered to Omaha to relieve General Ord and assume command of the Department of the Platte. Some of the region's newspapers applauded the move, confident that "Arizona Crook" would bring the Indians under control as he had done in the Southwest.[2]

Whatever the expectations of citizens and prospectors, Crook's assignment initially meant no change in the status quo. Until the government's "extinguishment of the Indian title" could be arranged, the treaty terms were still in force, and Crook was expected to keep unauthorized persons out of the Black Hills. After assuming command in Omaha on April 27, he made a quick trip to the Red Cloud Agency, in northwestern Nebraska south of the hills, then he and members of his staff went to Chicago for the June 3 wedding of the forty-four-year-old Sheridan and twenty-two-year-old Irene Rucker. Crook's only observation was that it "was a rather quiet affair" (Sheridan's father recently had died). Bourke, however, was "delighted" with Sheridan's bride, and at least one officer believed the marriage did much to calm the lieutenant general's foul temper.[3]

The geographical position of the Department of the Platte, slicing laterally through the center of the country and with a railroad running the entire width, meant that Crook often was in a better position to handle problems in other departments, and even in other divisions, than their own commanders. Eastern Nevada, in the Military Division of the Pacific, was more closely situated to the Platte than to California; at General Schofield's request, Crook sent infantry to Nevada to help suppress a minor outbreak of Indian trouble.[4]

Far more serious was the situation in the Black Hills. Although the region was in General Terry's Department of Dakota, it was most accessible through Nebraska and Wyoming, in Crook's jurisdiction. In July, Crook decided to personally investigate the situation. He took the train to Cheyenne, Wyoming, and from there traveled by ambulance to the Black Hills by way of Fort Laramie. It was a route he would come to know all too well over the next two years.

Crook found at least 1,200 miners and prospectors already working the gold fields. Talking with them, he found how much they resented "what they regarded as an interference with the rights of a sovereign citizen ... to go where he pleased and do as he pleased." The government, however, saw it differently, and on July 29 Crook issued a proclamation requiring "every miner and other unauthorized citizen to leave the territory known as the Black Hills, the Powder river, and Big Horn country by and before the 15th day of August."

On the face of it, the miners were being evicted in compliance with the treaty, but another section of the proclamation showed the order was, in fact, an empty gesture. In that section, Crook advised the miners, before leaving the area, to hold a meeting and establish a procedure to record their claims, against the day that "this territory shall have been opened," which is to say, when the Indians were expelled.[5]

In a letter to divisional headquarters, he suggested too much attention had been given to the grievances of the Indians, who he said were fed and clothed at government expense, and not enough to the grievances of settlers and miners, who had to support themselves. "I respectfully submit that their side of this story should be heard, as the settlers who develop our mines and open the frontier to civilization are the nation's wards, no less than their more fortunate fellows, the Indians."[6]

In September, a federal commission at the Red Cloud Agency met with the Indians in an effort to purchase the Black Hills, as well as the unceded Indian lands between the Powder River and the Bighorn Mountains of Montana and Wyoming. The government was prepared to offer $6 million in fifteen installments or, failing that, to lease mining rights for $400,000 a year. The Indians, however, demanded $600 million, an arbitrary figure they did not even comprehend. The council broke up amid confusion and recriminations, prompting Interior Secretary Delano to remark: "However unwilling we may be to confess it, the experience of the past summer proves either the inefficiency of the large military force under the command of such officers as general Sheridan, Terry, and Crook, or the utter impracticability of keeping Americans out of a country where gold is known to exist by any force of orders, or of United States cavalry, or by any consideration of the rights of others."[7]

Delano was right about "the utter impracticability" of keeping the prospectors out of the hills. Political and economic realities overrode any moral concerns about the rights of the Indians. As President Grant saw it, the interests of the nation now required the government to abrogate the Fort Laramie Treaty. On November 3, he met at the White House with Crook, Sheridan, and Secretary of War W. W. Belknap. They were joined by Interior Secretary Zachariah Chandler, newly appointed following Delano's resignation, and by Assistant Interior Secretary Benjamin R. Cowan. Although details of the meeting were never officially divulged, all agreed that it would be impossible to keep the miners out of the Black Hills. Consequently, the Indians would have to yield the region and, if they refused, the hills would be taken by military force. Chandler had no qualms about using the army, and the generals and the War Department were prepared to cooperate. Grant now issued confidential orders to the cabinet secretaries and generals stipulating that no further efforts would be made to keep citizens out.

Crook did not return to Omaha immediately after the conference, but instead accompanied Sheridan to Camp Supply in the Indian Territory. There they conferred with Ben Clarke, at thirty-four already a veteran scout whom Sheridan trusted implicitly. He told Clarke that he expected war with the Sioux, and wanted him to scout for Crook when the time came. Although Clarke replied that he knew nothing of the country in the northern plains, Sheridan insisted that he be ready to head north.

On December 6, the Interior Department ordered all Indians affiliated with the Nebraska and Dakota agencies to be within the control of their agencies, or within the boundaries of their reservation on or before January 31, 1876, or be regarded as hostile. At the request of General Sherman, Sheridan polled his commanders about the state of preparedness for a winter campaign. Terry was not at all certain; much of the area of operations was desolate, open prairie exposed to the full force of the bitter northern winters. Crook, however, had been secretly preparing since returning to the Platte. His base of operations would be Cheyenne, which had the combined advantages of railroad service, a military depot, and the nearby post of Fort D. A. Russell. This post, and Fort Sanders at the town of Laramie, about forty-five miles to the west, would provide the cavalry contingents, and he polled the commanders to determine the number of new horses needed. Crook also dispatched every available mule from the Nebraska and Wyoming posts to the Cheyenne Depot, and assembled wagons from throughout the department at Fort Laramie, about ninety miles north of Cheyenne. On January 3, Sheridan was able to report, "Gen. Crook is of the opinion that military operations can be undertaken in his Dept. against bands of hostile Sioux Indians [whenever] in the opinion of the Indian Bureau such action become necessary."

One day after the January 31 deadline, Secretary Chandler turned jurisdiction of non-agency Sioux over to the War Department. Six days later, the army was authorized to commence operations. One old pioneer who served as a scout in the ensuing conflict later said, "Of all the wars in which the United States has been engaged, the least justification is found in the Sioux War of 1876.

The Interior Department can never wash its hands of this crime."[8] Hundreds of soldiers and Indians would die in the government's seizure of land that had been guaranteed to the Indians in perpetuity.

Sheridan's plan called for a three-pronged offensive designed to catch the Indians between converging columns of troops. Terry's troops were situated in western Montana and in Dakota, and Sheridan envisioned a column of Montana troops moving east under Col. John Gibbon, and a column of Dakota troops moving west under Custer. A third column, from Crook's department, would move northward from Wyoming. In theory, the plan was sound, and had proven successful during the Red River War of 1874–75, when columns of troops moving into the same area from four different directions had battered the southern plains tribes into submission, effectively breaking Indian resistance in Texas and Oklahoma. The flaw was climate. Sheridan's own experience was in the southern plains, and he had no grasp of the severity of winter in Montana. So while Crook was almost ready to move, Terry's troops were snowbound and would be idle until well into March. Disappointed, Sheridan nevertheless was determined to get Crook's forces into the field, and Crook was willing to accommodate.[9]

On February 17, Crook and his staff, accompanied by Scout Ben Clarke, left Omaha by train, arriving in Cheyenne the following day. Preparations were well advanced. The column, formally designated the Big Horn Expedition and under the overall command of Col. Joseph J. Reynolds, Third Cavalry, would consist of five companies each of Second Cavalry and Third Cavalry, and two companies of Fourth Infantry. Part of these were already assembled at Fort D. A. Russell. Other components were at Fort Sanders and Fort Laramie; and the remainder at Fort Fetterman, eighty miles beyond Fort Laramie. All would assemble at Fetterman. Tom Moore, Crook's chief packer in Arizona, already had the mule train organized and equipped.[10]

Few had any illusions about the coming campaign. Bourke noted in his diary: "We are now on the eve of the bitterest Indian war the Government has ever been called upon to wage: a war with a tribe that has waxed fat and insolent on Gov't bounty, and has been armed and equipped with the most improved weapons by the connivance or carelessness of the Indian Agents."[11]

On February 21, Nickerson returned to Omaha. The following day, Crook and the remainder of his staff left Cheyenne for the overnight ride to Fort Laramie. Upon arrival, Crook began interviewing scouts and guides. He had been unable to obtain Lakotas because they were less fractious than the Apaches. Indeed many reservation Lakotas were sympathetic to those the government had declared hostile and decided to remain neutral, at least for the time being. Consequently, Crook had to content himself with white civilians who lived in the region.

The most fascinating was Frank Grouard, a large man whose polyglot features created much speculation about his origins. His own story, and one most likely true, was that he had been born in Polynesia twenty-three years before, the son of an American missionary and an island noblewoman, and had been brought to California when he was two years old. In 1865, he became a freight transporter in Montana and was captured by the Oglalas, with whom he lived for six years. Ben Arnold, who hired on as a scout and messenger, recalled that Grouard "could speak perfect Sioux and could even pass most places at a full blood." His knowledge of their languages, customs, and country prompted Crook to hire him as chief scout at $125 a month, about $25 above the going rate.

Shortly after this meeting, Bourke's writings begin to mention an Oglala chief named Crazy Horse. It may be that Crook first learned of Crazy Horse from Grouard, who had a grudge against the chief stemming from his Oglala captivity; until now Bourke's writings and Crook's official correspondence centered around the Hunkpapa chief Sitting Bull, the principle advocate of resistance to the government, and the Oglala chief Red Cloud, who had fought the government to a stand-still in the years immediately following the Civil War. Whatever the case, the knowledge of Crazy Horse's existence suited Crook perfectly. His personality required enemies—real people against whom he could focus his energies, and whom he could blame if things went wrong. Perhaps Grouard, who seemed adept at recognizing human failings and playing them for his own ends, saw this in Crook and offered up Crazy Horse. Whatever the case, as the campaign progressed Crook began to see Crazy Horse as a sort of boogie man, a super Indian responsible for everything that went awry for the army. In doing so, he helped create the modern mystique surrounding the war leader.

Grouard was one of thirty scouts contracted at Fort Laramie, and to Bourke, most of them seemed "as sweet a lot of cutthroats as ever scuttled a ship. Half-Breeds, Squaw-men, bounty-jumpers, thieves and desperadoes of different grades from the various Indian agencies." He did note, however, that a "respectable minority" such as Grouard, Ben Clarke, and Louis Richaud seemed dependable. Major Thaddeus Stanton, a paymaster, was placed in charge of this "corps d'elite" as chief of scouts.

Besides soldiers and scouts, there was also one newspaper correspondent, Robert Strahorn of the *Rocky Mountain News*, an experienced journalist in

Denver who wrote dispatches under the pseudonym "Alter Ego." He also sold dispatches to newspapers in Chicago and New York, and to the *Cheyenne Sun* and *Omaha Republican*. Like Joe Wasson in Idaho, Strahorn took an active part in Indian fights, and would stay with Crook for the duration of the Sioux War. Strahorn was the professional journalist of the expedition, but several officers and enlisted men supplemented their army pay by selling accounts of Crook's campaigns to newspapers.[12]

From Fort Laramie, the command marched northwest for two days until it reached Fort Fetterman, the outer limit of government authority. Beyond was nothing but wilderness. Ten years earlier there had been three forts—Reno, Phil Kearny and C. F. Smith—to the north, but these had been abandoned in compliance with the terms of the Fort Laramie Treaty, and subsequently destroyed by the Indians. Fort Fetterman was the final staging point and, on February 27, Tom Moore's pack trains arrived from Cheyenne, and several cavalry contingents rode in from the other posts.

In answer to an inquiry from Custer, Crook gave his date of departure and troop strength, although he added that he had no reliable information on the country, and therefore could not determine any line of operations until he actually was in the region between the Bighorns and the Powder River. He had heard nothing from General Terry, and so was not certain what was happening with the Montana and Dakota columns. Although disappointed that two or three columns would not be operating simultaneously, he appears to have had little confidence in Terry because his preparations were those of a commander who did not necessarily expect support.[13] If Crook had mixed feelings about the situation, he was not alone. In his diary, Bourke noted: "The same wise system of logistics which did so much to shatter the power of the hostile *Apaches* in *Arizona* is now to be brought into play to conquer the haughty *Sioux*. But we have not the same knowledge of country which proved so invaluable in that campaign, nor the same unerring Indian auxiliaries who led us into the dens and fastnesses of the enemy with clock-like accuracy."[14]

Bourke's comment goes far to explain why Crook's tactical performance in the Northwest and in Arizona was so successful, while in the northern plains it often was mediocre. Arizona and the Columbia River region were smaller areas by comparison, and had extensive white settlement. Thus the terrain generally was known to the soldiers, and they never were more than a few days' march from support. The situation was entirely different in eastern Montana and northern Wyoming. There was no white settlement and, beyond Fort Fetterman, it was hundreds of miles to the next military post. This was the exclusive domain of the Indians, many of whom were hostile. Crook admitted as much, telling Ben Arnold, "We are outsiders and unacquainted with the country, and the Indians know every nook and corner of it."

On March 1, the Big Horn Expedition marched out of Fetterman and headed north. Total strength of the expedition was 883 soldiers, civilian scouts, guides, and packers. Four hundred mules in five trains would carry provisions and equipment on the march. A large train of wagons and ambulances, and a herd of cattle for fresh meat, accompanied the expedition during the initial stages and would be left at the ruins of old Fort Reno, where Crook planned to establish a depot.[15]

Officially at least, the expedition was under the immediate command of Colonel Reynolds. Crook accompanied the troops in his capacity as commander of the department, and therefore as an observer. He later explained that he had been told that an expedition against northern Indians in winter and early spring was impossible, and he "wished to demonstrate by personal experience whether this was so or not." He also implied other reasons, but did not elaborate. Part of Crook's motive may have been lack of confidence in Reynolds, who some officers felt was not up to the rigors of Indian fighting. Crook was also aware that Reynolds had been accused of graft while commanding the Department of Texas several years earlier, and his name was now linked to corruption in the War Department. Part also may have been Crook's own personality; despite his earlier protestations that he was "tired of the Indian work," he essentially was a field commander rather than an administrator, and may have been loathe to sit behind a desk while others did the fighting. Whatever the reason, it soon became clear that Reynolds would head the expedition in name only, and all command decisions would come from Crook.[16]

As the command moved northward into the Wyoming winter, the men were assessing their general. Captain Anson Mills, Third Cavalry, who would figure prominently in Crook's Sioux campaigns, and whose webbed Mills belt ultimately would be adopted by many of the armies of the world, called Crook "a cold, gray-eyed and somewhat cold-blooded warrior, treating his men perhaps too practically [i.e. ruthlessly] in war time." That opinion—or worse— would come to be shared by many of the men during the ensuing months. Frank Grouard, whose relationship with Crook was that of a civilian employee, believed Crook was "the master of every emergency where coolness and courage were essential." That, too, would be acknowledged—if grudgingly— by many of the troops.[17]

To avoid attracting attention, Crook handled the command as he had done in Arizona, marching it at night and resting during the day. "The scenery," Bourke wrote, "was dreary; the weather bitter cold; the bluffs on either side bare and sombre prominences of yellow clay, slate and sandstone." The infantrymen were least affected during the marches, because the constant motion of their legs and swinging of their arms kept their blood circulating. The cavalrymen, however, sat nearly motionless for hours and were in danger of freezing to death in their saddles. To protect themselves, they bundled themselves in so much wool and fur that Bourke commented they could hardly be recognized as soldiers.

Indian sign abounded. The first night out, Indians wounded one of the cattle herders and stampeded forty-five head. Because of that, extra sentinels were posted, nervous men who tended to shoot "at anything and everything which looked like a man." The scouts found lodgepole trails headed in the directions of Fort Fetterman and the Red Cloud Agency, indicating bands of Indians trying to comply with the government's ultimatum even if the deadline had already expired. Many of these groups were so remote that the deadline had passed before they learned of the ultimatum, and so only now were moving toward the military posts or reservations. On the fourth day, smoke signals were observed in the hills ahead.

After five days, the expedition reached the ruins of Fort Reno, where Crook established his depot. The wagons were parked, and the infantry was left to guard them. From here on, the command would depend on the mule trains, traveling lightly, each man wearing only the clothes on his back. Each soldier was allowed one buffalo robe or two blankets. Half rations for fifteen days would consist of bacon, hardtack, coffee, and sugar. That night a group of Indians tried to stampede the stock, but the outer sentries drove them off. Frustrated, they fired into the camp for about half an hour. Crook, who had already turned in and did not stir from his blankets, forbade the men to return fire, saying the muzzle flashes would give away their positions. The only casualty was a soldier grazed slightly on the cheek, and Crook's determination not to let the Indians interfere with his sleep boosted morale.[18]

At 7 P.M. on March 7, the cavalry left, moving northwest and covering thirty-five miles before bivouacking at 5 A.M. the next day. In camp, however, a blizzard blew in, and Crook ordered the men to move five miles to a more sheltered position. The storm continued to batter them as they broke camp and continued their northward march. "Mustaches and beards coated with pendent icicles several inches long and bodies swathed in raiment of furs and hides made this expedition of cavalry resemble a long column of Santa Clauses," Bourke commented. Continuing northwest, they passed the ruins of Fort Phil Kearny, its cemetery crowded with victims of the Red Cloud War ten years earlier, including the remains of Capt. William J. Fetterman and eighty men, who were wiped out when they blundered into an Indian ambush on December 21, 1866. At times air was so cold that the mercury congealed in the bulb of the thermometer, prompting Bourke to observe that it was at least 39 degrees below zero. Horses were coated with ice.

On March 16, Maj. Stanton and his scouts chased two young warriors. Crook halted the command and ordered coffee for the men. He surmised they were out hunting, which meant their camp would be nearby. The halt was designed to make them think he was resting his men before pushing on toward the Yellowstone, and lull them into complacency. Then, with a forced night march, the troops might be able to locate and attack their camp.[19]

Crook determined to give Reynolds a chance at hunting down the Indians without supervision. Reynolds's record as a Union Army officer had been respectable, and Crook hoped that a victorious Indian fight would redeem his reputation after the allegations of graft in Texas. He would take six companies of cavalry and scouts, and follow the trail of the warriors. If he found the village, he was to attack. If not, he would return and rendezvous with Crook, who would remain behind with the mule trains and four companies of cavalry.

Reynolds moved out and followed the trail until about 2:30 A.M., when he called a halt while Frank Grouard scouted ahead. Just before daylight, Grouard spotted a large village on the Powder River. Reynolds organized his command into battalions of two companies each. A battalion under Capt. Henry E. Noyes, Second Cavalry, would attack the village and capture the Indian pony herd. That commanded by Capt. Alexander Moore, the same officer whose blunder had cost Crook the chance to cut off the Apache raiding party at Sulphur Springs Valley in Arizona three years earlier, would occupy the ridge behind the village and cut off escape. Captain Anson Mills's battalion was to be in reserve, but Reynolds changed his mind and detailed him to back Moore.[20]

The fight was a fiasco. Men and horses were exhausted, and the "charge" was little more than a slow trot. Moore blundered in his attempt to secure the bluffs, moving instead into the valley and allowing the Indians to regroup and counterattack. Noyes took one company against the pony herd, detailing his second company to hit the village, then failed to support that company when it got into trouble. Finally, Mills brought his battalion to the rescue, and the troops pushed into the village. In one of the tipis the scouts found a sick old

woman who told them what apparently she surmised they wanted to hear—
that this was the Oglala village of Crazy Horse.

In order to travel lightly, the column had carried no rations, and overcoats
and blankets had been left behind with the train. Now, at Reynolds's orders,
the soldiers burned everything in the village, including food, buffalo robes,
and blankets that they would desperately need over the next twenty-four
hours. While the soldiers were busy with their destruction, the Indians moved
down the bluffs and counterattacked, driving the exhausted troops back the
way they came with the loss of several men. Despite the pleadings of several
officers, Reynolds allowed no effort to recover the dead, and at least one
wounded soldier was taken alive and tortured even as the troops withdrew.
To aggravate the problem, Reynolds failed to secure the captured pony herd;
that night, the Indians stampeded the animals and recovered most of them.
There were bitter mutterings in the ranks as the column met Crook the next
day.[21]

Crook was furious. The expedition, begun so hopefully, had turned into a
fiasco. The recovery of the pony herd restored mobility to the Indians and, in
the words of Nickerson, "was equal to nullifying the effect of the entire expedition." Crook's first act upon returning to Fort Fetterman was to file charges
against Reynolds, Moore, and Noyes, which he summed up as:

1st. A failure on the part of portions of the command [i.e., Noyes and Moore]
      to properly support the first attack.
2d.   A failure to make a vigorous and persistent attack with the whole command.
3d.   A failure to secure the provisions that were captured for the use of the
      troops, instead of destroying them.
4th. And most disastrous of all, a failure to properly secure and take care of the
      horses and ponies captured, nearly all of which again fell into the hands
      of the Indians the following morning.

Weighed against this was Crook's belief that they had achieved complete
surprise, which was only partly correct; alerted by the two warriors, the
Indians were half-expecting some sort of a problem, and had sent out scouts
of their own who had missed the soldiers coming in. Crook was also satisfied that the village with all the equipment and large quantities of ammunition was destroyed.[22]

In the last case, Crook was correct. Destruction was more or less complete.
Unfortunately, the village did not belong to Crazy Horse but consisted prima-

rily of Cheyennes under the ranking chief Two Moons. Until now, they had not considered themselves part of the quarrel between the government and the Lakota Sioux. They had learned late of the government ultimatum, and had been making their way by back trails to Fort Laramie. It was merely by chance that two of their warriors had run into Crook's expedition while out hunting. Now that their village and provisions were destroyed, they made their way toward Crazy Horse's people who, in fact, were camped some fifty miles to the east. Crazy Horse received them, but their destitution put a strain on his own resources and, at his suggestion, both Oglalas and Cheyennes moved some thirty-five miles to the north, to join Sitting Bull's Hunkpapas. There, the combined tribes agreed they had no alternative but war.

The decision was not solely a reaction to the attack. Almost a year earlier, in response to the white incursions, Sitting Bull had begun efforts to forge more unity among the northern tribes. Despite the alliance between the Lakotas and the Cheyennes as nations, the Lakota side was represented primarily by the Oglalas and Miniconjous; the Cheyennes and other Lakota tribes knew little of each other. Sitting Bull worked to strengthen ties between his Hunkpapas and the Cheyennes, obtaining pledges to act in concert and working to identify the common enemies. So when the Oglalas and Cheyennes joined the Hunkpapas after the Reynolds fight, all had a reasonably clear agenda. They would remain together to present a defensive front against any further government expeditions.

Meanwhile, a group of mixed-bloods arrived at the Cheyenne agency with the facts of the fight. Not only had Reynolds hit the wrong village but outraged Indians were threatening swift reprisals. This information was sent to General Terry, who forwarded it on to Sheridan. Sheridan passed it on to Crook without comment. For Crook, however, this was unacceptable. The newspapers had already reported that his troops had hit Crazy Horse's village, and these accounts were never retracted. Unwilling to admit the blunder, he spent the rest of his life insisting he had struck a blow against Crazy Horse.[23]

Whatever the blow to Crook's ego, the immediate problem was morale. The already fractious Third Cavalry was divided even more because of the charges against its commanding officer and one of its company commanders. Upon returning to Fort D. A. Russell, a large number of enlisted men deserted, claiming they would not serve under officers who abandoned their dead and wounded to the Indians. The proceedings against Noyes moved rapidly, because his case was the least complicated. He had simply been too attentive to his orders to secure the pony herd, when common sense dictated that he should have assisted the companies in the village. His trial was held at D. A. Russell almost immediately upon the expedition's return, and he received an administrative reprimand. The trials of Reynolds and Moore should have been held with equal expediency to end the matter and rebuild confidence. Unfortunately, they were delayed until January 1877, undermining morale even further.[24]

Despite what Nickerson called "the intervention of some of the highest authorities in the land to hush the matter up," newspapers began portraying the Reynolds fight as something less than the total victory that Crook wished to present to the public. While these accounts usually blamed Reynolds for the disappointing results, headlines such as "Crook's Chagrin" and "Partial Failure" did little to ease the blow to his pride. He was determined to avenge the humiliation by seeking out Crazy Horse, and either destroying him or reducing him to impotence.[25]

While Crook sat in his office in Omaha and pondered his next move, events were developing to the north. When Two Moons and Crazy Horse opted to seek out the Hunkpapas in the wake of the Reynolds fight, they joined others who were banding together. The encampment would have been substantial in any case; the annual council of the Lakota nation, where the various tribes gathered in a week-long reunion, normally was held in June, and would be hosted by the Hunkpapas. This year, however, they gathered earlier and in larger numbers to seek collective security from the soldiers, until they numbered about 460 lodges, containing perhaps three thousand people, of whom about eight hundred were warriors. This great camp was forced to move almost every day, because the mass of people and huge pony herds soon would have stripped the ground bare and exhausted the resources had they remained in one place for any length of time.

Meanwhile, the weather in Dakota and Montana had cleared sufficiently for Terry's troops to enter the field. The first was Colonel Gibbon's column from western Montana, which began its march eastward along the Yellowstone River in April. Even more delayed was the Dakota column, which finally left Fort Abraham Lincoln, across the Missouri River from Bismarck, on May 17. Part of the holdup was due to command problems. Although Custer headed the cavalry wing of the Dakota column, the expedition was commanded personally by General Terry, who had not led troops in the field since the close of the Civil War eleven years earlier. The change was ordered by President Grant, whom Custer had offended earlier in the year by hinting that his brother, Orvil Grant, was involved in corruption involving government contracts. In fact, Grant initially had ordered Custer to remain behind, but intercession by General

Terry had saved him from that humiliation. Nevertheless, the president was determined to diminish Custer's status by placing an unwilling Terry in charge of field operations.

Both Terry and Gibbon had the great asset that Crook lacked on his Big Horn Expedition—Indian scouts. In Gibbon's case, scouts hired at the Crow agency proved invaluable by actually locating the Lakota-Cheyenne encampment twice as it moved through the Yellowstone country. Each time, Gibbon's excessive caution cost an opportunity to hit the camp, although in view of later events on the Little Bighorn River, this might have been just as well.

As summer approached, the great encampment drew support from agency Indians as large bands collectively known as summer roamers or summer wanderers began leaving the Great Sioux Reservation. These were Indians who habitually spent their winters near the agencies and then, as summer approached and the provisions they had laid in the previous year ran low, left the reservation to attend the annual council and spend the remainder of the summer hunting. Normally indifferent to the government, this year they were even more defiant because they had heard of the Reynolds fight, and most Indians considered it a victory for the Cheyennes.[26]

Besides the summer wanderers, a food shortage at the agencies was prompting many to leave. Government rations were late and, upon arrival, were inadequate. Crook warned Sheridan that unless some effort was made to feed the Indians, they would have no choice but to leave and join the hostiles. Sheridan's hands were tied because rations were the responsibility of the Indian Bureau; the best the lieutenant general could do was offer sympathy. Although the Red Cloud Agency was guarded by troops at Camp Robinson, and the nearby Spotted Tail Agency by those at Camp Sheridan, between eight hundred and a thousand warriors and most of their families left Red Cloud in early May, and about 350 individuals bolted Spotted Tail. As these bands moved west to join the hostiles, they sometimes attacked isolated ranches. Travel on the roads leading into the Black Hills from Nebraska and Wyoming became dangerous. Frustrated, Crook wired Sheridan, "Can't you do something about this[?] Indications are that we shall have the whole fighting force of the Sioux to contend with."[27]

The army could expect little support in the East, where opposition was building against the war and against the government Indian policy as a whole. The depression wrought by the financial panic was now in its third year, and the military expeditions were seen as an expense the government could ill afford. As evidence mounted of corruption in the system, many viewed the

Indian policy as costly failure. A growing number of citizens also believed that the government—in this case at least—was clearly in the wrong.[28]

Dissent extended even to Omaha, headquarters of the Department of the Platte. The *Omaha Herald,* which increasingly espoused Indian rights, thundered, "Our latest Indian war was as needless as it is proving to be cruel and damaging. The movement of Gen. Crook in the winter has driven the Indians upon the war path. The failure of the campaign resulted in the failure to awe the red men and renewed their confidence in their ability to resist *the lawless spirit of encroachment in which this whole Black Hills occupation originated* [italics added]."[29]

Opposition notwithstanding, Crook prepared for another expedition which, this time, he expected to coordinate with Gibbon and Terry. Every available cavalry unit in the Department of the Platte, from as far away as Omaha and the Salt Lake basin, was ordered to the mustering point at Fort Fetterman. Crook, meanwhile, left Omaha on May 9, arriving in Cheyenne the following day. From there, he traveled to the Red Cloud Agency by way of Fort Laramie in an effort to obtain Lakota scouts. When this effort was frustrated by agent James S. Hastings, who was suspicious of the military, he returned to Fort Laramie and sent a telegram to Sheridan, asking the lieutenant general to obtain the services of from two hundred to three hundred Crow warriors, to meet him at old Fort Reno on May 30.

Agent Hastings's attitude annoyed Sheridan, who distrusted both the Indians and their agents. In order to control the Red Cloud Agency, and prevent any further efforts to leave the reservation and join the hostiles, he transferred eight companies of the Fifth Cavalry, under command of Lt. Col. Eugene Carr, from General Pope's jurisdiction to the Department of the Platte. These companies, which included many veterans of Crook's Apache campaign, would cover the road between Red Cloud and the war zone.

Despite the pressure he was under, Crook was most relaxed during trips around the department as he organized his expedition. The time on the road allowed him to think and exchange ideas with members of his staff and selected traveling companions who, in this case, included correspondent Robert Strahorn. Between Fort Laramie and Red Cloud he had pondered the difference between this war and the campaigns in Arizona, and now understood the enormous contrast between the two groups of Indians. The populous tribes of the northern plains, he observed, "would never stand the punishment as the Apaches had done." The Apaches had few possessions other than what they could carry on their persons, and could endure any privation as they fought to preserve their independent way of life. Consequently, they had to be hunted down and reduced piecemeal. The Lakotas and Cheyennes, on the other hand, had accumulated great wealth in ponies, buffalo hides and robes, food supplies, and trade goods. The destruction of several large villages, with their provisions and pony herds, would reduce them to poverty and shatter their ability to make war. Henceforth, his objective would be the location and destruction of villages.[30]

On May 28 at Fort Fetterman, Crook formally assumed command of the column, which was designated as the Big Horn and Yellowstone Expedition. It included ten companies of Third Cavalry and five companies of Second Cavalry, under overall command of Lt. Col. William B. Royall of the Third, an experienced veteran whose serv.ve dated back to the Mexican War; and three companies of Ninth Infantry and two of Fourth Infantry under command of Maj. Alexander Chambers of the Fourth. Bourke and Nickerson accompanied as aides-de-camp. Scouts were commanded by Capt. George M. Randall, Twenty-third Infantry, who had campaigned successfully with Crook in Arizona. Altogether there were 992 officers and enlisted men, augmented by packers, wagon drivers, civilian scouts, and other hangers-on.

A large cadre of news correspondents also joined at Fort Fetterman. Besides Strahorn and the various soldier-journalists, the group included Joe Wasson, who was sending dispatches to papers in New York, San Francisco, and Philadelphia; John F. Finerty of the *Chicago Times,* who would write one of the most complete accounts of Crook's campaigns; T. C. MacMillan of the *Chicago Inter-Ocean*; and Reuben Davenport of the *New York Herald.* Davenport was an investigative reporter in the modern sense. Unlike the others, who were eager to preserve their "insider" status with Crook, he asked detailed, frequently annoying questions, often conveying an impression of naiveté when, in fact, he was absorbing everything. Unconcerned with popularity, Davenport presented the situation as he saw it in dispatches, regardless of whom they might offend. This trait, as well as the fact that his boss, James Gordon Bennett, was a promoter of Custer—not to mention his own decision to mess with the Third Cavalry, which was still divided over Crook's decision to court martial Reynolds— ultimately made Davenport an outcast.

The expedition left Fort Fetterman the following afternoon. "The long black line of mounted men stretched for more than a mile with nothing to break the somberness of color save the flashing of the sun's rays back from the carbines and bridles," Bourke recalled. "An undulating streak of white told where the wagons were already underway, and a puff of dust just in front indicated the line of march of the infantry battalion." The scenery was familiar because this

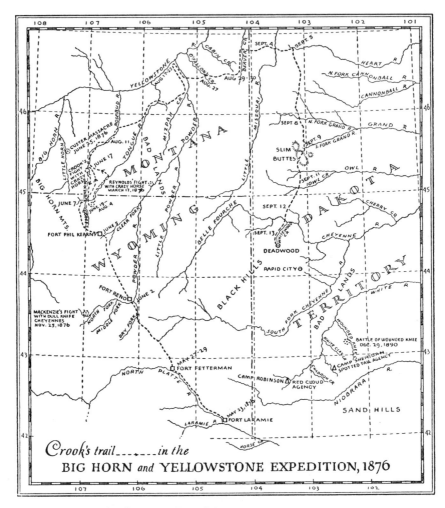

Crook's trail .... in the
BIG HORN and YELLOWSTONE EXPEDITION, 1876

The Big Horn and Yellowstone Expedition, 1876.

FROM MARTIN F. SCHMITT, *GENERAL GEORGE CROOK, HIS AUTOBIOGRAPHY.* COURTESY
UNIVERSITY OF OKLAHOMA PRESS.

was the line they followed the preceding March. Despite the late season, a snowstorm blew in from the Bighorn Mountains on May 31, freezing water in the
pots and generally making life miserable. As the column approached the ruins
of Fort Reno, the officers discovered a woman, Martha Jane Cannary, better
known as Calamity Jane. Dressed in male attire, she had hired on as a teamster.
She was given improvised women's clothing and placed under guard until she
could be sent back to Fort Fetterman.[31]

Crook had expected to meet his Crow Indian scouts at Fort Reno, but when they failed to arrive, he sent Frank Grouard, and scouts Louis Richaud and Baptiste (Big Bat) Pourier to look for them and to contact the Shoshones. Meanwhile, as the troops continued northward, they saw smoke signals ahead and encountered fresh pony tracks. In camp, entire companies were placed outside the perimeter to intercept any Indians who might try to stampede the horse herd. On June 4, they were joined by a party of sixty-five Black Hills miners who would prove a valuable asset when the time came to fight. Passing Fort Phil Kearny and the site of the Fetterman Massacre, Crook continued northward. Rain and hail pelted the command on June 7, and a soldier died from a wound sustained a week earlier when his revolver accidentally discharged into his thigh while he was chopping wood. He was buried with as much honor as could be mustered in the wilderness. Correspondent Finerty commented, "It was, indeed, a sad destiny that led this young man to die, accidentally, it is true, by his own hand, the first of Crook's brigade to lay his bones in the terra incognita of Wyoming."

The following night, Crook camped on the Tongue River, impatiently awaiting the Crow scouts. About 11 P.M., an Indian called out from a bluff above the camp. Ben Arnold, pulled out of bed and still half asleep, answered in Lakota, and the Indian broke off the talk. This convinced Crook that the Indian had been a courier from the Crows, and Arnold's mistake further delayed their arrival. The next afternoon, though, hostile Indians fired into the camp, riddling tents and equipment. Two horses and a mule were wounded, and two soldiers were grazed by stray bullets. By the time the cavalry managed to get saddled, the Indians had disappeared.[32]

It was a minor incident, more annoying than damaging, but, as time passed, it was remembered far out of proportion to its actual significance. Fourteen years later Bourke would write, "This attack was only a bluff on the part of 'Crazy Horse' to keep his word to Crook that he would begin to fight the latter just as soon as he touched the waters of the Tongue River."[33]

Bourke's remark shows how much the image of Crazy Horse had grown in the minds of Crook and his adherents in the years since the expedition. Contemporary accounts make no mention of this threat, or indicate that Crazy Horse was inclined, or even in a position of leadership, to make such a threat.[34]

By June 11, Crook's 1,900 horses and mules had exhausted the grass around the camp on the Tongue, so he moved seventeen miles south to Goose Creek, a tributary of the Tongue, in the foothills of the Bighorns. It was a pleasant site, with plentiful forage and water, and cool temperatures.[35] Designated Camp

Cloud Peak, for its close proximity to the tallest mountain in the range, this would be Crook's depot for much of the summer, and the expedition settled into a relaxed, almost safari-like routine. Men hunted and fished, and played checkers on makeshift boards, or whist. Crook was an avid whist player, and indulged his equally avid enthusiasm for hunting and fishing. He also joined a couple of his officers in a search for rare birds and butterflies. Once they returned with a prairie owl that quickly became the camp mascot; he was named "Sitting Bull." The Black Hills miners picked up earlier in the march prospected the nearby gullies for signs of gold.

Crook's hunting and fishing concealed anxiety. He had heard nothing from Grouard, Big Bat, and Richaud since sending them out from Reno. Aside from the blundered parley between the unknown Indian and the sleepy Arnold, there had been no indication of Crows in the vicinity, and an officer sent back to Fort Phil Kearny, where the Shoshones were expected, returned empty-handed. Lt. Thaddeus Capron of the Ninth Infantry observed, "The Gen'l is quite uneasy and nervous, and it is thought that he is feeling very anxious about the safety of the guides that were sent out from Reno." There was more than the safety of three men at stake. The longer the command waited, the more rations it consumed, thus limiting the range of the expedition; for without Indians and experienced whites and mixed-bloods who knew the country and the enemy, Crook would be fighting blind.

Three days later, however, Grouard, Richaud, and Big Bat returned with about 176 Crows, each of whom brought two ponies, one for general work and the other for hunting and war. They had held off meeting Crook on the Tongue after the sleepy scout answered their courier in Lakota, and the move to Goose Creek, away from where they believed the hostiles were camped, caused them to question whether the soldiers really intended to fight. Nevertheless, they came, and Crook allowed them to bivouac in the midst of the soldiers, where soon they were cooking a supper of bear meat and venison.

The Crows advised Crook that Gibbon was camped on the north bank of the Yellowstone opposite the mouth of the Tongue, but could not cross because of high water. The hostile camp, they said, was on the Tongue or one of its tributaries. Crook believed that, with a forced march, he could locate, attack, and destroy them. At officers' call, he announced that he intended to leave the wagons at Goose Creek, and march north in light order with only four days' subsistence rations for each officer and man. Each man would have a hundred rounds of ammunition and one blanket. Infantrymen would be mounted on mules. If the Indian camp was attacked and taken, they would resupply from the stores found there.³⁶

Crook apparently did not even consider a coordinated movement with Terry and Gibbon, but depended entirely on locating and taking the camp on his own. Then, resupplied from the hostile Indian stores, he could move on and link up with the Dakota and Montana columns, accepting their accolades and leaving them to clean up. If, however, he did not locate the camp, four days' rations were not sufficient to reach Terry and Gibbon; he would be forced to return to Goose Creek to reprovision. No effort was made to communicate with Terry, who was left to presume that Crook was on his way north in a coordinated effort with the Dakota and Montana columns. In this way, Crook contributed to the subsequent disaster at the Little Bighorn.³⁷

No sooner was the conference concluded than the Shoshones arrived, a total of eighty-six warriors under their renowned chief, the seventy-eight-year-old autocrat, Washakie. They were accompanied by three Texans who lived among them—Tom Cosgrove, Nelson Yarnell, and Bob Eckles. Cosgrove had been a Confederate cavalry captain, and his influence was evident. According to Finerty, the Shoshones rode into camp "in column of twos, like a company of regular cavalry. . . . They carried two beautiful American flags and each warrior bore a pennon. They looked like Cossacks of the Don, but were splendidly armed with government rifles and revolvers." With the current .45-caliber Springfield rifles, they were better armed than the Crows, who carried the older .50-caliber.

In council, the Crows and Shoshones expressed their grievances against their hereditary enemies, the Lakotas and Cheyennes. Both expressed long-term friendship with the whites. They stipulated, however, that they would scout in their own customary fashion without hindrance by the troops. Crook readily agreed. The Indians began their war preparations, chanting and dancing into the night. Elsewhere in camp, Crook suffered his second casualty when Pvt. William Nelson, Third Cavalry, died in the field hospital of unspecified causes.³⁸

The next day was spent getting the infantrymen used to riding the cantankerous mules, much to the amusement of the Indians, who occasionally demonstrated that they had no trouble at all. The packers, on the other hand, had a relatively easy time getting their mules ready. Indians checked their weapons and various other war implements. Wagons were parked in a corral, with each wagon positioned for defense. At 5 A.M., June 16, the column moved out. The Crows and Shoshones were ready for battle with their ancient enemies, and drew admiration from the whites.

"Crook was bristling for a fight," correspondent Finerty wrote. He had the general notion that the hostiles were near the confluence of Rosebud Creek and the Yellowstone, but Anson Mills was less certain. Years later, he observed, "I did not think that General Crook knew where they were, and I did not think our friendly Indians knew where they were, and no one conceived we would find them in the great force we did."[39] Another officer subsequently stated, "[Crook] knew the Indian and his nature well, no man in our day knew him better, but he never yet had fought the mounted warriors of the great plains."[40]

He was about to get a rude awakening.

ELEVEN

ROSEBUD GEORGE

THE COMMAND MARCHED DOWN Goose Creek, then across the Tongue River. They followed the Tongue a short distance, then turned up a tributary stream. The cavalry was in the lead, with the mounted infantry in the rear. After twenty-five miles, the column broke for coffee and a two-hour rest. Large herds of buffalo were visible on the surrounding hills. Indian scouts killed thirty, and the hump, tenderloin, tongue, heart, and ribs were packed. In the distance, they heard rifle fire indicating the Lakotas and Cheyennes were also hunting, but there was no contact between the two groups. The march resumed, the troops and scouts crossing the divide separating the valleys of the Tongue and Rosebud Creeks. They camped that night on the Rosebud, having covered forty-two miles. "Men and animals very tired," Lieutenant Capron wrote in his diary. Despite orders of silence and no fires, the Indian scouts immediately began roasting the day's buffalo meat, and danced and sang war songs well into the night. Crook was furious but knew better than to interfere.

Late that night, Tom Cosgrove, Frank Grouard, and some Crows ran across a hunting camp whose occupants had fled in such haste that they left their fire burning and abandoned an India rubber blanket. Although the scouts correctly surmised the hunting camp was hostile, they did not realize the hunters had fled back to their main camp, which had moved away from the Rosebud toward the Little Bighorn, and was now only twenty miles northwest of Crook's camp. This was the core of hostile Indian fighting power. Thus positioned, and learning that soldiers were in the vicinity, this great assembly of warriors—Lakotas, Cheyennes, and their allies—exulted in the prospect of a fight. Initially, the chiefs counseled restraint and adherence to the plan of defensive war. The young men, however, were too worked up, and ultimately the chiefs yielded to the inevitable and prepared for battle.[1]

Reveille sounded in Crook's camp at 3 A.M. on June 17. With fog obscuring fires, every man was allowed some coffee. Animals were saddled and packed, and the Indian scouts, less eager than before, were hurried along. At first light, they moved out to look for signs of the hostiles, while the soldiers waited for the order to march. At 6 A.M., the infantry started ahead with the cavalry falling in behind. Up the trail, the valley began to narrow and the path grew more twisted and rugged, forcing men and animals to move in single or double file. After four miles, it opened out into a wide bottom land, but by now the column was so strung out that Crook called a halt to allow the rear to catch up. The Third Cavalry was sent across to the east bank of the stream, while the Second Cavalry and infantry remained on the west bank directly opposite. This compacted the troops into a single area on either side of the Rosebud, so that when the stragglers came in the command would be more concentrated and move with closed ranks. The terrain sloped away from the bottom land on both sides, and rolled up toward rocky bluffs, beyond which was open country. Ahead, the valley narrowed into yet another canyon, similar to the one just cleared. Pickets were sent up to the bluffs. Animals were unsaddled and allowed to graze, while some of the soldiers dozed. Crook sat down to a game of whist with some of his officers.

Up among the bluffs to the west, shots rang out. At first the soldiers took no notice, assuming Indians were hunting buffalo. Those on that side of the creek could not see beyond the bluffs at their back, but across the creek the men of the Third Cavalry had a better view, and Mills saw Lakotas charging down toward the troopers. Almost simultaneously, a couple of Crows came riding hard toward Crook's bivouac, shouting, "Sioux! Sioux!" While scouting above the bluffs, they had collided with the Lakota and Cheyenne advance, and fighting had broken out.

Mills immediately ordered his battalion to saddle up. Meanwhile, the pickets had opened fire on the hostiles, and skirmishers were sent out to reinforce them while the troops saddled. On Crook's orders, Mills crossed the creek with his battalion and moved up the bluffs to hold them. Crook, meanwhile, established his headquarters with the infantry, and began deploying two of the companies to the right along a line just under the ridge at the extreme north end of the valley. He hoped the Crows and Shoshones would draw the hostiles in among the soldiers. Instead, the hostiles were trying to draw individual companies of cavalry up among the bluffs, where they attempted to cut them off and destroy them piecemeal, much as they had done with Fetterman almost ten years earlier. "In one word," Bourke later wrote, "the battle of the Rosebud was a trap."[2]

Elsewhere, the remaining infantry companies were sent to cover left and center, then move up to the plateau to meet the Lakotas and Cheyennes head on. "When we reached the crest of the plateau," Nickerson wrote, "there appeared in our front a formidable band of those justly celebrated Sioux and Cheyenne warriors, magnificently mounted, and in all the splendor of war paint and feathers. Every hill appeared to be covered with their swarming legions, and up from every ravine, and out of every little vale, more seemed to be coming."

"The country was very rough and broken," Crook stated in his report, "the attack made in greater or less force on all sides and in advancing to meet it the command necessarily became much separated."

The hostiles and soldiers battered each other back and forth as the battle broke into three separate fights. Royall had a portion of the cavalry on the west, Crook had the main force on the bluffs in the center, and Capt. Frederick Van Vliet, Third Cavalry, had two companies on the south. Royall attempted to push beyond the bluffs, but the Lakotas followed their usual strategy of retreating in front of a cavalry charge, then doubling back around and separating the soldiers from support. Mills remembered that the Indians "swung around and over-whelmed them, charging bodily and rapidly through the soldiers, knocking them from their horses with lances and knives, dismounting and killing them, cutting the arms of several off at the elbows in the midst of the fight and carry-ing them away." Seeing that Royall was in trouble, Crook sent infantry to support him as he fought his way back.[3]

Finally, Crook ordered Mills up the north canyon to attack the phantom Indian camp that he still believed lay beyond. First, Tom Moore took the pack-ers and Black Hills miners into the rocks leading into the canyon to provide cover, then Mills started in with nine companies of cavalry. He was to locate and capture the camp and hold it until Crook arrived with the rest of the command. Mills marched six miles until the canyon opened out onto another valley. Like Crook, he was convinced that the camp was nearby and that he was on the verge of finding it when Nickerson overtook him and ordered him to return. Disappointed, Mills doubled back above the canyon, returned to the main command, and reported to Crook. "I never saw a man more dejected," Mills remembered.

"General," he asked, "why did you recall me? I had the village and could have held it."

"Well, Colonel," Crook replied, addressing Mills by his brevet rank, "I found it a more serious engagement than I thought. We have lost about fifty killed and wounded, and the doctors refused to remain with the wounded unless I left the infantry and one of the squadrons [of cavalry] with them.... I knew I could not keep my promise to support you with the remainder of the force."[4]

The Battle of the Rosebud lasted about six hours and ended primarily because the Indians were no longer interested in fighting. They had lost at least thirteen men, perhaps more, an uncomfortably high figure for a nomadic, tribal people who could not easily replace fallen warriors. Officially, and despite his earlier high estimate, Crook listed his losses as ten killed, including one Shoshone scout and twenty-one wounded, among them Capt. Guy Henry, whose face was shattered by a bullet. In view of the six hours of hard fighting, Frank Grouard may have been closer to the truth when he figured Crook's losses at about fifty soldiers and Indian scouts. Whatever the case, some of the officers began comparing notes and "realized for the first time that while we were lucky not to have been entirely vanquished, we had been most humiliatingly defeated."

Crook still believed the camp was beyond the north canyon and, in a council that evening, urged his Indian scouts to help him locate it for a dawn attack. The Indians, however, balked. The canyon, they insisted, was a perfect spot for an ambush, where the hostiles would have cover and they would be exposed. They were also disconcerted by the inability of the troops to distinguish them from the Lakotas; apparently there had been several near misses from friendly fire.

Probably the Indian scouts also understood that Crook was in no condition to further pursue the march. He was down to fifty rounds of ammunition per man and had just enough rations to get back to Goose Creek. The hostile Indians had left him in possession of the field, prompting him to insist, for the rest of his life, that he had won a victory. But in reality, his only option was retreat, whereas the hostiles could move about the countryside at will. This was obvious to Sheridan, who ordered additional cavalry from Fort Douglas, Utah, and Fort Sanders, Wyoming, to reinforce Crook at Fort Fetterman. Sheridan also sent Col. Carr with the Fifth Cavalry to cover the crossing of the South Cheyenne River just west of the Black Hills and to head off any attempt by the reservation Indians to join the hostiles.[5]

Back on the Rosebud, the dead were buried in a deep trench near the edge of the creek. The bodies were covered with stones, mud and dirt, and a fire was built over the mass grave and allowed to burn all night. The next morning, the entire command marched over the burial to obliterate any trace, so that the Indians could not desecrate the bodies. Travois were rigged for the wounded, and Crook began the trek back to Wyoming. As Ben Arnold observed, "After June 17 Crook, to all practical purposes, was out of the campaign." Nevertheless, Crook had learned a valuable lesson—the Indians were far more unified and in far greater numbers than the military believed, and were willing and able to fight large units of soldiers. This instilled in him greater caution, perhaps even too much caution.

The column arrived at Goose Creek on June 19. After several days' rest, the wounded were sent back to Fort Fetterman with the wagon train and two companies of infantry. They were accompanied by correspondent MacMillan and Nickerson, both of whom were ill and had been advised by the surgeons to leave the expedition. Crook planned to remain in camp until he could replenish and receive reinforcements, and perhaps hear from Terry and Gibbon. It apparently never occurred to him to advise Terry of his setback on the Rosebud. Not needed for the time being, the Crows and Shoshones departed for their own country, promising to return in time for the next march against the hostiles.[6]

In camp, the expedition once again took on the air of a safari. On June 22, Bourke noted that fifty trout were caught over a two-day period, and "more could have been taken, I think, were it not for the splashing of men bathing and animals drinking in the water which must have frightened the timid little fish." Crook, Captain Van Vliet, and Capt. Andrew Burt, Ninth Infantry, took a small party up Cloud Peak "to hunt and fish," leaving Royall in command of the camp.

The following day, Lt. Walter Schuyler, whom Crook had befriended in Arizona, arrived from Fetterman to serve as one of the general's aides-de-camp. His old friends from Arizona days greeted him and asked for the latest news of the outside world. Among the items of interest was news that the Republicans had nominated Rutherford Hayes as their candidate for president of the United States.[7]

In the north, General Terry finally had linked with Gibbon on the Yellowstone earlier in the month. On June 17, while Crook was fighting the Indians near the headwaters of the Rosebud, sixty miles downstream a scouting expedition of Seventh Cavalry under Maj. Marcus Reno came across a trail that had been made several days earlier as hostiles headed upstream. Five days later, on June 22, Terry sent Custer with the entire Seventh Cavalry south along the Rosebud to investigate the trails, while he and Gibbon took the infantry up the Bighorn. Terry's instructions were sufficiently vague to allow Custer freedom of action if the situation required, but he apparently intended this to be primarily a reconnaissance to locate the Indians and push them toward the infantry. If they escaped, they could go in only one direction—south, where Terry assumed they would run into Crook. Terry, however, reckoned without two factors. First, he failed to consider Custer, who resented his subordinate position and was eager to break out on his own. And second, although Sheridan had forwarded Crook's report of the Rosebud fight, Terry had not received it and was unaware that Crook had retreated back to Wyoming.

The Indian camp, meanwhile, had shifted to the banks of the Little Bighorn where, on the afternoon of June 25, Custer attacked. The troops and horses were exhausted after a three-day forced march, and the command was divided so that, when the attack fell apart, the battalions were unable to assist each other. Five companies with Custer were wiped out to the last man, and seven companies under Reno were mauled so badly that, after their rescue by Terry on June 27, the Seventh needed a complete reorganization.[8]

Oblivious to those events, Crook's men continued to relax at Goose Creek. The day of the Custer disaster, Bourke wrote, "Colonel Mills brought in this afternoon one hundred trout caught by himself and assistants. Other parties were equally successful. What was so lately a luxury is now become a component of daily ration." Two days later, the big news seems to have been that Crook and party killed a cinnamon bear. The only indication of a military expedition was that the cavalrymen saddled their horses twice daily and exercised them at walk, trot, and gallop. The camp periodically was taken down and moved, primarily so the large number of horses and men would not exhaust the resources of any one spot and also, at least according to Bourke, to keep the men in practice setting up and taking down tents, saddling horses, packing mules, and performing various other duties of a soldier in the field. There was no particular sense of urgency, and there seems to have been no effort to hurry the anticipated provisions. Crook was wasting time that would better have been spent reorganizing and preparing to move north again in order to link with Terry. That, after all, was the reason he was in Wyoming.[9]

While Crook hunted and fished at Goose Creek, there was a change in the Fifth Cavalry. Nominally the regiment was commanded by Col. William H. Emory, who had been on detached duty since 1868. Consequently, for the past eight years, Lieutenant Colonel Carr had exercised actual field command, and was largely responsible for the regiment's excellent combat record on the frontier. Now, however, Colonel Emory was retiring and, following army seniority rules, Lt. Col. Wesley Merritt was promoted to full colonel and given command of the regiment. His first assignment was to take ten of the Fifth's twelve companies from Red Cloud and join Crook at Goose Creek, after which Crook would resume his campaign.

Merritt assumed command of the Fifth Cavalry in camp northwest of the Red Cloud Agency on July 1, to the consternation of the men; it had been presumed that he, like Emory, would keep out of the way and leave the fighting to Carr. Instead, he took over working command of the regiment, even though he had not led troops in combat since the end of the Civil War.[10]

Outwardly, Carr took the change in stride, and prepared to work with the new commander. Privately, however, he was furious. Still unaware of the Custer disaster on the Little Bighorn, Carr complained to his wife:

> It is of course a great humiliation to me to have him [Merritt] come in and take command in this manner & I feel it most keenly and cannot help thinking what a pity it is that I have no one to speak for me and advance my rights & interests but I must bear it as I may. . . .
>
> It seems curious that the government should find it necessary to spend large amounts of money & some blood to teach Terry, Crook, Gibbon, Merritt & others how to fight these prairie Indians when there are Custer & myself who know how to do it and are ready & willing.[11]

Merritt, however, required little teaching. He moved the camp closer to the trail between Red Cloud Agency and the war zone, and began sending out scouting details. On July 12, he was ordered to Fort Laramie to refit, and then join Crook at Goose Creek. Shortly after starting for Laramie, he received a message from Camp Robinson that about eight hundred Cheyennes and a large number of Lakotas planned to break out of Red Cloud. Turning his regiment around, he made a rapid forced march to head them off. The reports had been exaggerated, and when Merritt encountered the hostiles on War Bonnet Creek in northwestern Nebraska, on July 17—exactly one month after the Rosebud fight—there were only about two hundred. Nevertheless, these were ready for battle, and Merritt obliged. The fight was little more than a skirmish, yet it stopped the outbreak and drove the Indians back to the agency. Moreover, Merritt won the confidence of his officers and men.[12]

Back at Goose Creek, some mixed-bloods arrived on June 30 with news of a fight in which every soldier had been killed. Crook's officers believed it was the story of their own fight at the Rosebud, which had made its way around the plains with embellishments. Even so, the rumors seem to have shaken Crook from his lethargy because, the following day, he sent Frank Grouard and Big Bat to the Crow Agency to prod his scouts into returning. They traveled only twenty miles before the large number of hostile Indians in the immediate vicinity forced them back. Crook did not learn of Grouard's information until July 4, because he had been in the mountains on a "reconnaissance" that consisted largely of hunting and fishing. Nevertheless, three days later, he sent a party under Lt. Frederick W. Sibley, Second Cavalry, to scout the headwaters of the Little Bighorn. After a two-day absence, Sibley's hungry, battered troops returned on foot, having encountered more than four hundred Cheyennes. They had been pinned in a small valley and forced to abandon their horses and equipment in order to escape.

On July 10, Crook received dispatches from Sheridan advising him of Custer's annihilation at the Little Bighorn. To compound the shock, that night hostiles set fire to the grass around the camp, a harassment that continued virtually every night until heavy rains saturated the ground. The only good news was the return of Washakie with about 220 Shoshones and half-breeds. At Washakie's request, Crook detailed soldiers to ride with his warriors so they would not be mistaken for hostiles. The Shoshones organized their own expedition, and located the site of Sibley's fight and the grave of an important Cheyenne chief who had been killed. The command was also joined at intervals by Utes and the returning Crows.

Three bedraggled couriers arrived from Terry on July 13, with dispatches describing the Custer fight, and reinforcements and supplies began arriving from Fort Fetterman the following day. Crook also received dispatches from Sheridan, advising that Merritt was en route with ten regiments of the Fifth Cavalry and instructing Crook to remain in camp until their arrival. Crook passed the information along to Terry, telling him that once Merritt arrived, he would take the field immediately, and proposing to link with Terry's troops.[13]

After almost a month of inaction, Crook suddenly became impatient. Although outwardly calm as usual, the rapid turn of events—the continual grass fires set around his camp by hostiles, the Custer debacle, Sibley's fight—and time to reflect on his own narrow escape at the Rosebud appear to have shaken his confidence.[14] He anxiously awaited Merritt and the Fifth Cavalry, and as time passed without any word from them, he telegraphed Sheridan:

I find myself Inmeasurably [*sic*] embarrassed by the delay of Merritts Column as the extreme hot weather of the last few days has so completely parched the grass excepting that on the mountain tops that it burns like tinder[;] besides our delay is a source of uneasiness and dissatisfaction to our indian allies[.] on powder[,] tongue & rosebud rivers the whole country is own fire & filled with smoke[.] I am in constant dread of an attack[.] In their last [attempt] they set fire to the grass and as much of it was still green [it was] extinguished without difficulty[,] but should it be fired now I dont see how we could stay in the country[.] I am at a loss what to do[.] I can prevent their attack by assuming the aggressive but as my effective strength is less than (1200) twelve hundred exclusive of indian allies I could do but little beyond scattering them which would render it impossible to subdue them until cold weather narrowed their limits & in the meantime they could do an incalculable amount of damage to the settlements[.][15]

His ego received another blow with the arrival of newspapers, including copies of the *New York Herald* with correspondent Davenport's dispatch on the Rosebud fight. Davenport had been with Royall during the fight, and shared Royall's view that his battalion had been cut off and mauled because Crook delayed in providing support. The dispatch infuriated Crook, who called it "villainous falsehoods." He was even more outraged by an editorial in the *Herald* that bluntly stated he, Crook, had allowed himself to be surprised and beaten, and that in the future he should be reduced to a subordinate role. Davenport caught the full force of Crook's wrath, becoming an outcast among the inner circle of officers and staff and treated like a pariah by the other correspondents who were eager to preserve their "insider" status.[16]

Merritt finally arrived on August 3, bringing the expedition to about two thousand men drawn from the entire Third Cavalry, ten companies of the Fifth, and four of the Second, as well as a full brigade of infantry drawn from the Fourth, Ninth, and Fourteenth Regiments, and about three hundred packers, civilian scouts, and Indians. Crook hoped to strike north, trapping the hostile bands between himself and Terry, but realized they could escape if his movements were impeded by the 160 supply wagons.[17] Consequently, on August 4, an order was passed down through the various units:

All tents, camp equipage, bedding, and baggage, except articles hereinafter specified, to be stored in the wagons, and wagons turned over to care of chief quartermaster by sunrise to-morrow. Each company to have their coffee roasted and ground and turned over to the chief commissary at sunset to-night. Wagons will be left here at camp. A pack-train of mules will accompany each battalion on the march, for the protection of which the battalion will be held responsible. The regiment will march at seven A.M. to-morrow, "prepared for action," and company commanders will see to it that each man carries with him on his person one hundred rounds carbine ammunition [rifle ammunition in the case of the infantry] and four days' rations, overcoat and one blanket on the saddle [backpack for infantry]. Fifty rounds additional per man will be packed on mules. Four extra horses, not to be packed, will be led with each company. Curry-combs and brushes will be left in wagons. *Special instructions for action:* All officers and non-commissioned officers to take constant pains to prevent wastage of ammunition.[18]

The Big Horn and Yellowstone Expedition finally returned to the field on August 5. The first two days were hot. The summer had been dry, and grass and brush were burning in the surrounding hills, the fires sometimes caused by act of nature and sometimes set by the Indians to burn off the grass and cause the army horses to starve. August 8 dawned chilly, but the air was heavy with smoke from grass fires ahead; it became so thick that the troops had difficulty seeing beyond fifty yards in any direction. Next morning the soldiers awoke to a slight drizzle that provided some relief, but by midmorning it turned into a cold, driving rain, and the trail was churned into heavy mud. That night was bitterly cold and the troops, restricted to overcoats and blankets and without tents, were miserable.

Thirty miles from the confluence of the Rosebud and the Yellowstone, the column finally linked with Terry's, and Crook's men cleaned up and drew rations from Terry's train. Yet the difference between the two columns was soon evident. The bulk of Terry's cavalry was the badly mauled Seventh, which still needed reorganization after the Little Bighorn. And his pack train consisted of wagon mules that were not accustomed to carrying loads, were poorly packed, and, according to Bourke, dropped or lost more equipment in a single day than Crook's well-trained mules and packers had ruined from the beginning of the campaign.

The bad weather continued as the two columns moved together, following an Indian trail leading east from the Rosebud and back along the Tongue. In camp, Terry's men were well provided against hunger, cold and rain, but Crook's troops had to exist on subsistence rations and improvise shelter. The command continued on to the Powder, which it followed down to the Yellowstone, where

Crook planned to replenish from Terry's steamers. On reaching the confluence of the Powder and the Yellowstone, however, Crook found the supplies inadequate for his needs, so Terry sent the steamers along the river to gather more from various depots.

Because Crook's men were in Terry's department, the senior brigadier general held overall command. The result of the combined expedition was disappointing. There were simply too many soldiers, wagons, mules, and other impediments to track down the mobile Indians. The government Indians, who recognized the problem, became impatient, and Washakie bluntly informed Crook that the Shoshones were prepared to abandon the march because they were tired of being held back by Terry's inefficient transportation.[19]

They were not alone in their dissatisfaction. Lieutenant Charles King, one of Crook's Arizona associates who had come up with the Fifth Cavalry, complained in a letter to his father (himself a former army officer): "I may say to you that 40,000 men maneuvered, marched and held back as we have been since Terry assumed supreme command would never catch, kill or scare 40 Indians. The command is superb. The men eager. The officers skilled and willing—but the caution of Headquarters surpasses everything—When it will end I don't know."[20]

The grain-fed government horses were giving out. Even before Crook linked up with Terry, the hardship was starting to tell on the animals, and as the columns pushed on with no relief, they began to collapse. "Most of the men had to lead their animals during three fourths of the march," Finerty wrote. "Very frequently a played-out horse would fall as if shot, and the rider was compelled either to abandon the equipments or pack them on a mule. All the led horses were in use owing to frequent deaths of the line animals, and dozens of dismounted cavalrymen toiled painfully along the steep, rugged hills in the rear of the column." The entire line of march was littered with dead or abandoned horses.[21] The soldiers were little better off. Coffee had become so scarce that each man brewed his share in his tin drinking cup. Rations were reduced to sugar, bacon, and hardtack.[22]

On August 20, the Shoshones, Utes, and Crows had had enough. Most had never been so far from home, and they worried that with so many of their warriors accompanying the troops, their own camps would be exposed to attack by hostile bands. Most of the whites and mixed-bloods remained with the column, but the Indians departed. That night, the troopers were hit by the worst storm yet. "For hours the rain poured down," Bourke wrote, either as heavy drops which stung by their momentum; as little pellets which drizzled through canvas and blankets, chilling our blood as they soaked into clothing; or alternating with hail which in great, globular crystals, crackled against the miserable shelter. . . . No stringing together of words can complete a description of what we saw, suffered and feared during that awful tempest. The stoutest hearts, the oldest soldiers, quailed . . . the exposure began to tell upon, officers, men, and animals . . . no one who followed Crook during those terrible days was benefited in any way.[23]

After several days, the generals received word that Indians had attacked Terry's depot at the mouth of Glendive Creek, and had fired on a steamer on the Yellowstone. That news, together with the burdensome job of moving almost five thousand men and their equipment through the wilderness, prompted them to separate. Terry turned north and crossed the Yellowstone to intercept the Indians in that direction, while Crook continued to follow the main Indian trail until it broke up into smaller trails, most heading toward the agencies or toward the Black Hills. Believing the Black Hills settlements were exposed to attack, he made up his mind to follow the Indians in that direction. At 7:50 A.M., August 24, after replenishing one last time from Terry's steamers, Crook began the man-wasting trek known to history as the Starvation March or Horse Meat March.[24]

The column moved northeast and then eastward, backtracking along Terry's line of march from Dakota the previous spring. After twelve exhausting days, they were on the Heart River, and the food was running low. Fort Abraham Lincoln, on the Missouri River, was 160 miles to the east. The northern edge of the Black Hills was two hundred miles to the south. Finerty asked Crook what he planned to do.

The general pulled on his beard as he thought for a moment, then said, "We are five full marches from Fort Abraham Lincoln. We are seven, at least, from the Black Hills. By going to the Missouri we lose two weeks' time. By marching on the Hills we gain so much. I march on the Black Hills to-morrow. Between going to and coming back from Fort Abraham Lincoln we should lose more than half our horses."

"How much rations have you left?" Finerty inquired.

"Only two days' and a half [at] half-rations, but we must make them last for seven, at least. It must be done. The Indians have gone to the Hills and to the Agencies. The miners must be protected and we must punish the Sioux on our way to the south or leave this campaign entirely unfinished."

Finerty could scarcely believe what he was hearing. "You will march 200 miles in the wilderness, with used-up horses and tired infantry on two and one-half days' half rations!"

"I know it looks hard," Crook replied, "but we've got to do it, and it shall be done." He explained he had sent a courier to Fort Abraham Lincoln to telegraph Sheridan for supplies to meet the column in Crook City or Deadwood, mining communities recently established in the Black Hills. In the meantime, half-rations would be issued, and they could supplement them by hunting. "All will be glad of the movement after the march has been made. If necessary," he concluded, "we can eat our horses."[25]

Crook's comment that the troops would be "glad of the movement" was—at the very least—overly optimistic. The country was largely unknown; actual distances and the availability of forage and water were questionable. "Many are opposed to it," Capron laconically commented in his diary. But Crook had two reasons—the Indian trails headed in that direction, and it would take him away from any possible contact with Terry, in whom he and most of his men had lost confidence.[26]

The march south began under leaden skies, through a region of water thick with sediment and one with little wood or grass for fuel. Supper was coffee, assuming the men could build a fire large enough to brew it. The officers of Crook's staff managed to gather enough grass to twist into little bundles. Then they dug a hole in the ground and began burning the bundles of grass, with their cups around the edge until the water boiled. "It is simple enough, but takes patient labor," Schuyler wrote. The water, however, had so much salt and sediment that Bourke called the coffee "decidedly repulsive." Schuyler described the next morning's breakfast as "water and tightened belts."

Rain poured as the column marched to the North Fork of the Grand River, where the soldiers found better grass. Even so, the horses were giving out because the men were no longer physically able to give them the care they needed. Normally, on a steep grade, cavalrymen would dismount and lead the animals to ease their load. Now, however, they were so exhausted and malnourished they could not even sit straight and slumped in their saddles, letting the horses carry the full load. On September 5, Crook had ordered that abandoned horses were to be shot for food, then the order extended to the most jaded service horses, which were sent to the commissary for butchering. Horse meat became a staple, sometimes flavored with wild onions the men found growing in the vicinity.[27]

The infantrymen were less concerned about the horses because they did not depend on them. Some joked that if the trek continued much longer they would eat all the cavalry horses. If anything, however, they suffered even worse than the cavalry as their shoes fell apart and pounds of muddy clay stuck to their feet with every step. Schuyler wrote his father: "I have told you what *I* experienced on this march, but you can gather from that no realization of the suffering of the men, and particularly the infantry. I have seen men become so exhausted that they were actually insane, but there was no way of carrying them, except for some mounted officer or man to give them his own horse; which was done constantly. I saw men who were very plucky, sit down and cry like children because they could not hold out."[28]

On September 7, Crook decided to send Mills with Frank Grouard, and 150 of the strongest men and best horses of the Third Cavalry, to escort the Commissary Department to the Black Hills settlements to purchase food and quinine for the sick. Lieutenant John W. Bubb, commissary officer, and Tom Moore would have charge of fifteen men and sixty-one mules.

Mills departed about 7 P.M. His orders from Crook apparently were verbal, which has led to dispute as to how he was to conduct the expedition. In his report, Mills insisted that Crook "instructed me to lose no opportunity to strike a village." Bubb, however, remembered hearing Crook tell Mills to avoid a fight with any large village, to bypass it instead and continue on to the Black Hills for supplies. Unbeknownst to Crook, however, his troops were in the midst of a large group of Indian camps scattered among the surrounding valleys. Collectively, they were formidable, and close enough to assist one another. Their leaders included Sitting Bull, Crazy Horse, and other great chiefs.[29]

Unaware of the peril, Crook planned to remain in camp all the next day and rest his men. Fortunately for Mills, he changed his mind, perhaps because the discovery of more Indian sign caused him to realize that Mills might need support. Breaking camp, he pushed the command ahead, marching it forty-two miles. That night, Crook celebrated his forty-eighth birthday while sitting under a rocky overhang that protected his campfire and received congratulations from his officers. "It was rather a forlorn birthday party," Bourke wrote, "nothing to eat, nothing to drink, no chance to dry clothes, and nothing for which to be thankful except that we had found [fire] wood, which was a great blessing."[30]

Discontent was growing. That night, Colonel Merritt overheard one of the orderlies complain that Crook "ought to be hung," and Merritt repeated the remark to Carr. Carr himself wrote his wife that he hoped Crook might "be brought to trial before he can take any more action about us. I have a sort of desire to be located somewhere in these hills to protect [the settlements] but the desire is faint."[31]

The most scathing indictment came from Pvt. Alfred McMackin, who moonlighted as a correspondent for the *Ellis County Star* in Hays, Kansas. McMackin told his readers:

> So far the result of this expedition has been nothing but disaster, and a deple-
> tion of the public purse. Custer and his 300 brave soldiers still remain
> unavenged, and the Indian Question is further from solution than ever. Whether
> General Crook (or "Rosebud George," as the boys jocularly call him) displayed
> that sound military judgment necessary in the management of as important a
> concern as the present expedition, may be judged from the fact that while his
> forces were within easy distance of the hostile Indians from June 19th to August
> 5th, lying idle, and having the best scouts whose services could be obtained in
> the country, he allowed the Indians to withdraw from his front without any
> knowledge of the time they had left.

Crook's performance led McMackin to speculate that the general was suffering "from slight attacks of abberration of the mind, to which [he] has of late
evidently been subject."[32]

McMackin was one of several soldier-journalists who contributed to the
Star, and it is significant that all were in the ranks of the Fifth Cavalry, where
resentment against Crook was particularly strong. The men of the Fifth were
fully aware that they had borne the brunt of the fighting during Crook's offensive in Arizona, and believed he had won his general's star with their blood.
Now they were convinced they were being allowed to starve, while Crook gave
undue attention to the well-being of the mule packers and various other civilians attached to the expedition. Some of the regiment's Hibernian troopers
expressed their resentment in a new stanza to a popular soldier's song of the time.

> But 'twas out upon the Yellowstone we had the d——dest time,
> Faix, we made the trip wid Rosebud George, six months without a dime.
> Some eighteen hundred miles we went through hunger, mud, and rain,
> Wid backs all bare, and rations rare, no chance for grass or grain;
> Wid 'bunkies shtarvin' by our side, no rations was the rule;
> Shure 'twas ate your boots and saddles you brutes, but feed the packer and the
>   mule.
> But you know full well that in four fights no soldier lad was slow,
> And it wasn't the packer that won ye a star in the Regular Army, O.[33]

Crook's column resumed its southward march "strung out in a long column of twos, some afoot, some astride," King remembered. They had not gone far when couriers arrived with news that Mills had attacked an Indian camp at an uplift called Slim Buttes, about seventeen miles ahead. Although he possessed the camp, the Indians were fighting to retake it, and he needed assistance. Crook gathered up most of his serviceable cavalry and pushed ahead. The prospect of a fight seemed to reinvigorate the men. Moving out about 7 A.M., they reached the Indian camp about four and a half hours later.³⁴ After the long, terrible march, "everyone was mad enough to fight well," Schuyler wrote to his father.

> I have never seen such a sight as was presented in the captured village, when 2000 men were scattered through it in orderless confusion, picking up buffalo robes and other articles, and burning the lodges; while at the head of a gulch a hundred yards away, a circle of men were held at bay by a handful of Indians in a hole; and off to the south the pickets were engaged. Occasionally a bullet would come in among us, but no one appear to mind it much, though all stood horrified for a moment when [Charley "Buffalo Chips"] White,—a scout, was heard to wail out,—"My God, I've got it," and seen to fall shot through the heart.³⁵

White was one of three of Crook's men killed in the fight. A large number were seriously wounded, including Lt. Adolphus von Leuttwitz, Third Cavalry, a tough Prussian veteran of three armies, whose leg had to be amputated in a makeshift hospital set up in one of the larger tipis. Many of the Indians, including a large number of women and children, had been killed during the undisciplined shooting into the ravine. When the officers managed to restore order, Big Bat and Grouard called for the survivors to surrender and most, glad to be alive, came out.

About 4 P.M., a large band of Indians began moving down the bluffs. They were from a nearby camp that had been summoned to help early that morning when Mills attacked. They moved toward the pony herd, but the sight of 1,600 soldiers deploying unnerved their chiefs, and they retreated. Some of the cavalry tried to chase, but their horses were not up to it.

Crook was furious with Mills, who had located the camp the night before but had not bothered to send back to the main camp for support. Most of the officers, while admiring Mills's valor, agreed with Crook that his eagerness to attack could have led him and his men into a debacle similar to that at the

Little Bighorn. The memories of the Custer fight were emphasized by the plunder found in the camp—military equipment, personal items belonging to men killed with Custer, and horses branded with the marks of the Seventh Cavalry.

The assembled column moved out at 6:30 A.M. the next day, marching over the graves of White and the two soldiers to obliterate them. The wounded were carried on travois behind mules. One battalion of the Fifth Cavalry remained behind of finish destruction of the Indian camp.

"It went sorely against my grain to see hundreds of magnificent buffalo robes and skins destroyed," King wrote his mother, "but we had no way of carrying them. Our poor horses could barely stagger and we were eating those who couldn't get along so it was sufficiently hard on them to carry what they already had."

An incident emphasized the shortages. When the fire detail finally finished and started out of the ruined camp, it had to fight off an attack by a small group of Indians. No effort was made to follow them because there wasn't enough food. In fact, it was estimated that all the dried meat taken in the Indian camp would be enough to sustain the two thousand men for two days at the most.

Rain continued to pour and the mud clung to boots. Mules stumbled, throwing the wounded into the wet, churned-up clay. Hostiles stalked the column, ready to pick off any stragglers, but many men were so exhausted they were willing to risk a chance to rest. The rear guard managed to find most of them, prodding them along with pushes, kicks, and occasionally bayonet point. Even so, one man who fell behind was discovered by the Indians and killed. On the afternoon of September 13, Crook's exhausted men collapsed on the Belle Fourche just north of Deadwood, and soon the wagons loaded with food rolled into camp.[36]

"The cheer that went up when the herd of beef cattle came in sight was magnificent," Schuyler wrote. "The wagons with flour and vegetables arrived soon after, accompanied by delegations from the towns in the Hills, who came out to welcome the army that had come through so much hardship to save them from massacre." Crook ordered double rations.[37]

In fact, the ordeal of the soldiers had a far more devastating effect on the Indians than simply blocking them from the settlements. Crook's continual marching forced the hostile bands to keep moving. They had to stay together, and were unable to send out large hunting parties to lay in supplies of food for the winter. To avoid the troops, they doubled back across the wasteland they themselves had created by burning the grass; now their own ponies were starving, and the fires had driven away the game. And wherever they moved, they seemed to run into more soldiers. Realizing their situation was hopeless, many started toward the agencies to surrender.[38]

TWELVE

A Bloody Campaign
of Attrition

Even as Crook's men endured the Horse Meat March, the government was working inexorably to bring the war to a conclusion. Custer's defeat at the Little Bighorn humiliated the nation, particularly because news of the disaster arrived in the midst of the national centennial celebration in Philadelphia. Custer, Crook, Terry, Sherman, and President Grant were vilified in the press. An outraged public demanded retribution, and much of the earlier objection to the war was stifled. Sherman began shifting troops from elsewhere into the war zone, and successfully lobbied Congress to strengthen the army by an additional 2,500 enlisted men.

Among the regiments sent north were the Fourth Cavalry under Col. Ranald Mackenzie, and Col. Nelson Miles's Fifth Infantry. These troops had emerged victorious from the Red River War of 1874–75, which broke the power of the southern plains tribes, and Mackenzie and Miles were perhaps the army's leading experts on Indian warfare. They were accustomed to winning. The specter of famous northern chiefs like Sitting Bull and Crazy Horse neither frightened nor impressed them, and they thoroughly prepared themselves and their men for the task ahead.

Both had been transferred up from General Pope's jurisdiction. Miles went from Kansas to Montana where, theoretically, he would serve under Terry, although in fact he exercised independent command. Mackenzie was ordered from the Indian Territory of Oklahoma to Camp Robinson, to take charge of the District of the Black Hills in the Department of the Platte. His command eventually totaled eighteen companies, which, besides his own regiment, included units of the Third and Fifth Cavalry, Fourth Artillery, and Ninth and Fourteenth Infantry. With his arrival, the center of operations against the Oglalas and Cheyennes began to shift from Fort Laramie to Camp Robinson.[1]

Mackenzie's emotional instability had deepened since he and Crook served together in the closing days of the Civil War. He was beset with bouts of irrationality, particularly after suffering a severe head injury in a wagon accident at Fort Sill the previous year, and was suspicious to the point of paranoia. Foultempered and autocratic, he often exasperated superiors with seemingly incessant criticism of the army system and endless demands on military resources. Even so, his talent and usefulness outweighed his faults, and Sherman and Sheridan considered him indispensable for a major Indian campaign.[2]

Even before Mackenzie departed for Camp Robinson, Sheridan had managed to secure the Interior Department's approval for the military to take over the various agencies of the Great Sioux Reservation, as well as the Red Cloud and Spotted Tail Agencies in Nebraska. On August 15, President Grant signed a rider to the annual Sioux appropriation bill, requiring the Indians to forfeit the Black Hills and all rights to the unceded Indian territory of Montana and Wyoming. They would also be required to receive their supplies on the Missouri River, well inside the area of government control, and send a delegation to the Indian Territory to consider possible relocation there. An additional million dollars was attached to the bill for rations alone, but no future appropriations would be released until the Indians relinquished the land, granted right-of-way for three roads across the remaining reservation, and agreed to make themselves self- supporting by white standards. In other words, they must agree to the government's terms or starve.[3]

So far, Red Cloud had remained at the agency, even though his sympathies were with the hostiles. Now, however, he and his followers left the agency, as did a band under Red Leaf. Both groups were camped on Chadron Creek about twenty miles northeast of Camp Robinson. Determined to render the Indians impotent, Sheridan first concentrated troops at Robinson to awe and intimidate those who remained at the agency, and impress on them the futility of resistance. Then, on September 21, he met with Crook and Mackenzie at Fort Laramie to draft further plans. In Crook's department, the Indians at the Red Cloud and Spotted Tail Agencies would be disarmed and unhorsed, and in Dakota, Terry's troops would do likewise at the Sioux agencies along the Missouri River. A scenario was devised whereby Mackenzie would demand that Red Cloud and his followers return to the agency and place themselves under its jurisdiction. When Red Cloud refused (as they knew he would), he would recommend the agencies be sealed off, the outlying bands (specifically those of Red Cloud and his adherents) be rounded up and returned to the agencies by force, and all Indians, friendly and otherwise, be disarmed and stripped of their ponies.

Sheridan also had secured congressional authorization for two new forts, one in Terry's department and the other in Crook's. Crook initially had planned to operate out of the Black Hills during the coming winter campaign. Instead, Sheridan instructed him to establish a major cantonment near old Fort Reno as a preliminary to the new post, and use it as his base.

The conference broke up the following day, and Mackenzie returned to Camp Robinson to prepare for the subjugation of the agencies. Sheridan and Crook remained at Fort Laramie, where the latter began organizing his winter campaign, and tended to the piles of routine departmental paperwork brought from Omaha, where it had accumulated while he was in the field. Crook also helped Sheridan play host to several visiting Japanese officers.

At Robinson, everything went according to plan. Mackenzie recommended the roundup of Red Cloud, and general disarming of the agency bands, and Sheridan and Crook endorsed the action. On October 23, Mackenzie surrounded the bands of Red Cloud and Red Leaf on Chadron Creek and marched them back to the agency. When Crook arrived, however, he balked at disarming and unhorsing all the Indians, applying the order only to the followers of Red Cloud and Red Leaf. "The other bands," he explained, "have been loyal to us, and to have disarmed them with the others, would simply have arrayed the white man against the Indian and placed the loyal and disloyal on the same footing." Allowing loyal Indians to keep their arms was a pledge of good faith on the part of the army and, he pointed out, their warriors began enlisting as scouts "in large numbers."[4]

Back in Chicago, Sheridan was furious at Crook's deviation from the adopted plan. "The action of Gen. Crook in disarming the Redcloud and Redleaf bands of Indians at the Redcloud Agency is highly approved," he wrote in his endorsement to Crook's report. But he added, "His neglect to disarm and dismount other bands at that Agency is disapproved, and all the theories in this report seem to be given as a plea for not having performed what he promised and what was expected of him, and which would have been good policy and true humanity."[5]

To Crook, however, "true humanity" meant maintaining faith with the Indians who had remained loyal to the government throughout the campaign, even though this often had set them against their own people. Spotted Tail's position was particularly embarrassing, because Crook named him head chief of the two agencies, replacing Red Cloud, whom Crook deposed. This elevation in rank required Spotted Tail to lead the delegation visiting the Indian Territory, and the mere mention of resettlement in Oklahoma infuriated him. Crook, however, was adamant, and in a special council, he bluntly told the chiefs what was expected of them under the new order imposed by the government. Realizing he was part of that new order, Spotted Tail agreed to look over the Territory, but warned Crook not to construe that as accepting relocation.[6]

The agencies were only one of the problems Crook faced. High on his list of priorities was his reputation, which he apparently felt was being smeared by Reuben Davenport's latest dispatch to the *New York Herald*. Headed "General Crook's Sham Simplicity of Life," it accused Crook of playing the ascetic in public while privately preoccupied with his own comfort. Davenport also took a swipe at the officers and correspondents of Crook's inner circle, whom he called the general's "familiars and toadies."[7]

Attempting to justify his lack of preparation for the march, Crook told Cuthbert Mills of the *New York Times*: "How could any one anticipate such a season of rain, when we had been lying idle all the summer without having a drop fall upon us? We had to go on once we left Goose Creek, at any cost. The Indians were not where we expected to find them. Would it do to turn back again, after lying idle so long, with the old cry that our rations would give out, or something else prevented our going on?"

Crook acknowledged that his train had not been large enough, that his rations were not adequate for a thorough search of the country, and he did not have enough capable scouts.[8] Yet he alone was responsible for the fact that his troops had spent virtually all of July sitting idle at Goose Creek. The summer had been squandered, and when he finally realized that he had to return to the field, preparations were haphazard and totally inadequate. For that, and for the immense wastage of men and animals, he had only himself to blame, although he would never admit it.

All that, however, was behind, or at least Crook was attempting to place it behind. In the same interview he changed the subject to Crazy Horse, whom he considered personally responsible for his setback at the Rosebud, and for virtually everything else that had gone wrong during the summer. He told Mills that Crazy Horse

should be followed up and struck as soon as possible. There should be no stopping for this or that thing. The Indians cannot stand a continuous campaign. I cannot tell whether we can go on yet. That depends on our getting the things we want. The best time to strike them is in the winter. They cannot remain together in large bodies at that season. The necessities of subsistence compel them to separate, and then is the time to throw a large force on each band and crush them all in detail. . . .

The system of moving without a wagon-train is the only proper one for a campaign of this character. a mule-train can go anywhere; there is no rear to protect at the cost of largely reducing your fighting force. Our train was not large enough. That will be remedied.[9]

In Washington, General Sherman was less concerned with newspaper dispatches than with concluding the war. If Crook could defeat Crazy Horse, and if all the Lakotas could be disarmed, dismounted, and concentrated around Fort Randall on the Missouri River in what is now eastern South Dakota, the government's only concern would be feeding them until they learned to grow their own food. In the meantime, Sherman envisioned miners and settlers becoming established in northern Wyoming and in the Black Hills, displacing the Indians in those areas and rendering further resistance futile.[10]

Crook believed Crazy Horse and Sitting Bull were somewhere in southern Montana or northern Wyoming, in the vicinity of the Rosebud and the Powder. On November 4, at Fort Laramie, he formally organized the Powder River Expedition. The following day, he departed for Fort Fetterman where, on arrival, he called a council of the Indian scouts. Most were Sioux, Pawnees, and Arapahos, with a scattering of Crows, Cheyennes, and Bannocks. Crook assured them they would be allowed to use their own scouting methods, and they would continue to enjoy his friendship and support after they were discharged. But he bluntly warned them that their traditional way of life was over, and they should plan to become self-supporting rather than depend on government annuities.

Crook's achievement in getting the various tribes to serve together as scouts cannot be overstated. Old hatreds were deep, particularly between the Pawnees and the various Sioux groups. The Pawnees were suspicious of any joint endeavor, and claimed the Sioux were pretending friendship only for the opportunity to recover horses previously captured by the Pawnees. Nevertheless, they agreed to cooperate, although from time to time in the coming expedition, Crook would be called on to settle disputes.[11]

The expedition left Fort Fetterman on November 14. It included a brigade of cavalry under Mackenzie, and a brigade of infantry and artillery commanded by Lt. Col. Richard Irving Dodge, Twenty-third Infantry. The cavalry brigade consisted of thirteen companies divided into three battalions. Dodge's brigade included four companies of artillery and eleven companies of infantry in two battalions. Altogether there were 61 officers, 1,436 enlisted men, 367 Indian scouts, 400 pack mules with 65 packers, 168 wagons, and 7 ambulances. Bourke believed it was "the best equipped and best officered of any with which I have ever served," and was particularly well-equipped against cold weather. The destination was the new cantonment Sheridan had ordered. Four companies of infantry, detailed from Fort Laramie, were on the post, which was designated Cantonment Reno. Located on Middle Fork of the Powder River, it was about eighty-five miles northwest of Fetterman and three miles south of old Fort Reno.[12]

Colonel Dodge, who commanded the infantry and artillery brigade, was one of the more remarkable officers to serve under Crook during this expedition. Although older (fifty, with some thirty years in the service), he had much in common with Bourke. He was a scholar whose interests covered not only Indians but natural history. He wrote several books about the West and Indian life, along with a scientific paper on the buffalo that is still a definitive work. Dodge was also an accomplished diarist, whose brutally frank assessments of Crook offer an interesting counterbalance to Bourke's usual praise of the general.[13]

The first day's march passed without incident. In camp the following evening, November 15, Dodge went to see Crook, who pulled him into a game of whist. The visit gave Dodge a chance to observe Crook's lifestyle which, together with what he considered the general's indifferent handling of the march, destroyed any illusions he might have had. Crook, he decided, wanted to give the image of a man

who utterly contemns anything like luxury or even comfort—yet he has the most luxurious surroundings, considering the necessity for short allowance that I have ever seen taken to the field by a Genl Officer—there is no doubt of his courage, energy [or] will—but I am loath to say I begin to believe he is a humbug—who hopes to make a reputation by assuming qualities foreign to him. One thing is most certain. He is the very worst mannered man I have ever seen in his position. Though his ill manners seem to be the result rather of ignorance than of deliberate will—I believe him to be warm hearted—but his estimate of a man will I think be discovered to be founded not on what that man can or will do for the Service, but what he can or will do for Crook. . . .

The Cav[alr]y & Inf[antr]y are nobodies. The Indians & pack mules have all the good places [in camp]. He scarcely treats McKenzie & I decently, but he will spend hours chatting pleasantly with an Indian, or a dirty scout—I don't blame Davenport of the Herald one bit. He stated what he saw & is cordially hated for it. I can['t] state what I see except in this private journal.[14]

It took four days to reach Cantonment Reno. The Indian scouts ranged out thirty to forty miles on each side of the column. The only thing they noticed was the tracks of three horses that, when overtaken, proved to be ridden by whites. Part of the march was made into a snowstorm which, to the well-equipped column, was only a minor inconvenience. Soon after arriving at Reno, Tom Cosgrove rode in with about a hundred Shoshones. Washakie was not among them, but had sent his sons.

The morning after arriving, Crook assembled the Indians for another council, prompted to a large extent by the old animosities. The Sioux complained that the Pawnees were treating them coldly. The Shoshones had a list of grievances against the Sioux, and everyone seemed to hate the Arapahos. The languages alone were a formidable barrier to cooperation, Arapaho being so obscure that when their chief, Sharp Nose, aired his grievances, it had to be translated first into Lakota, and then into English. Crook's words required four different interpreters so that everyone could understand. Many of the grievances were petty, as when the Pawnees, who appeared in the full uniform of army scouts, objected that some Lakotas and Cheyennes wore the war dress of their own people.

Crook managed to smooth over most of the problems, impressing on them "the importance of being friends, temporarily at least," because they would serve together and might need each other in battle. Finally, Three Bears, first sergeant of the Sioux, stood up and carried a horse over to Sgt. Frank White of the Pawnees. "Brother," he said, "we want to be friends and as an evidence of my sincerity I give you this horse." White responded with gratitude, and the two groups became considerably more friendly, shaking hands, talking and visiting with each other, and with the Arapahos. The Shoshone response to the Pawnees, whom they had never met, was less animosity than curiosity. The Pawnees had come up from the Indian Territory and therefore were familiar with the Comanches, who were related to the Shoshones. Consequently, the Shoshones were able to learn much about their kinsmen to the south.[15]

After the council, Dodge made a curious entry in his diary, "We have had no end of trouble today with drunken men, & tonight three shots have been fired in camp. I asked Genl C .to shut up the Traders Store, but he being a personal friend (it is said they are partners in a sheep ranche in Oregon) of the trader refused, & said I could regulate it."[16]

The allegation of some sort of partnership with W. B. Adair, the trader, is the first indication that Crook may have been involved in nefarious activities, an accusation that again would surface in an unrelated incident several years later. The general's comment that Dodge "could regulate it" served no real purpose because, as Crook must have known, Dodge's authority extended only to members of his brigade but not to cavalry, teamsters, or others. There is no proof that Crook had any sort of business arrangement with Adair, but as Wayne Kime points out in his notes to Dodge's journal, Crook took no action on complaints that Adair's activities damaged business for E. Tillotson, the authorized post trader at Fort Fetterman.[17]

On November 21, the Lakota scouts rode in with a young Cheyenne prisoner named Beaver Dam, whom they had captured some fifty miles west of Cantonment Reno. As Crook interrogated him, rumors flew about the camp that all the Cheyennes were planning to come in and surrender. Beaver Dam, however, told Crook that he was a member of a band of five lodges, and as soon as he was missed, they would break camp and head for Crazy Horse, who was encamped on the Rosebud. Most of the Cheyennes, he said, had already crossed to the other side of the Bighorn Mountains. With that information, Crook wired Sheridan, "Crazy Horse and his band are encamped on the Rosebud near where we had the fight with them last summer. We start out after his band tomorrow morning."[18]

Crook moved his troops northward across country and through the snow to the banks of the Crazy Woman, where he would leave his wagons. At daylight November 23, camp was struck, and the packers were loading the mules for the day's march when a white flag was spotted on one of the bluffs. It was carried by Sitting Bear, a Cheyenne who had been sent from Camp Robinson a month earlier with an ultimatum to Crazy Horse. He had found Crazy Horse on the Rosebud exactly where Beaver Dam had placed him, but while there, news arrived from the Yellowstone that Sitting Bull had clashed with Miles and now was heading north toward Canada. On the way back, he ran into a member of Beaver Dam's band, who confirmed that they had become frightened when he did not return, and were now on their way to warn Crazy Horse.

This meant that the element of surprise was lost, and Crook was convinced that Crazy Horse was probably moving his camp. On the other hand, Sitting Bear told him about a large Cheyenne camp deep in the Bighorns near the headwaters of the Crazy Woman. He decided to keep the infantry in place, and send Mackenzie with all but one company of cavalry, and all the scouts to round them up. Mackenzie departed at noon, and the others sat down to wait. Camp was warm and comfortable, the troops having discovered a vein of coal nearby, and Dodge remarked that it looked "like Pittsburg [sic]."[19]

Crook spent much of the time hunting, and his tendency to range out alone in hostile country worried his officers and friends. "He will be picked off sometime," Dodge noted in his diary. Remembering that Custer also liked to hunt alone, he commented that Crook "is as restless as Custer in a different way. Custer was all dash & daring when there was anything to be made by it, in glory, or public opinion. Crook is just as daring, but in pursuits of his own quiet enjoyment in hunting. He will ride out miles by himself or with one orderly, & that, when he knows that hostiles are likely prowling about. One Indian will waylay & shoot a single man, when five or six will not attack two men."[20]

On November 26, a courier rode in with news that Mackenzie had captured a large Cheyenne camp with its pony herd, although most of the Indians had escaped into the rocky bluffs overlooking the area. Mackenzie was asking for infantry with long rifles to dislodge them. Crook started Dodge and the infantry toward the village, then followed with this headquarters guard. The command pushed some twenty-five miles into the Bighorns, bivouacking on Willow Creek, a tributary of the Powder River. The following morning, Crook had proceeded a few miles when he was met by five of Mackenzie's Indians, who told him that the hostile Indians had fled, and Mackenzie, having destroyed the village, was returning with his dead and wounded. The troops started back toward their main camp on the Crazy Woman, arriving the afternoon of November 28.

Mackenzie came in about 11 A.M. the next day. He had lost one officer, Lt. John A. McKinney (for whom Cantonment Reno was subsequently renamed), and six troopers, with twenty-six wounded. Although most of the hostiles escaped, this was the main Cheyenne camp, whose principal chiefs were Dull Knife and Wild Hog. Once again, the troopers found an extensive array of trophies from the Custer fight, as well as from raids against the Shoshones. The camp's destruction devastated the Cheyennes, and effectively ended them as a major fighting force.[21]

The Dull Knife Fight, as it became known, together with Miles's successes against Sitting Bull in the north, signaled the beginning of the end of the Great Sioux War. Even the chronic complainers were jubilant. Commenting to his sister, Carr wrote, "It is in these mountains that the Indians like to live and there are so many cañons, precipices & rocks, that it is very hard to get at them, but we have made it so hot for them of late that most of them are glad to come in & eat uncle sam's rations & behave."[22]

In Washington, Sherman wrote Sheridan, "Please convey to Generals Crook and Mackenzie my congratulations, and assure them that we appreciate highly the services of our brave officers and men who are now fighting savages in the most inhospitable regions of our continent. I hope their efforts this winter will result in perfect success and that our troops will hereafter be spared the necessity of these hard winter campaigns."[23]

Unaware of this praise, Mackenzie was in a severe depression. He was accustomed to lightning attacks with minimal casualties, and the loss of so many killed and wounded left him badly shaken. He took Lieutenant McKinney's death particularly hard. McKinney had joined the regiment four years earlier as an irresponsible young man with the beginnings of a drinking problem and, under Mackenzie's guidance, had become a reliable and efficient officer. Mackenzie had spent a sleepless night after the fight, pacing back and forth, listening to the moans of the wounded in the field hospital, and the next morning, had worried to his orderly about the number of casualties.

The funeral for the dead, which was held in the Crazy Woman camp on Thanksgiving Day, November 30, seemed to unbalance him even more. When Dodge went to see him after the service, he found Mackenzie almost incoherent, calling the fight a failure and even mentioning suicide. Dodge calmed him down, but reported the problem to Crook, who "was greatly worried & soon left my tent, I think to send for Mac & get him to play whist or something."[24]

If Sherman and Sheridan expected any sort of follow-up, they were disappointed. The next day, Crook marched the command back to Cantonment Reno. On December 3, and with no notice, he ordered a move twenty-eight miles to Buffalo Springs on the Dry Fork of the Powder. "I was disgusted," Dodge complained in his diary, "but there is no use in being so with Crook's orders. He really does not know ahead what he intends to do. Makes up his mind at the last moment, & then acts at once—expecting everybody else to do the same. He has nothing to do but make up his mind. I have to take care of my men. I had clothing to draw & other things to attend to."

Dodge expected some sort of expedition to develop from Buffalo Springs, but Crook seemed to flounder in indecision over the next several days. Perhaps he was concerned about Mackenzie's ability to command. But when couriers arrived with congratulatory telegrams from Sherman and Sheridan, Mackenzie's good spirits returned, and Crook decided to move. They would march by

Pumpkin Buttes to the Belle Fourche, then down that river to its forks, from there to the Little Powder, and on to the Big Powder. The Indian scouts would fan out in all directions, and if they found a village, the troops would attack it and resupply from hostile stores. Otherwise, they would return to Reno by December 28.

The expedition spent the next three weeks wandering over northeastern Wyoming. Although better rationed and equipped than during the Horse Meat March, the constant, aimless marching nevertheless wore down men and animals. The scouts returned with nothing, and the lack of information was disheartening. Finally, Crook determined that if any hostile camps still existed, they were too far away to attack. On December 21, he decided to end the expedition. He called the scouts together, thanked them for their help, and released them to return to their reservations. The next day, the men of the Powder River Expedition began the long trek back to Fort Fetterman, finally arriving on December 29.[25]

Crook, Mackenzie, and some of the headquarters staff continued on to Cheyenne, where Mackenzie departed for Washington. He had been ordered to the capital because of unrest over the hotly contested presidential election. At the outset, it appeared that Hayes had been defeated by Democrat Samuel J. Tilden. Yet there was enough doubt in several states, particularly in the South, that both sides charged fraud. Ultimately, the election was given to Hayes, but only after the Democrats received several concessions, not the least of which was the end of congressional Reconstruction (which was a failure in any case) in those southern states where it still remained. Crook's friend and admirer would succeed General Grant as president on March 4, 1877, and Mackenzie returned to Camp Robinson.[26]

In Cheyenne, meanwhile, Mary Crook arrived from Omaha to join her husband, and a court-martial board convened for the long-delayed trials of Colonel Reynolds and Captain Moore for the fiasco on the Powder River the previous March. Testimony in the Reynolds case began January 8, and was filled with acrimony and recrimination. Reynolds contended that Crook was equally liable for the affair, because he divided the command and failed to cooperate on the expedition. Testimony in Moore's case began January 16. Three days later both cases were concluded. Reynolds was found guilty of disobeying orders, misbehavior before the enemy, and conduct to the prejudice of good order and discipline, and was suspended from rank and command for one year. Moore, who was found guilty of conduct to the prejudice of good order and discipline but acquitted of a charge of disobeying orders, was suspended from command

and ordered confined to the limits of his post for six months. In view of their past records (more likely in view of Reynolds's record in the Union army), President Grant remitted their sentences and restored them to duty, although their careers were finished. Reynolds retired five months after the trial, and Moore left the service in 1879.[27]

The same day the court-martial convened in Wyoming, Miles attacked and defeated Crazy Horse at Wolf Mountain in Montana. Flushed with his success, he lobbied Sherman for command of a department, either the Dakota or the Platte, promising that once he was in charge he could end the war by summer. It was typical of Miles that he considered himself more qualified to command than two brigadier generals, yet his enormous vanity was backed by substance. A self-made soldier, he had worked as a clerk before entering a volunteer regiment of the Union Army as a first lieutenant. The military proved to be his true calling, and by the time the war ended he had been brevetted to major general. Success made him contemptuous of university men like Terry and West Pointers like Crook. He championed himself shamelessly, earning the enmity of virtually every senior officer in the army, most of whom were quick to point out Miles's lack of any formal military training. Although married to Sherman's niece, a connection he exploited at every opportunity, it rarely did him much good because Sherman was among the long list of officers who despised him. But whatever his faults, Miles was, together with Mackenzie, the most successful Indian fighter in the army.[28]

Miles considered Terry well-meaning but inept, and he loathed Crook, in part because he was one of the colonels who had been bypassed when Crook was jumped two grades from lieutenant colonel to brigadier general, and in part because Miles considered him an incompetent publicity seeker who orchestrated events for the benefit of the press, often at the expense of Terry's troops, who did not get such coverage. Summing up his opinion of Crook (whom he did not mention by name), he wrote:

> I would suppose that a General officer could find some other employment than questioning a lying Indian and giving his statements to the press in such a way as to reflect discredit upon a small part of the army [i.e., Terry's department] not under his command. It will be remembered that with all the resources of a Dept. this same officer started with the great 'Powder River Expedition' of twenty-two hundred men to subjugate or destroy this same body of Indians and that after the engagement of Mackenzie with the Cheyennes, and when within a few days march of Crazy Horse's camp he turned round and marched

back to Reno & then down toward Bell Fourche where there has not been a camp of hostile Indians in two years, camped fourteen days on a sage brush plain & returned to winter quarters, having accomplished nothing, but given the Indians renewed confidence. These insinuations come with very poor grace from a man who was a failure during the [Civil] war and has been ever since.[29]

Miles's statement reflected Sherman's own disappointment that Crook had not made a greater effort to follow up on Mackenzie's fight. Although he toyed with the idea of placing Miles in charge of all field operations, ultimately he decided against it, accepting Sheridan's view that the only way to end the war would be through the campaign of attrition then being waged.[30]

Crook, meanwhile, again sought to justify himself. In his report of the Powder River expedition, he complained that "the want of proper transportation on account of meagre appropriation allowed me for this purpose has been and now is the cause of the most serious embarrassment." The report made its way up the channels until it reached General Sherman, who would have none of it.

"General Crook was certainly empowered to provide for his command as liberally as any General that ever took the Field at any time," he wrote to Sheridan, adding, "If his men were not properly provided with everything, it was his own fault." Sherman was running out of patience. Neither Crook nor Terry had lived up to his expectations, and any success so far was largely through the efforts of Mackenzie and Miles.[31]

Sheridan replied that Mackenzie and Miles would command field columns, Miles to keep pressure on any bands that remained free in his area, and Mackenzie to protect the Black Hills and settlements of Wyoming and Nebraska. He wanted Terry to remain in St. Paul to supply Miles, and Crook either in Cheyenne or Omaha to provide for Mackenzie. He was relying on the two colonels because he, like Sherman, had lost confidence in the generals. Expanding on Sherman's remarks, Sheridan wrote, "Last summer the commands of Gens. Terry and Crook were abundantly supplied; more supplies and men were given than they asked for or than were necessary and where any suffering occurred or opportunities were lost it was from their own actions. They were each abundantly strong to have met and defeated the Indians; and there is no excuse for failure on account of throwing off on each other."

He was particularly disgusted with Crook for the wastage of men and animals on his various ramblings, and did not hesitate to let Sherman know it.

It was beyond the range of possibility for Crook to have supplied a cavalry command, or to have even kept it out during the winter, unless it had been provided with huts and stables [and] forage at Reno before the late fall or winter came on, which he rendered impossible by his [Horse Meat] march around the Black Hills which not only consumed the time necessary to provide for the winter but broke down his command. The fact of the case is, the operations of Gens. Terry and Crook will not bear criticism, and my only thought has been to let them sleep. I approved what was done, for the sake of the troops, but in doing so, I was not approving much, as you well know.[32]

Sheridan's remarks appeared well-founded, particularly because Indian depredations in the northern part of the Black Hills actually stepped up during the first two months of 1877. The reasons were twofold: a substantial number of Indians along the Yellowstone had yet to be subjugated; and the opening of the Black Hills for settlement brought an ever-growing number of whites, enhancing the opportunities for plunder. Following a series of raids in mid-February, the mayor of Deadwood pleaded for military protection, and Crook ordered an expedition into the region from Camp Robinson. For the next two months, troops marched through the vicinity of Deadwood and Spearfish, initially engaging in several skirmishes and recovering hundreds of head of stolen livestock, mostly sheep. As time passed, however, resistance declined, and Crook ordered extreme care to avoid clashing with groups of friendly Indians who were contacting the hostiles to try and convince them to surrender. In April, the expedition returned to Camp Robinson and disbanded.[33]

Despite the raids, the attrition campaign was beginning to tell on the bands of Indians that were still roaming free. For them, it was no longer a question of maintaining their independence, but only whether they would surrender to Crook or Miles. Hoping to gain prestige for ending the war, both commanders sent emissaries to the various bands urging them to come in and surrender; otherwise they would resume large-scale operations in the spring.

The Cheyennes saw no other option. Some moved north toward Miles's camp on the Tongue River (later Fort Keogh), while others headed south. On February 24, the Cheyenne chief Little Wolf led a small band into Camp Robinson, the first group of what would soon become a large movement. Crook sent Spotted Tail with some two hundred chiefs, subchiefs, and warriors to meet with the hostile bands that still were out. The most important, as far as Crook was concerned, was Crazy Horse, who was Spotted Tail's nephew. Spotted Tail told the Oglala chief that if his band did not surrender before spring, Crook would move against them, using not only Crow and Shoshone scouts but Lakotas and Cheyennes as well. Realizing that Crook had won over his own people, Crazy Horse agreed to come in April, when the grass was high enough for the ponies to travel. Continuing their trek, Spotted Tail and the chiefs delivered the same message in the various hostile camps along the Little Powder and Little Missouri Rivers, returning on April 5 with 917 people ready to surrender. Crook expressed his appreciation by commissioning Spotted Tail as a lieutenant in the regular army.

Red Cloud, who had been in Spotted Tail's shadow since the latter had replaced him as head chief of the agencies the previous October, now saw a chance to regain prestige. Spotted Tail, he reasoned, had gained Crazy Horse's assurances of surrender, but had not brought him in. Like Spotted Tail, he was related to Crazy Horse, with the added advantage that he was an Oglala, while Spotted Tail was Brule. This, he contended, would have more effect and encourage Crazy Horse to surrender sooner rather than later. Crook agreed, telling Red Cloud to remind Crazy Horse that the longer he delayed, the sooner the troops and Cheyennes would come looking for him. The emphasis on the Cheyennes was for Spotted Tail and Red Cloud as much as for Crazy Horse because, as Bourke noted in his diary, " *'Red Cloud'* and *'Spotted Tail'* are especially afraid of the ascendancy *General Crook* has gained over the *Cheyennes and Arapahoes.'* Unless they did something to gain Crook's attention and gratitude, their own people would come out second best.[34]

On April 14, a huge assembly of Sans Arcs and Miniconjous surrendered at Camp Sheridan near the Spotted Tail Agency. Crook, who was at Red Cloud, about twenty miles away, hurried over to Sheridan, where he unfurled the guidon of Company I, Seventh Cavalry, captured at Little Bighorn and retaken at Slim Buttes. After surrendering and stacking their weapons, they continued on to Spotted Tail.

Describing the scene, Bourke wrote, "The village was arranged in the form of a circle and the parade in the center, (of 200 to 250 yds. diameter,) was one dense, black mass of humanity. Not alone in the village, but streaming far out over the hillocks beyond, were the crowds of *'Brules'* and *'Loafers'*, with the crowds, equally great almost, of *'Minneconjous'* and *'Sans Arcs'*. The number present was not less than 3000, little and big, and may have run up as high as 4.000."[35]

A week later, Dull Knife arrived at Red Cloud with 524 Cheyennes, the largest capitulation to date. Most were survivors from Mackenzie's attack almost five months earlier, and were in such poor condition they were ready to surrender unconditionally. The women set up camp while the warriors continued to the agency, where they halted in front of Crook. One of their chiefs, Standing Elk, told him, "I want to give you my gun. I want to shake hands and give you my gun. All my young men here want to give you their guns to-day. We want to shake hands and bury the hatchet." With that, he handed Crook his Henry rifle, and the warriors following him stacked their weapons. Bourke noted the devastating effect of the war.

> Their property is of no value. They are almost entirely without blankets and with only very scant supply of robes. They have many widows and many people with frozen feet: both these are melancholy survivors of their fight with *Mackenzie.*
>
> Their apologies for lodges are made of old remnants of canvas, old hides and robes, and even pieces of gunny sacks—just such things as they could pick up in the old camps of *General Crook's Expedition.* I saw not one perfect lodge. The squaws are also compelled to carry water in skin bags, as they have not a single utensil of any description.[36]

Two days later, couriers brought news that Crazy Horse was on his way, and by May 2 he was only thirty miles from the agency. His band was exhausted and starving, but virtually intact. Troops were sent out to meet them with rations and a herd of cattle. They pitched camp, ate, and rested, then moved on to Camp Robinson, where Crazy Horse surrendered shortly after noon, May 6. Ironically, Crook was not on hand to accept the surrender, but had returned to Omaha, and from there had gone to Washington.[37]

Crook appears to have been willing to let the Cheyennes remain in their old territory, provided they gave up their arms and ponies. But almost immediately after their surrender, the army, at the Indian Bureau's insistence, began transporting them to the Indian Territory. The Lakotas, largely through the efforts of Red Cloud and Spotted Tail, managed to delay their move to the Missouri River.

Crook finally met Crazy Horse during a council at the Red Cloud Agency on May 25, where the question of relocation was raised. Crazy Horse pushed for an agency in the Bighorns or in the Powder River country, and other chiefs sought one in the vicinity of Bear Butte, near what is now Sturgis, South Dakota. Crook tended to agree that relocation to the north was preferable to the Missouri River or the Territory, but added he could only make recommendations. He suggested the chiefs themselves should travel to Washington and discuss it with President Hayes. Emphasizing his own relationship with the president, he believed that Hayes might be receptive to their views. They agreed to form a delegation and visit the capital in the fall.

The council included review of a battalion of Indian scouts, organized by Lt. W. Philo Clark, Second Cavalry. Consisting largely of Lakotas, Cheyennes, and Arapahos, the battalion included, as first sergeants, Sharp Nose, Red Cloud, Little Wound, Spotted Tail, and Crazy Horse. Besides routine scouting, the job of these newly enlisted Indian soldiers was to spy on the northern tribes—and each other—to detect any possible conspiracy against the government. The system seemed to work, and on August 1, Crook was able to report, "Crazy Horse, Little Big Man . . . and other noted hostile chiefs are at the Red Cloud and Spotted Tail Agencies, and to all appearances are now as peaceable and well disposed as any of the Indians there."[38]

The calm was not to last, largely because of Crazy Horse's growing influence among the agency Indians. The traditional agency chiefs saw a threat to their prestige and their standing with the government, and used Clark's spy system to spread rumors of an impending outbreak. The Indians began to divide into factions for and against Crazy Horse, with the anti-Crazy Horse groups centering around Red Cloud and Spotted Tail. The rift even entered Crazy Horse's own camp, where his old friend and ally, He Dog, abandoned him and joined the Red Cloud faction, and Little Big Man distanced himself. The anti-Crazy Horse factions played both sides. While feeding false information to Lieutenant Clark, they also undermined Crazy Horse's faith in the government, telling him, among other things, that Crook's proposed trip to Washington was a ruse to murder him.

Crook, of course, received only the information given to Clark. He especially wanted Crazy Horse in the delegation to Washington, and when Crazy Horse balked, he took it as a sign of bad faith. The refusal, together with Clark's rumors of possible trouble, apparently resurrected the specter of Crazy Horse that had haunted Crook during the war.

Crazy Horse was on his mind when he learned of the Nez Perce outbreak in Idaho. Ordering the chief closely watched, he started for Camp Brown, in western Wyoming, via Fort Laramie. Clark, meanwhile, sought Crazy Horse's assistance as a scout against the Nez Perces. Crazy Horse's affirmative response, however, was mistranslated by Frank Grouard to the effect that he intended to settle scores against the whites, and Clark was suspicious enough to believe it. Informed of the situation when he reached Fort Laramie, Crook ordered Crazy Horse's arrest, then turned around and headed back for Camp Robinson to take charge personally. He intended to send Crazy Horse to Omaha, and from there he urged his removal to some remote internment, preferably the old Spanish castle at Fort Marion, Florida, a favorite detention center for undesirable Indians.

By the time Crook arrived at Robinson, however, the issue was resolved, albeit violently. Crazy Horse had been arrested on September 5, and when the soldiers attempted to put him into the guardhouse, he slashed out a knife. Little Big Man grabbed his wrists from behind, and they tumbled out the door. In the scuffle, Crazy Horse cut Little Big Man and broke free, just as a member of the guard detail ran up with bayonet fixed on his rifle. Crazy Horse either stumbled and fell, or was thrown, onto the bayonet. Mortally wounded, he died about midnight.[39]

With Crazy Horse dead, and the Nez Perce outbreak confined largely to the Department of the Columbia, Crook accompanied Red Cloud, Spotted Tail, and other chiefs to Washington, where they met with Hayes on September 27.[40] The president's positive attitude was due, no doubt, to Crook, who had been arguing since summer that the Lakotas be allowed to remain on some portion of their homeland. Hayes explained that they would have to move to the Missouri at least for the winter, because their rations had already been stockpiled there. Then, in the spring, he promised to send a commission to help the chiefs select spots for their agencies somewhere within the remaining boundaries of the old Great Sioux Reservation. Lest there be any misunderstanding of the gravity of the situation or the determination of the Indians, Crook wrote army headquarters, "It is my firm conviction that unless the promises . . . are strictly complied with, serious trouble will ensue."

The government understood. The commissioners arrived in the spring of 1878, and while they met with the chiefs, Hayes's secretary of the interior, Carl Schurz, successfully lobbied Congress to abandon any plans to transport them to the Territory. Crook, in the end, had kept his word that the Lakotas could retain some of their old land. It was too late, however, for the Cheyennes, who had already been moved. It was also too late for another tribe, the Poncas, who had been uprooted from their ancient homeland on the Missouri and removed to the Territory so the land could be given to the Lakotas. Over the next several years, the removal of Cheyennes and Poncas become a sort of turning point, not only in government–Indian relations, but for George Crook personally.[41]

THIRTEEN

"It is an Outrage"

~~~

In late 1877, Crook stopped by Spiegel Grove, the Hayes estate at Fremont. The house, begun almost twenty years earlier by Sardis Birchard as a simple frame summer home, was expanding into a large, elegant mansion as the Hayes family and its varied interests grew. Located in a twenty-five-acre park, it was surrounded by tall, ancient trees, and late that summer President Hayes had begun naming individual trees for prominent house guests. On this visit, an especially imposing oak was named in honor of Crook. The George Crook Oak, with a dedicatory plaque affixed to the trunk, still stands only a few yards from the veranda.[1]

The visit, no doubt, was a pleasant break from the problems that faced Crook back on the frontier, where the end of the Great Sioux War marked a turning point in the Indian campaigns. The most powerful indigenous nations were broken, and the complete subjugation of the West by the government was simply a matter of time. Yet the very inevitability of white dominion led to further outbreaks. As settlers felt more confident in encroaching on Indian lands, even the friendly tribes were pushed to the limit of endurance. Already the Bannocks of the Northwest were becoming restless under the unrelenting white pressure.

The Bannocks' relations with the government were generally cordial, and some had served as scouts during Crook's expeditions against the Sioux in 1876. Nevertheless, grievances had been building over a period of years. The critical issue was food. By an 1868 treaty, the Bannocks had agreed to share a reservation with the Shoshones; their agencies were located at Fort Hall and Ross

Fork in Idaho. The agreement allowed them to continue living off the land, particularly in an area called the Camas Prairie, a lush, well-watered valley about ninety miles east of Boise. The valley was named for the profusion of camas, an edible flowering bulb that grows wild in much of the region west of the Rocky Mountains. One particular camas species, the quamash *(camassia quamash)*, was the food staple of the Bannocks and other tribes of the Northwest. The bulbs proliferated after the spring rains, and a single Indian woman could gather several bushels a day. The bulbs could be baked in a hole in the ground, or dried, pounded into flour, and baked into bread.

The problem arose when settlement of the surrounding area depleted the game, and government allowances were not adequate to make up for the difference. Additionally, the rations were not evenly distributed, with the Shoshones receiving more per capita than the Bannocks. The situation was aggravated further when whites began running their hogs in the Camas Prairie to feed on the bulbs, even though this was in violation of the 1868 treaty. The Bannocks faced the possibility of famine.[2]

Tensions over food shortages led to a general restlessness, and during the Nez Perce War of 1877, the army put the Bannocks under surveillance, even though some fifty of their warriors were serving as scouts against the Nez Perces. The garrison at the military post of Fort Hall, some fifteen miles from the agency, was strengthened. Random acts of violence broke out during the summer and fall of 1877. A Bannock girl was raped, and on August 8, her brother retaliated by shooting and seriously wounding two teamsters, who apparently were unconnected with the crime. When the brother was arrested at the Fort Hall Agency on November 23, one of his friends, a man named Tambiago, retaliated by shooting to death one Alex Rhoden, who was delivering cattle to the reservation. The agency was placed under military occupation, and Tambiago was arrested and sent to Malad City, Idaho, for trial. Then, on January 16, 1878, territorial militia surrounded two Bannock villages, confiscating thirty-two firearms and three hundred ponies, and taking Tambiago's father and two brothers to Fort Hall for internment.[3]

Although Idaho initially was part of the Department of the Columbia, since 1875 the southern part of the territory around Fort Hall had been attached to the Platte and therefore was under Crook's jurisdiction. On April 2, 1878, Crook visited the Ross Fork Agency and met with Capt. A. H. Bainbridge, Fourteenth Infantry, commander of the military contingent, agent W. H. Danilson, and the leading men of the Bannocks and Shoshones. Despite the shootings, Crook was convinced that the majority of the Bannocks wanted peace. He agreed with the agent, Danilson, that the confiscation of the ponies was ill-advised and unnecessary; it would not affect Bannock fighting ability, but would hinder their spring planting. Likewise, he urged return of the firearms, which he said were old fashioned and more suitable for hunting than fighting.

Crook, however, did see trouble in the food situation. In a report to divisional headquarters in Chicago, he wrote, "In my conversation with Mr. Danilson, and from the complaints of the Indians, I learned that the rations issued at this Agency are entirely inadequate; hitherto' it has been the practice to permit the young men to hunt the buffalo in the Big Horn and Yellowstone country, but the rapid settling up of that region as well as the country around this Agency, makes any such dependence for the future most precarious, and I therefore urgently recommend an increase [equal] to the amount now allowed the Sioux and other Indians." He also stated that he considered the continued military presence unnecessary, and suggested that the troops return to their posts.[4]

The government denied the requisition for additional rations on the grounds that "no appropriation had been made." Crook considered this incredible because, as he saw it, the Bannocks had never been supplied with even half of what they needed.[5]

Tambiago, meanwhile, was convicted of Alex Rhoden's murder, and sentenced to hang on June 28, 1878, in the Idaho Territorial Prison. On recommendation of the commander at Fort Hall, Crook sent Tambiago's father and brothers to Omaha Barracks for internment until after the execution. By the time Tambiago was hanged, however, he and his family were no longer the issue. Pressed beyond the limits of their endurance, several groups of Bannock warriors had already decided they had no option but war. Parties of Bannocks and Paiute allies bolted their reservations, combined forces, and swept across Idaho and into Oregon.[6]

Crook believed government incompetence was responsible for the war. In an angry letter to divisional headquarters, he pointed out that most Bannocks at the agencies went hungry three days out of every seven because of inadequate rations.

> [The Indians] know nothing, and can understand nothing, of such things as the "failure of an Appropriation", or the cumbersome and dilatory complications of administrative "red tape"; they only know that we have promised faithfully to feed and clothe them and teach them to earn their own living, and they insist upon our living up to our contract, or they will, if driven to the war-path, wreak vengeance upon the unprotected ranchmen and miners near them.

Then, too, they are dissatisfied because while they, who have been for years our steadfast friends and allies, are nearly starving, the Sioux—so lately our bitter enemies—have twice the amount of supplies provided them.[7]

Crook's feelings about the government Indian policy were well known within the military. Now, however, he was no longer content to keep it within channels. He went public. In an interview with Thomas Henry Tibbles of the *Omaha Daily Herald,* Crook commented that Indians often had to choose between fighting and starving.

"The buffalo is all gone," Crook told Tibbles, "and an Indian can't catch enough jack rabbits to subsist himself and family, and then there aren't enough jack rabbits to catch. What are they to do? Starvation is staring them in the face. . . . I do not wonder, and you will not either, that when these Indians see their wives and children starving, and their last sources of supplies cut off, they go to war. And then we are sent out there to kill them. It is an outrage."[8]

While Crook's humanitarian instincts damned the government for bringing on yet another Indian war, as a soldier he prepared for the possibility that he might have to fight the Bannocks. He considered it a remote possibility because in August, after two months of war, only 150 warriors were absent from the agency, and these were poorly armed. In their initial outbreak, they had crossed into Oregon, which was in the Department of the Columbia, and therefore had become General Howard's problem. So when Archie McIntosh wrote from Arizona, offering to return to Idaho and once again scout for his old friend, Crook replied that it was not serious enough for a major campaign. Aside from strengthening the garrison at Fort Hall, he made no effort to move after the hostiles. Howard had adequate forces in the Columbia, and Crook preferred to use his troops as a deterrent to outbreaks in Idaho. After a visit to the Ross Fork Agency in July, he was able to report that the Bannocks and the Shoshones had three hundred acres of wheat, and about fifty acres of potatoes and vegetables, and the yield looked promising. As time passed, it became obvious there would be little further disturbance in Idaho.[9]

Eventually, the hostile warriors were chased out of Oregon and back into Idaho. They were rounded up and disbursed among various military posts in the Divisions of the Missouri and Pacific, sufficiently distant from their home territory for a cooling-off period before they were allowed to return home.

If Crook was growing to dislike his role as an Indian fighter, other duties were more pleasant. In the spring of 1878, a vacancy opened for major and assistant adjutant general. Over seventy captains sought the promotion, including

Azor Nickerson. His service as Crook's senior aide-de-camp and chief of staff brought him powerful support, including that of the governors of three states and four territories, and four federal senators. On June 16, Crook telegraphed President Hayes, "I urgently solicit Captain Nickerson's appointment as a favor to myself and assured that he is the best selection that can be made. His record during and since the [Civil] War, his severe wounds, cultivated mind and high tone of character as known to me for more than (12) years, are the qualifications upon which I base my recommendation." Crook's word apparently swung Hayes's decision, because later in the day he sent a second telegram thanking the president for appointing Nickerson. A month later, on July 17, Nickerson was formally relieved of his responsibilities with the Department of the Platte. Crook issued a general order stating his "deep sense of obligation for the valuable and distinguished services rendered him by Major *Nickerson,* during the twelve years that that officer has been a member of his military family."[10]

Another friend to be rewarded was Washakie. Throughout the latter half of the 1870s, Camp Brown, Wyoming, often was known locally as "Fort Washakie" because it was identified with the old Shoshone chief. It was situated in his reservation, and he used it as a mustering point for scouts going to assist the soldiers in their various campaigns. On December 30, 1878, at Crook's request, the government officially upgraded the camp to a permanent post and naming it Fort Washakie in commemoration of his steadfast friendship.[11]

Always there loomed the specter of another Indian outbreak, and on the night of September 9, 1878, it came when the Cheyenne bands headed by Little Wolf broke camp in the Indian Territory and started north. The year in the territory had been devastating. Unlike their Southern Cheyenne cousins, they were a mountain people who drew most of their sustenance from hunting. The low, hot, malarial plains of Oklahoma, where much of the game had been exterminated, sickened them almost immediately on their arrival. Within two months, nearly two-thirds of the 999 people in their camp were ill, and during the winter of 1877-78, forty-one died. The lone physician, charged with the care of five thousand Northern and Southern Cheyennes, and Arapahos, had not been provided with medicine. The Northern Cheyennes received rations for only nine of the twelve months of the fiscal year, and the cattle provided for beef were thin and rangy with very little meat. After enduring it as long as they could, they packed and left.[12]

The band totaled no more than three hundred people, of whom about sixty or seventy were warriors, and the rest women, children, and old people. About a hundred miles north of their agency, they were overtaken by troops who ordered them back. They refused, and in the ensuing fight, the soldiers were driven back. The Cheyennes continued northward, out of the Territory and into Kansas. When they needed transportation, they stole horses, and when they ran out of food, they took cattle. Reaching the Sappa and Beaver Valleys of northwestern Kansas, where white settlement was heaviest, they went on a rampage. At least forty whites were killed, along with any livestock they could not take. Homesteads were pillaged, and any goods that could not be carried were destroyed.[13]

Although the Indian Territory and Kansas were in General Pope's jurisdiction, there was no question that, if the Cheyennes were not stopped, they would cross over into the Department of the Platte. No one could guess what that might lead to, and Crook had to put personal plans on hold and prepare for war. Most of his plans centered around Webb Hayes, who had invited Crook to his class reunion, after which they planned to go hunting in the Bighorns. Now, however, Crook had to forgo Webb's reunion, and he felt that with the Cheyennes on the loose and heading who-knew-where, hunting in the Big-horns would be "risky." On the other hand, he believed they might be able to hunt in the Medicine Bow range, although he said the chances of bagging big game would be considerably less.[14]

There is no indication that the hunt took place, and probably it did not. When the Cheyennes crossed into Nebraska, thereby coming under Crook's jurisdiction, the Department of the Platte was woefully unprepared. Many of the units were scattered in the northern part of the department, still mopping up stray groups of hostiles, and others had been loaned to the Department of Dakota for the same reason. The bulk of the remaining available troops were strung out along the Union Pacific line.

The first detachment of troops into the field was a small unit consisting almost entirely of infantry "drawn from the various posts" all the way from Omaha to Salt Lake City. These assembled at Sidney, Nebraska, mounted on cavalry horses sent over from Fort McPherson, and placed under the command of Maj. Thomas T. Thornburgh, Fourteenth Infantry. The Fifth and Third Regiments of Cavalry had been in the field since May, and consequently had pack trains and Indian scouts already assembled. Merritt was ordered to take the Fifth to Fort Laramie, while Maj. Caleb Carlton and the Third were sent to Camp Robinson. Other units returning from Dakota arrived at Camp Sheridan.

The Cheyennes, meanwhile, had crossed the North Platte River, after which they split into separate bands, the main group going with Little Wolf and the remainder with Dull Knife. Both headed into the sandhills of west-central

Nebraska. So far they had managed to travel more than five hundred miles virtually unopposed. For the public, reading lurid accounts of Cheyenne depredations during the march through Kansas, this situation was unacceptable. Anti-Indian feeling was strong, and there were demands for the heads of Crook, Pope, Sherman, and virtually anyone else even remotely responsible.

On October 23, however, two companies of the Third under Capt. J. B. Johnson encountered Dull Knife's band. After several hours of negotiation, Johnson managed to convince the Cheyennes to surrender their livestock and weapons. Some of the young warriors objected to the disarmament, but Dull Knife managed to keep them under control, and Johnson did not order them individually searched. That afternoon, Major Carlton arrived and informed the Cheyennes they would be moved to Camp Robinson. Knowing this would be the first stop on a trip back to the Territory, the Cheyennes balked, telling Carlton they would die first. After rejecting an alternative of Camp Sheridan, they returned to their camp and prepared to fight, presumably with weapons they had concealed during the initial disarmament.

Both sides eyed each other throughout the next day, and Carlton sent for more troops from Robinson and Sheridan. On the morning of October 26, the Cheyennes found themselves surrounded, and Carlton informed them they must now follow him back to Camp Robinson. They reached the post that night, and the Indians—forty-six adult males, sixty women, and forty children— were interned in an unused barracks building.

The Cheyennes told Carlton they had left the Territory because they had been starved. They said the Northern Cheyennes still in the Territory planned to break out and join them. Carlton telegraphed the information to Crook, who forwarded it on to Chicago. The reply was to return the Cheyennes to the Territory, but on being informed of the government's decision, Carlton told Crook they were so adamant in their refusal it would "be necessary to tie and haul them." On November 14, he sent another telegram, advising Crook that Red Cloud had suggested confiscating all knives; otherwise, the Cheyennes "would kill themselves to keep from going south."[15]

The government's concern was two-fold: failure to make an example of the Cheyennes would lead to a breakdown of the reservation system; and Kansas authorities demanded retribution against those involved in the depredations. There seemed ample reason for punishment. The Cheyennes possessed a substantial amount of obvious plunder—clothing, bedspreads, pictures, tableware, and the like. Initially, they claimed it had been taken by members of Little Wolf's band, who had traded it to them later. But some of the chiefs confided that at least fifteen of the young warriors interned at Camp Robinson had been involved in the raids.

On December 3, Sheridan notified Crook that the commissioner of Indian affairs wanted the Cheyennes removed to "such place in Kansas as would enable the civil authorities to identify those who had been engaged in the horrible series of outrages in that State." Accordingly, they were to be transported to Fort Leavenworth, after which those not singled out for prosecution would be sent back to the Territory, and ringleaders of the outbreak would be interned at Fort Marion. Formal orders were issued on December 20. Crook passed them on to Capt. Henry Wessells, Third Cavalry, commanding Camp Robinson, instructing him to "use due discretion in speaking of this matter to Indians or others."

Wessells emerges as the villain of the affair, particularly after Karl Malden's portrayal of him as a martinet in advanced stages of alcoholic delirium in the 1964 film *Cheyenne Autumn,* very loosely adapted from Mari Sandoz's book of the same name. His correspondence, however, shows him to have been reasonably concerned about the Indians' welfare, but largely hamstrung by bureaucracy and conflicting jurisdictions. He notified Crook that the physical condition of the Cheyennes was generally good, with only a few being ill. On the other hand, he said he would need about twenty-five blankets. Seven wagons would be necessary to move their personal equipment, tents, rations, and forage to the railroad at Sidney, besides which, he believed, about seventy-five of the women and children would need to be transported in wagons.

More immediately, the Indians desperately needed clothing. Wessells had plenty on hand, but it came from military stores, and he lacked the authority to issue it to the Indians, who were under the Interior Department's jurisdiction. He telegraphed Crook for permission to distribute enough from his stores to protect the Indians from the severe cold. Crook also complained about the situation, pointing out to Sheridan that the temperature in the area around Camp Robinson had been below zero for several days, and it would be "inhuman to move these Indians as ordered." Meanwhile, the Indians were growing suspicious. Dull Knife had bluntly stated that he would die before going back, and Crook said that Carlton believed it would be necessary to handcuff the men in order to move them quietly.[16]

A few days later, eleven Cheyenne prisoners captured near Red Cloud's new agency at Pine Ridge, Dakota Territory, were sent to Robinson for inclusion in the transport, and on January 3, Wessells notified departmental headquarters that he was ready to move them as soon as clothing was provided. While the clothing issue was debated at higher levels, Wessells and the Cheyennes reached a complete impasse. They were adamant that they would die before returning to the Territory, and on January 4, Wessells ordered their food and fuel stopped, believing they would give in when they got cold and hungry enough. He told Crook that most of the resistance came from the younger warriors (presumably those who might have faced prosecution in Kansas).

"Dull Knife is inclined to give up," he telegraphed Crook, "but the young men won't allow it. I offered to feed the young children, but the Indians won't allow it." Frustrated, Wessells took even more drastic action by cutting off the water supply. The thirsty Cheyennes then scraped the frost off the window glass. They had reached the point of siege mentality in which they had one final weapon against the whites—their lives.[17]

Crook's patience with the government was wearing thin. "Among these Cheyennes," he later wrote in his annual report, "were some of the bravest and most efficient of the auxiliaries who had acted under General Mackenzie and myself in the campaign against the hostile Sioux in 1876 and 1877, and I still preserve a grateful remembrance of their distinguished services which the Government seems to have forgotten."[18]

In a telegram to Sheridan, he expressed his disgust at being forced to do the Indian Bureau's dirty work, "It is hard to ask the military to perform this disagreeable duty, more especially if this removal had been made (2) two months ago, the great suffering which must ensue and much of their opposition to going would have been obviated. Cannot the Indian Dept. send some one to superintend the movement and we simply furnish the escort[?]"[19]

The Indian Bureau, however, was silent on the matter. Sheridan agreed with Crook about the impracticality of moving the Cheyennes during cold weather, and advised him to use his own judgment. It soon became a dead issue, though, because, unknown to Wessells, the Cheyennes prior to their surrender had concealed at least five rifles and carbines and perhaps eleven revolvers. The long arms were hidden under the floor of the barracks, and the revolvers had been dismantled, with larger pieces such as cylinders, barrels, and frames hidden in the women's clothing, and the smaller pieces—hammers, triggers, and such—worn openly as ornaments by the children. On the afternoon of January 9, the Cheyennes gathered the pieces and reassembled them and, at 10 P.M., opened fire and made their break. One sentry was killed outright, and another mortally wounded, and two soldiers were wounded. About eighteen Cheyennes surrendered as soon as the fighting started, and another thirty-five were recaptured almost immediately. Forty were killed, and the remainder fled to the bluffs northwest of the post. The prisoners included the head chiefs Wild Hog, Crow, and Left Hand. Dull Knife was said to have been killed, but nobody was sure.

Wessells dispatched a company of soldiers who found the Indians entrenched in the hills about fifteen miles away. Skirmishing was almost constant, and two companies were dispatched to back up the one already sent out. Confronted with the troops and faced with starvation, the Cheyennes slowly began to surrender. By January 12, the number of prisoners had reached seventy, and about forty were dead, mostly young warriors. The army's losses were four killed and eight wounded. Crook telegraphed Wessells, "Follow them with all your available force and don't leave their trail until they are recaptured, as much depends on this. The Cheyenne captives should remain where they are for the present." Then he sent Schuyler to investigate the situation at Fort Robinson (Camp Robinson had been upgraded to fort on December 30, 1878).[20]

Schuyler spent several days interviewing the prisoners. The chiefs admitted the young warriors had been involved in the raids in Kansas, and feared hanging if they were sent to Fort Leavenworth. "The cutting down of their rations only made them more desperate, because it proved that the Government would not change its determination," Schuyler reported. Equally terrifying was the prospect of being sent to Fort Marion, because the Indians equated the sultry coast of Florida with a death sentence. Any fugitives who managed to get through the military cordon would try to make their way north and join Little Wolf, who they believed was camped on the Powder River. Meanwhile, Red Cloud's Oglalas at Pine Ridge were demanding that the Cheyenne women and children prisoners with any Sioux blood be sent to their reservation. Crook agreed, telling Sheridan "the effect would be good."[21]

Little Wolf, in fact, did reach the Powder River area in March 1879. Here he was intercepted by Miles's troops, who took Little Wolf's band to Fort Keogh, on the Yellowstone in Montana. Rather than deal with the Indian Bureau over their disposition, Miles simply enlisted the Indians as scouts. This was typical of Miles who, as Sheridan noted, had little regard for regulations. He likewise had enlisted those Cheyennes who surrendered near the end of the Great Sioux War, presenting the government with a *fait accompli,* while Crook, the West Pointer, had followed procedure and obeyed the Indian Bureau's instructions to send his Cheyennes to the Territory. In fact, while Crook, Wessells, and Sheridan worried over the Dull Knife band, first at Fort Robinson and then in the hills after the outbreak, Miles considered the period "uneventful" in his area, and did not even mention the surrender of Little Wolf's band in his memoirs.[22]

Of the Indian prisoners at Fort Robinson, about eight or ten remained unaccounted for, some probably killed by soldiers who never recovered their bodies, and others apparently starved to death in the hills. Wild Hog and six others were sent with their families to Fort Leavenworth. The case against them was thrown out of court, and they were returned to the Indian Territory. Most of the remainder were sent to Pine Ridge, and from there transported to Fort Keogh. Eventually, those still in the Territory were allowed to move to Pine Ridge, and later relocated to a new Northern Cheyenne Reservation on the Tongue River. Contrary to rumor, Dull Knife had not died in the breakout, but managed to escape with his family into the hills. Three weeks later they surrendered at Pine Ridge, and were sent to the Tongue River, where the old chief was allowed to live quietly until his death in 1883.[23]

As far as General Sheridan was concerned, the entire blame for the fiasco at Fort Robinson belonged on Crook's head. He wrote Sherman:

> It is apparent that trouble was apprehended in moving the prisoners south and proper precautions should have been taken in anticipation of an outbreak. This was not done.
>
> *Writing Confidentially* I am sorry to say that but very few things have been well done in that Department since Crook came in command of it.
>
> The troops complain that he has a want of confidence in them & they have a corresponding want of confidence in him, and from these existing circumstances we must expect indifference and bad results. [Emphasis is Sheridan's][24]

Part of Sheridan's rancor was due to his continuing anger over Crook's failure to disarm all the agency Indians at Red Cloud and Spotted Tail in 1876. This, he believed, set a bad precedent which the Cheyennes used to their advantage in the Fort Robinson outbreak.[25] For all his protestations on their behalf, Crook must share some of the blame for the sufferings of the Cheyennes. Although not responsible for the decisions of the government, or its failure to provide clothing, he was responsible for the actions of subordinates in his department. As Sheridan hinted, he failed to supervise properly their internment at Fort Robinson, placing entirely too much of the burden on Wessells. Discussing the matter with an investigating board convened later that spring, Wessells pointed out that he had advised both Crook and Sheridan of his decision to cut off food and fuel to the Cheyennes, and neither had said a word.[26] Crook apparently realized his own awkward position, because in his annual report he took the unusual stance of justifying not only Wessells' actions, but those of the Cheyennes as well.

> I may say here that this measure criticized by the rules for the *theoretical* management of Indians seems to have been a severe one; but I ask, and I claim to have had as much experience in the management of Indian tribes as any man in his country, what alternative could have been adopted? During the 27 years of my experience with the Indian question, I have never known a band of Indians to make peace with our Government and then break it, or leave their Reservations without some ground of complaint; but until these complaints are examined and adjusted they will constantly give annoyance and trouble.

Then, in a slap at the government's acceptance of Little Wolf's refuge with Miles, and of various hostiles who slipped through the cordon and reached the Dakota reservations, he wrote:

> It seems to me to have been, to say the least, a very unnecessary exercise of power to insist upon this particular portion of the band going back to the Reservation while the other fragments of the same band which surrendered to the troops on the Yellowstone or escaped to the Red Cloud or Spotted Tail Reservations have been allowed to remain North unmolested, more especially since we have every reason to believe that the latter were the principal actors in the outrages perpetrated in Kansas, and know that they murdered several persons since the surrender of those confined at Fort Robinson.

That said, Crook concluded his report by writing:

> At present, affairs in the Department are in a very satisfactory condition, the only trouble being with the Utes of the White River Agency, Colorado, (to which point troops from this Department have just been sent) and which trouble I hope may soon be adjusted.[27]

Colorado was in the Department of the Missouri, but when the trouble with the Utes came to a head in September 1879, General Pope had no troops in the immediate vicinity. The conflict arose out of clashes between N. C. Meeker, the well-meaning but ignorant and autocratic agent at White River, and the Ute chiefs under his jurisdiction. By September 10, the situation had deteriorated to the point that Meeker wrote the governor of Colorado, claiming an uprising was imminent and employees were in danger of massacre, and asking for troops. The message was forwarded to the Interior Department, which requested troops to protect the agency and arrest the Indians who resisted Meeker's policies. The nearest post was Fort Fred Steele, at Rawlins, Wyoming, 175 miles to the north, under command of Major Thornburgh, who previously had assembled troops to deal with the Cheyenne outbreak. Because of his proximity to the agency, and the fact that he probably knew more about the Utes and the country between Fort Fred Steele and the agency than any other officer in the Platte, Thornburgh was ordered to protect Meeker and enforce his regulations on the Indians. He was also instructed to arrest the Indian "ringleaders" and hold them pending an investigation.[28]

Thornburgh left Fort Fred Steele with three companies of cavalry and one of infantry on September 21. His orders were to "advance with prudence." Four days later, he reached Fortification Creek, Colorado, in the Ute country, where he established his supply camp. His arrival panicked the Indians. Most apparently believed the dispute at the agency to be simply a disagreement between Meeker and a few of their tribe, and did not realize that the frightened agent had sent for troops. To them, the arrival of soldiers meant that they were to be uprooted and relocated. On September 26 at Bear River, Thornburgh met with some of their chiefs who promised to go with him to the agency, although they wanted to know why the troops had come. He tried to explain his mission, and reported to Omaha that he did not anticipate trouble. He was wrong. Three days later, just south of the Milk River, Thornburgh was ambushed and killed along with nine soldiers and two civilian employees. Four officers, thirty-four troopers, and a scout were wounded, and most of the animals were killed. The battered command managed to retreat back to the river, where they dug in for a siege and sent word to Fort Fred Steele for reinforcements. At the same time, the Utes attacked the agency, where they killed Meeker and nine employees and carried off the white women and children.

Crook, who was in Chicago at the time, ordered Merritt at Fort D. A. Russell to relieve the battered command. Then he started back to Omaha, and from there continued on to Fort Fred Steele. Merritt arrived at the Milk River on October 5, having marched 170 miles in just under forty-eight hours. The Utes scattered into the hills. Merritt occupied the agency, and then began planning a campaign to hunt them down. With every available man in the department being sent to the front, Crook estimated he would have about fifteen hundred men, and ordered him to prosecute the campaign "with greatest vigor." The White River Utes would face these troops alone because Uintah and Uncompahgre Utes wanted no part of the quarrel.[29]

Once again the government's inability to formulate a clear policy one way or the other interfered with Crook's planning. Secretary Schurz appointed General Charles Adams of Colorado as a special commissioner to meet with the Utes, arrest those responsible for the Meeker murders, and negotiate a peace. No mention was made of those who had ambushed Thornburgh and caused so much death and injury among the troops. Meanwhile, what, Crook wondered, was Merritt supposed to do? Complaining to Sheridan, he said, "It seems to me [Merritt] is placed in a delicate position[.] should he meet the indians and act upon dishonest proffessions of friendship [by those Indians?] it will give them a great advantage over him[.] six companies of cavalry should reach Rawlins today[.] shall they be sent forward[?]"[30]

Crook was beginning to see both Indian and soldier as victims of government incompetence at best and perfidity at worst. Even before the Ute trouble, he had written to newspaperman Thomas Henry Tibbles:

> If you were to collate from treaties all the promises made to the red men and contrast them with our performances you would have to admit that there was a very serious margin of compacts broken and unfulfilled, upon which the Indians could ground their distrust and contempt. We send them too many commissioners; there is no class of men for whom the Indian has less respect. Better select one tribe and stick closely to the letter and essence of the compacts we have entered into with it; such an example would not be lost upon adjacent tribes. Our method is different. Let a tribe remain at peace, we starve them. Let them go to war and spring suddenly upon our scattered settlements, we make every promise, yield every concession. Thus the Indian learns that by being "bad" he is all the more certain to be the recipient of kind treatment.[31]

The Indians having been provoked to war by this policy, the soldiers then were required to go out and fight them. Tibbles had thought of this at the station in Omaha earlier in the month, when he went to see Crook off for Fort Fred Steele. Crook, he wrote,

> made no remark about the unpleasant duty, but his whole demeanor showed that he felt exceedingly sad. I could not but remember a remark he had made to me the first time I ever conversed with him. Then, as now, we had an Indian war on our hands. I remarked that it was a hard thing for the Army to be constantly called upon to sacrifice their lives settling quarrels brought about by thieving contractors and agents of the Indian Department. I will never forget how his eyes flashed as he replied: "I will tell you a harder thing, Mr. Tibbles. It

is to be forced to fight and kill the Indians when I know that they are clearly
in the right."[32]

General Adams arrived in October, meeting first with the Utes and then
with Merritt. The Indians claimed they did not want the war and whenever
there had been a fight—even with Thornburgh—they contended the whites
had fired first. The captive women and children were returned, and Adams asked
Merritt to refrain from any movement; otherwise, he said, the Indians might
raid the settlements. This last request was easily complied with because Merritt,
at that point, was too low on rations to mount a campaign in any case. After
Adams left, things grew quiet. A few Indians were spotted in the hills, but
seemed to be mainly watching to see what Merritt would do.[33]

The entire situation was now in the hands of the Interior Department,
which ultimately closed the White River Agency and forced those Indians to
move to the Uintah Ute Agency in Utah. The White River reservation then was
thrown open to settlement. For the army, however, the entire affair was just one
more example of civilian incompetence in the Indian Bureau. Already, Congress
was considering the possibility of transferring the Indian Bureau to the War
Department. Crook wholeheartedly endorsed the idea, comparing the existing
system of divided responsibilities and conflicting jurisdictions with a ship having
two captains.

Schurz, however, blocked the change, believing he could rid the Indian
Bureau of the fraud, graft, and corruption while keeping it under civilian
control, which he believed was more enlightened than that of the military.
Despite his honest efforts, the clean-up was only marginal. As Martin F. Schmitt
observed in his supplement to Crook's autobiography, "The Indian plum was
too rich to leave unplucked."[34]

FOURTEEN

THE PONCA AFFAIR

GENERAL CROOK'S REACTIONS TO THE Cheyenne outbreak, and the Ute and Bannock risings were the first indications of a new determination to protect the Indians. His entire approach to the problem, indeed to the Indians as people, was changing. For many years his attitude had been one of paternalistic condescension, the attitude of a "civilized" person toward an "unlettered savage." Now, however, he was developing respect for the Indian as a rational human being in his own right. Much of this metamorphosis may be attributed to Bourke. As his biographer, Joseph Porter, has noted, Bourke was the scholar of Crook's official family, whose extensive reading of history and anthropology helped the general formulate ideas or gave intellectual justification to notions he already held.[1]

In the mid-1870s, Bourke shared the opinion of many anthropologists of his day that the tribal culture of the Indians would have to be destroyed before the Indian could progress as an individual. History, he believed, provided many cases where progress was possible only through a transition from a hunting to a pastoral culture, and from there to an agricultural society. The transition should be forced on the Indians if they were unwilling to accept it otherwise. Within a few years, however, experience and knowledge of Indian culture had completely altered his views. No amount of political pressure or military force could compel the Indians to give up ideas and traditions that had sustained them for centuries. The Indians, Bourke concluded, would have to be eased into the mainstream with patience and compassion, not by force.[2]

Crook came to share this last view and believed it should be implemented. No longer content to limit himself to official remarks on a policy he considered inhumane, he now openly advocated recognition of the Indians' basic rights as human beings and residents of the United States. Although his commission as a soldier required him to continue executing the government's policies, he had enough rank, seniority, and prestige to voice his own opinions. The fact that Rutherford Hayes was in the White House no doubt also provided him with some sense of added security.

The decisive turn of events came with the Ponca affair of 1879, when Crook the Indian fighter cast his lot permanently, publicly, and unequivocally with the Indian rights activists. It was, Bourke observed, "the most important [event] occurring within General Crook's jurisdiction after the pacification of the Sioux."[3]

The Ponca case went back to the Fort Laramie Treaty of 1868 when, by bureaucratic error, Ponca lands on the Missouri River in what is now northeastern Nebraska were included in the Great Sioux Reservation.[4] The Lakota Sioux then treated the Poncas as trespassers, attacking them and attempting to expel them from their own country. Rather than correct the problem, the government aggravated it when, during the Great Sioux War in 1876, it decided to relocate the Poncas in the Indian Territory and permanently turn their homeland over to the Lakotas. For the government, this was expedient because the Poncas were a docile people who had never been at war against the United States, while an immense amount of money and manpower was still being expended to fight the Lakotas. Secretary Schurz rationalized that they had to be relocated for their own protection because the Lakotas were their ancient enemies. And finally, it suited the government's policy of relocating and concentrating as many tribes as possible into the Indian Territory, where presumably they would not stand in the way of white expansion and development. Four leading chiefs—Standing Bear, White Eagle, Standing Buffalo, and Big Chief—appealed personally to President Hayes, who, to his later regret, followed Schurz's advice that the relocation was in the Poncas' best interests.

Not all the Poncas accepted the situation quietly. Standing Bear advocated resistance, and was interned at Fort Randall, Dakota Territory, until he grudgingly agreed to comply. The relocation, which began in the spring of 1877, was devastating. Much of the livestock was lost in transit. Members of the tribe died en route and many more, weakened by the hardships of the march and unaccustomed to the hot, malarial climate of Oklahoma, died after arriving. Within two years, one-third of the Poncas were dead and the majority of the survivors were disabled.

During the removal and relocation, Standing Bear lost two daughters, as well as his wife's mother and grandmother. The subsequent death of his only son, in the early spring of 1879, was more than the old chief could tolerate. Unwilling to bury him in a strange country, Standing Bear decided to take him back to the ancient homeland. Thirty members of the tribe joined the march north on foot, followed by a wagon carrying the son's body. Upon their arrival in Nebraska, they sought out the Omahas, a closely related tribe, who welcomed them to their reservation and allowed the Poncas to settle and plant crops. Inoffensive as this might have been, it nevertheless was in direct defiance of a government edict, and Secretary Schurz requested that the War Department arrest Standing Bear and return him and his followers to the Territory. As commander of the Department of the Platte, the responsibility fell on Crook.[5]

Troops were sent to the reservation where, over the objections of the Omahas, the Poncas were arrested and taken to Fort Omaha for internment. On March 30, 1879, they were visited and interviewed by Thomas Henry Tibbles, now assistant editor of the *Omaha Daily Herald*. Their position, simply stated, was that they wanted land and homes of their own such as any resident of the United States should have the right to expect.

Tibbles was the man to make their case. Already he had made the *Herald* a platform for Indian rights and, going against the wisdom of the day for an essentially western city, had stirred the Omaha community's interest in the cause. At thirty-nine, he was an established crusader, fighting for abolition in antebellum Kansas as a member of James Lane's Free-State Militia, and as a scout and correspondent in the Civil War. After the war, he was a circuit-riding preacher in Kansas and Nebraska, where he raised funds for victims of the 1874 grasshopper plague. Retiring from the ministry in 1877, he became a full-time newspaperman, carrying his zeal for equality and reform over into journalism.[6]

The day after Tibbles's visit, Crook received the Poncas in his office. Besides his staff and the Indian leaders, those present included several Ponca women and children, Tibbles, and Charles Morgan, an Omaha Indian who served as interpreter. Bourke noted that Standing Bear was "tall and commanding in presence, dignified in manner and very elegantly dressed in the costume of his tribe." He wore a blue flannel shirt with brass buttons, and collar and cuffs trimmed in red. He had blue flannel leggings, deerskin moccasins, and was draped with a red and blue blanket decorated with a broad band of beadwork. The part in his hair was painted red, and the two braids over his shoulders were

covered with otter fur. Bourke was most impressed, however, with his neck-
lace of grizzly bear claws. The others were dressed "in the costume of whites,"
although they all wore green blankets. Following the introductions, the Poncas
sat in a semi-circle on the floor.

Standing Bear opened by stating the situation of the Poncas, their removal
to the Indian Territory, their subsequent appeals to the president, and conditions in the Territory, culminating with the decision to return to Nebraska.
Then he came to the point, "If a white man had land, and some one should
swindle him, that man would try to get it back, and you would not blame him.
Look on me. Take pity on me and help me to save the lives of the women and
children. My brothers, a power, which I cannot resist, crowds me to the ground.
I need help."

Acknowledging the Indians' plight was just as they had stated, Crook told
Standing Bear, "It is a very hard case, but I can do nothing myself. I have received
an order from Washington and I must obey it. They have all the facts in Washington, and it would do no good for me to intercede." To the contrary, he said any
effort on his part "is likely to do more harm than good."

Faced with the inevitable, Standing Bear asked that the government cover
the expenses of their return to the Territory. He indicated that he expected
funerals to count heavily among the expenses because "half of my people here
are sick, and of course they will die before we get there, and they must be
buried."

Crook replied that he could only provide rations for the trip, and allow the
Poncas to take their livestock. "It is a very disagreeable duty to send you down
there," he said, "but I must obey orders."[7]

Sympathy for the Poncas was growing. The day of Crook's meeting with
Standing Bear, the pastors of the Baptist, Methodist-Episcopal, Presbyterian,
and Congregational Churches of Omaha telegraphed Secretary Schurz that
their congregations had passed resolutions calling on the government to rescind
the transportation order and allow the Poncas to settle with the Omahas.[8]

Despite his official position, Crook had no intention of letting the matter
drop. He appears to have called on Tibbles, and together the two men formu-
lated a plan. In his autobiography, *Buckskin and Blanket Days*, written in 1905,
Tibbles claims that Crook began the conversation by saying, "During twenty-
five or thirty years that I've been on the plains in government service, I've been
forced many times by orders from Washington to do most inhuman things in
dealing with the Indians, but now I'm ordered to do a more cruel thing than
ever before. I would resign my commission, if that would prevent the order

from being executed—but it would not. Another officer would merely be assigned to fill my place. I've come to ask if you will not take up the matter. It's no use for me to protest. Washington always orders the very opposite of what I recommend."

Crook believed that Tibbles, as an editor of "a great daily newspaper," was in a position to reveal the travesty against the Poncas to the American people, who would then demand justice. "If we can do something for which good men will remember us when we're gone," he concluded, "that's the best legacy we can leave. I promise you that if you'll take up this work, I'll stand by you."[9]

Although some historians contend that Tibbles, at the very least, embellished the conversation for dramatic effect, they do not question that Crook was genuinely interested in the Poncas and very likely the moving force behind the landmark legal case that Tibbles initiated on their behalf. It was in character with Crook, who stood by Tibbles just as he had promised. As Tibbles later wrote, "The outcome of General Crook's appeal to me was that our government reversed its hundred-year-old policy toward a whole race of people."[10]

Tibbles, meanwhile, telegraphed his coverage of the Ponca case to the metropolitan newspapers, and before long received positive responses from Chicago, St. Louis, and New York. Public sympathy was aroused and, interestingly enough, much of it came from the West. The western sense of fair play had been stirred when, as Bourke noted, the Poncas trekked north from the Territory "at their own expense across the country, walking every foot of the way, molesting nobody, and subsisting upon charity. Not a shot was fired at any one; not so much as a dog was stolen." Westerners were accustomed to "white tramps by the thousands, whose presence excited no comment." Here, however, were "Indians going along peaceably back to their old habitat to seek work and earn their own bread."[11]

Citizens of Omaha formed a committee to help the Indians. From Nebraska, the movement spread into Dakota Territory, where the churches of Yankton, the territorial capital, petitioned the federal Senate to allow the Poncas to settle in their old homeland. Two western senators, Algernon S. Paddock of Nebraska and Henry M. Teller of Colorado, took up the Ponca cause, even though Paddock generally disliked Indians and once had introduced a bill calling for their extermination.

In the East, the publicity of the Ponca case, and the efforts by the Omaha and Yankton groups, galvanized the Indian rights activists and gave them a new sense of purpose. Public opinion on the government's Indian policies had always been ambiguous but, prior to the Civil War, humanitarians were preoccupied with the abolition of slavery. After the war permanently settled that issue, the erstwhile abolitionists turned their attention to Indian rights, but they could not agree whether the best policy was removal and concentration, or assimilation. The Ponca removal brutally demonstrated the failure of removal and concentration, and reaction from the humanitarians was swift and intense.[12]

Tibbles believed the fate of the Poncas hinged on equal protection guarantees under the Fourteenth Amendment of the Constitution, and required a lawsuit to establish whether these guarantees applied to Indians. He approached two attorneys, John L. Webster of Omaha, who was widely respected in Nebraska, and A. J. Poppleton, chief attorney of the Union Pacific Railroad and a constitutional scholar. Both agreed to take the case pro bono, and prepared a petition of habeas corpus on behalf of the Poncas, which was served to Crook on April 8.

The case of *United States ex. rel. Ma-chu-nah-zah (Standing Bear) vs. George Crook* opened in Omaha before U.S. District Judge Elmer S. Dundy on April 30. Crook was named as defendant in his capacity as departmental commander, and therefore the military officer legally responsible for confining the Indians. The solemnity of the occasion was emphasized when he appeared in the dress uniform of a brigadier general, instead of his usual civilian suit. Standing Bear, likewise, understood the significance of the hearing, and wore the full regalia of a Ponca chief.

The petition on behalf of the Poncas contended that at the time of their arrest and imprisonment at Omaha Barracks, they were residing peacefully within the United States, supporting themselves through their own labor, and not constituting any threat or burden to the government or society in general. Consequently, it held that their "imprisonment and detention is wholly illegal" and demanded their release.[13] The government's response was that the Indian was not a "person" in the sense of having legal standing in court, and therefore could not bring suit against the government. Indian Commissioner E. A. Hayt summed up the official position in a letter to Schurz stating that, if the reservation system was to be maintained, Indians could not simply come and go as they pleased. Otherwise, he said, the West soon would be rife with vagabond and lawless Indians who would spread discontent among those engaged in useful pursuits.[14]

Hayt's letter was entered as part of the government's case, and drew a contemptuous reply from Standing Bear. He produced his own letter from Hayt attesting to his position as chief and his character, carefully noting that the commissioner was simply affirming a good character that Standing Bear himself had spent a lifetime building. The chief then dismissed Hayt as an officious bureaucrat who created major disruptions in his life for reasons that were, at best, trivial.[15]

Initially, Crook had little to say. When served notice of the Ponca suit, his position had required him to respond that he confined the Poncas under a lawful order from his superiors, issued in accordance with the government's legally enacted Indian policy. On the second day of the trial, however, he was infuriated to learn that some government bureaucrat had inserted an appendix to his response, which appeared in the record over his signature. It said, in part, that the Poncas "have not adopted and are not pursuing the habits and vocations of civilized life." Knowing this statement to be blatantly false, he demanded through Maj. Horace B. Burnham, departmental judge advocate, that the appendix be stricken. He contended he had never authorized it, and did not want it to appear attached to his name. Judge Dundy rejected the demand, pointing out that it was not entered as Crook's own views, but rather reflected his official position as a representative of the government. Crook continued to protest, but to no avail.[16]

The closing arguments appear to have been classics of lengthy nineteenth-century oratory. Tibbles recorded that Standing Bear's attorneys, Webster and Poppleton spoke six hours and four hours, respectively, while U.S. Attorney G. M. Lambertson spoke for five hours. Finally, Dundy allowed Standing Bear to address the court. The old chief stretched out his right hand, then turned to the judge and said:

> That hand is not the color of yours, but if I pierce it, I shall feel pain. If you pierce your hand, you will also feel pain. The blood that will flow from mine will be of the same color as yours. I am a man. The same God made us both.

He described his feeling of isolation and helplessness in the Indian Territory, comparing it to a great flood about to overwhelm him and his family. By contrast, his ancient home was a refuge against the flood.

> But a man bars the passage. He is a thousand times more powerful than I. Behind him I see soldiers as numerous as the leaves of the trees. They will obey that man's orders. I too must obey his orders. If he says I cannot pass, I cannot. The long struggle will have been in vain. My wife and child and I must return and sink beneath the flood. We are weak and faint and sick. I cannot fight.

With that, he bowed his head, then looked back up at Judge Dundy and said, "You are that man."

Recalling the scene in his memoirs, Tibbles wrote, "I saw tears on Judge Dundy's face. General Crook sat leaning forward, covering his eyes with his hand. Except for women's sobs there was absolute silence for a moment, then the whole room rose at once with a great shout. Among the first to reach Standing Bear was General Crook. The entire audience came crowding after him to shake the chief's hand."[17]

A week later, Dundy issued his decision, declaring "that an *Indian* is a PERSON within the meaning of the laws. . . . " Just as Indians were expected to obey the laws of the United States, the judge said, so were they entitled to the protection of those laws. "In what General Crook has done in the premises no fault can be imputed to him. He was simply obeying the orders of his superior officers as a good soldier ought to do," Dundy noted. But he added that those orders lacked necessary legal authority and therefore were not binding on Standing Bear and his followers. Instead, their detention was in violation of the law, and Crook was ordered to release them.[18]

Lambertson appealed the decision to the Federal Circuit Court. In response, the Omaha Committee sent Tibbles east to raise money for legal costs. The activists wanted to take the case to the Supreme Court, where they hoped to get a ruling restoring the Ponca's home territory, returning those Poncas still in the Indian Territory, and ending all government control of Indians. Schurz, however, was one jump ahead, and convinced Lambertson to withdraw the appeal and drop the case. In a letter to a then-little-known citizen named Helen Hunt Jackson, the secretary contended that the Poncas ultimately would lose in the appeals process, and that money collected toward legal expenses might better be used for education of Indian children.[19]

Although Helen Hunt Jackson's name would come to symbolize the reform movement, at this point she was only marginally involved. In fact, there is no indication that she had been particularly interested in humanitarian work of any kind until the fall of 1879, when Standing Bear accompanied Tibbles on a second tour of the East and she heard the chief speak in Boston. She embraced the cause with the enthusiasm of a new convert and, for the next six years until her death in 1885, it would become her all-consuming passion.

Corresponding with Schurz, whom she called "that false souled man," and with Crook, whom she respected, she began gathering historical material on government–Indian relations. On January 27, 1880, she wrote a friend, "I begin today, my solid work . . . going back, *100 years*—to tell sharply & succinctly the history of our *'Century of Dishonor,'*—in a small book." The "small book" would be published a year later as *A Century of Dishonor,* a scathing albeit slanted 514-page indictment of the government's Indian policies from the beginning of the United States as a sovereign nation.[20]

Schurz emerges as the villain of the Ponca affair, but in reality his views were as humane as those of the Indian rights activists. Both sides had the same goal— to make the Indians self-sustaining. Schurz believed it could only be done through government stewardship, a long process of weaning them away from a tribal life by slow degrees until—ultimately—they could be treated "like other inhabitants of the United States under the laws of the land." Until then, they could not be permitted to "take their chance" in the fast-paced, technologically advanced world of the late nineteenth century. He was quick to point out that there was no corner of the country that did not have some sort of conventional economic value, and railroads were rapidly making all parts of the country accessible, regardless of how the Indians might feel about it. He likewise noted that many whites still advocated a policy of extermination, thereby requiring government protection of the Indians.

Thoughtful reformers understood that Schurz's moderate approach was the more realistic than the radical transition proposed by the extremists and therefore the lesser of evils. The activists, however, believed the first step should be "to establish the rights of the Indians as citizens under the 14th amendment," then address the needs of assimilation. The extreme faction, consisting primarily of various reform-minded businessmen and philanthropists of Boston, would settle for nothing less than the total end to government control over the Indians. As far as they were concerned, Schurz and the Indian Ring were resisting Indian citizenship for the sole purpose of perpetuating their own positions. To expedite their cause, the extremists formed the Boston Indian Citizenship Association, better known as the Boston Committee, which challenged Schurz at every turn. The result was that actual efforts to aid the Indians were stalled while the two factions maligned each other.[21]

The Indian question was becoming so entangled in ideology that Crook feared the Indians themselves might be neglected to the point of starvation, or destroyed in wars of desperation, while the various factions argued over a solution. Like the Boston reformers, he was suspicious of Schurz; yet his own experience on the frontier made him pragmatic enough to realize that the government could not immediately withdraw supervision of Indian affairs while Indian wars still raged. Nevertheless, his actions in the Standing Bear case indicate that he saw no reason why Indians such as the Poncas, who had already given plentiful evidence of adaptation, could not be removed from government control. The problem was the government's seeming refusal to distinguish between the tribes that clung to their traditional ways, and those that were adapting to the realities of a white-dominated society.

"It seems to me to be an odd feature of our judicial system," he wrote to Tibbles, "that the only people in this country who have no rights under the law are the original owners of the soil. An Irishman, German, Chinaman, Turk or Tartar will be protected in life and property, but the Indian commands respect for his rights only so long as he inspires terror for his rifle."

The principal chiefs, Crook noted, realized that the traditional life was over. No longer able to hunt, they were "anxious to obtain cattle, seeds and implements and to have their children educated. They see the necessity of adopting the white man's ways and of conforming to the established order of things. But, I am very sorry to say, they have, to a very great degree, lost confidence in our people and their promises."[22]

In the midst of the controversy, Crook found a chance to return to the wilderness and to observe Schurz first-hand when the secretary decided to tour the Department of the Platte. Although Schurz's stated purpose was to negotiate a land cession from some Idaho tribes in a continued attempt at relocation and concentration, he was particularly interested in seeing Yellowstone National Park, established only a few years earlier. According to the *Salt Lake Tribune,* Schurz wanted "to examine the feasibility of making roads and leasing ground for hotels and other improvements." He was also "strongly inclined to have one part of the Park set aside as a preserve for some of the animals which will soon be extinct unless some precaution is made to save them." As departmental commander, Crook was detailed to accompany him, and he invited Webb Hayes for the trip.[23]

Crook, Bourke, and Webb Hayes arrived in Ogden, Utah, August 10, 1880, to find Schurz with a large retinue that included his staff, a nephew visiting from Germany, and various others. The secretary's two daughters also were at the depot but opted to continue on to Washington, no doubt to Crook's great relief as they would have been an additional encumbrance.

If the Indian rights extremists considered Schurz too hard on his indigenous charges, an incident at the depot showed that many westerners considered him far too lenient. When the Utah and Northern Railroad provided a special car for the party, Bourke noted that the "arrangement gave great umbrage to a big strapping fellow, calling himself Maguire who, much to my quiet enjoyment, wanted to whip the Secretary as a mark of esteem, I suppose. Mr. Maguire was very tipsy, but very plucky, nevertheless."

The following day the party arrived at Ross Fork, where Schurz met with a delegation of Shoshones, Bannocks, and affiliated tribes in a futile effort to get them to relinquish their nearby reservation at Lemhi and consolidate with the tribes at Fort Hall. Summing up the attitude of the Indian delegation, the chief, Din-Doy, told Schurz, "You have given me ten agents. None of them has ever been fit for anything."

From Fort Hall, the party continued on to Beaver Canyon, Idaho, terminus of the rails 258 miles north of Ogden. A detachment of Fourteenth Infantry was waiting with ambulances for the people and a light wagon for their baggage. Moving east across the Camas Prairie, so recently the cause of the Bannock rising, Crook, Schurz, Webb, and another guest went shooting, and bagged "a number of plump young prairie chickens." Finally, they came to the divide between the headwaters of the Columbia and the Missouri, where the supreme packmaster, Tom Moore, met them with all their equipment ready. "Our accommodations on this trip are decidedly regal," Bourke noted. "We have one wall tent for every two persons and a hospital tent for dining room." In all, there were seven army wagons, three ambulances, fourteen mounted infantrymen, Shoshone guides Jack Hurley and Mike Fisher, a hospital tent, seven wall tents, and fifteen common tents. The seventeen pack mules, together with horses and draft mules, brought the number of animals to seventy-six. On the first night, cook Timothy Foley prepared tomato soup, baked salmon trout, mashed potatoes, prairie chicken, stewed sage hens, pork and beans, hot biscuits, fresh butter, pickles, olives, peaches and pears, cheese, whiskey, claret, tea and coffee. Schurz provided the champagne.[24]

In Yellowstone, the party was joined by Park Superintendent Philetus W. Norris and Government Forester Harry Yount. Catching their first sight of the geysers, even the most jaded western veterans were overwhelmed by the power and beauty of nature. Bourke observed that Major Stanton, "who hasn't said a prayer for a quarter of a century, tried to mumble a Pater Noster, but he got it so badly mixed up with the Star Spangled Banner that I don't think it did him much good." For himself, Bourke commented:

In cities, sophistry, cynicism, infidelity thrive; there rascality and intrigue too generally are successful and the despondent mind may well doubt the existence of an All-Wise and All-Good Master of the World. But in these grand mountain ranges, the human soul is brought face to face with its Creator, admires His

Power, concedes His wisdom and humbly hopes for His justice and mercy. "The heavens declare the Glory of God, the firmament showeth His handiwork."[25]

Bourke's attitude toward Schurz mellowed during the trip. The secretary, he concluded, "is a very genial companion, puts on no airs whatever, and exerts himself to make everything run along smoothly." The German-born Schurz was "a wonderfully fine linguist and speaks our language with classic precision. He is a very good shot and by his skill has done much for our table. He rides well, is very wiry and can stand almost any amount of fatigue."[26]

The hunting and fishing continued. At Yellowstone Lake, Webb Hayes caught a large trout and, without moving from his position, flipped it into a hot spring and cooked it. On the other hand, neither Webb nor Crook cared to discuss a morning encounter that brought them rushing, exhausted, into camp. The most they would say was that they came upon a grizzly bear and Crook, separated from the bear only by a large rock, crawled up to get a shot, using a rifle borrowed from a soldier. According to Bourke, "Genl. Crook took a careful aim, pulled trigger, the cartridge failed to explode and. . . . "

That having been said, Crook changed the subject, commenting, "The scenery was the grandest I ever saw in my life."

"But, General," someone said, "tell us about the Bar. Did he run you into camp?"

"The scenery," Crook repeated, "was the most beautiful man every looked upon. Why, Sir, there are springs up there which are rivers, Sir. Rivers."

"But, General, how about the Bar?"

"The scenery," Crook said, now growing very red in the face, "was grand, but I am too hungry to talk about it now. Let me have some lunch."[27]

Despite the conviviality of the western tour, the Ponca situation remained. Judge Dundy's ruling had relieved the government of immediate responsibility for Standing Bear's band. No longer wards of the government, they were not allowed to settle on the reservation and so had to stay on an island in the Niobrara River, depending for their survival on the charity of the Omaha Committee. Meanwhile, the Poncas in the Indian Territory had grown accustomed to their new surroundings and were becoming uneasy at the idea of another relocation, even if it meant returning to their homeland. The fact was, there was nothing to which they could return. On the Dakota reservation, the old agency buildings had been demolished, as had most of their homes, and a shift in the Missouri River had eroded much of the good farmland on its banks. In the Territory, however, they had new homes, rations, livestock, and farm equipment. They had recovered from the trauma of the move, and the birth rate now exceeded the death rate. Once again, the tribe was growing.

In October 1880, the Ponca chiefs from the Indian Territory notified the Interior Department they wanted to visit Washington. Schurz made the arrangements and, in early December, they met with President Hayes, advising him that their people were willing to surrender their reservation in Dakota and remain in the Territory. This brought charges from the extremists that Schurz was manipulating the chiefs.

The controversy was polarizing Indian affairs to such a degree that President Hayes decided to appoint a special commission to travel to the Territory and investigate the Ponca situation there. First, he arranged with the Boston Committee to accept its recommendations for up to half the commission members, provided the committee cover their expenses. For his part, lack of a contingency fund to compensate commission members forced Hayes to look to the army or the Interior Department for government representatives. On December 10, the president summoned Crook to Washington to meet with him "in regard to the Ponca Indians." Five days later Crook arrived in the capital, where he had dinner with the Hayeses and General and Mrs. Grant. The following day, Hayes named him chairman. Besides Crook, the commission was composed of Nelson Miles, now brigadier general, representing the army; William Stickney of the Board of Indian Commissioners for the Interior Department; and the Boston Committee's man, Walter Allen of Newton, Massachusetts, who also served as Washington correspondent of the *Boston Advertiser*.[28]

Despite Crook's chairmanship and the Boston Committee's input, Helen Hunt Jackson was unimpressed. "For God's sake," she wrote Sen. Henry Lauren Dawes of Massachusetts, chairman of the Senate Indian Committee, "don't let that Committee go, as it stands. Carl Schurz has organized it—not a man in it can be absolutely trusted not to be either hoodwinked or influenced, except Gen. Crook—& possibly Walter Allen.—I don't know him.—Gen. Crook is an army officer—and must be silent, as he has been again & again or lose his commission. He loves the Indians & is their true friend—but he can't serve them now. . . . No Govt. Committee—met by Govt. Agents, and *their selected interpreters,* will ever know the truth. That is just the way these Poncas have been cheated before."[29]

Mrs. Jackson's misgivings notwithstanding, the commission began its hearings in Washington on December 24, when its members and Interior Department officials met with the visiting chiefs. Then, on January 5, 1881, they began hearings with the Poncas of the Territory. Instead of whitewashing the government, the members were determined to get at the facts, and without outside influence. Only commissioners, members of the tribe, and interpreters were allowed; those "connected with the Interior Department, and not members of the tribe," were excluded. Miles asked especially pointed questions. He pushed the agent into conceding that the Poncas on the reservations of the Territory had the right to consult legal counsel, and asked the chiefs specifically about the death rate. Nevertheless, the conference upheld the existing notion that the Poncas of the Territory had adjusted and preferred to stay. After completing their work in the Territory, the commissioners continued to Nebraska, where Standing Bear and his associates were equally adamant that they would not return.[30]

Despite those findings, the commission's final report blistered the government's removal of the Poncas, saying that it had been undertaken with ineptitude and mismanagement, and caused "great hardships and serious loss of life and property . . . without sufficient cause. It was also without lawful authority, inasmuch as the law requiring the consent of the Indians as a condition precedent to their removal was overlooked or wholly disregarded."

Even so, Crook, Miles, and Stickney accepted the view that those living in the Territory, 521 in all, preferred to stay there and be allowed to remain, although they suspected that it was largely because they had given up all hope of ever regaining their homeland. Likewise, they recommended that the 150 or so who had returned to Nebraska and Dakota be allowed to exercise their preference and remain there.[31]

In a one-man minority report, Allen dissented in the question of the Poncas of the Territory. "It is proper to inquire," he wrote, "first, how far this decision is to be regarded as a free determination."

> Had they a fair chance to make a choice? Did they have an uncompelled option in the matter? Had the government ever informed them that they could return to their old homes if they wished to do so? It had done no such thing. . . .
>
> Careful questioning discovered that they understood that the agreement they had made would give to them in the Indian Territory all the proceeds of the sale of the old reservation, and that the Poncas in Dakota would not share the proceeds unless they came to live in the Indian Territory.

In other words, Allen was stating that the Poncas in the Territory were being paid to stay put.[32]

Secretary Schurz likewise had come to believe that his insistence on removing the Poncas to the Territory had been a mistake, and was working to rectify
the situation. He submitted a draft of recommendations to President Hayes,
who revised them and presented them to Congress on February 1, 1881. They
included preparing the Indians for citizenship by offering a general education
to the young of both sexes; allocating land to the Indians "in severalty, inalien-
able for a certain period"; awarding fair compensation for lands not required for
individual allotments, to be held in trust for their benefit; and granting full citizenship with all rights and responsibilities.

"The time has come," Hayes told Congress, "when the policy should be to
place the Indians as rapidly as practicable on the same footing with the other
permanent inhabitants of our country." The cause was taken up by Senator
Dawes, who six years later would secure a severalty act that was to be the first
step on the long, torturous road to full citizenship.[33]

For Crook, the Ponca Affair was pivotal. Throughout most of his life, he had
regarded civilian Indian rights advocates as meddlesome and impractical. He
would spend his last decade as one of their most influential supporters.[34]

FIFTEEN

ARIZONA

"Justice to All—Indians as Well as White Men"

Aᴌᴛʜᴏᴜɢʜ 1880 ᴜsʜᴇʀᴇᴅ ɪɴ ᴀ ᴘᴇʀɪᴏᴅ of relative quiet in the Department of the Platte, Crook's image as an Indian fighter got a new boost. A year earlier, Charles King had been invalided out of the army because of wounds received in the Nez Perce War in Idaho—the first of several retirements that would punctuate his seventy years of military service. Seeking to supplement the $2,100 annual retirement pay, King accepted an offer from the *Milwaukee Sentinel* to write a series of articles on life in the Fifth Cavalry during the Great Sioux War. The *Sentinel* reprinted the articles in a paperback pamphlet entitled *Campaigning with Crook: The Fifth Cavalry in the Sioux War of 1876*. Ten years later, in 1890, Harper and Brothers of New York republished it in book form together with three of King's short stories under the title, *Campaigning with Crook and Stories of Army Life*. King's glowing account, along with Bourke's *On the Border with Crook* and correspondent John F. Finerty's Sioux War memoir, *War-Path and Bivouac*, all of which are still in print, are largely responsible for Crook's image as the Spartan, modest, taciturn Indian fighter.[1]

In the Platte, meanwhile, the interval of tranquillity meant that Crook's responsibilities to the government were primarily administrative. Not only did this allow time to indulge in hunting and fishing, but time to develop his business interests as well. Throughout his career, Crook looked for ways to supplement his army salary. As a young lieutenant in California, he had invested in a ranch, and continued to be involved to some extent in ranching the remainder of his life. He also looked for other opportunities.

One of his ventures was a gold mine, an investment that lured many men of moderate means in the nineteenth century West. In his case, it was the Murchie mine near Nevada City, California, named for five brothers who discovered it in the early 1850s. The mine had never paid well enough to justify extensive operations and, in 1861, the Murchie brothers established a mill that proved a better investment. Nevertheless, in January 1880, Crook was ready to have a go at the gold mine and, with Sheridan, Bourke, King, Gen. Delos B. Sacket of Chicago, and several others, he formed a consortium to lease it. A corporation was established with Andrew Snider, former post trader at Fort Ter-Waw and one of Crook's hunting partners, as president. Walter Schuyler, who was due a substantial amount of leave and had great hopes for the mine, went to oversee the operation. He was accompanied by Oliver Crook, the general's nephew, who later told Martin Schmitt, "General Crook was an easy mark, Colonel Schuyler a would-be mining operator, and both of them, with very high salaries, died broke."[2]

Schuyler's first impressions were hopeful, which was good because some of the stockholders apparently had put all their available funds into the project, and would have had trouble coming up with another assessment. A rosy report was also good for Crook because, despite Snider's titular position as president, the general's letters to his furloughed aide leave little doubt that he was the moving force behind the scheme. On March 11, Crook told Schuyler, "While working the mine endeavor to give a good impression to outsiders as to the value of the property & in the mean time get all the statistics of the mine and those of the neighborhood, total yield of the County both from Ledge & Placer & everything that will so to show that our property is in one of the best localities in the Country &c. This may all be useful in trying to sell our property in the future."[3]

The history of the mine so far was not good. Under the Murchie brothers, yield had sometimes reached as high as $17 per ton of ore, but more often was closer to $5 a ton, and extending the shaft to a depth of a hundred feet was no more profitable. By the time Crook and friends got involved, the shaft had been pushed to three hundred feet, without enough yield to justify the expense.[4]

At this point, Sacket intervened, having been convinced to invest in a new method for extracting more gold from the same amount of ore. Known as the Maynard Process for Extracting Gold and Silver from Refractory Sulphurets, it was touted by an acquaintance of Sacket, Charles Knap, who had purchased three-quarters of the rights from the inventor, a Professor Maynard. Sacket not only believed that this would save the Murchie investment, but urged Crook to lease other mines in the vicinity.[5]

Schuyler was first to realize where all this was leading and began looking for a way out. He believed at least $50,000 would be necessary to put the mine on a paying basis. When Crook wrote to him in April suggesting they shut down the mill, Schuyler apparently hoped this meant abandoning the property entirely, but Crook was adamant that the mine must continue operating. Grasping at straws, Schuyler lobbied first for a transfer to Arizona, and then to China, but Crook would have none of it because "the Murchie holders here have great confidence in your integrity & judgement & none more so than Gen. Sheridan." This was not the type of news that a lieutenant, suddenly worried about his future, needed to read, particularly with his leave now extended for the economic benefit of the two generals who controlled that future. Crook pointedly mentioned this, telling Schuyler, "You have not suffered a particle in reputation by your connection with the mine, but should you leave it now, it would leave room for hard things to be said about you, besides I doubt if Gen. Sheridan would help you in the matter just now."[6]

Crook, meanwhile, investigated the Maynard Process, and the samples assayed at $30.74 a ton in New York. Encouraged, the stockholders came up with the money for another assessment. Crook warned, however, that the resources of some were already strained to the limit. Several had borrowed money to pay for this one, and he said it could not be done again.

On July 27, Sheridan, who had little patience for figures, grew tired of trying to decipher Schuyler's weekly reports, and sent Crook a list of questions about the operation. The letter caught Crook in the middle of an inspection tour-cum-camping trip, and he passed Sheridan's inquiries on to Schuyler to handle.[7]

All the while, the hapless lieutenant struggled on. By December, the shaft had reached four hundred feet and made a strike. Crook was overjoyed, writing that the news "has made us all feel good here, Bourke builds all kinds of 'Castles in the air' & can hardly wait the arrival of regular reports."[8]

The excitement was short-lived. More money would be needed, and it wasn't available. In March 1881, underground operations were suspended, and the ore already mined was processed. The end of the year brought a profit of fifteen thousand, which paid off the debts but did not allow dividends to the shareholders. As the principal player in the scheme, Crook found his position particularly embarrassing and, true to form, he looked for a scapegoat. The obvious candidate was Schuyler, and on December 31, Crook sent him a confidential letter from New York. "I think it better, all things considered, that you resign your position as A.D.C. I write you this now in order that you may assign your own reasons for the step. I was in hope of seeing you here so as to explain, but I leave this morning for Washington on my way West. Please present my kindest regards to your Father & Mother & rest of the family."⁹ With that, Schuyler was out, and Crook went out to California himself to close the mine. Some sort of friendship apparently remained, however, because after Crook's death Schuyler inherited part of his diaries and some of his papers.¹⁰

Crook continued to hunt and fish with his friends whenever their schedules could be coordinated with his. He invited Rutherford Hayes to join him at Fort Bridger for a trip to Yellowstone in July or August of 1881, but the former president's calendar was already full. Nevertheless, Crook wrote Hayes hoping that he would be able to break free at a later date "as you will always find me in hand for any kind of recreation or business within the limits of my Dept. unless Indian troubles should prevent[;] if you should like with a party to visit the 'National Park' I can fit you out nicely[.] all that is necessy is to let me know a little before hand."

Meanwhile, the recent attempt on the life of Hayes's successor, President James A. Garfield, by a disgruntled office seeker "cast a gloom over the whole country." Repeating local gossip, Crook told Hayes, "It is said here that the Mormons secretly rejoice over it, but I have no means of ascertaining its correctness, as they are a closed corporation on such questions."¹¹

Garfield died of his gunshot wounds and was succeeded by his vice president, Chester A. Arthur. A few months later, in late 1881 and early 1882, Crook's supporters began lobbying the new president for his appointment as major general. Although there were no openings at the time, a petition to Arthur from the congressional delegates of most of the Western territories urged him to consider Crook "in case of vacancy." The cause was also taken up by several senators and representatives of western states.¹²

Crook himself was testing the waters to determine his prospects. He was particularly interested in General Grant's views because, despite his lackluster performance as president, he still had great influence in the army. Discussing the situation with Webb Hayes, he wrote, "I think it wise for your Father to see Grant in person, because writing before knowing how he stands might do harm. I wish your Father could see Gen. Sheridan, as I know of no one who could get the information better than your Father. Secretary Lincoln [Robert Todd Lincoln, secretary of war] would doubtless have considerable influence in the matter. Gen. Sheridan & I are on good terms, but I have no means of knowing how he stands on the subject of this promotion."

A month later, he sent Webb a few more thoughts. He said that John Hay, prominent attorney and friend of Abraham Lincoln, the secretary of war's father, "is a good Card if properly marked & I have no doubt but what he understands just what to do." Several officers were senior to Crook, including Howard, Terry, Pope, and Brig. Gen. Irvin McDowell. Although Crook did not mention Howard or Terry, the failures of McDowell and Pope during the Civil War were common knowledge, and he believed Grant would not support them.[13]

Crook's effort met serious opposition. Within the army, many officers were frustrated by his accolades, most of which they thought—with good reason—to have originated with Bourke. Toward the end of March, a printed, unsigned flier was circulated, purportedly expressing the views of "Eighty Six Officers of the Army." The identity of the author or authors is unknown, but it contained enough "insider" information, and long-standing service-related resentment to suggest that it indeed came from within the officer corps. A copy found its way into Crook's file in the Adjutant General's Office.

New York,
March 29th 1882

To his Excellency
The President of the U.S.

Being officers of the Army we are debarred from expressing opinion respecting the promotion of a meritorious officer, and from protesting against the advancement of an unworthy one; consequently we are compelled to appeal to you.—our Commander in Chief—anonymously, hoping the serious nature of our subject may lead you to pardon this breach of decorum.

We learn from the press of the country that the name of Brig. Genl. George Crook is being mentioned to you, for your favorable consideration in filling the [next] vacancy in the list of Major Generals.

We would most respectfully call your attention to the fact that this officer was advanced to his present rank from the grade of *Lt. Col.,* to the prejudice of every Colonel of the line!

We further beg leave to inform you that this promotion was made by your Excellency's predecessor, Genl. Grant, the cause of whose mistake in this instance was *credulity!*

He believed the articles which were constantly appearing in the different journals of the country to the credit of Genl. Crook, were reliable. Had he known that those puffs were penned by a *staff officer* of Genl. Crook's, and that they contained statements which were wholly untrue, and which were contrary to the opinion and knowledge of every officer of the Army, we feel he would have hesitated before making that honorable distinction.

Had Genl. Merritt preferred charges against Genl. Crook (as he should have done) in 1876, for the imbecility he exhibited during his campaign against Sitting Bull, he would not now figure as an aspirant to promotion.

Doubtless the "many letters" you receive favoring this officer, emanate—as of your [sic]—from his headquarters; and we earnestly beg of you to maturely consider our protest before taking a step which would do much injustice to many worthy officers.

It is disgraceful that he should belong to the Army at all! But it would be insulting, should his imbecility and dishonesty be rewarded by promotion.

We remain, your Excellency's

Most Ob'd't Servants,

EIGHTY SIX OFFICERS OF THE ARMY,[14]

The situation was further complicated in April, when an obscure officer of the Third Cavalry at Fort Fred Steele attempted to file charges against Crook. The officer, Capt. John P. Walker, was then under arrest following a protracted quarrel with the post commander, Maj. A. W. Evans, Third Cavalry. The previous December, Walker had filed charges against Evans for "arbitrary and cruel treatment" of a private in Walker's troop. No action had been immediately forthcoming and, on March 21, Walker sent a letter to departmental headquarters demanding to know the status of his complaint against Evans and accusing the departmental command of discrimination against him.

Now that he was under arrest, Walker turned on Crook, charging him with neglect of duty. Specifically, he contended that Crook delayed action on his charges against Evans without ordering trial, and had failed to answer his inquiries into the matter. The complaint was forwarded to Omaha, where Crook endorsed it to the effect that Walker was a chronic agitator who had been shrewd enough, until recently, to avoid charges. Walker, he continued, had submitted many previous complaints, most of which were filed away at departmental headquarters "simply to prevent annoyance to the War Department." In Chicago, Sheridan shrugged the whole matter off with the comment, "It should be remembered that this officer, Captain Walker, was for some time an inmate of the Insane Asylum."[15]

No further action appears to have been taken. Nevertheless, Walker's charges, together with the flier from the "Eighty-Six Officers," indicated that the long-simmering dislike for Crook within the army was becoming more open. When all the recriminations were done, however, it really made no difference. There were no vacancies among the major generals and none were foreseen in the immediate future.

During Crook's entire tenure in the Platte, the Apache situation in Arizona deteriorated to an alarming degree. Although sporadic raiding had continued throughout the 1870s, the coming of the railroad did much to pacify the territory, and the improved transportation had rendered several military posts redundant. Consequently, a new series of outbreaks surprised many citizens who had come to believe their territory was relatively safe.

Part of the trouble was due to conflict between the military, which had rounded up the Apaches and put them on the reservation, and the civilian agents now responsible for them. Far worse, however, was the fact that the government continued the policy of removal and concentration that Crook had protested in Arizona in 1874. Washington intended to remove virtually all Apaches from their various familiar reservations in Arizona and New Mexico, and concentrate them at San Carlos where, as Bourke sourly observed, "the water is salt and the air poison, and one breathes a mixture of sand-blizzards and more flies than were ever supposed to be under the care of the great fly-god Beelzebub."

The policy was designed by the bureaucrats to bring peace by keeping all the Apaches in one place, in part to educate them and make them into the white definition of "productive citizens," and in part so that the government could keep an eye on them. But as Apache Wars historian Dan Thrapp noted, it had the opposite effect. Resentment of the removal was at least partly responsible for the ensuing outbreaks by the Warm Springs Apache chief Victorio, and the Chiricahua leaders Geronimo, Nana, Chato, and Chihuahua.[16]

Throughout the late 1870s, the Apaches at San Carlos simmered. Sporadic raiding broke out, largely to ease the monotony of reservation life. It culminated in September 1879, when Victorio and several followers rampaged and headed west into the mountains. Within a few months they were joined by more than three hundred Chiricahuas and Mescaleros, and the war spread from Arizona into Mexico, New Mexico, and Texas. Victorio was killed with much of his band by Mexican troops in October 1880, but the remnant, under Nana, continued the raids. Never having more than forty or fifty warriors, the ancient, rheumatic Nana wreaked havoc across the Southwest for another year, tying up hundreds of troops and ad hoc citizen militiamen, and inciting other discontented reservation Apaches.[17]

The defining moment of Apache-government relations came on August 30, 1881, when a detachment of troops and Indian scouts from Fort Apache under

Eugene Carr, now colonel of the Sixth Cavalry, arrested Nakai'-dokli'ni, a medicine man and a prophet who preached a message of Apache renaissance. The scouts were nervous. Their trusted commander, Lt. Charles Gatewood, was on leave, and his place had been taken by the less familiar Lt. Thomas Cruse. Their first sergeant, Alchise, a son of Cochise and himself a subchief, also was absent. And, like other Apaches, the scouts had been affected by the religious excitement centered around Nakai'-dokli'ni. Realizing their loyalties would be severely strained, Cruse advised Carr to leave the scouts at the fort. Ignoring the suggestion, Carr took them along, and the medicine man was taken into custody without incident at his camp on Cibicu Creek, about forty-five miles northwest of the fort. That night, however, as the troops settled down in their camp, Nakai'-dokli'ni's followers moved in. In the ensuing fight, the unthinkable happened—several of the scouts turned on the soldiers. When the shooting stopped, Nakai'-dokli'ni was dead, and eight whites were killed or mortally wounded. Because the scouts who had opened fire on the troops were technically soldiers themselves, they were charged with mutiny. Three—Sgts. Dandy Jim and Dead Shot, and Corporal Skippy—were hanged at Fort Grant, and two others were dishonorably discharged and sentenced to long terms in the military prison at Fort Alcatraz, California.[18]

The Cibicu fight unleashed pent-up hatreds on both sides. A few hours after Carr's troops returned to Fort Apache on the afternoon of August 31, Indians fired into the fort itself and, very briefly, the post was under siege. Over the coming weeks, roving bands murdered soldiers and civilians wherever they were found. On the white side, the incident created panic in the Southwest, and strengthened the notion that no Apache could be trusted. Although Brig. Gen. Orlando Willcox, commander of the Department of Arizona, successfully put down a new outbreak, many of the Apache leaders were still on the loose. The raids continued, citizens were organizing their own militias, and the reservation Indians were restless. In Bourke's opinion, "no military department could well have been in a more desperate plight." The government decided a change was needed, and in July 1882, Crook was ordered back to Arizona.[19]

After closing out his affairs in Omaha, Crook formally assumed command of the Department of Arizona on September 4. One of his first acts was to reaffirm his faith in the Apache scouts. "The great difficulty in the solution of the Apache problem," he wrote to divisional headquarters, "is in catching the Indians, which if done at all must be mainly through their own people." That said, he mounted his favorite mule, Apache, and started for the reservations. The Indians, he believed, realized the power of the federal government and the overwhelming demographic superiority of the whites. They knew they could never drive the whites from their country, so if they did go to war, there had to be other reasons. He wanted to meet with them and learn those reasons, and determine the extent of the problem.[20]

At San Carlos, Crook initially found the Apaches "sullen and distrustful," but after berating them for their lack of trust, they agreed to talk. Meeting with him privately, under the assurance that nothing they said would be put into writing, they spoke freely. Several of the scouts involved in the Cibicu mutiny were still at large, and when he raised the subject, the Indians insisted the attack was premeditated by the white soldiers, and that at least one of the scouts hanged at Fort Grant had been unjustly condemned. Although Crook did not necessarily believe them, they were so adamant that he felt it better to forego any further attempts to arrest and punish scouts. Given the overall circumstances of the fight, he believed that if the Indians had seriously meant trouble "not one of our soldiers would have gotten away from there alive."

As for the general unrest, Crook noted, "They all agreed that affairs could not well be worse, that one officer of the govt. would tell them one thing and another, something else, until finally they lost confidence in everybody and not knowing who or what to believe lent a credulous ear to every story which Mexicans or other irresponsible parties throughout the country concocted: they were constantly told that they were to be disarmed and then they were to be attacked as at Cibicu." Climate, lack of adequate food and water, and the inefficiency of the agents were other complaints. As a partial solution, he recommended closing the reservation, and relocating the Apaches "in places congenial to their dispositions and more healthful for them." There they could be allocated property and taught to farm, and fed until they became self-sustaining.[21]

The loss of confidence disturbed Crook, who prided himself on the trust he engendered among the Indians. One of his first priorities was to restore that trust. On October 5, he issued General Orders No. 43, which stated in part:

Officers and soldiers serving in this department are reminded that one of the fundamental principles of the military character is justice to all—Indians as well as white men—and that a disregard of this principle is likely to bring about hostilities, and cause the death of the very persons they are sent here to protect. In all their dealings with the Indians, officers must be careful not only to observe the strictest fidelity, but to make no promises not in their power to carry out; all grievances arising within their jurisdiction should be redressed, so that an

accumulation of them may not cause an outbreak. . . . When officers are applied
to for the employment of force against Indians, they should thoroughly satisfy
themselves of the necessity for the application, and of the legality of compliance therewith, in order that they may not . . . allow the troops under them to
become the instruments of oppression.[22]

The agent at San Carlos, Joseph C. Tiffany, had very little grasp of the situation. Although he often has been accused of being in league with a "Tucson
Ring" of businessmen who made money from bloated agency contracts, he
may have been more incompetent than corrupt. He also was an autocrat reminiscent of the cruel Victorian schoolmaster of a Dickens novel. He attempted
to suppress Apache customs and ceremonies, jailed Indians for trivial offenses,
and was not above slapping or kicking them. The abuses were such that, within
a few weeks of Crook's arrival, Tiffany became the subject of a federal grand
jury investigation. The grand jury report was, as Thrapp noted, a rare instance of
white men censuring a white man for mistreating Indians. It was also an endorsement for those who felt the reservations were better off under military control.[23]

The report, printed in the *Tucson Star,* stated in part:

> The investigations of the Grand Jury have brought to light a course of proce-
> dure at the San Carlos Reservation under the government of Agent Tiffany,
> which is a disgrace to the civilization of the age and a foul blot upon the
> national escutcheon. While many of the details connected with these matters
> are outside our jurisdiction, we nevertheless feel it our duty, as honest American
> citizens, to express our utter abhorrence of the conduct of Agent Tiffany and
> that class of reverend [s]pecultors who have cursed Arizona as Indian officials,
> and who have caused more misery and loss of life than all other causes
> combined. We feel assured, however, that under the judicious and just manage-
> ment of General Crook, these evils will be abated, and we sincerely trust that
> he may be permitted to render the official existence of such men as Agent
> Tiffany, in the future, unnecessary. . . . For several years the people of this
> Territory have been gradually arriving at the conclusion that the management
> of the Indian reservations in Arizona was a fraud upon the Government; that
> the constantly recurring outbreaks of the Indians and their consequent devas-
> tations were due to the criminal neglect or apathy of the Indian agent at San
> Carlos; but never until the present investigations of the Grand Jury have laid
> bare the infamy of Agent Tiffany could a proper idea be formed of the fraud
> and villany [*sic*] which are constantly practised in open violation of law and in
> defiance of public justice.[24]

Apathy and neglect, as least where Indians were concerned, were not criminal offenses, and Tiffany never was convicted of any crime. Nevertheless, he was replaced by P. P. Wilcox of Denver. Crook sized up the new agent, and quickly established a good working relationship. Wilcox was inept but honest, and while he disliked Indians, he was determined to do his best. His best seemed to consist primarily of leaving the operations of the agency to his capable clerk, Col. S. B. Beaumont, who cooperated with the military and made certain the Apaches received their due.

Among other things, Beaumont informed the military authorities that the scales used to weigh beef deliveries had never been checked. A test revealed them to be overweighted so that each week the contractor was paid for about 1,500 pounds more beef than was delivered. It was also discovered that the contractor allowed the cattle to go thirsty for day or so before delivery, then watered them on the way to the slaughter pens to boost their weight at the time of sale. "The Government," one officer observed, "was paying a pretty stiff price for a half a barrel of Gila River water delivered with each beef."

Such close scrutiny of reservation supply contracts brought calls from the local business community for Wilcox's removal. The fact that his appointment was political, as was Tiffany's, automatically gave him additional enemies among Tiffany's political allies. Newspapers were pro-Tiffany or pro-Wilcox, depending on editorial policy. Rallying to the agent's defense, Crook wrote Secretary of the Interior Henry Teller, "Mr. Wilcox has to contend against a nest of the vilest bummers, men for whom no words in the dictionary are too strong, the remnants of the old Indian ring of this Territory, who never made an honest penny in their lives, but grew fat on the proceeds of Indian hostilities. These men are vampires who gorge themselves on the blood of their fellow creatures, & no[w] still hang about the San Carlos Agency, and so long as one is there to be found just so long are you going to have trouble."

Crook also sent a letter to U.S. District Attorney J. W. Zabriskie, encouraging him to clamp down on corruption. Telling Zabriskie that it was easier to prevent outbreaks than to put them down, he said the only way to avoid trouble was for legal authorities to take action "against the villains who fatten on the supplies intended for the use of Indians willing to lead peaceful and orderly lives."[25]

The emphasis on weeding out corruption was part of a general reorganization of the department. One of Crook's first acts was to overhaul the pack trains, which were in deplorable condition. To save time assembling troops in an outbreak, he closed several small subposts, and concentrated their soldiers in larger garrisons. He also restructured the scouts, doubling their number to 250. One company was placed under the experienced Lieutenant Gatewood of the Sixth Cavalry, and the other under Capt. Emmet Crawford, Third Cavalry. Crawford knew little about Apaches, but he learned quickly, and his bearing, courage, and nobility soon won their confidence.

A count at San Carlos and Fort Apache showed 1,400 males capable of bearing arms. Taken together with about five hundred Chiricahuas and Warm Springs Apaches, who had been in Mexico since leaving the reservation the previous spring, the potential for trouble was obvious. To better control those on the reservation, Crook ordered every male able to bear arms to wear a metal tag inscribed with his number and the letter of his band. All were to be enrolled according to the information on their tags, with roll calls every few days. When not on active duty, scouts would return to their bands, keeping their officers informed of the mood and activities of the bands.

"So complete has been the success of this system," Crook wrote in his annual report, "that I am confident it would be impossible for an Indian to leave the Reservation, or to commit any outrage or depredation, without my being informed of the fact very soon afterwards." He also noted that these measures had been taken with the "hearty co-operation" of Agent Wilcox.[26]

While Crook's mandates may have helped control the Indians on the reservation, the great problem lay with those who were off, particularly the Chiricahuas who were depredating in Sonora from strongholds in the Sierra Madre. "The Mexicans," he wrote, "do not seem to be making much headway against this particular band which is likely at any moment to return across the border." Although a recent convention between the United States and Mexico allowed the military forces of either country to cross into the other in pursuit of Indians raiders, he saw very little improvement because "we can only follow Indians on hot trails, whereas to ensure success campaigning against them must be incessant."

To get the most accurate information, he organized a detachment of spies or "secret scouts." The official record of these parties is very sketchy, but according to Lt. Britton Davis, Third Cavalry, who commanded those at San Carlos, the detachment consisted of five men and two women. Two of the men were assigned to Gatewood at Fort Apache, with the remainder at San Carlos. Besides keeping an eye on the reservation Indians, they would go into Mexico, mingle among the Chiricahuas, and learn their locations, numbers, plans, and other information. They generally reported to Gatewood or Davis through Al Sieber, Archie McIntosh, Sam Bowman, and Mickey Free, the latter an Irish-Mexican boy captured in 1860 and reared by Apaches. Davis, who was born in Brownsville, Texas, spoke Spanish, as did some of the Apaches. They often preferred to deal directly with him rather than go through Mickey Free who, with one foot in each camp, was trusted by neither the whites nor the Apaches. Sieber described him as "half Mexican, half Irish and whole son of a bitch."[27]

Throughout the remainder of 1882 and the opening months of 1883, Crook was able to report quiet in Arizona. Depredations continued in Sonora, and the Mexican consul at Tombstone complained they originated with Apaches leaving San Carlos "for the purpose of invading the State of Sonora." Matias Romero, the Mexican minister to Washington, protested to the U.S. government that Crook was not adequately controlling them. In reply, Crook wrote:

> The Indians committing the outrages from time to time reported in Sonora and Chihuahua, are a band known as the Chiricahuas, who under their leaders Ju[h], and Hieronimo [sic] broke out from the San Carlos in April last year, just 5 mos. before my return to this Dept.
>
> They have since remained in the Territory of Mexico and have been the occasion of much damage to the unfortunate people living within the scope of their murderous raids.

He noted that, under General Howard's agreement with Cochise in 1872, they had been "specially exempt" from his jurisdiction. He had opposed this exemption at the time and, he mentioned pointedly, his predictions that it would lead to trouble had proven correct. After enumerating his efforts to control the Apaches at San Carlos, he pointed out that most of the Mexican allegations were based on unsubstantiated reports in the Tombstone newspapers. Then he took another swipe at the Tucson Ring, which he blamed for the false reports.

> Interested parties have often been at the bottom of these falsehoods; of these persons it is useless for me to say a word, they are jackals preying upon human flesh and making a pittance from wars and rumors of war.
>
> Peace is abhorrent to their ghoulish natures, and if they cannot have a genuine Indian outbreak, they can at least start baseless reports of Indian outrages.[28]

The calm on the U.S. side ended in early March, when Chato and Geronimo led a large raiding party out of their stronghold in the Mexican Sierra Madres. Once on the move, they separated into two parties. Geronimo took about fifty into Sonora, killing large numbers that included Americans employed at the mines and ranches, driving hundreds of rural residents into the larger towns, and completely paralyzing business in much of the state. Chato, meanwhile, led twenty-six into Arizona to obtain ammunition. Chato's band crossed the border near the Huachuca Mountains on March 21, and that same evening killed four whites about twelve miles southwest of Fort Huachuca. Over the next two days, five more were killed before the band scattered to frustrate pursuit parties. Reassembling miles away, they crossed into New Mexico, killing several people on the way. On March 28, Chato's band stumbled across Judge Hamilton C. McComas, his wife, Juniata, and their six-year-old son, Charley, traveling in a buckboard from Silver City to Lordsburg. The parents were killed, and Charley was carried off into captivity.

The raid created an uproar. Crook concentrated his troops into southern Arizona. Gatewood's scouts were sent to Fort Huachuca, while Crawford was told to try and head the raiders off at the border. Davis's scouts would secure San Carlos. Because the crisis involved two territories in separate military divisions, General Sherman ordered Ranald Mackenzie, now brigadier general in command of the District of New Mexico, to disregard divisional boundaries and work with Crook.[29]

On March 31, Crook received a telegram from divisional headquarters stating, "Instructions just received from the General of the Army authorize you under existing orders to destroy hostile Apaches, to pursue them regardless of department or national lines, and to proceed to such points as you deem advisable. He adds that General Mackenzie's forces will co-operate to the fullest extent."[30]

Crook, meanwhile, had telegraphed his counterpart in the Sonoran capital of Hermosillo, asking for information on the movements of the main Chiricahua band in Mexico, and inquiring about the disposition of Mexican troops "so that we may fully co-operate against the savages."[31]

Back at San Carlos, there was a new development. The night before the McComas killings, one of Chato's band, a White Mountain Apache named Pe-nal-tshn (sometimes called "Tzoe"), deserted and made his way to the reservation, where he was arrested by Lieutenant Davis. Eager to get any information on the bands loose in Mexico, Crook ordered Pe-nal-tshn taken to Willcox, where he personally interviewed the Apache. Pe-nal-tshn, whom the soldiers called "Peaches" because of his light pink complexion, insisted that when the Chiricahuas bolted the reservation, he had accompanied them only because his two wives were among them. Both women had been killed in a fight with the

Mexicans and, with no further incentive to stay, he had accompanied Chato's band as a virtual prisoner. He managed to escape during the night, and made his way to San Carlos. Whether Peaches was telling the truth, or whether he simply wanted to return to the reservation and downplayed his involvement in the raids, is debatable. Whatever the case, he became Crook's indispensable scout in the ensuing campaign.[32]

Peaches provided invaluable information about the Chiricahuas in the Mexican Sierra Madre, and Crook began formulating plans for a campaign. After conferring with Mackenzie in Albuquerque, he took the newly completed Sonoran Railway to Guaymas and Hermosillo to confer with the Mexican authorities. Meeting first with Maj. Gen. Bonifacio Topete, in charge of Apache operations in Sonora, then jointly with Topete and his superior, Maj. Gen. José Guillermo Carbo, as well as the governor of Sonora, Maj. Gen. Luis Torres, Crook was assured of their cooperation.[33] As a representative of his government, General Carbo pointed out that he could not grant Crook permission to cross the border on an extended campaign in defiance of the treaty. On the other hand, he said that if the U.S. forces found it necessary, he would not object, provided Crook had his Indian scouts wear some sort of identification, and notified General Topete of his intentions. Crook replied that, henceforth, his Apaches could be recognized by red headbands. After a lavish dinner in their honor, Crook and his staff boarded the train, returning to the U.S. before their Mexican hosts could renege on the commitment.

Crook next went by way of El Paso to the city of Chihuahua, where he met with Col. Luis Terrazas, who had defeated Victorio, and with Brig. Gen. Ramon Raguero, Governor Mariano Samaniego, and Mayor Juan Zubrian. Like the officers in Sonora, those in Chihuahua "received me most cordially and gave assurances that they would in every possible way aid in the subjugation of the Chiricahuas, who had for so many years murdered and plundered their people as well as our own."[34]

In Washington, the authorities were having second thoughts about the order to disregard national lines. Although the Mexicans in Sonora and Chihuahua might "recognize that a literal construction of the terms of [the] present convention between the U.S. and Mexico, will bring about failure in the settlement of pending Indian hostilities," the government in Mexico City was another matter. Minister Romero appeared amenable to military action, but the convention was then being renegotiated, and the U.S. was eager to avoid any confrontation. On April 28, Secretary of War Lincoln instructed Crook through General Sherman that "*no* military movements must be made into, or within the Territory of Mexico" contrary to the existing agreement, which meant no action for any reason other than active pursuit of a specific raiding party. The message was delivered to Crook at San Bernardino Springs, on the international boundary. He replied, "It is my intention to start tomorrow morning in pursuit of the savages in accordance with the treaty," an outright lie because he was hunting the entire Chiricahua population rather than pursuing a band of raiders.[35]

Already, he had made his final deployments "to guard the rear and flanks, and protect the settlers of Arizona from counter raids during our absence," and on May 1, he crossed the border. He would be on his own, completely out of communication for forty-one days. The bulk of the fighting force was the 193 Apache scouts commanded by Crawford, with the assistance of Gatewood and Lt. J. O. Mackay, Third Cavalry. Sieber was chief scout, assisted by Sam Bowman and Archie McIntosh. Mickey Free and Severiano, a Mexican raised by Apaches, were interpreters. The only regular troops were a company of Sixth Cavalry, consisting of forty-two enlisted men and two officers, a surgeon and a hospital steward, under command of Capt. Adna R. Chaffee. Crook's staff consisted of Bourke as adjutant, and Lt. Gustav Joseph Fieberger, Corps of Engineers, aide-de-camp. The packtrain was comprised of more than 350 mules. True to form, Crook also took a correspondent, A. Frank Randall of the *New York Herald*.

"This force," Crook wrote, "was the maximum which could be supplied by the use of every available pack animal in the Department, and the minimum with which I could hope to be successful in the undertaking upon which I had engaged. We had supplies, field rations, for sixty days, and one hundred and fifty rounds of ammunition to the man." To reduce baggage, officers and men carried only such clothing and bedding as was absolutely necessary, and instead of keeping up their own messes, the officers shared the food of the packers.[36]

The command moved down the San Bernardino, a branch of the Yaqui River, following a trail that Peaches said was made by the Chiricahuas. The whole country had been devastated, and large areas of what had once been cultivated land was now overgrown by mesquite and cane. Footprints of Chiricahua moccasins became commonplace, showing the tribe roamed the area with impunity. By contrast, the trails of Mexican mule trains indicated close guarding by soldiers. On May 6, Crook's command passed through the villages of Bavispe, San Miguel, and Basaraca, where they were welcomed "with exuberant joy." He observed: "The condition of these little Mexican communities was deplorable. Apache attacks were to be looked for at any moment. No man would venture far away from the vicinity of his own hamlet. All the available force of the settlements was constantly on the alert watching for an enemy as cunning, as stealthy and bloodthirsty as so many Bengal tigers." The local authorities offered their own people as well as four guides familiar with the foothills of the Sierras. Crook declined, however, in part because transportation and supplies were not available, and in part because he had more confidence in his own scouts.

Two days later, the command entered the Sierra Madre and began moving eastward up the canyons, past the ruins of ancient civilizations. As they marched, the troops began to see scattered plunder from the raids in Mexico, such as dresses, saddles, bridles, letters, and commodities. At one point, the Chiricahuas had burned the grass, and the command marched ten miles before reaching forage and water. The trail wound up the face of a mountain, forcing the men to dismount. The ten miles took twelve hours. Five mules lost their footing and plunged into a ravine. Three were killed outright and two had to be shot. They came to an abandoned camp that Peaches said had been their stronghold while he was with them. On May 10, the troops covered only nine miles. Still the trail was growing fresher, beaten down by the hooves of stolen horses and cattle. Before long, it became littered with carcasses of freshly slaughtered steers and horses, and occasionally they would see live animals wandering about.

The next day, Peaches said they were nearing the stronghold of the Chiricahuas. The scouts held a conference with Crook and pointed out that the pack train was falling behind. They proposed that the white troops stay with the train while they moved ahead. Crawford and his officers took 150 dismounted scouts with provisions for four days. They were accompanied by Sieber, his assistants, and the interpreters. If they came on a party of hostiles, they would kill as many as possible and take the rest prisoners. If they found a fortified position, they were to attack and send back to Crook for the soldiers. A few hours later a runner returned with a message from Crawford to move the command ahead about fifteen miles, where there was an excellent campsite on a tributary of the Bavispe River.[37]

The troops remained in the camp, resting men and animals. "Crawford, with the tireless scouts and himself as tireless, is still ahead," one officer wrote in his diary. On May 14, another courier arrived with a message from Crawford to bring the supplies up the trail nearer to his camp. He said he had found signs indicating he could surround the Chiricahua stronghold, and "was satisfied that the hostiles do not know of Crook's presence in the Sierra Madres." Rations were sent ahead to Crawford, and the command moved out the next morning.

They had gone six miles when yet another courier approached and handed Crook a note, which read, "15:h—1:10 P.M.—Indian scouts ran upon one buck and ten squaws and killed them before I intended to attack the camp, but I must now. Crawford." About the same time, they heard gunfire far ahead. Crook ordered Chaffee to mount his men and ride to Crawford's aid. A short time later, the gunfire died out. The command pushed on, making camp after night-fall as the scouts began drifting back with stories of the fight.[38]

Crook's official report states that the scouts captured a camp belonging to Chato and Bonito. The bodies of nine hostiles were found, although Crook noted that the rugged country provided ample shelter for Chiricahua snipers, so that a thorough search was impossible. Five "half-grown girls and young boys" were captured in the fight, along with about forty horses and mules. There was ample evidence of raids on both sides of the border. Besides what Bourke called "traditional riffraff of an Indian village,"—saddles, bridles, meat, mescal, blankets, and clothing—the soldiers found gold and silver watches, a couple of family albums, and $2,000 in U.S. and Mexican money. Correspondent Randall wrote that one of the albums contained pictures of the McComas family.

The camp was destroyed, but now Crook faced a dilemma. He could not hope to chase down those who had escaped because every rock provided cover for snipers who could destroy the command piecemeal. He could either return to the United States with what had been accomplished so far and try again later, or he could accept a surrender if it were offered. The Chiricahuas them-selves provided the answer on May 17, by sending up a smoke signal. Six women came in, but Crook told them that he would only discuss terms with the men.

A woman prisoner said there had also been a white boy about six years old called "Charlie," captured in Chato's recent raid, who had run away with the old women when the scouts attacked. To the soldiers, this could only mean Charley McComas. The woman said if she were allowed to follow them, she could bring back the whole band, including "Charlie," within a couple of days. She was given enough hard bread and meat to last two days, and sent back out, accompanied by one of the Chiricahua boys.

Early the next morning, Chihuahua came in. "He is not a chief," Crook reported, "but is one of the most prominent men of his tribe, noted for intel-ligence and bravery.... He told me where the different chiefs were raiding." Like the woman, Chihuahua said Charley McComas had run off when the attack started, but had been "alive and in good spirits."[39]

On May 24, several captive Mexican women and children came into camp. Taken on a raid in Chihuahua, and abandoned after the attack, they had been living on garbage around the abandoned camps. The women said that during their captivity, they had been worked, beaten, and raped. Still, there was no sign of Charley McComas or his body. He simply disappeared and, despite unconfirmed rumors over the years, was never heard from again.[40]

Back in the United States, the ominous silence from Mexico led to wild speculation. Hearsay abounded that Crook's command had been slaughtered. A report from Tombstone said the scouts had mutinied and precipitated the massacre. The *Boston Globe's* headlines trumpeted:

CANBY, CUSTER, CROOK

Slaughter of the Third Indian
Fighter and His Men.[41]

Meanwhile, unaware that the newspapers had declared him dead, Crook was winding down the campaign. After Chihuahua's surrender, "the Chiricahuas came in rapidly from all points of the compass—men, women and children. All the chiefs surrendered, gave themselves up." How this was accomplished is not known. Bourke is silent on the matter, other than to say that one night during supper, Geronimo "was ushered in to have a talk with General Crook." There is some speculation that Crook might have initiated the parleys by going up into the mountains alone and personally meeting with the chiefs. This might account for subsequent stories that Crook had been captured and gave generous terms in exchange for his life. Whatever the case, his prisoners ultimately included Geronimo, Chato, Bonito, Loco, Cochise's son Naiche (whom Crook always called "Natchez"), and Ka-e-te-na (i.e., Cayetano), a Mexican Sierra Madre Apache whom none of the soldiers or scouts recognized. The only leading chief missing was Juh, who had quarreled with the others and departed the camp before the attack. When the chiefs told Crook they wanted to make peace, "I replied that they had been committing atrocities and depredations upon our people and the Mexicans, and that we had become tired of such a condition of affairs and intended to wipe them out; that I had not taken all this trouble for the purpose of making them prisoners; that they had been bad Indians, and that I was unwilling to return without punishing them as they deserved; that if they wanted a fight they could have one any time they pleased." As an added threat, he said Mexican troops were moving in from both sides, "and it was only a matter of a few days until the last of them should be under the ground."

That said, he gave them several days to think it over. Finally, Geronimo led the others in and begged to be taken to San Carlos. After another lecture, in which Crook made a great display of thinking the matter over, he agreed to take them to the reservation. Geronimo, however, wanted to wait until all the Chiricahuas came in. Crook refused. He already had 384 prisoners and six Mexican captives, and his rations were becoming dangerously strained. Geronimo then said he wanted to go out and bring in those still hiding. Given the overall situation, Crook had little choice but to agree. But he told Geronimo that his party would have to overtake him on the trail, or "move along the mountains until they reached San Carlos," avoiding Mexican patrols on the way. He refused to give passes because if Geronimo's men were killed by the Mexicans, and the passes were found on their bodies, it could create diplomatic repercussions.[42]

The troops, scouts, and prisoners recrossed the border on June 12 to a tumultuous reception, mixed with relief. Every major community hosted dinners, and the victorious general was much in demand for newspaper interviews.[43] In contrast to earlier reports of mutinous scouts, the newspaper headlines now said:

A Hurrah for Crook—His
White and Red Soldiers.

———

Rejoicing Throughout Ari-
zona[44]

Among the congratulatory messages was one from Henry Heth, whom Crook had defeated at Lewisburg in 1862. "I have watched, with interest, your career for many years," Heth wrote, adding, "your deserved promotion as a Brigadier Genl: in the U.S. Army gave me [illegible] pleasure." Bringing up the old subject of Lewisburg, he added, "I know your prowess as a fighter." Franz Sigel, who now edited a German-language newspaper, sent an article he wrote about Crook's expedition, with the hope that someone in Crook's command could read German and translate it for him.[45]

Crook, meanwhile, took steps to ensure minimal official reaction from Mexico. A day after his return, and while still in the field, he wrote a letter of appreciation to General Topete for the "kind attention" the U.S. forces received in the Mexican villages. "This expression of friendliness, I attribute largely to your influence," he said. He concluded by assuring Topete, "and all the gentlemen with whom I have the good fortune to come in contact while in Sonora," of an equally hospitable reception in Arizona.[46] He also pondered the fate of his prisoners. He opposed the popular notion of bringing the most recalcitrant raiders to trial, saying, "Vengeance is just as much to be deprecated as a silly sentimentalism."

> To attempt to punish one or a dozen of the tribe for deeds of which all were equally guilty, would be a gross act of tyranny, while to attempt to punish *all* after they had surrendered in good faith, would be not only perfidious, but would involve us in a war with a small but desperate handful of men who would then fight with the recklessness of buccaneers under the black flag.
>
> The Chief is no more guilty than every member of his band, since he has often less influence than individual members, being merely their mouthpiece, or spokesman. To punish individuals guilty of particular crimes could be done, were it possible to get evidence, but from the nature of things this is impossible.[47]

Crook traveled to Washington to confer with Lincoln and Secretary of the Interior Teller, who signed a memorandum giving the military responsibility for policing the entire reservation. The outward show of cordiality covered disappointment that Crook had not brought in all the hostiles, particularly Chato and Geronimo. The western press charged that Crook's entire command had been captured during the campaign, and that he bought his way out by offering easy terms to Geronimo. Crook believed these allegations originated in an interview with Teller, which he took "as evidence that the Interior Department was not in sympathy with my views." The situation was aggravated when Agent Wilcox, who had assured Crook of cooperation, complained first that the agency Indians did not want the Chiricahuas at San Carlos, and then that the military presence undermined his authority. Bristling, Crook replied that the agreement between the two departments gave the military responsibility "under *direction* and with the *approval* of the Indian agent." Fed up with bureaucracy, he proceeded with the organization of agency police. Crawford was placed in complete charge, assisted by Gatewood. True to Crook's expectations, the remaining Chiricahuas soon began straggling in.[48]

The Sierra Madre Campaign had taken a toll on others besides Crook. Bourke's health was declining and a medical examination showed he was unfit for duty. On July 7, he began an extended leave, the first real time off he had had in fourteen years. On July 25, the long-time bachelor and staunch Roman Catholic married Mary Horbach, thirteen years his junior and the Episcopalian daughter of a prosperous Omaha businessman. The couple enjoyed a five-month wedding trip in Europe, and when Bourke returned to duty at Whipple Barracks, in January 1884, Crook noticed a definite improvement in his health.[49]

During Bourke's absence, there had been a shuffle in command. In the fall of 1883, General Sherman announced his impending retirement, which meant Sheridan would move up to command the army. Although Sherman's retirement would not become effective until the following February 4, he decided to vacate command on November 1, 1883, to give Sheridan time to settle in and prepare to represent the War Department when Congress reconvened at the beginning of 1884. The change meant a shake-up of the divisional commands, with Schofield moving to Chicago as commander of the Division of the Missouri, and Pope appointed major general to succeed Schofield in the Division of the Pacific.[50] Now Pope would be Crook's immediate superior.

SIXTEEN

GERONIMO

CHATO SURRENDERED ON FEBRUARY 7, 1884, and Geronimo arrived later in the month. Crook's annual report for that year was unusually brief, only ten printed pages, compared to forty-one for 1883. Calling the military situation in his department "eminently satisfactory," he wrote, "The last of the Chiricahua Apaches is now on the Reservation and, for the first time in the history of that fierce people, every member of the Apache tribe was at peace."[1]

Crawford essentially ran the reservation, assisted by Lt. Charles P. Elliott, Fourth Cavalry, provost; Lt. Franklin O. Johnson, Third Cavalry, quartermaster; Lt. Thomas B. Dugan, adjutant; and Dr. Thomas Davis, contract surgeon. Friction between the civil and military authorities continued, however, and Elliott wrote that the military "was a very unwelcome restraint upon the agents" in some of their nefarious business dealings with the civilian community outside of the reservation. "The discord at headquarters multiplied the difficulties, but Capt. Crawford had mastered them, and his watch over the agent and his employees was as strict as that over the Indians, and he allowed no interference with the police control of the reservation."

The only potentially serious problem was averted when, on a tip from Crook's Indian spies, the scouts arrested the Mexican Apache Ka-e-te-na for promoting dissention. He was tried and convicted by an Apache jury, and sentenced to three years on Alcatraz. When it was later suggested he might be paroled back to the reservation, Geronimo and Chato blocked the possibility on the grounds that he stirred up too much trouble.[2]

At Sheridan's behest, Crook addressed the graduating class at West Point on June 16, 1884. Reminding them that many would be sent to the Indian frontier, he offered advice that summed up his entire philosophy:

> Make them no promises which you cannot fulfill; make no statements you cannot verify. When difficulties arise, as they occasionally will, endeavor to be so well informed of all the circumstances of the case, that your action may be powerful and convincing . . . just and impartial. Let the Indian see that you administer one law for the both white-skinned and the red-skinned, that you do this without regard for praise or censure, and you will gain his confidence because you have shown yourself worthy of it.[3]

At the time Crook made this speech, there were "almost exactly" five thousand Apaches concentrated on the sixty-by-ninety-mile reservation at San Carlos. They had begun developing farms, the produce of which was sold to the garrisons at the reservation and at Fort Apache. Explaining the program to Herbert Welsh, corresponding secretary of the Philadelphia-based Indian Rights Association, he wrote, "No sermon that was ever preached on the 'Dignity of Labor' could print upon the savage mind the impression received when he sees that *work* means *money,* and that the exact measure of his industry is to be found in his pocket book."[4]

Although immense effort was spent constructing irrigation ditches, and there was a shortage of tools, the program was beginning to succeed. Some crops near Fort Apache were damaged by frosts, and those closer to the San Carlos agency were lost to high water in the Gila River. Nevertheless, Crook reported in 1884 that the Apaches had grown 3,850,000 pounds of corn, 550,000 pounds of barley, 54,000 pounds of beans, 20,000 pounds of potatoes, 50,000 pounds of wheat, 200,000 pumpkins, 50,000 watermelons, and 40,000 muskmelons, as well as onions, cabbage, and peppers. "The two Chiefs—*Geronimo* and *Chato*—who last year were our worst enemies—have this year made the greatest progress and possess the best tilled farms," Crook boasted.[5]

In November 1884, Agent Wilcox resigned and was replaced in December by C. D. Ford. The new agent promised Crawford assistance in expanding the farm program, and said he would cooperate wherever possible with the military. But no matter how sincere any agent might have been, the real problem lay in the determination of the Interior Department to wrest complete control of the Indians away from the military. As an employee of the Interior Department, Ford had to carry out its policies, and within a month, he and Crawford were feuding. Ford protested a project by the Yuma Indians to dig an irrigation ditch on the Gila River opposite the agency, and on January 17, he confiscated their picks and shovels. Crawford also reported that the chief of the agency police and the resident farmer were interfering with his duties "and talking to Indians in such a manner as to greatly weaken my authority on the reservation among Indians and employees. They are upheld in this course by the agent." Furious, Crook wrote General Pope, demanding "that either I be sustained in my administration or relieved from my responsibility [for policing the agency]." Pope passed the letter on to the War Department with the recommendation that Crook's authority be expanded.[6]

Crook's letter reached Washington at a time when the War and Interior Departments were conferring in an effort to achieve some sort of harmony. To facilitate discussions, the War Department advised Crook that he had exclusive jurisdiction over the Indians who had been captured or surrendered and were regarded as prisoners of war. His control over all other Indians, however, extended only to law enforcement, and did not include their farming activities, which were to be supervised by the agent. As for Crook's request that he be relieved from Indian supervision, the department said it "must in the public interest be held in abeyance for the present."[7]

Crook replied that since his authority had been undermined, he could no longer be responsible "for the behavior of any of the Indians" on the reservation. In San Francisco, Pope agreed, commenting, "If General Crook's authority over the Indians at San Carlos be curtailed or modified in any way there are certain to follow very serious results, if not a renewal of Indian wars and depredations in Arizona."

Crawford, meanwhile, realized that he could no longer effectively police the reservation. The public defiance of his authority by the police chief, and the curtailment of his power by the agent had cost him prestige and, by extension, the respect of his Apache charges. He requested that he be relieved at San Carlos and allowed to join his regiment, which was being transferred to Texas. Crook agreed, with the bitter comment that it was "better to place new people in charge than to continue the old management with emasculated powers." Captain Francis E. Pierce, First Infantry, was named to succeed him.[8]

Pierce lacked Crawford's experience with Apaches, and did not grasp the discontent that was already brewing on the reservation. There was no question that the majority of the Apaches desired peace, and that many of the past problems were caused by ill-considered government policies, as well as

inefficiency and corruption. The change in command at San Carlos frightened them because they believed that Crook, whom they feared but trusted,
had left them as well. The one licensed trader on the reservation took advantage of his monopoly to overcharge them, and there were allegations that
annuities were being held in the agent's warehouse at San Carlos while the
Apaches suffered shortages. Dissatisfaction was especially strong among the
Chiricahuas, who had spent generations at war in Arizona and Sonora. The
warrior tradition was too strong to be broken by a season or two of successful farming, and the curtailment of military authority diminished their
awe of the soldiers. In advocating his program as the only viable solution,
Crook placed too much faith in himself, and grossly underestimated the
Chiricahuas.

Britton Davis later attributed the problem to three small factions centered
around Mangus, a son of the great mid-century Apache chief Mangas Coloradas,
Chihuahua, and Geronimo. The complaints of Mangus and Chihuahua were
petty, and neither seriously wanted trouble. "Geronimo's dissatisfaction" Davis
wrote, "was deeper seated and far more serious."[9]

Even as he dealt with Indian problems, Crook had to make a major change
in his staff. After twelve years as aide-de-camp, Bourke felt the time had come
to move on. When he joined Crook in 1873, he had been an obscure young
officer with a highly developed curiosity about southwestern Indian culture. By
1885, however, he was a highly respected anthropologist, and a fellow of the
American Association for the Advancement of Science. Because Crook enjoyed
his company, he was kept on as aide-de-camp even though much of his time
was now spent on anthropological research. Herein lay the problem: Bourke
was concentrating on his own fieldwork at San Carlos or Fort Apache, even
though his rightful place was with the general at Whipple Barracks. This obvious favoritism created problems with the other officers, so that in May Bourke
asked to rejoin his regiment. He was assigned to command Camp Rice (later
Fort Hancock), a one-company cavalry post some fifty miles east of El Paso,
Texas. Captain C. S. Roberts, Seventeenth Infantry, who had served as Bourke's
assistant, now assumed the full duties as Crook's aide-de-camp.

Bourke's transfer was short-lived. Powerful easterners, including historian
Francis Parkman, Jr., believed he was more valuable to the government as an
anthropologist than as a soldier. At Parkman's behest, Secretary of War William
C. Endicott ordered Bourke to rejoin Crook in Arizona. He arrived at Fort
Bowie on October 17, in time to serve with Crook in what proved to be the
last campaign for both men—the Geronimo War.[10]

Like many Apache war leaders, Geronimo was an older man, in his early to mid-sixties. He probably was born in the early 1820s, near the upper Gila Mountains on the Arizona side of the boundary with New Mexico. He was a Bedonkohe Apache, part of the collection of tribes generally classed as Chiricahua. Although his own name was Goyahkla, the Mexicans called him Geronimo (Jerome), and eventually the Apaches themselves took it up. His family was prominent, and he was related by marriage to both Juh and Nana.

By Geronimo's time, Apaches and Mexicans had been fighting for generations. Murder and plunder were commonplace, and each side raided the other for slaves. About 1850, Geronimo's wife, mother, and three children were part of a group massacred by Mexican troops at Janos, in Chihuahua. From that point until the end of his life, Geronimo nursed a deep hatred for Mexicans, taking vengeance on them at every opportunity.

Initially, the Apaches had no quarrel with the United States, and confined most of their raiding to Mexico. But the development of mines in southern Arizona brought skirmishing between Apaches and miners, and troops were sent to subdue the Indians and concentrate them on reservations. The conflict culminated in the murder of Mangas Coloradas by soldiers under a flag of truce. Geronimo was one of the leading candidates to succeed him.[11]

What prompted Geronimo's outbreak from San Carlos in 1885 is uncertain. He believed Crook had abandoned them, and he feared for his life—those were among the excuses he later gave. Undoubtedly, he did feel insecure in the unfamiliar world of the reservation. Boredom almost certainly was a factor, as was vanity. He was an active man. Raiding offered excitement, and gave power and prestige. Whatever the reasons for Geronimo's behavior, they were aggravated by alcohol. The Apaches were manufacturing *tiswin,* the native liquor brewed from corn or barley. Crook had prohibited the industry, saying it "not only developes their worst and most brutish qualities, but when indulging in it they barter or sell anything in their possession for it." He noted the renewed manufacture as "an unmistakable sign of dissatisfaction."[12]

On the morning of May 15, the leading chiefs and subchiefs appeared before Davis's tent with about thirty of their followers. They claimed to have spent all night drinking, although Chihuahua was the only one who appeared visibly drunk. No women or children were present, which meant they had something serious on their minds. The scouts gathered in groups of four or five with their carbines. Defiantly, the chiefs aired grievances about regulations prohibiting *tiswin* and wife-beating. The undercurrent, however, was fear of the future and uncertainty about whether Crook actually was in command.

Davis assured them that Crook still was definitely in charge, and he would telegraph their grievances and ask for instruction. Then he wired Captain Pierce at San Carlos:

> There was an extensive tiswin drunk here last night, and this morning the following chiefs came up and said that they, with their bands, were all concerned in it: Geronimo, Chihuahua, Mangus, Natchez, Fele and Loco. The who[le?] Business is a put up job to save those who were drunk. In regards to the others, I request instructions. The guard house here is not large enough to hold them all, and the arrest of so many prominent men will probably cause trouble. Have told the Indians that I would lay the matter before the General, requesting at the same time, that their captives in Mexico [i.e., members of their band held by the Mexicans] be withheld. I think they are endeavoring to screen Natchez and Chihuahua.[13]

Had Emmet Crawford still been in charge, he would have taken some sort of immediate action that would have impressed the chiefs without unduly upsetting them. Pierce, however, was unsure of himself, and went to Al Sieber for advice. Sieber was sleeping off his own all-night drinking and gambling binge. Exhausted, nursing a hangover, he read the telegram and handed it back to Pierce with the remark, "It's nothing but a tizwin drunk. Don't pay any attention to it. Davis will handle it." Then he went back to sleep. Pierce pigeonholed the telegram, and it was months before Crook learned of it.[14]

On the night of May 17, Pierce telegraphed Crook that Geronimo, Mangus, and their followers were preparing to leave the reservation. He planned to depart immediately with enough troops and scouts to head them off. Before Crook could reply, however, the telegraph line between San Carlos and Fort Apache was cut. By the next afternoon, after service was restored, Crook learned that Geronimo, Mangus, Nana, Naiche, and Chihuahua had left at dark the previous day, pursued by two companies of Fourth Cavalry under Capt. Allen Smith, and White Mountain and Chiricahua scouts commanded by Gatewood and Davis.

Crook ordered all available troops into the field, and alerted Col. Luther P. Bradley, commander of the District of New Mexico. Telegrams went out to all the newspapers in the region to warn citizens. Troops were told to follow the trails and disregard departmental and international boundaries. Having heard the Chiricahuas were heading toward the Black Range in New Mexico, Crook himself traveled to Fort Bayard near Silver City, New Mexico. His official reason was that Fort Bayard was more conveniently located for directing troops in southeastern Arizona than the posts in Arizona itself, which was true. New Mexico, however, was not in his department, nor even in the Military Division of the Pacific; but it was part of the war zone, and Crook assumed de facto command on the assumption that ultimately he must be given formal jurisdiction of the entire region.

In twenty-three days of hot pursuit, from the time of the outbreak until Geronimo entered Mexico, the Chiricahuas had the advantage. Two years of peace had stimulated development of ranches, and the Indians could find plenty of food to steal and stock to replace their worn-out ponies. The soldiers, on the other hand, were restricted to their government-issue mounts, and had to carry rations. "The vigor of the pursuit may be understood from the fact that probably more than one hundred and fifty horses and mules were found on the different trails, which had been worn out and killed or abandoned by the Indians in their flight," Crook reported.

The Chiricahuas, meanwhile, had separated. Naiche and Chihuahua, realizing their mistake, intended to take their people back to San Carlos but, finding their way blocked by troops, turned about. Now committed to the outbreak, Chihuahua resumed raiding, cutting a swath of destruction through southern Arizona and New Mexico, and committing many of the depredations for which Geronimo later was blamed. Elsewhere, Geronimo had crossed into Mexico, and was taking his people back up into the Sierra Madres.

On June 5, after it became obvious that the Chiricahuas were retreating toward Mexico, Crook went to Deming, New Mexico, east of Lordsburg, to prepare an expedition to follow them. Crawford was transferred back, and took his scouts and a company of cavalry down toward the Guadalupe Mountains of Texas. Davis, who had been following the trail with his White Mountain and Chiricahua scouts, was ordered to report to Crawford. On June 11, the combined command, consisting of ninety-two scouts and a company of Sixth Cavalry, crossed into Mexico and headed toward the Sierra Madres.[15]

Crawford's command was soon augmented by a second expedition under Capt. Wirt Davis, Fourth Cavalry, with his own company, a hundred scouts, and pack trains with sixty days' rations. Working separately, the two groups would comb the Sierra Madres and adjacent ranges, attempting to surprise the hostiles in their camps.

Crawford's scouts were in fine form. They had their trusted first sergeant, Alchise, as well as Ka-e-te-na, whom Crook brought back from Alcatraz because the hostiles trusted him and he might be useful in negotiations. That, as it turned out, was an excellent decision. "He is thoroughly reconstructed," Crook later

wrote, "has rendered me valuable assistance, and will be of great service in helping to control these Indians in the future. His stay at Alcatraz has worked a
complete reformation of character."

On June 23, a detachment of Crawford's scouts, led by the now-loyal Chato,
hit Chihuahua's camp in the Bavispe Mountains. Because of the terrain, Chato
could not surround the camp, and most escaped, but the scouts did capture fifteen women and children and several horses, and recovered a substantial amount
of plunder. Elsewhere, Wirt Davis's scouts located and attacked Geronimo's
camp in the Sierra Madre. Another fifteen women and children were captured.
Davis hit another camp on September 22, losing one of his scouts in the
ensuing fight.

The pressure in Mexico drove the hostiles back into the United States, pursued by Wirt Davis and Crawford. The animals of both the hostiles and the
soldiers were giving out, but the Indians managed to steal fresh ponies from a
camp of cowboys on a fall roundup. Well mounted, they crossed into Mexico,
while the soldiers had to return to their bases for remounts. This was one of
several instances where the hostiles were nearly run down but managed to get
fresh animals by hitting ranches, and Crook blamed the ranchers for their lack
of caution.[16]

Throughout the fall, the troops chased the Indians more or less in circles
across Arizona, New Mexico, and the northern Mexican Republic. Stock raids
became so chronic that Crook complained the Indians could steal with virtual
impunity. In November, the situation deteriorated even further when Josanie,
reputedly a younger brother of Chihuahua, crossed the border into New
Mexico. In the first few days, his band created havoc, killing both whites and
friendly Indians. Then, for three weeks, they remained quiet, until November
23, when they were seen within a few miles of Fort Apache. They cut the telegraph wire from the fort, then struck San Carlos, killing several reservation
Apaches. This was done, presumably, to punish those who remained peaceful
and to frighten more Indians into joining them. Their only setback came on
December 9, when they were attacked by a company of Eighth Cavalry and
ten Navajo scouts under command of Lt. Samuel Warren Fountain. Although
Fountain inflicted no casualties (he initially thought he had), he did capture
fifteen horses and all their supplies. Josanie retaliated by stepping up his depredations. Remounting his men with stolen horses, he lured Fountain into a trap,
killing five of his men and wounding two.

By the time Josanie recrossed into Mexico near the end of December, his
followers had killed thirty-eight American settlers, about twelve reservation

Indians, and an unknown number of Mexicans. As far as is known, he lost only one member of his band, killed by White Mountain Apaches near Fort Apache.

Josanie's raid created an uproar. It was particularly embarrassing for Sheridan, who was defending Crook against accusations that he was not doing enough to run down the hostiles. Sheridan believed San Carlos was a base for marauders, and trouble would continue as long as the Apaches remained there. He advocated closing the reservation and moving all the Indians elsewhere. Before taking any action, however, he traveled west to confer with Crook. Picking up Colonel Bradley in Santa Fe, he arrived at Fort Bowie on November 29. Emmet Crawford, who was preparing to take two hundred scouts out to hunt for Josanie, was called into the conference and vehemently opposed any effort to close down the reservation. He said the services of his Apaches were essential to any campaign, and it would be impossible to ask them to scout for him when their families were being uprooted and driven from their homes.

Sheridan decided to put the idea of closing the reservation on hold. He did transfer New Mexico from the Department of the Missouri to the Department of Arizona, giving official sanction to what Crook essentially had already done. They agreed on a more aggressive policy toward chasing the Indians into Mexico, and strengthened Crawford's force.[17]

Crawford and Wirt Davis continued their operations in Mexico. Now, however, a new complication arose. General Torres, the governor of Sonora, complained to Crook that Crawford's scouts were harassing Mexican nationals. On January 11, Crook sent a message to the governor, expressing his regret if any trouble actually had arisen, and promising Torres that he would forward the dispatches to Crawford for an investigation and whatever action was necessary.

Unfortunately, the protests were too late for Crawford. A day earlier, after an eighteen-hour march, his scouts located Naiche's camp situated among the rocks about fifty miles southwest of Nacori, Sonora. Despite its nearly impregnable position, the four companies of Indians deployed so as to nearly surround the camp. Near daylight, some of the burros in the Chiricahuas' herd began braying, and three hostiles came out to check on them. They saw the soldiers and exchanged shots. The scouts opened up from every side, forcing the Chiricahuas to flee the camp. After a two-hour running fight, the hostiles sent in a woman who said Naiche and the others would come in for a talk the next morning. Crawford agreed, knowing the hostiles had lost their food, camp equipment, and animals, and had little choice but to surrender.

At daylight, before the hostiles could come in, the scouts began shouting an alarm. Suddenly gunfire erupted. Crawford's second in command, Lt. Marion

P. Maus, First Infantry, thought Wirt Davis's scouts had attacked by mistake, and he ran out to stop them. He then discovered it was a detachment of troops from Chihuahua. Although the Americans waved white handkerchiefs and identified themselves in Spanish, the firing kept up for about fifteen minutes. When it stopped, Crawford and Maus went out about fifty yards toward them and explained who they were. The Mexicans assured them there would be no more shooting, and Crawford told Maus to go back and make sure the American scouts did not fire.

As Maus turned, the Mexicans fired another volley. He dove for cover, and when he looked out, Crawford was down. He had a head wound and part of his brain was spilled onto the rocks. Tom Horn, one of the company chief scouts, and two Indians scouts were slightly wounded, and one scout was severely wounded. In the return fire, the Mexicans appeared to have lost four killed and five wounded. "It is remarkable no others were shot," Maus wrote in his report of the fight. Noting that the Mexicans expressed regrets over what they considered to be an error in identification, he added emphatically, "*There can be no mistake; these men knew they were firing at American soldiers at this time.*"

Crawford died seven days later without ever regaining consciousness, and was temporarily buried in Mexico. Maus, meanwhile, had assumed command and reopened negotiations with the Chiricahuas. Their resistance was wearing down, and they were ready for Crook himself to come to Mexico for a meeting to discuss the future. For the time being, Nana surrendered along with several others, including family members of Geronimo and Naiche. As incentive for the others to come in, Crook got assurances from the civil authorities that Nana would not be prosecuted.[18]

Amid Crook's worries over Geronimo and his followers, the prospect of advancement appeared as General Pope neared his retirement date of March 1886. Based solely on seniority, General Howard was his obvious successor, followed by Terry. But Crook, who was third on the list, and Miles, who was fourth, had better records on the frontier. The Crook-Miles rivalry was aggravated on February 9, when Winfield Scott Hancock died unexpectedly, creating a second vacancy among the major generals. Ultimately, the appointments went to Howard and Terry, leaving Crook and Miles to marshal their efforts toward the next vacancy.[19]

Regardless of whether Crook moved up, Bourke began to consider his own future. Aware of the deteriorating relations between Crook and Sheridan, he understood that his continued association with Crook might adversely affect his own career. He now had his own professional reputation to guard, and he kept his options open with the Bureau of Ethnology. On March 22, he asked to be relieved as soon as he and Crook returned from Mexico, and requested assignment near a large library to facilitate putting his field notes into shape.[20]

The council with the Chiricahuas took place at Cañon de los Embudos, near the border in the northeast corner of Sonora. The hostiles were camped on a height about five hundred yards beyond Maus's camp, separated from it by a ravine. Arriving on March 25, Crook noticed that the Chiricahuas, "though tired of the constant hounding of the campaign, [were] in superb physical condition, armed to the teeth, and with an abundance of ammunition. In manner they were suspicious, and at the same time independent and self-reliant." Every major chief was present except Mangus, who had separated with his band several months earlier.[21]

Crook and his staff met with the Chiricahua chiefs after lunch. The confrontation had a new twist; it was recorded on camera by Tombstone photographer Camillus S. Fly, who moved about the group taking pictures and even asked Geronimo and the others to shift positions or turn their heads or faces. All the Indians cooperated except Chihuahua, who ducked behind trees. Bourke noticed that every man and boy wore two cartridge belts, and most were well dressed with new shirts and blankets. Geronimo was nervous. Sweat rolled down his face and over his hands, and he fidgeted with a leather thong he was holding.

Geronimo began with a list of grievances and excuses. Among other things, he said that Chato and Mickey Free had told him "that the Americans were going to arrest me and hang me, and so I left." He added, with some justification, that he was blamed for virtually every incident, regardless of whether he actually was involved.

Crook demanded to know what that had to do with killing innocent people on his raids. As for the camp rumors, he said, "There is not a week that you don't hear foolish stories in your own camp, but you are no child, you don't have to believe them. You promised me in the Sierra Madre that peace should last, but you have lied." He reminded Geronimo that he had defended him from the revenge and accusations of the whites. The hard feeling against Geronimo had almost died out when he broke out of the reservation, but now it was more bitter than ever. For that reason, Crook said, "the white people say I am responsible for every one of those people who have been killed."

"That's why I want to ask you who it was that ordered that I should be arrested," Geronimo replied.

"That's all bosh," Crook snapped. "There were no orders for anyone to arrest you."

The two leaders exchanged accusations awhile longer, and the first day's council ended with nothing settled.²²

Early the next morning, Bourke and several others wandered over to the Chiricahua camp. They noticed Geronimo was meeting with Ka-e-te-na and all the warriors. They argued all day, considering their options and the idea of unconditional surrender. Alchise and Ka-e-te-na moved among them, playing on their fears, encouraging their hopes, and setting factions off against each other. Crook, meanwhile, was considering his own options, and realized that if the Chiricahuas proved stubborn, they could hold out a long time in their camp, which was a natural fortress. He sent a message to Sheridan, explaining that surrender appeared unlikely unless they were allowed to return to their old status on the reservation. That night, Chihuahua offered to come down and surrender. Crook, however, asked him to remain with the Chiricahuas for the time being, foment dissent, and undermine Geronimo's position.²³

On March 27, Chihuahua sent a secret message to Crook saying he was certain all the Chiricahuas would surrender. They offered three options. First, if they were sent east to Fort Marion or some other internment post, their confinement would not exceed two years, and they would be accompanied by their families. Nana would be exempt and allowed to remain in Arizona because of his age. The second option would be to return to their old status at the reservation. If either of these was unacceptable, they would resume fighting. Whatever the others did, Chihuahua would bring his people down and surrender unconditionally at noon. Realizing he had to make an immediate decision, Crook agreed to the two-year internment.

When discussions resumed later that morning, Chihuahua opened by saying he wanted to return to the security of the reservation and live quietly. "Whenever a man raises anything, even a dog, he thinks well of it and tries to raise it right and treat it well," Chihuahua told Crook, "so I want you to feel toward me and be good to me, and don't let people say bad things about me. Now I surrender to you and go with you." He added that his people could decide for themselves if they would follow him back to San Carlos.

Naiche added, "What Chihuahua says, I say. I surrender just the same as he did. . . ."

Crook said he planned to return to Fort Bowie the next day, and would leave Alchise and Ka-e-te-na with the scouts to escort them to the fort. He advised them to depart the next day also, because there were no rations for them.

Chihuahua agreed to move as fast as he could, but claimed his livestock was in poor condition and could not travel fast. He added he would send word to Crook each day.

"All right," Crook replied. "Ka-e-a-te-na [*sic*] can write your letters for you."

This left Geronimo as the only holdout. Faced with the inevitable, he shook hands with Crook, saying, "I give myself up to you; do with me what you please; I surrender. Once I moved about like the wind; now I surrender to you and that is all."

Crook accepted the surrender amicably, but cautioned Geronimo about paying attention to rumors. "There are some people who can no more control their talk than the wind," he remarked.

Geronimo wanted to hear from Ka-e-te-na and Alchise on behalf of the scouts. Alchise said he was "a small man" whose words didn't matter. Ka-e-te-na begged off because of a sore throat.

When Crook replied that all statements would be put into writing so they would be binding, Alchise spoke on behalf of his erstwhile enemies. "They have surrendered," he said. "I don't want you to have any bad feelings toward them. They are all your friends now. . . . You are our chief. The only one we have. There is no other. No matter where you send these Chiricahuas, we hope to hear you have treated them kindly."[24]

When General Sheridan learned that Crook had agreed to a two-year confinement, he was furious. As far as he was concerned, Geronimo should have been turned over to civil authorities in Arizona, tried for his depredations, and—hopefully—hanged. Crook's report arrived at the worst possible time. His young wife, Irene, was critically ill with peritonitis, and for awhile her survival seemed doubtful. Although she did recover, Sheridan was still badly shaken when the surrender terms reached him, and his biographer, Paul Andrew Hutton, speculates that anxiety might have partly dictated his reaction.[25]

After conferring with President Grover Cleveland, Sheridan wired Crook, "The President cannot assent to the surrender of the hostiles on the terms of their imprisonment East for two years with the understanding of their return to the reservation. He instructs you to enter again into negotiations on the terms of unconditional surrender, only sparing their lives. In the meantime . . . you are directed to take every precaution against the escape of the hostiles, which must not be allowed under any circumstances."[26]

By the time that message had been drafted and sent, Sheridan's worst fears were realized. Before daylight March 27, Alchise and Ka-e-te-na woke Crook and told him that many of the Chiricahuas were drunk. During the night they had acquired mescal from a bootlegger named Tribollet, who operated just inside the border in Mexico. Hurrying to the Chiricahua camp, they saw, according to Bourke, "four or five Chiricahua mules, already saddled . . . wandering about without riders. Pretty soon we came upon 'Geronimo,' 'Kuthli,' and three other Chiricahua warriors riding on two mules, all drunk as lords."

At San Bernardino, they learned from Frank Leslie, Wirt Davis's chief scout, that Tribollet had sold thirty dollars' worth of mescal to the Chiricahuas in less than an hour. When Leslie called him on it, Tribollet boasted that he could have sold a hundred dollars' worth at ten dollars a gallon in silver. The bootlegger, apparently angry that his clientele was returning to military control on the agency, told them horror stories of the fate that awaited them at San Carlos, and that night, Geronimo, Naiche, and a small band of followers fled. Maus pursued them, joined on the trail by two returning Chiricahuas who apparently had second thoughts about escaping. After two days, the soldiers lost the trail in the mountains.

Crook had no doubt that Geronimo and Naiche had surrendered in good faith, and had fled because they were "filled with fiery mescal, and alarmed by the lies of a designing man. . . . " Nevertheless, the damage was done.[27]

This was too much for Sheridan, who was adamant that the scouts were as guilty as any of the marauders. He distrusted Indian scouts in the first place, and had taken a dim view of Crook's enlistment of them in the Great Sioux War. As for Apaches, the so-called Cibicu mutiny had only strengthened his suspicion that they could not be trusted. Now the escape of Geronimo seemed proof. "It seems strange," he wrote Crook in an initial draft, "that Geronimo's party could have escaped without the knowledge of the Scouts. I feel ashamed of the whole business." After reflecting awhile, he deleted the last sentence from the final dispatch. Nevertheless, his feelings were clear.[28]

Crook, however, would tolerate no criticism. "There can be no question that the scouts were thoroughly loyal and would have prevented the hostiles leaving had it been possible," he replied. "When they left their camp with our scouts they scattered over the country so as to make surprise impossible, and they located their camp with this in view, nor would they remain in camp at one time. They kept more or less full of mescal."[29]

Sheridan was running out of patience. He had spent much of the last fifteen years protecting this maverick who seemed to feel that he alone was capable of resolving the complicated question of Indian-white relations that had plagued the Americas for almost four centuries. His thirty-five-year-old friendship with Crook, so often strained in the past, was now nearing the breaking point. In a short, curt telegram, he told Crook he had received no acknowledgment of the president's instructions and demanded to know the prospects of recapturing the escapees.

To Crook, on the other hand, it seemed incredible that Sheridan could not understand what he had to deal with. The Apaches' position had been such that "a thousand men could not have surrounded them with any possibility of capturing them," he replied. "They were armed to the teeth, having the most improved guns and all the ammunition they could carry. The clothing and other supplies lost in the [June 23] fight with Crawford had been replaced by new blankets and shirts obtained in Mexico."

As far as Sheridan was concerned, this was simply another attempt at self-justification. He had visions of Geronimo cutting new trails of death and destruction throughout the Southwest. Crook had at his disposal forty-six companies of infantry and forty companies of cavalry, which Sheridan considered ample. He demanded to know what Crook intended to do with them.

Replying on April 1, Crook said, "I believe that the plan on which I have conducted operations is the one most likely to prove successful in the end. It may be, however, that I am too much wedded to my own views in this matter, and as I have spent nearly eight years of the hardest work of my life in this Department, I respectfully request that I may be now relieved from his command."[30]

Sheridan, likewise, felt it was time for Crook to go. Arizona was in chaos, and he was determined to bring the wars to an end. Crook's request for transfer was approved. He was assigned to the Department of the Platte, and Nelson Miles was appointed to succeed him.[31]

It was time for Bourke to go as well. Emmet Crawford's body had been exhumed and returned to the United States, and on April 2, Bourke boarded the train at Bowie Station to escort Crawford back to his home in Nebraska for burial. Then, after a reunion with his own family in Omaha, he continued on to Washington to prepare his report on Indians of the Southwest. He would never again serve under Crook.[32]

Bourke's arrival at Bowie Station coincided with the arrival of the first group of Chiricahuas. Sheridan ordered that they be transported to Fort Marion "under the terms directed by the President," which is to say their lives would be spared with no other conditions observed. He also pointedly told Crook, "The present terms not having been agreed to here and Geronimo having broken every condition of the surrender, the Indians now in custody are to be held as prisoners and sent to Fort Marion without reference to previous communications and without in any way consulting their wishes in the matter."

Crook, who would continue in command until Miles arrived, began making arrangements. He did not inform the Indians that President Cleveland had abrogated the surrender agreement because it would discourage any more hostiles from coming in and thus prolong the war. At 4 P.M., April 7, the first train, carrying Chihuahua, Nana, and Josanie, together with twelve other men, thirty-three women, and twenty-nine children, left Bowie Station for San Antonio on the first leg of the journey to Florida.[33]

On April 11, Crook turned the command over to Miles and, a day later, departed for Omaha. Miles began reorganizing and preparing for new expeditions, but the Chiricahuas struck first, devastating the Santa Cruz Valley in Arizona. Troops pursued them across the border, forcing them deep into Sonora. Over the next several months, soldiers and Apaches rode back and forth, and for awhile it seemed Miles would accomplish no more than Crook. Miles turned to Crook's Apache scouts to guide his troops, and on August 25, they led Gatewood to Geronimo's camp in Mexico. Gatewood delivered an ultimatum from Miles that if Geronimo surrendered, he and his followers would be sent with their families to Florida to await the president's decision on their future. Otherwise, the troops would fight them until a finish.

The old warrior was worn down from the constant pursuit, and faced increasing pressure from Mexican forces. On September 3, he met with Miles and capitulated. On Sheridan's recommendation, President Cleveland had decided that Geronimo and his followers be held in Arizona for trial before a civil court. Gatewood, however, had promised Geronimo his life, and Miles, like Crook, intended to honor the pledge. The hostiles were loaded on trains and started out of Arizona toward internment in Florida before the government or local authorities had time to dictate otherwise.[34]

Attention had already turned to the reservation Indians at San Carlos. Arizona was rapidly developing, and citizens were pressuring for the giant reservation to be opened for settlement. Miles agreed that the reservation, which he considered a haven for renegades, should be closed, and advocated relocation of the Indians to the Indian Territory. Sheridan and Cleveland, on the other hand, favored internment. Ultimately, the Indians of San Carlos, friendly and otherwise, were transported to Fort Marion, essentially as prisoners. They even included the scouts who, over the years, had done as much as any soldier to secure peace in the Southwest. Crook was enraged by the decision. Until the end of his life, he never forgave Sheridan or Miles.[35]

The citizens of Arizona honored Miles with banquets, balls, and a special presentation sword. Bancroft, who was completing his history of Arizona and New Mexico at the time, observed, "General Miles is the hero of the day, naturally, and justly to the extent that he has well performed his duty, but unfairly in so far as his service of a few months is made to outweigh the still more valuable work of Crook for years."[36]

Perhaps, though, the final word belongs to the Apaches themselves, and was best stated by old Juh's son, Asa Daklugie, "The thing that embittered Geronimo was the promise that Crook made as to his band's going east for two years and then being returned to their homes. . . . Crook was our enemy; but though we hated him, we respected him, and even my uncle thought he would keep his promise. I think that he was honest in his promise but that he was not permitted to keep it. . . ."

Regarding another general, Daklugie was emphatic, "If Crook was disliked, you should know how much more bitterly Miles was hated; he was regarded as a coward, a liar, and a poor officer. His claim for having captured Geronimo? If any man deserved credit for that, it was Lieutenant Gatewood. Did Miles come within any reasonable distance to confer with Geronimo? He stayed close to Fort Bowie."[37]

SEVENTEEN

DIVISION COMMANDER

EN ROUTE TO OMAHA, Crook was feted with receptions, received callers, and found the acclaim "very enjoyable."[1] Relieved at last from the burdens of Indian warfare and looking forward to primarily administrative responsibilities, he was coming out of his shell. His diary entries for the period show that he attended the theater, wedding receptions, and other social events.[2] During an inspection of Fort Niobrara, Nebraska, he wrote, "It was very pleasant to see so many old friends. Had a hop this evening which put me in mind of old times in Arizona."[3]

Mary's social activities, on the other hand, were beginning to diminish. She suffered from gout and neuralgia that occasionally confined her to bed. Sometimes she would attend a function, only to leave early.[4]

Crook's health likewise was failing. Throughout the fall and winter of 1885–1886, he complained in his diary of colds, headaches, and other ailments. He also had recurring malaria. On January 6, 1887, a medical examination revealed "heart enlarged & top of right lung affected." A year later, he wrote, "My chest hurt last night and I spit blood. [I] look wooden. . . . spit blood tonight again." He did not mention whether he consulted a physician for the pains and blood.[5]

Most likely, he was suffering a delayed reaction to the hardship and privation of the terrible summer of 1876. As he passed his sixtieth birthday, Crook was aging, but was not an elderly man even by the standards of his time. He had always been robust, and his passion for camping, hunting, and fishing kept him in excellent physical condition. But the Horse Meat March devastated those who had taken part in it. Bourke, who himself would die two weeks before his fiftieth birthday, largely from the aftereffects of the march, noted that within fifteen years more than half the officers who had participated in the campaign were no longer in the service. Most had been young men and career officers in 1876; the march simply wore them out. The sudden decline in General Crook's health may indicate that he too was joining that statistic.[6]

He apparently was beginning to consider his role in history, and how future generations might judge his actions. The near-disaster at the Rosebud was a particularly sore subject that, even after ten years, kept him brooding. He was furious when, in the summer of 1886, two Omaha papers attributed a statement to William Royall, now colonel of the Fourth Cavalry, that Crook took to be critical of his handling of the fight.[7]

The matter came to a head one night in August at his house in front of a group that included Guy Henry, who had been badly wounded in the fight, Capt. Cyrus S. Roberts of the Seventeenth Infantry, and Lt. Lyman Kennon, who had replaced Bourke as Crook's aide. According to an account in Kennon's diary, Royall was leaving and the others followed him out. He sat down on the steps and said to Crook, "These are all your friends, I suppose."

Henry replied, "I am Gen[era]l. Crook's friend, but no more than I am your friend[,] Col. Royall."

Crook then started in, "It has come to my knowledge from Washington and elsewhere, Col. Royall, that you have been going around the country making remarks and statements of a nature disparaging to me. This does not seem to me to be generous or in good taste. For ten years I have suffered silently the obloquy of having made a bad fight at the Rosebud, when the fault was in yourself and Nickerson. There was a good chance to make a charge, but it couldn't be done because of the condition of the cavalry. I sent word for you to come in, and waited two hours, nearer three, before you obeyed. I sent Nickerson three times at least. Couriers passed constantly between the points where we were respectively. I had the choice of assuming the responsibility myself for the failure of my plans, or of court-martialing you and Nickerson. I chose to bear the responsibility myself. The failure of my plan was due to your conduct."

Royall replied, "I have never had any reason to think my conduct at the Rosebud was bad. Nickerson came to me but once and then I moved as soon as I received the order." Turning to Henry, he asked, "Did I not move as soon as I could after Nickerson came, Col. Henry?"

"Yes, I think you did," Henry acknowledged.

"I was with the leading battalion," Royall continued. "I went with it where the enemy was thickest. I was not responsible for the scattered condition of the cavalry. As to what I said in the interview with the reporter, I did not mention your name." With that he produced the clipping.[8]

Backed into a corner, Crook let the matter drop. Very likely the accusations he leveled at Royall and Nickerson were an effort at self-justification. As Martin Schmitt noted in his addendum to Crook's autobiography, Nickerson's account of the fight never mentioned being sent after Royall. And considering how quickly Crook initiated charges against Reynolds, Noyes, and Moore after the botched fight on the Powder River, it is unlikely he would have hesitated in charging Royall and Nickerson after the Rosebud had he the slightest grounds for doing so. The allegation against Nickerson is particularly absurd when one considers the effort Crook had made for his promotion two years after the Rosebud.[9]

Later that summer Crook did order a court-martial for Maj. Frederick W. Benteen, Ninth Cavalry, commanding officer of the recently established post of Fort Du Chesne, on the Uintah River in Utah. Benteen was well known in the army. As senior captain of the Seventh Cavalry in 1876, he had commanded one of the surviving battalions at the Little Bighorn. Prior to that, he had headed the anti-Custer faction in the regiment, and continued to vilify Custer after his death. He was prone to drink (a trait not uncommon among frontier officers), and his bluntness and irascible disposition won him few friends.

Publicly at least, Benteen tended to blame Custer for the disaster at the Little Bighorn. Even so, historian John M. Carroll speculated that, privately, Benteen may have faulted Crook for retreating to Wyoming after the Rosebud, in effect leaving the Seventh to operate blindly in Montana, and that Crook may have resented Benteen as a "living reminder" of his failure on that occasion. Whether or not that was the case, there appears to have been some sort of preexisting animosity between the two men that ultimately led to Benteen's court-martial and suspension from service.[10]

The trouble began in 1886 when Benteen was ordered to construct Fort Du Chesne, to keep an eye on the Utes who had been relocated there from Colorado after the uprising of 1879. From the outset he had difficulty with the post trader, George H. Jewett, who also held various supply and construction contracts, and who boasted openly of "connections" at departmental headquarters in Omaha. The situation was reminiscent of the Powder River Expedition of 1876, when Dodge had problems with trader W. B. Adair, who supposedly had a private business arrangement with Crook. On January 3, 1887, the *Kansas City Times* published a letter purportedly submitted by "a member of the Ninth Cavalry belonging to one of the troops stationed at Du Chesne . . . having been discharged from the service by expiration of his term."

According to the letter, Crook himself had selected the site, a barren plot of land only ten miles from a much more suitable location. That done, he hastily departed, leaving the troops to their own devices. The letter also cited ineptitude by the departmental officers responsible for materials for the post and supplies and provisions for the garrison. The men did not have adequate food, shelter or clothing. Construction materials arrived, but without tools. Horses and mules were unshod, and the blacksmith had to cut up wagon tires and iron bed frames to make shoes. The letter went on:

> After months of delay, contracts were let. All the stoves at the post are coal burners, so the only fuel contracted for is wood, and rotten cottonwood at that to save $2 a cord, when the extra $2 would have purchased cedar. . . . There is plenty of fine timber about forty miles from there, but the only sawmills the government has sent them [are] old and worn out ones, not worth the price of getting them into that country. One of them has already blown up, killing one man and injuring two others. . . .

At Benteen's behest, the departmental inspector, Maj. R. H. Hall, Twenty-second Infantry, came to investigate and, according to the letter writer, placed the blame on Benteen himself.

> Were I in Major Benteen's place I would not rest until the whole matter was thoroughly investigated, not by any whitewashing board, but by an officer who is not dependent upon favors from department headquarters.[11]

The letter infuriated Crook. Although Benteen swore under oath he had nothing to do with writing it, there can be little doubt he was behind it. No soldier of the Ninth had recently been discharged at Fort Du Chesne, and Benteen was known to have written a similar letter blistering Custer after the Washita Fight of 1868. Four days after the letter was published, a court-martial board was ordered to try Benteen on charges of drunkenness on duty, with six specifications dating back almost four months to September 25, 1886, and for "conduct unbecoming an officer and a gentleman," specifically that Benteen had undressed to expose "his person" and used "obscene and profane language" during a quarrel with citizens in the post trader's store.[12]

The trial began at Fort Du Chesne on February 7, 1887, and lasted sixteen days. Benteen contended that he was a scapegoat because Sheridan had taken Crook to task for delays in completing the post. Crook then attempted to shift the blame to Benteen, and in early January had suggested, through Major Stanton, departmental paymaster, that Benteen might want to take a six-month leave of absence until the heat was off. After the letter was published in the *Kansas City Times,* however, Crook had been publicly embarrassed and decided to ruin Benteen. Based on these contentions, Benteen challenged the jurisdiction of the court "on the grounds that Brigadier General George Crook, commanding the Department of the Platte, who orders the Court, is virtually, nay, actually the prosecutor."[13]

The court ignored the objections, and the trial continued. Jewett himself served as a witness to Benteen's drunkenness, and the trader's name came up several times elsewhere. Benteen contended that Jewett blocked a competing bid for construction at the post, and had complained to Stanton that he could not keep his position as trader unless Benteen was relieved as post commander. During testimony, questions were raised regarding contractual dealings between Jewett and Second Lt. L. J. Hearn, post quartermaster. Hearn had been relieved of his duties, although the official explanation was that he was to be replaced by a more experienced officer.[14]

In the end, Benteen was found guilty of three of the six specifications on the charge of drunkenness. As for the second charge, although the court concluded he was not guilty of exposing himself, there nevertheless was enough evidence to convict him of misconduct for quarreling. He was sentenced to dismissal. The verdict and sentence went to Crook, who hinted that some clemency might be extended in view of Benteen's past service, but recommended "some discipline." Sheridan agreed, and passed the case on to President Cleveland, who changed the sentence to one year's suspension on half-pay. When the suspension ended, Benteen retired voluntarily.[15]

Whatever its implications, the Benteen case was an administrative matter, and with the Indians at peace in the Department of the Platte, administration was Crook's primary concern. Congress had finally allocated enough money to provide ammunition for regular target practice and Crook, with his enthusiasm for shooting, emphasized marksmanship. He believed drill should be modernized, with particular attention to campaign conditions in a particular locale. Soldiers on the frontier, he maintained, should be prepared to fight on the frontier. Yet as the frontier developed, and more amenities became available, those amenities should be available to soldiers. In his inspections, Crook noted that many posts which had once been adequate, and quarters which had been comfortable by local standards, were no longer suitable. As long as civilians increasingly had access to modern conveniences, he saw no reason these should not be made available to soldiers as well.[16]

The rights of the Indians were another issue that increasingly occupied Crook's attention. The time had come, he believed, to step up the assimilation process. He had not forgiven Miles and Sheridan for what he believed was a betrayal of his promises to the Apaches.[17] Justifying his own position in an article for the *Journal of the Military Service Institution of the United States,* he wrote, "The Apaches had such a deep-seated distrust of all Americans that four points of policy at once obtruded themselves. First, to make them no promises that could not be fulfilled. Second, to tell them the exact truth at all times. Third, to keep them at labor and to find remuneration for that labor. Fourth to be patient, to be just, and to fear not."[18]

He also put his views into a lengthy letter to the assistant adjutant general of the army, dated December 27, 1886, and incorporating page after page of official exchanges during the Apache campaign. The letter summed up his operations from 1882 to 1886, in which he particularly defended the Apache scouts, and he wanted it published in pamphlet form. Sheridan, however, advised Secretary of War Endicott that it simply was a restatement of old arguments, and contained little in the way of new information. "To publish the letter," Sheridan remarked, "would be merely to lay before the public a matter which there is no military reason whatever for bringing to their knowledge, and would re-awaken a discussion in the public press of a subject which now appears to have passed from their attention."[19]

Consequently, Endicott refused to authorize publication. Outraged, Crook wrote army headquarters, "Against this decision, I deem it my duty respectfully to protest. It is true as stated by the Lieutenant General, that the letter contained little in the way of military information not embodied in reports previously rendered. But it is also true that not all of these reports have been given to the public. As some of them that were published contained an implied censure of my acts, it seemed but simple justice that I be allowed to present the facts which justified my action. There can be no reason, military or otherwise, for the suppression of these material facts in a matter which has received a large share of public interest and attention."[20]

Eventually, the pamphlet was published as *Resume of Operations against Apache Indians, 1882 to 1886.* That, together with Crook's earlier Apache article in the *Journal of the Military Service Institution,* aggravated the hard feelings that already existed between him and Miles. Crook was determined that the Apaches should be returned as soon as possible from their exile in Florida. Miles, apparently feeling cornered by Crook's position, upheld the status quo, especially where Geronimo was concerned. In sending the old warrior to Florida, Miles contended he was carrying out a presidential order as an alternative to hanging him, an action that President Cleveland had bluntly stated he "would prefer."[21]

Crook was leaning more and more toward stating his views on Indian management in magazine articles, speeches, and other private outlets, because he had grown uneasy about putting them in official correspondence. Some of his views expressed in government documents had been extracted and published as his official opinion, although in conflict with the policies of the government. He did, in fact, support the franchise for the Indians, and in an essay on the subject, he wrote, "The American Indian is the intellectual peer of most, if not all, the various nationalities we have assimilated to our laws, customs and language. He is fully able to protect himself, if the ballot be given, and the courts of law [are] not closed against him."[22]

He got an opportunity to state publicly his position before a wide audience in February 1887, when the Boston Indian Citizenship Committee invited him to speak in a series of public meetings at the committee's expense.[23] Crook and Kennon arrived in Boston on February 23 and, after a tour of the city's historic sites, they met with members of the committee to plan Crook's speaking schedule and the appropriate publicity. Also present for the meetings were Thomas Henry Tibbles, and his wife, Susette La Flesche, also known as Bright Eyes, who was the daughter of an Omaha chief.

Crook's first lecture was scheduled for February 26 at Shawmut Church, but he had to cancel because he was ill. By the afternoon of February 28, he was able to speak at the Old South Church, in front of what the committee felt was a "good audience." Afterwards, he had dinner in Cambridge at the home of committee treasurer H. O. Houghton, then spoke again at Memorial Church, where the famed minister Edward Everett Hale presided.[24] Emphasizing the right of the Indian to be treated with the dignity due any human being, Crook told the audience:

> One question today on whose settlement depends the honor of the United States is, "How can we preserve him?" My answer is, "First, take the government of the Indians out of politics; second, let the laws of the Indians be the same as those of the whites; third, give the Indian the ballot." But we must not try to drive the Indians too fast in effecting these changes. We must not try to

force him to take civilization immediately in its complete form, but under just laws, guaranteeing to Indians equal civil laws, the Indian question, a source of such dishonor to our country, and of shame to true patriots, will soon be a thing of the past.[25]

The following day, Crook, Tibbles, and Bright Eyes spoke at the Unitarian Church in Wintonville. On March 2, Crook and Tibbles visited the Bunker Hill monument. That afternoon, they met with the committee to discuss what Crook called the "Florida matter," the internment of the Chiricahuas at Fort Marion. The committee's position, which Crook supported, was to give them a reservation where they could become self-sustaining. That evening, Crook spoke at a church in Springfield to "a large and responsive audience." He and Kennon spent the night at the Springfield Arsenal and, the next morning, toured the workshops and "saw how the entire Springfield Rifle was [made] by machinery."[26]

Crook wound up his tour on March 5 with a farewell dinner hosted by the committee, and two days later returned to Omaha. On the average, he had made one speech a day, although occasionally he managed two. He had shown himself to be a popular speaker, and his message was well-received.[27]

The regular daily schedule of an administrative post allowed Crook time to work on his memoirs. In 1886 and 1887, he wrote the largest part of his autobiography, which would remain unfinished at the time of his death. He was particularly interested in how history would view his actions at the Opequon, and he continued to fume about what he saw as Sheridan's failure to give him credit for his part in the battle. On March 21, 1887, on the stagecoach from Fort Robinson to Fort Laramie, Lieutenant Kennon wrote in his diary, "Gen. C[rook]. thinks Sheridan has never properly acknowledged his indebtedness to Gen. C. for his work in the Valley. Sheridan made no move without consulting Genl. C. Their headquarters were side by side—by Sheridan's wish."[28] Throughout that spring, Crook dwelt on it, his anger growing until he became permanently embittered.[29]

Elsewhere, the Indian rights movement was finally beginning to bear fruit. In response to several years of lobbying by the Boston Committee and the Indian Rights Association, Congress passed the Dawes Severalty Act (also called the Dawes Allotment Act), which ended tribal ownership of reservation lands and divided them into family and individual land holdings. Hailed as a breakthrough (which, given the alternatives of extermination or total dependancy on the government, it was), the act gave 160 acres of tribal land to Indian heads of household, 80 acres to single Indians over eighteen, and 40 acres to minors.

"This bill," wrote Herbert Welsh of the Indian Rights Association, "secures to the Indian the right to own land in individual allotments, and opens to him the door to the full rights of citizenship." Indeed, this was part of the intent. The government would hold the land in trust for twenty-five years, while preparing the Indians to become citizen-landowners. After that, they presumably would be able to handle their own affairs and administer their individual holdings on their own.

The Dawes Act was based on the assumption that only the Anglo-Saxon concept of individual land title had any value in civilized society, and totally ignored the fact that some tribes had done very well with communally owned land. It also committed the very error that Crook, in his Boston addresses, had warned against by attempting to force an entire set of alien values on the Indian. It assumed the Indians would gratefully abandon their own values for those of the whites, and thereby obtain self-sufficiency in a white world. Finally, once the allocation was completed, there would be a substantial amount of surplus land that would be purchased from the Indian reservations and resold by the government for homesteading and development. Before the end of the decade, Crook would feel the repercussions of the Dawes Act, when he would be called upon to assist in the break-up of what remained of the old Great Sioux Reservation.[30]

As 1887 drew to a close, the prospect—indeed this time the likelihood— was that Crook would be appointed major general. Terry's health was failing, and it was obvious he soon would retire. Crook now was senior brigadier general, and therefore the likely choice for the vacancy. The only serious rival was Nelson Miles, who was second in seniority, and by February 1888, an initially large field of hopeful contenders had narrowed to Crook and Miles. Both began a campaign of self-promotion interspersed with smearing each other with accusations of doctoring official correspondence concerning that great bone of contention, the Geronimo campaign.

Crook had two decided advantages over Miles: eight year's seniority as brigadier and, whatever the allegations of the Geronimo campaign, a solid reputation as an Indian fighter. Miles, meanwhile, had alienated the Cleveland administration by helping Geronimo cheat the hangman. Likewise, Miles's openly contemptuous attitude had arrayed much of the army command against him. Crook, on the other hand, may have had few close friends among the other generals, but neither had he made any serious enemies. Even Sheridan preferred him over Miles as the lesser of evils. On April 6, 1888, the Senate confirmed Crook's appointment as major general.[31]

The confirmation fanned Miles's hatred for Crook. In a venomous letter to his wife's brother-in-law, Sen. J. D. Cameron in Washington, Miles blasted Crook's administration of Arizona, and offered yet another hint that Crook might have been involved in some sort of nefarious business dealings.

> The difference between my policy and that of General Crook is perfectly plain. He had no confidence in the troops and so expressed it. The troops had no confidence in him. He stated officially that they could not protect the settlements "a half mile away from their camps." The posts and troops were stripped of transportation and a large amount of it was concentrated up at Prescott two hundred miles from where it was needed and beyond reach when emergency arose. Of course that disbursed great quantities of public money at Prescott, and the very men that are howling to have his policy re-established are men who were making money by that kind of management. He had hundreds of Indians employed as scouts to whom were issued tens of thousands of rounds of ammunition (over 100,000).
>
> All that has been changed: the scouts were disarmed and sent home, the troops were effectually and properly equipped and made to understand that they could break down and subjugate Indians. Of course it looks to me that Crook's promotion was a vindication of his course, and you will see . . . the efforts of the interested parties that are being made to have him re-assigned to this Territory with increased rank and of course, being wedded to *his* policy, as he stated at the time he asked to be relieved, it might reasonably be expected that *his policy will be re-established.*[32]

The letter is odd, because it was unlikely that Miles actually believed Crook would return to Arizona; command of the Military Division of the Missouri was virtually automatic with Crook's appointment. Indeed, signing his oath of office as major general in Omaha on May 1 was one of Crook's last acts as commander of the Department of the Platte.[33] Five days later, he arrived in Chicago and assumed command of the division, temporarily moving into the Calumet Club until Mary arrived and they could establish their residence at the Grand Pacific Hotel. The following day Sheridan, who was en route to Cincinnati, stopped by for a visit, and on May 9, attended a banquet for Crook at the Calumet. The next day, they met again at the club to play euchre. Aware that these meetings were merely a courtesy between generals, Crook noted them in his diary without elaboration or comment.[34]

This appears to have been the final meeting between Crook and Sheridan. Some months earlier, Sheridan had been diagnosed with progressive heart disease, and on May 26 suffered a series of near-fatal heart attacks. In view of his condition, Congress rushed through a fourth star, raising him to full general, a rank held up to then only by Washington, Grant, and Sherman. By now, however, Sheridan was bedridden. He died on August 5.[35]

Sheridan's death did not lessen Crook's obsession with the Shenandoah Campaign. On September 28, 1888, he began dictating a short memoir of the campaign to Kennon, who took it down in his diary with the idea of writing a book. He also arranged for Kennon to interview various officers who had participated, and himself contacted Brig. Gen. George A. (Sandy) Forsyth on Kennon's behalf, to see if anyone had been present in Grant's meeting with Sheridan during the campaign.

When Kennon asked advice about publication, Crook replied, "I am glad you are getting along so well with your work. I have been thinking about the same thing[,] of your getting in communication with the Century [Magazine] people with the view of having your book published in it." He asked Rutherford Hayes to use his influence to get the work published in a magazine, but the former president replied that he wanted "to think the matter over."[36]

In March 1889, Kennon's research took him to Lynchburg, Virginia, where Jubal Early was living in the squalor of elderly bachelorhood. At Early's suggestion, they met in Kennon's room in the Norvelle-Arlington Hotel, the Confederate general's reason being that the accommodations were better than his own room.[37]

"He was an old man," Kennon noted in his diary, "bent very considerably, with a bright eye that had something of a twinkle in it, and seemed altogether very pleasant. He was somewhat bald, with white hair cut short, and a long, white beard." He wore a gray coat, with gold cufflinks decorated with a Confederate flag in enamel. Kennon noted that Early "had a habit of spitting thro' his teeth, in which he displayed a great degree of skill."[38] Early took an immediate liking to the young soldier, and Kennon no doubt rose in his estimation when he asked the old general for a photograph, which Early gladly gave him.[39]

According to Kennon, Early was pleased that Crook had risen to major general, and said he believed the honor was overdue. "He was certainly the ablest of the men I had to deal with. It was he that came in and whipped me after I had beaten the other two corps at Winchester. With open country, and cavalry on both my flanks, and Crook, too, I couldn't hope to stay there. And at Fisher's Hill again, it was Crook who came in on my left and upset my dismounted cavalry, and they in turn upset the infantry. But I got even with him at Cedar Creek about a month later, when his troops were the first I broke up about five o'clock in the morning." With that, Kennon noted, "The old man's eyes twinkled at the recollection."[40]

Aside from sharing his young aide's enthusiasm for the Shenandoah project, Crook seemed to be preoccupied with how history would view his actions during the campaign. This may have reflected a growing awareness of his own mortality. His health was deteriorating, Mary frequently was ill, and others besides Sheridan were beginning to die. Perhaps the most tragic was Ranald Mackenzie. Overcome by the mental instability that plagued him during the Great Sioux War, he had been forced into retirement in 1884. He existed in the dark world of insanity for not quite five years, dying on January 19, 1889, at the age of forty-eight.[41]

Mackenzie's passing is oddly absent from Crook's diary, which normally mentioned the deaths of his contemporaries. He did, however, respond to the death of Lucy Hayes, who suffered a severe stroke on the afternoon of June 21, 1889. She lingered for a little more than three days, dying at 6:30 A.M., June 25. The news reached Crook in Nebraska four days later, and he immediately wired his condolences.[42]

As Major General Crook settled into his new command, the atmosphere at divisional headquarters became decidedly unmilitary, which brought applause from a *Chicago Herald* reporter who wrote:

> There is precious little red tape around Crook's headquarters, and none what-
> ever of that military exclusiveness which is so often exasperating to the ordi-
> nary civilian doing business with the Army. The doors are all wide open, and the
> visitor simply walks in. He doesn't see anybody in uniform. Everybody from
> Gen. Crook down is in citizen's dress. No orderly, no messenger, no formality
> of any kind. If you don't interrupt the general in the midst of a good story he
> will be very glad to see you and tell you so most cordially. Everybody that knows
> General Crook knows that he is a typical American and a democrat, and that
> some spirit of democracy pervades his whole headquarters.[43]

The close proximity of Chicago to Ohio allowed Crook to join the Ohio Commandery of the Military Order of the Loyal Legion, a veterans' organi-zation for officers of the Union Army. He explained to Hayes that he had "repeatedly refused" to join the Nebraska Commandery in Omaha, because he wanted to join the commandery of his home state.[44]

On the other hand, the new position created a rift with Bourke. Three times during 1888, Crook had supported his former aide's candidacy for promotion from captain to major. Each time, Bourke was passed over because of what he believed was animosity from the Cleveland administration. Meanwhile, upon assuming division command, Crook asked Bourke to join his staff in Chicago. Bourke, however, was now settled into his anthropological work and declined. Thus, in 1889, when Benjamin Harrison became president, and Bourke saw a better chance for promotion, he found he had lost Crook's support.

Bourke was bitter about the change in Crook's attitude, and when it came up in a conversation, he noted, "Crook acted as if he felt thoroughly ashamed of himself, as he had every reason to be." Thereafter, although they continued to deal with each other from time to time, the relationship was decidedly cool, and Bourke communicated with Crook through Kennon whenever possible.[45]

Early in 1889, Congress again took up the question of Indian lands. The previous year, a government commission had proposed to divide what remained of the old Great Sioux Reservation into six separate reservations centered on existing agencies, Standing Rock, Cheyenne River, Crow Creek, Lower Brule, Pine Ridge, and Rosebud. The new boundaries would leave nine million surplus acres, which the government planned to purchase at fifty cents an acre, plus a thousand bulls and twenty-five thousand cows to facilitate the tribes' entry into stock raising. The Indians flatly rejected the proposal, and the commission recommended outright seizure of the reservation.

Realizing the government ultimately would prevail, a delegation of chiefs visited Washington to negotiate the best deal they could. To some degree they were successful, because the final terms were better than those originally offered. The law dividing the reservation, which was approved by Congress on March 2, 1889, expanded the Dawes Act by giving each Sioux head of household 320 acres; single persons over eighteen, and orphans under eighteen, 160 acres; and other single persons under eighteen, 80 acres. If the land was suitable only for grazing, rather than cultivation, the allotment would be doubled. Land not allocated would fall under public domain and be opened to homesteaders at $1.25 per acre for the first three years, seventy-five cents for the next two years, and fifty cents thereafter, with the money going into a trust fund for the needs of the Indians. The other provisions of the Dawes Act, such as the twenty-five-year trust, would remain in force. The government would bear all administrative costs.

Because the government no longer recognized Indian tribes as sovereign nations, any accord would have the status of an agreement rather than a treaty. Nevertheless, before taking effect it would have to be ratified by three-fourths of the adult males in each of the six proposed new reservations. To convince the Indians to agree, a new commission was named consisting of Governor Charles Foster of Ohio, chairman; Sen. William Warner of Missouri; and General Crook.

The commission left Chicago on May 29, 1889, stopping first at the Rosebud, where members established a pattern they would follow at the other agencies, offering a feast to put the Indians into a receptive frame of mind. Nevertheless, they encountered strong opposition. Although some historians have argued that the Indians did not understand the conditions of this agreement any more than they had understood the first Sioux treaty with the government almost seventy years earlier, they nevertheless understood the motives of the whites. They remembered well that any agreement in the past had resulted in the slow but inexorable expropriation of their land until they now had only a fraction of their original domain. They were also acutely aware that where the Dawes Act already had been implemented, there had been little real benefit. And at all the main agencies the powerful old chiefs, such as Red Cloud, Iron Nation, Touch-the-Clouds, Sitting Bull, and American Horse, feared their influence would diminish if individual members of the tribes became landowners.

Crook responded as he had always done, by playing the various factions against each other. He manipulated the "progressive" chiefs (those who recognized the reality of their position) against the non-progressives. Negotiations at the Rosebud took four days, and at one point, some of the warriors threatened to kill anyone who signed. Nevertheless, after a particularly stormy session on June 7, the Indians agreed. Crook wrote Kennon, "Our success at Rosebud agency has virtually solved this whole question, but much laborous [*sic*] & vexatious work is still before us, but I hope we will not be detained as long at any one of the other agencies as we were at Rosebud."

Arriving at Pine Ridge, he managed after some argument to win over American Horse, who, facing the inevitable, led his band in signing. At Standing Rock, Sitting Bull tried to speak against the agreement, but Crook stopped him and blocked his effort to "stampede" the Indians away from the council. With Crook firmly in control, the Standing Rock Sioux also signed. Ultimately, 4,463 of the 5,678 eligible males, slightly more than the required three-fourths majority, signed the agreement, and the division of the Great Sioux Reservation became reality.

Crook congratulated himself on fulfilling his mission, but beneath the diplomacy, he had left no doubts among the Indians that if they failed to sign the agreement, the government would take the land anyway. The Sioux themselves were bitterly divided, and when Congress reduced the Sioux appropriation, the situation became worse. Those who had signed felt betrayed, and were themselves viewed as traitors by those who had held out. In desperation, many of them embraced the rising Ghost Dance movement, setting the stage for their destruction at Wounded Knee, some nine months after Crook's death.[46]

EIGHTEEN

THE LAST BATTLE

—∽∽∽—

There is no doubt that, while we were prisoners of war, he
did what he could in our behalf.

—ASA DAKLUGIE
quoted in Eve Ball, *Indeh: An Apache Odyssey*

Ever since leaving Arizona, General Crook had worried about the fate of
the Apaches. His concern became even greater after whole bands, both hostile
and friendly, were transported to internment in Florida. The majority were sent
to Fort Marion at St. Augustine, where they were lodged in an old Spanish
fortress built almost two hundred years earlier. The exterior of the thick
masonry walls was about 270 feet on each of the four sides, and enclosed an
interior square of about 180 feet to a side. It was surrounded by a tidal moat
with one drawbridge leading to a barbican, and a second drawbridge from the
barbican to the sallyport.[1]

Bourke, who was posted to Washington to continue his studies of Southwestern Indians, complained about conditions at Fort Marion to Herbert Welsh
and, in 1887, accompanied Welsh and Philadelphia attorney Henry Paul on a
visit to the post.[2] They found 447 prisoners crowded into the compound, living
in filth, in tents erected on the ramparts and in the square. Only eighty-two
were men, with the remainder being women and children. Another forty-four
children were in the U.S. Industrial School at Carlisle Barracks, Pennsylvania,

where the government had decided to send Apaches between the ages of twelve and twenty-two. Among those at the fort, the death rate was more than double the birth rate, and all but one of the dead were women and children. Elaborating on his figures, Welsh noted, "It is an interesting fact, and one to which I desire to call especial attention, and upon which I desire to lay the strongest possible emphasis, that of the 82 men not more than 30 have been guilty of any recent misdoing, whilst many of the remainder were employed in our Army as regularly commissioned scouts, first by General Crook, and afterwards by General Miles, to assist the soldiers in following up and finally securing the surrender of Geronimo and his hostiles."[3]

Geronimo himself had been confined to Fort Pickens at Pensacola, together with sixteen of his men, while their wives and children were in Fort Marion. "*This separation,*" Welsh noted emphatically, "*is a direct violation of the terms on which Geronimo surrendered to General Miles.*"[4]

In exposing conditions at Fort Marion, Welsh had the encouragement of both Bourke and Crook. Because of Bourke's position in Washington, and the fact that his lesser rank made him more vulnerable than Crook, Welsh did not refer to him in his pamphlet, although Bourke greatly influenced the content. In fact, he was largely responsible for the success of Welsh's visit, using his friendship with many of the prisoners to convince them to talk openly.

Crook, while supportive of Welsh, hoped for greater things. A year before her death in 1885, Helen Hunt Jackson had published her most famous work, *Ramona*, a novel centered around the plight of the California Indians. Although the book had not achieved the reform that Mrs. Jackson had sought, it neverthelessdrew attention to the problem. Crook saw more drama in the betrayal of the Apaches than in Mrs. Jackson's tragic romance of mission Indians in California, and believed that an Apache novel similar to *Ramona* would do more to stir the public than a recitation of facts.[5] There is no indication, however, that Crook or any of his contemporaries attempted an Apache novel.

Crook's opinion notwithstanding, Welsh's visit created enough public outcry to force the Cleveland administration to act. In April 1887, most Apaches from Fort Marion were transported to Mount Vernon Barracks, about thirty miles north of Mobile, Alabama. The families of Geronimo and others confined at Pensacola were sent to join them at Fort Pickens until May 1888, when they too were all moved to Mount Vernon. The situation in Alabama, however, was no better than in Florida, and in some ways it was worse. The land was unsuitable for farming, there was nothing for them to do, and rations were not adequate. The Apaches were used to the open spaces of the Southwest, and the

Florida coast at least had offered a view. The dense pine forests of southern Alabama, on the other hand, made them feel claustrophobic and only emphasized their imprisonment. One of the Apaches later said, "We had thought that anything would be better than Fort Marion with its rain, mosquitoes, and malaria, but we were to find out that it was good in comparison with Mt. Vernon Barracks. We didn't know what misery was until they dumped us in those swamps. There was no place to climb to pray. If we wanted to see the sky we had to climb a tall pine."[6]

Virtually everyone agreed that Mount Vernon was not a permanent solution, but no one could agree on a viable alternative. In March 1889, however, President Harrison took office, and his newly appointed secretary of war, Redfield Proctor, determined to settle the matter once and for all. Major General John M. Schofield, who had succeeded Sheridan as general-in-chief, summoned Crook and Bourke to discuss the matter. In April, they met with Charles C. Painter, the Indian Rights Association's agent in Washington. At the behest of Herbert Welsh, Bourke and Painter investigated possible relocation sites in North Carolina, and inspected Mount Vernon Barracks, where they found conditions appalling and the death rate excessive.[7]

Crook, meanwhile, spent the remainder of the spring and summer tending to the affairs of his division. After the partition of the Great Sioux Reservation, he attended a review of the troops in the Department of the Platte at Fort Robinson, then went hunting in Wyoming with Webb Hayes. All the while, however, he had one eye on the Apache situation, and was biding his time. Then, in the fall of 1889, while escorting a Sioux delegation to Washington, he took a side trip to Governor's Island, New York, to discuss the matter with General Howard, who, as commander of the Military Division of the Atlantic, had jurisdiction over the Apaches.[8]

Howard was a willing ally who, Crook learned, had already taken the initiative. Frequently receiving reports from the post commander about poor conditions at Mount Vernon, he enlisted Proctor's support for an investigation that was handled by his son, Lt. Guy Howard, Twelfth Infantry. Lieutenant Howard determined that the Apaches could scarcely be expected to remain for another year at Mount Vernon with its deplorable conditions and high mortality rate. Instead, he recommended they be relocated to a suitable tract of land no later than March 1, 1890.

By the time Lieutenant Howard submitted his report on December 23, 1889, Bourke and Painter had recommended purchasing a portion of Cherokee reservation in the Great Smoky Mountains of western North Carolina. The reservation consisted of a hundred thousand acres, and the Cherokee leaders indicated they would sell twelve thousand to assist the Apaches. Secretary Proctor liked the idea and suggested Bourke take some of the Apache chiefs to North Carolina to confer with the Cherokee leaders. Now, however, opposition rose in North Carolina. To settle the matter, Secretary Proctor sent Crook to determine the suitability of the Cherokee land, and then go on to Alabama and meet with the Apaches.[9]

As Crook headed south, he took the opportunity to visit the old battlefields of the Shenandoah Campaign. It was his first time back since the war and, visiting Opequon on Christmas Day, he realized the field had changed so much that he had trouble recognizing many of the main features. The next day, he visited Cedar Creek and Fisher's Hill, and found that they had changed as well. Nevertheless, the sight of the old grounds brought his resentment toward Sheridan to full fruition. In his diary, he noted:

> After examining the grounds & the positions of the troops after the 25 years which have elapsed & in the light of subsequent events it renders Gen. Sheridan's claims & his Subsequent actions in allowing the General public to remain under impressions regarding his part in these two battles, when he knew they were fiction all the more Contemptable [sic]. The adulations heaped on him by the grateful nation for his supposed genius turned his head which added to his natural disposition caused him to bloat his little carcass with debauchery & dissipation which carried him off prematurely.[10]

On December 28, Crook, Kennon, and Sen. Zebulon Vance of North Carolina inspected the Smoky Mountain country around Bryson City, to determine whether it might be suitable for an Apache reservation. Although it was better than Mount Vernon Barracks, and the cool, forested mountains in some ways resembled the mountainous regions of the Apaches' own country, there was not enough arable land to support their farms.[11]

Crook continued on to Mount Vernon Barracks, arriving on January 2. Some of the Indians recognized him, and as word spread through the post, they came running to see him, crowding around, laughing, and reaching out to touch him. He called for a council outside the school building to meet with the leaders. He was interested in the reasons that Naiche and Geronimo had violated their surrender, and asked detailed questions to try and establish that the scouts were instrumental in ending the outbreak. He was particularly concerned about the circumstances surrounding the removal to Florida.[12]

Geronimo started to speak, but Crook bluntly stated he wasn't interested. He did, however, listen to Naiche, who shrugged off the question about the outbreak with the laconic remark, "We talked to each other about it. We were drunk."[13]

Opinions varied as to the importance of the scouts, depending on whether the speaker was a former hostile or a former scout. When it came to the removal to Florida, however, everyone had essentially the same story of federal perfidity. The peaceful Chiricahua leaders had accepted a summons to Washington, where they had met with government leaders to discuss their future. Presuming they were going home, they were taken instead to Carlisle for a week, after which they started back west. At Fort Leavenworth, however, they were halted and detrained. Soon after, the remaining Chiricahuas arrived from Fort Apache, and together the entire band had been sent to Fort Marion. They had lost their farms and livestock in Arizona, had not been reimbursed, and now lived aimlessly with little hope for the future.[14] Summing up the feelings of the entire group, Chihuahua told Crook, "I am getting so my limbs feel as if they were asleep. I would like to have some better place than this. I would like to have a place where I could have a farm and go right to work, so that my children can have plenty to eat; and I would like to have tools to go right to work with them. I have a daughter away at school and have other near relatives. I want to see them soon. Won't you make it so I can see them very soon[?]"[15]

Crook started to Washington to prepare his report on the Chiricahuas. En route, a problem with the trains caused considerable delay in Lynchburg, and he decided to call on Jubal Early. As a near-contemporary, Crook held an opinion of the crotchety, un-Reconstructed Confederate far different from that of the younger, more impressionable Kennon. Early was now seventy-three and, Crook noted, "bitter and violent as an adder." Nevertheless, they visited until after midnight. To Crook, Early was almost a pathetic figure who was "living entirely in the past. He has fought his battles so many times that he has worked himself into the belief that many of the exaggerated and some ridiculous stories he tells are true."[16]

Crook's report, prepared for him by Kennon, was submitted to Proctor on January 6, 1890. He noted that, although the Apaches at Mount Vernon gave all appearances of being "healthy and strong," the mortality rate was "much more than normal and would seem due to homesickness, change of climate and the dreary monotony of empty lives." They wanted to become self-sufficient, and he felt they could if given the opportunity. Indeed, he pointed out, many were on the verge of becoming successful farmers in Arizona when they were unjustly and unnecessarily uprooted and transported to Florida.

"By far," he continued, "the greater part of the tribe remained true to the Government in the outbreak of 1885, and the most valuable and trustworthy of the Indian scouts were taken from among them. For their allegiance all have been rewarded alike, by captivity in a strange land."

Crook admitted it would be impractical to send them home. Although he believed they would try to be law-abiding, the strong feelings against Apaches in Arizona might lead to trouble. In that case, he said, "it would be utterly impossible ever to get them to surrender again, and to exterminate them in war would cost thousands of lives, to say nothing of the loss of property that such a war would necessarily entail." Instead, he recommended their relocation to the Indian Territory where the environment, if not identical to Arizona, was at least more congenial to Apaches than the East.

Besides the immediate problem of Mount Vernon, Crook criticized the government policy of sending children to Carlisle, where tuberculosis was rampant. The Apaches considered the forced removal of their children cruel enough, but equated Carlisle with a death sentence. Of the 107 Apache children who had been sent to the school since the internment, twenty-seven were dead. Shortly after the move to Mount Vernon, seven children were returned to their families, all in the final stages of tuberculosis. Later that year, another twelve dying children arrived from Carlisle. The disease spread among the Indians at Mount Vernon, adding to an already growing death rate. Opposing further removals to Carlisle, Crook wrote Secretary Proctor that the Apaches loved their children, and were terrified that they would be removed and sent to Carlisle to die.[17]

Although a federal law from 1879 prohibited Indians from Arizona or New Mexico from living in the Territory, Senator Dawes responded to Crook's report by introducing Senate Joint Resolution 42, allowing the Apaches to settle there. On January 20, President Benjamin Harrison transmitted Crook's and Lieutenant Howard's reports, together with a favorable recommendation by Proctor, to both houses of Congress. In his message, the president pointedly remarked that some of the Apaches had faithfully served the government in chasing down Naiche and Geronimo, and it was disgraceful that the government now confined them with their erstwhile enemies. He concluded with his own earnest recommendation "that provision be made by law for locating these Indians upon lands in the Indian Territory."[18]

The next day, Dawes steered the resolution through Senate approval, and on January 23 it was submitted to the House Committee on Indian Affairs. Initially,

Nelson Miles had supported the idea of moving the Apaches to the Territory. When called on to testify, however, he changed his position. The Indian Territory, he contended, was too close to their old haunts of New Mexico and Arizona, and they might break for their homeland.

Miles's remarks brought General Howard into the fray. Howard, whose Christianity was real and sincere, had two concerns. First, his son's report convinced him of what he had long suspected, that the Apaches were living under conditions that should not be thrust on any human being. Second, although Howard normally was capable of forgiving most affronts and shrugging off virtually any quarrel, Miles was for him the exception because of disputes that began when Miles served under him during the Nez Perce campaign of 1877. Howard downplayed Miles's opposition, convincing Secretary Proctor and General Schofield that it was based on personal grievances, and he advised Crook to cultivate the eastern press to offset Miles's influence in the West. Taking the advice to heart, Crook began lining up support. Commenting that the Apaches were thoroughly broken and defeated, and never again would be a threat to the peace, he ripped into Miles for his inconsistency, and dubbed the western press "Miles' Literary Bureau."[19]

Miles reacted immediately, marshaling opposition to the bill with the support of the press in Arizona and New Mexico. The only suitable place, he maintained, was North Carolina. Crook countered that the only reason for Miles's opposition to the Territory "was anything to beat me." Bourke was inclined to agree; with all the recriminations, and with everyone taking sides, he concluded the welfare of the Apaches had become a secondary issue in the increasingly vicious quarrel between Crook and Miles.[20]

Crook, meanwhile, had returned to Chicago to handle the affairs of the division, leaving Kennon in Washington to promote Senate Resolution 42. They corresponded almost daily, Crook directing the effort from Chicago while attending to routine business. By now, however, his health was failing. He was ill during much of January, although by the end of the month, he told Kennon he was "pretty much recovered," and was planning a trip to the Indian Territory. Recovery, however, took longer than he anticipated for, on February 3, he wrote, "I haven't gotten over my 'grippe' yet & am in hopes that my trip will do me good."[21]

The effort to relocate the Apaches continued. Miles's supporters had three major objections to the removal. They reiterated the original two arguments, that the western Indian Territory was unhealthy, and that the Apaches might break out from the Territory and head for their homelands. Finally, and most importantly, Miles and his supporters insisted there had been no injustice to begin with—that the Chiricahuas had surrendered unconditionally and had no right of consideration at all, and that the attitude of the entire tribe was hostile.[22]

For Crook, this was too much. Pondering whether he should respond, he wrote to Kennon from the Indian Territory, "So long as [Miles's] 'Literary Bureau' confined itself to giving false impressions as to who was entitled to the settlement of the Apache question, I made no reply, but when he took advantage of my visit to the Chiricahuas to make misleading statements about these Indians whose outrageous treatment he was connected with, forbearance ceased to be a virtue. It would be of great[,] great importance if I could come to Washington to help people there to understand this whole Indian business."[23]

He also continued to smolder because the Apache scouts, who had loyally supported the government, were part of the dispute. The situation became even more aggravated, and Miles's position gained ground when the Mexican government submitted claims for what it considered to be depredations by the scouts while they were in Mexico.

The Mexicans, Crook complained to Kennon, "have trumped up a lot of charges so as to offset any claims we may ever make for the killing of Capt. Crawford which they too well know was a most villainous affair." Initially, Crook had hesitated at involving Gatewood, whose service on Miles's staff was calculated to keep him quiet, in Crook's view. As the controversy progressed, however, he began to believe that Gatewood "could be a very important witness" to the circumstances surrounding the surrender of Geronimo, and the role played by the scouts.[24]

Crook did not live to see the dispute resolved. Throughout February and early March of 1890, his health continued to fail. Besides his other ailments, he suffered from chronic gastritis that bloated his stomach and, on some occasions, was so severe that it caused irregular heartbeat. Usually his surgeon, Maj. Ely McClellan, was able to relieve the discomfort. Shortly before 7 A.M., March 21, Crook arose as usual in his suite in the Grand Pacific Hotel, went into the dressing room adjoining his bedroom, and began exercising with Indian clubs before breakfast. Suddenly, he was unable to get his breath. Calling for Mary, he lay down on a couch. A physician who lived in the hotel was called in but, after a few gasps, Crook died. He was sixty-one years old.[25]

As division surgeon, Dr. McClellan formally notified the Office of the Surgeon General in Washington, which forwarded a copy to the Adjutant General's Office. McClellan determined that heart failure was the official cause of death, although he qualified that by stating, "The General was absolutely temperate in his life. He drank nothing; did not smoke, and was remarkably abstemious in his habits, and I can only attribute the occurrence of the disease from which he suffered to the incidents of his many exposures in line of duty."[26]

Bourke, who was not a physician but who knew Crook, was ready to second the opinion, writing, "The real cause of death was the wear and tear of a naturally powerful constitution, brought on by the severe mental and physical strain of incessant work under the most trying circumstances."[27]

The funeral was held in the Grand Pacific, with many old friends and comrades attending. Despite his own failing health and a recent injury sustained in a fall from a trolley car, Rutherford Hayes came from Ohio to serve as honorary pallbearer for his friend and beloved former commander. Webb Hayes stood by Mary.

The coffin was taken to a train for the trip east to Maryland. Walter Crook, the general's brother from Dayton, accompanied the body. Thousands of people from the surrounding countryside crowded the streets of Oakland to witness the procession to the cemetery on March 24. Although the burial was private, three former Confederates received special permission to attend. They were members of McNeill's Rangers, come to pay their respects to the man they had captured twenty-five years earlier.

Crook's body remained in Oakland less than eight months. On November 11, he was reinterred in Arlington National Cemetery. The procession to Arlington was escorted by two companies of cavalry, and among those attending were General Schofield, Bourke, and Webb Hayes.[28]

Crook had not been dead a week when Miles began campaigning for promotion to the vacancy. His efforts were rewarded on April 6, when he was named major general. That, however, was not enough. He wanted the Division of the Missouri and, on September 1, 1890, he got that, too. As division commander, he once again reversed himself, and recommended the Apaches be relocated to Fort Sill, in the southwestern part of the Indian Territory. This time there was no argument. In the fall of 1894, as they were being transported the last few miles across the Oklahoma prairie to their new home, the Apaches heard coyotes howling for the first time in eight years. Overcome by emotion at the familiar sound, the women wept. In October 1895, Miles became the last general-in-chief of the army. He would outlive Crook by over thirty-five years, dying on May 15, 1925.[29]

If Miles saw Crook's death as a means of advancement, others saw a great loss. Only twelve days after Crook died, his old friend, Capt. Charles King, presented a tribute before the Wisconsin Commandery of the Military Order of the Loyal Legion. "[I]n all America," King said, "no name can ever be more intimately connected with the westward way of our glowing star of Empire— no name be held in higher reverence among the red men, or in deeper gratitude among the whites, than that of George Crook."[30]

Neither tributes nor diatribes answer the lingering question of whether Crook participated in any of the graft that permeated the military during much of the period known as the "Gilded Age." Information on his estate is sparse; if a will still exists, it has not been located, and little is available on probate of his estate. Crook made no secret that he fancied himself a businessman, a mine developer, and rancher, and he owned at least part interest in small western ranches throughout his life. He was not above using subordinates for his own affairs, as when he sent Lieutenant Schuyler to manage the Murchie mine. And there are three separate allegations—by Richard Irving Dodge in 1876, by Frederick Benteen in 1887, and by Nelson Miles in 1888—that Crook was involved in shady dealings with government contractors, and with businessmen who stood to profit by the military presence in the West, notwithstanding his own indignation at such corruption. There is no evidence, however, that any of these allegations were ever investigated.

Whatever the case, Crook apparently had very little money at the time of his death. As previously noted, his nephew said he "died broke." Only a day after his funeral in Oakland, a bill was introduced in Congress to grant Mary a widow's pension of $2,000 annually. The report accompanying the bill noted her claim for the pension "is no exceptional case, as other widows of generals of same rank have frequently been granted pensions of $2,000 per annum, and some even more." Between the pension and her own small inheritance, she was able to live comfortably and even tour Europe. She died on September 24, 1895.[31]

Looking back on Crook, a century and a decade after his death, he remains something of an enigma. The hagiography perpetuated by those who knew him, his own secretive personality that presented only the side he wanted to be seen, and his mercurial temperament have obscured both the man and his career. He was ambitious, egotistical, and vindictive. Beneath the modest demeanor, he craved appreciation and promotion, and would go great lengths to attain them. There is no question that he could be innovative, yet he was far from being a military genius. As a Union officer, he blundered, but the same could be said of many other Union generals, and some blundered far worse. Overall, he appears to have risen to his level of competence during the Civil

War, when he provided a solid, generally predictable support to the true genius of Sheridan and Grant.

In the Pacific Northwest, Crook established his reputation as an Indian fighter, albeit one who wasted men and animals far out of proportion to any gains. This was a scenario that would be repeated with less successful results in the northern plains in 1876. The campaign against the Sioux and Cheyennes also demonstrated that, while Crook might have understood the Indian mentality, he was not always able to convert that understanding into military action. His true fame as an Indian fighter came in Arizona. In dealing with Apaches, as enemies, as allies, and as wards of the government, he was without peer. It may even be argued that the success of his Grand Offensive of 1872–73 sustained the remainder of Crook's career.

In his "democratic" approach to the military—the easy-going atmosphere of headquarters, and the preference for civilian clothes—one is reminded of Brig. Gen. (later President) Zachary Taylor, who also preferred civilian clothes and had a casual view of ceremony. Taylor's attitude, however, reflected an earlier age when even professional officers might lean toward the citizen-soldier approach. It also reflected Taylor's own personality and sense of humor. During the Mexican War, when a presumptuous young lieutenant mistook him for a servant, Taylor charged the man a dollar to clean his sword before identifying himself. In a similar incident at Fort Laramie, a newspaper correspondent mistook Crook for the boss of a mule train. Crook's reaction—if any—is not recorded, but it is unlikely he would have played it as well as General Taylor. Crook was an autocrat, who used his rank to achieve his goals, reward his friends, and punish those who crossed him. He selected staff and companions according to their usefulness, and discarded them when they no longer served his purposes.[32]

Whatever Crook's faults, they were offset by his fundamental humanity. None could deny the faith he inspired among the Indians. In war, he could be as cruel as they, but he always respected them as human beings. Even his old enemy Red Cloud acknowledged as much, remarking, "He, at least, had never lied to us. His words gave the people hope. He died. Their hope died again. Despair came again."[33]

When news of his death reached the remnants of the Apaches still in Arizona, they "sat down in a great circle, let down their hair, bent their heads forward on their bosoms, and wept and wailed like children."[34]

NOTES

—⁓—

ABBREVIATIONS

ACP	Appointments, Commissions, Promotions
ADC	Aide de Camp
AG	Adjutant General
AAG	Assistant Adjutant General
AAAG	Acting Assistant Adjutant General
Arizona	Department of Arizona
MilDivMo	Military Division of the Missouri
MilDivPac	Military Division of the Pacific
OR	*Official Records of the Union and Confederate Armies*
Pacific	Department of the Pacific (pre–Civil War)
Platte	Department of the Platte
RG	Record Group
USA	United States Army

INTRODUCTION

1. Downey, *Indian Fighting Army*, 162.

2. Crook started at least three autobiographies. A brief manuscript of only fifteen pages appears to have been the earliest effort, and this was followed by a second attempt that reached fifty-five pages. The version completed by Schmitt, the longest and most detailed, apparently was begun in 1881 and was unfinished at the time of Crook's death nine years later. All are preserved in the Crook-Kennon papers in the U.S. Army Military History Institute at Carlisle Barracks.

3. See Porter, *Paper Medicine Man*, 12–13. Although historians are indebted to Bourke for his detailed, if slanted, account of daily life with Crook, this journalistic aspect of Bourke's life unfortunately has overshadowed his outstanding achievements as an anthropologist.

4. Nan Card, Rutherford B. Hayes Presidential Center, to the author, November 29, 1999.

5. *The General* is a biography of Lt. Gen. Robert L. Bullard, whom Millett uses as a case study in professionalism. This paragraph is based on the nine-page introduction, which is an essay on the professional officer corps as an institution within the army. Bullard, who entered West Point in 1881, represented the military generation that followed Crook's. See also Robert M. Utley, *Frontiersmen in Blue*, 34.

6. Nickerson, "Major General George Crook," 32, Schuyler Papers, WS 58. (This item is reproduced by permission of The Huntington Library, San Marino, California).

7. King, "Needed: A Re-evaluation," 225–26.

8. Schmitt, *General George Crook*, 82.

9. Haley, *Apaches*, 264–65; Robinson, *A Good Year to Die*, 56–57.

CHAPTER 1: FRONTIERSMAN

1. Schmitt, *General George Crook*, xx. When I was eighteen years old, I was a crewman on a desperately short-handed ship bound from Scotland to Norway across the North Sea in the dead of winter. To meet the minimum legal requirement for departure, we signed on three Scottish sailors, one of whom was named Crook.

2. Ibid., xx–xxi.

3. Ibid., xx–xxii.

4. Ibid., xxi; Hutton, *Phil Sheridan*, 3.

5. Schmitt, *General George Crook*, xx; Hutton, *Phil Sheridan*, 3.

6. Sheridan, *Personal Memoirs*, 1:7; Wallace, *General August V. Kautz and the Southwestern Frontier*, 10; King, *Major-General George Crook*, 3. King notes that of the forty-three graduates in Crook's class at West Point, six were from Ohio, giving that state one-seventh of the total.

7. Quoted in Schmitt, *General George Crook*, xxii.

8. Cullum, *Notes of the Biographical Register*, 2:329; Schmitt, *General George Crook*, xxii–xxiii; RG 393 Division and Department of the Pacific, Letters Sent, vol. 4: index. Hereafter cited as "Pacific, Letters Sent."

9. Utley, *Frontiersmen in Blue*, 33–34, 34 n. 59.

10. Schmitt, *General George Crook*, xxiii–xiv; Sheridan, *Personal Memoirs*, 1:9.

11. Sheridan, *Personal Memoirs*, 1:2, 11–12; Hutton, *Phil Sheridan*, 2; Sheridan to Brig. Gen. S. Thomas, AG, USA, August 3, 1861, Sheridan Papers.

12. Crook, Cadet Expense Book, March–April 1850; May–June 1851; July–August 1851; September–October 1851; various entries.

13. Ibid., various entries; Crook, Diary, various entries 1885–90.

14. Crook's file is designated RG 94 2229 ACP 1882, Crook George, Letters Received by the Appointment, Commission and Personal Branch, Adjutant General's Office, 1871–1894. Hereafter it will be cited as ACP—Crook.

15. Schmitt, *General George Crook,* 3, 6 n. 1; Wallace, *General August V. Kautz and the Southwestern Frontier,* 10–11. Crook's brevet rank was awarded because the antebellum army was still influenced by the old "minute man" tradition which held that citizen-soldiers drawn from civilian life were capable of military command. Consequently, the officer corps often was overburdened with men drawn from civilian life; with the number of officers restricted by law, academy graduates such as Crook often were brevetted to regiments as supernumeraries until a vacancy occurred. See Utley, *Frontiersmen in Blue,* 34.

16. Schmitt, *General George Crook,* 3–6.

17. Ibid., 6.

18. Ibid., 7, 10; Utley, *Frontiersmen in Blue,* 30–31. Among those who quit the service during this period were men who later became notable Union or Confederate generals, including U. S. Grant, George B. McClellan, Simon B. Buckner, Braxton Bragg, William T. Sherman, and Thomas J. (Stonewall) Jackson. Most had praiseworthy Mexican War records, but resigned because of frustration over their frontier assignments; Grant and Sherman were serving in California at the time of their resignations.

19. Schmitt, *General George Crook,* 10.

20. Ibid., 8–11, 21.

21. Ibid., 11; Strobridge, *Regulars in the Redwoods,* 62–63.

22. Schmitt, *General George Crook,* 13. Fort Jones was a year old, having been established on October 16, 1852. See Schmitt, 13 n. 15.

23. Frazer, *Mansfield,* 112.

24. Ibid., 165, 215; Utley, *Frontier Regulars,* 19.

25. Frazer, *Mansfield,* 166.

26. Schmitt, *General George Crook,* 21.

27. Nickerson, "Major General George Crook," 31–32, Schuyler Papers, WS 58.

28. Strobridge, *Regulars in the Redwoods,* 70–71; Schmitt, *General George Crook,* 17–19.

29. Strobridge, *Regulars in the Redwoods,* 71–72; Schmitt, *General George Crook,* 19–20.

30. Frazer, *Mansfield,* 165. Crook said he first met Hood in the fall of 1854. Col. Mansfield places them together in August of that year. Crook wrote his memoirs decades later. See Schmitt, *General George Crook,* 21.

31. Davis to Williamson, May 1, 1855, in Abbot, *Report,* 9. Because Williamson became seriously ill after the expedition to Oregon, the final report was prepared by Lieutenant Abbot (Abbot, Letter to the Secretary of War, May 6, 1857, in *Report,* 3).

32. Ibid., 13–14.

316

33. Ibid., pt. 1: 56, 59–60; Strobridge, *Regulars in the Redwoods,* 120–21.

34. Abbot, *Report,* pt. 1: 60–62; Strobridge, *Regulars in the Redwoods,* 121; Schmitt, *General George Crook,* 22.

35. Abbot, *Report,* pt. 1: 62; Schmitt, *General George Crook,* 21–22.

36. Abbot, *Report,* pt. 4: 49.

37. Schmitt, *General George Crook,* 23–24.

38. Abbot, *Report,* pt. 4: 105.

39. Ibid., pt. 1: 79–81; Schmitt, *General George Crook,* 24, 24 n. 14.

40. Abbot, *Report,* pt. 1, 56–110; ibid., 71; Strobridge, *Regulars in the Redwoods,* 122; Sheridan, *Personal Memoirs,* 1:39ff. Sheridan had a lifelong preoccupation with hostile Indians.

41. Abbot, *Report,* pt. 1: 102–10; Strobridge, *Regulars in the Redwoods,* 124; Sheridan, *Personal Memoirs,* 1:53–54.

42. Strobridge, *Regulars in the Redwoods,* 124.

43. Abbot, Letter to the Secretary of War, May 6, 1857, in Abbot, *Report,* 3.

44. Ibid., 3.

CHAPTER 2: INDIAN FIGHTER

1. Boorstin, *The Discoverers,* 627–29; Greeley, *Overland Journey,* 211; Utley, *Frontiersmen in Blue,* 101 n. 21. The Roman Catholic view had begun to change in the mid-sixteenth century after Pope Paul III declared Indians to be children of God and candidates for salvation. Subsequently, Catholic colonial powers such as France, Spain, and Portugal had to temper conquest with evangelism. By then, however, the Reformation had taken hold in central and northern Europe, and the pope's ruling had little, if any, impact on the Indian policies of Great Britain, the Netherlands, or—by extension—the United States.

2. Utley, *Frontiersmen in Blue,* 100–01; Bancroft, *Works,* 24:474–77; Clark, "Military History of Oregon," 26; Ruby and Brown, *Indians of the Pacific Northwest,* 165.

3. Bancroft, *Works,* 24:474.

4. Utley, *Frontier Regulars,* 101.

5. Schmitt, *General George Crook,* 16–17; King, "'A Better Way'": 240.

6. The causes of the war are discussed in detail in Schwartz, *Rogue River Indian War,* 69ff. See also Bancroft, *Works,* 30:369–74; Marks, *In a Barren Land,* 139–40; and Clark, "Military History of Oregon": 26.

7. Schmitt, *General George Crook,* 25–27. The story of the Second Oregon Mounted Volunteers is told in Harvey Robbins, "Journal of Rogue River War, 1855," where the captain is correctly identified. Crook referred to him as "Bowie."

8. Strobridge, *Regulars in the Redwoods,* 127; Schmitt, *General George Crook,* 31–32.

9. Maj. Gen. John Wool to D. R. Jones, AAG, Pacific, March 27, 1856, and Jones to Wyse, March 30 1856—both in Pacific, Letters Sent, 7:433–34; Schmitt, *General*

George Crook, 33–34 ; Bancroft, *Works,* 30:407–9; Ruby and Brown, *Indians of the Pacific Northwest,* 119–22.

10. Schwartz, *Rogue River Indian War,* 148–49.

11. Strobridge, *Regulars in the Redwoods,* 143–45; Judah to W. W. Mackall, AAG, Pacific, May 31, 1857, and Judah to Crook, May 27, 1857—both in RG 393, Letters Received, Department of the Pacific, hereafter referred to as "Pacific, Letters Received."

12. Schmitt, *General George Crook,* 38–39.

13. Crook to Judah, June 12, 1857, Pacific, Letters Received. Five men is the number given in Crook's report to Judah, written two days after the fight. In his auto-biography (Schmitt, 40), he gave the number as ten.

14. Crook to Judah, June 12, 1857; Dryer to Judah, July 6, 1857—both in Pacific, Letters Received; Schmitt, *General George Crook,* 40–41; Strobridge, *Regulars in the Redwoods,* 145–46; Crook, Diary, June 10, 1886.

15. Dryer to Judah, June 22, 1857, and Dryer to Judah, July 6, 1857—both in Pacific, Letters Received.

16. Dryer to Judah, July 6, 1857; Crook to Judah, July 8, 1857—both ibid.; Schmitt, *General George Crook,* 42–45.

17. Strobridge, *Regulars in the Redwoods,* 146–47; Schmitt, *General George Crook,* 48 n. 3; Crook to Judah, July 8, 1857, Judah to Crook, July 11, 1867, and Judah to Gardiner, July 11, 1857—all in Pacific, Letters Received.

18. Strobridge, *Regulars in the Redwoods,* 147; Schmitt, *General George Crook,* 48 n. 3. Fort Crook was occupied until May 1866.

19. Strobridge, *Regulars in the Redwoods,* 148ff; Schmitt, *General George Crook,* 48–52; Mackall to Henley, August 15, 1857, and Mackall to Crook, September 11, 1857—both in Pacific, Letters Sent, 4:232, 243–44.

20. Strobridge, *Regulars in the Redwoods,* 154; Schmitt, *General George Crook,* 55–56 n. 1. Fort Ter-waw was closed in 1861.

21. Strobridge, *Regulars in the Redwoods,* 154–57; Schmitt, *General George Crook,* 56–57; "with knives, bows and arrows": Crook to Mackall, November 24 and December 25, 1857, and Heintzelman to Crook, December 15, 1857—all in Pacific, Letters Received; Mackall to Crook, December 5, 1857, Pacific, Letters Sent, 4:285. Crook called the disaffected tribe "Tol-a-nas."

22. King, *Major-General George Crook,* 7. King points out that although Sheridan received his commission only a year after Crook, he had to wait five years longer for promotion to first lieutenant.

CHAPTER 3: VOLUNTEER OFFICER

1. Sheridan, *Personal Memoirs,* 1:122–24.

2. Schmitt, *General George Crook,* 83. Writing two decades later, Crook referred specifically to the Confederate warship *Alabama,* although he undoubtedly meant the

Sumter, which was the only Southern naval vessel at sea at the time. The *Alabama* was not commissioned until August 24, 1862. Both ships were commanded by Capt. Raphael Semmes, CSN. For a discussion of the *Alabama* and Semmes's interest in the California steamers, see Robinson, *Shark of the Confederacy.*

3. Schmitt, *General George Crook,* 83; Garrison, *Civil War Curiosities,* 151–52; McPherson, *Battle Cry of Freedom,* 326–29. Garrison points out that, of the officers who remained in the regular army after the outbreak of the war, only one in twenty achieved the rank of general, whereas fully half of the hundred or so West Pointers who joined state volunteer units became generals.

4. Schmitt, *General George Crook,* 83–84.

5. West Virginia was created in 1861 when forty pro-Union counties broke away from the Confederate-controlled part of the state, and formed their own government. It was admitted as a separate state in 1863.

6. Schmitt, *General George Crook,* 84ff.

7. Cox, "West Virginia Operations," 2:278. Jackson's Shenandoah campaign is explained in the Time-Life book *Shenandoah 1862.*

8. Cox, "West Virginia Operations," 2:278.

9. Ibid., 2:280–81; Schmitt, *General George Crook,* 89–92. During the Civil War, brevet promotions were honorific, to reward an officer for meritorious service. In many cases, the brevet promotion also carried responsibility of the brevet rank, and thus could be used to build a temporary officer corps during the war without burdening the service with an excessive number of senior officers after the war ended. Because brevets were issued in both the Regular Army and the Volunteers, and because the officer corps of the two branches were separate, a regular officer serving with the volunteers might conceivably carry four different ranks simultaneously, i.e., his active rank and brevet rank in the Regular Army, and active and brevet ranks in the Volunteers. In Crook's case, his position as colonel of a volunteer regiment had no bearing on his active rank in the Regulars, where he officially remained a captain, breveted to major and higher ranks until, ultimately, he was appointed brevet major general. In separate actions, he was promoted up through the line of Volunteers until, likewise, he reached the position of major general. When the war ended, however, he was mustered out of the Volunteers and reverted back to the active rank of captain in the Regular Army with the brevet honor of major general attached to his record.

10. Cox, "West Virginia Operations," 2:280; Schmitt, *General George Crook,* 92.

11. Crook, Sturgis and Pope quoted in Schmitt, *General George Crook,* 92–94.

12. Ibid., 94.

13. Palfrey, *Antietam and Fredericksburg,* 15; McClellan to Brig. Gen. Lorenzo Thomas, AG, USA, October 15, 1862, *OR,* Series 1, vol. 1, pt. 1:25.

14. Crook (in Schmitt, *General George Crook,* 95) spells it "Moore." The spelling used here is from various reports throughout *OR,* ser. 1, vol. 19, pt. 1.

15. McClellan to Thomas, October 15, 1862, *OR,* ser. 1, vol. 19, pt. 1: 25–26; Burnside to Brig. Gen. S. Williams, AG, September 30, 1862, ibid., 416; Cox, "Forcing Fox's Gap and Turner's Gap," 584–85; Schmitt, *General George Crook,* 95.

16. McClellan to Thomas, October 15, 1862, *OR,* ser. 1, vol. 19, pt. 1: 27; Palfrey, *Antietam and Fredericksburg,* 21–22, 27–29; Cox, "Forcing Fox's Gap and Turner's Gap," 585.

17. Palfrey, *Antietam and Fredericksburg,* 34; Cox to Lt. Col. Richmond, AAG, Right Wing, Army of the Potomac, September 20, 1862, *OR,* ser. 1, vol. 19, pt. 1: 458; Cox, "Forcing Fox's Gap and Turner's Gap," 585–86. The custom of paroling, rendered obsolete by twentieth-century warfare, allowed a captured soldier to return to his own lines pending formal exchange for enemy prisoners. Technically, then, although Moor was in Union custody he was under Confederate jurisdiction, and was thus prohibited from rendering any assistance to his own side until the exchange was completed. Crook would find himself in a similar situation later in the war.

18. Schmitt, *General George Crook,* 95–96.

19. Cox, "Forcing Fox's Gap and Turner's Gap," 586–89; Crook to R. P. Kennedy, AAAG, Kanawha Division, September 20, 1862, *OR,* ser. 1, vol., 19, pt. 1, 471; Cox to Lt. Col. Richmond, September 20, 1862, ibid., 460; Crook quoted in Schmitt, *General George Crook,* 96.

20. Schmitt, *General George Crook,* 96. Crook's losses, listed on his report (Crook to Kennedy, September 20, 1862, *OR,* ser. 1, vol. 19, pt. 1: 471) are as follows: Eleventh Ohio—seven killed, 34 wounded, three missing; Twenty-eighth Ohio—three killed, 12 wounded; Thirty-sixth Ohio—seven killed, 18 wounded.

21. Stackpole, *From Cedar Creek to Antietam,* 353–56.

22. Burnside to Brig. Gen. S. Williams, AG, September 30, 1862, *OR,* ser. 1, vol. 19, pt. 1: 418; Schmitt, *General George Crook,* 97.

23. McClellan to Thomas, October 15, 1862, *OR,* ser. 1, vol. 19, pt. 1: 29.

24. McClellan, *Report on the Organization and Campaigns of the Army of the Potomac,* 374. McClellan later reprinted this statement verbatim in his memoir, *McClellan's Own Story,* 587.

25. McClellan, *Report on the Organization and Campaigns,* 374, and *McClellan's Own Story,* 587; Stackpole, *From Cedar Mountain to Antietam,* 407.

26. Schmitt, *General George Crook,* 97; Cox, "Battle of Antietam," 632. Scammon's brigade was led by Col. Hugh Ewing now that Scammon commanded the division.

27. Palfrey, *Antietam and Fredericksburg,* 110–11; Schmitt, *General George Crook,* 97; Cox, "Battle of Antietam," 651.

28. Crook quoted in Schmitt, *General George Crook,* 97.

29. Cox, "Battle of Antietam," 632; McClellan, *McClellan's Own Story,* 602–3; Christ to Captain Hutchins, AAG, September 21, 1862, *OR,* ser. 1, vol. 19, pt. 1: 438. McClellan's *Report on the Organization and Campaigns of the Army of the Potomac* (389–90) varies slightly in detail, but essentially agrees with Burnside's dispositions of September 16. Burnside's report of the battle stated, "[I] directed General Cox to detail

General Crook's brigade to make the assault...." Burnside to Williams, September 30, 1862, *OR,* ser. 1, vol. 19, pt. 1: 419. (By the time Burnside wrote this report, Crook had been breveted to brigadier general of volunteers).

30. Cox, "Battle of Antietam," 651–53; Stackpole, *From Cedar Mountain to Antietam,* 407, 418–23; Schmitt, *General George Crook,* 98–100.

31. Crook quoted in Schmitt, *General George Crook,* 97, 100; Return of Casualties in the Union forces at the battle of Antietam, Md., *OR,* ser. 1, vol. 19, pt. 1: 198; Crook to Lt. Kennedy, AAAG, Kanawha Division, September 20, 1862, ibid., 472; Maj. Lyman J. Jackson, Eleventh Ohio Infantry, to Crook, September 20, 1862, ibid., 473.

32. Schmitt, *General George Crook,* 100–101, 100 n. 5, 101 n. 6.

33. An excellent summary of the early part of the Chickamauga campaign appears in Time-Life's *Chickamauga,* 9–13.

34. Crook's strength fluctuated that spring according to the needs of the Army of the Cumberland as a whole. The April return listed his division with an aggregate of 6,346 officers and men, but constant reassignments reduced it to 3,791 for May. See *OR,* ser. 1, vol. 23, pt. 2: 378.

35. Schmitt, *General George Crook,* 101; Rosecrans to Senior Officer of Gunboat (Care of General Crook), February 22, 1863, *OR,* ser. 1, vol. 23, pt. 2: 82; Crook to Col. C. Goddard, Chief of Staff/AAG, Army of the Cumberland, March 5, 1863, ibid., 110; Crook to Rosecrans, March 2, 1863, ibid., 99; Crook to Goddard, March 10, 1863, ibid., 130. The new troops also included the Twenty-first Indiana Battery of artillery, which was assigned to Crook in late February or early March. See A. Piatt Andrew III to "Dear Sister," March 5, 1863, in Andrew, *Some Civil War Letters,* 42–43.

36. Schmitt, *General George Crook,* 101–2; Crook to Brig. Gen. James A. Garfield, Chief of Staff, Army of the Cumberland, March 27, 1863, *OR,* ser. 1, vol. 23, pt. 2: 179–80. Garfield was one of four future presidents with whom Crook would be associated during the war, the others being U. S. Grant, Rutherford B. Hayes, and William McKinley, Jr. Like Crook, all were from Ohio. Garfield and McKinley would be assassinated while in office.

37. Crook to Garfield, May 27, 1863, *OR,* ser. 1, vol. 23, pt. 2: 366; Schmitt, *General George Crook,* 102.

38. Rosecrans to Burnside, June 2, 1863, *OR,* ser. 1, vol. 23, pt. 2: 381; Schmitt, *General George Crook,* 102.

39. Crook to Garfield, June 4, 1863, *OR,* ser. 1, vol. 23, pt. 2: 386.

40. Maj. Gen. David S. Stanley, Cavalry Division, to Turchin, June 4, 1863, ibid., pt. 2: 386; George E. Flynt, AAG/Chief of Staff, XIV Corps, to Maj. Gen. J. J. Reynolds, Fourth Division, June 26, 1863, ibid., 466; Crook quoted in Schmitt, *General George Crook,* 102–3.

41. Schmitt, *General George Crook,* 103; Crook to "Soldiers of the Kanawha Brigade [*sic*]," July 30, 1864, George Crook Papers, (A24), University of Oregon; Andrew to "Dear Sister," August 3, 1863, in *Some Civil War Letters,* 67.

42. Crook to Maj. W. H. Sinclair, AAG, Cavalry Command, September 29, 1863, addenda, *OR,* ser. 1, vol. 30, pt. 1: 919. The composition of his division is in ibid., 47.

43. Stanley to Garfield, September 6, 1863, ibid., pt. 1: 887; Stanley to Garfield, September 13, 1863, ibid., 890; Crook to Sinclair, September 8, 1863, ibid. 917; Crook to Sinclair, September 29, 1863, ibid., 918–19; Mitchell to Garfield, October 3, 1863, ibid., 891; Schmitt, *General George Crook,* 103–5, 104 n. 1. In his memoirs Crook claimed that, being next in rank, he succeeded Stanley. If so, it was only until Mitchell arrived. Crook's memory proved faulty on McCook, for he continually identified "Gen. A. D. McCook" as commander of the First Division of the Cavalry Corps. Maj. Gen. Alexander McCook was, in fact, commander of the XX Corps. Crook meant Col. Edward M. McCook, who led the First Division under both Stanley and Mitchell. Crook's writings indicate some sort of personal animosity toward McCook, but whether it was with Alexander or Edward cannot be determined at this late date. The confusion is further compounded by the fact that Crook must have known Alexander McCook reasonably well because they both were from Ohio and were classmates at West Point (see Wallace, *Gen. August V. Kautz and the Southwestern Frontier,* 11).

44. Halleck to Stanton, November 15, 1863, *OR,* ser. 1, vol. 30, pt. 1: 38; Mitchell to Garfield, October 3, 1863, ibid., 393; "take posts at once": Crook to Sinclair, September 29, 1863, ibid., 918–19 ; Time-Life, *Chickamauga,* 61–62; Schmitt, *General George Crook,* 105.

45. Schmitt, *General George Crook,* 105–6.

46. Crook to Sinclair, September 29, 1863, *OR,* ser. 1, vol. 30, pt. 1: 918–19; Schmitt, *General George Crook,* 106–7. Crook (Schmitt, 107) contended that General Mitchell, in his verbal report to Rosecrans, had expounded on "the valorous deed of his command. How he could have the cheek, after what has passed, surpassed my understanding." Crook is not clear whether he was chagrined by the withdrawal, or whether Mitchell was denying him proper credit. If credit was the problem, Crook had little cause for complaint, for Mitchell's written report (Mitchell to Garfield, October 3, 1863, *OR,* ser. 1, vol. 30, pt. 1: 894) stated, "Brigadier-General Crook, commanding Second Division, deserves the gratitude of the country for the gallant manner in which he discharged his duty throughout the entire advance, as well as on the battlefield of Chickamauga."

47. Halleck to Stanton, November 15, 1863, *OR,* ser. 1, vol. 30, pt. 1: 39–40. Crook's activities during this period are detailed in Schmitt, *General George Crook,* 107–13.

48. Schmitt, *General George Crook,* 114; Williams, *Hayes of the Twenty-third,* 166–67.

CHAPTER 4: THE SHENANDOAH CAMPAIGN

1. Warner, *Generals in Blue,* 447–48. For opinions of Sigel by contemporaries, see Eby, *A Virginia Yankee,* 229–30, 230 n. 12.

2. Pond, *Shenandoah Valley,* 9–10.

3. Ibid., 9–10; Grant to Ord, March 29, 1864, Simon, *Papers of Ulysses S. Grant,* 10:233; Grant, *Memoirs,* 478–79; Schmitt, *General George Crook,* 114.

4. Ord to Grant, March 30, 1864, Simon, *Papers of Ulysses S. Grant,* 10:235n; Grant to Ord, March 30, 1864, ibid.

5. Pond, *Shenandoah Valley,* 10–12; Crook to Averell, May 1, 1864. Miscellaneous Papers, The Rutherford B. Hayes Library (Crook Collection, microfilm edition); Crook to Capt. T. Melvin, AAG, May 23, 1864, *OR,* ser. 1, vol. 37, pt. 1: 10. Crook faced a shortage of mounts and, because none were available locally, requested permission to purchase horses in Ohio. Grant passed the information to Secretary of War Stanton, who authorized the purchase "wherever he can procure them" and ordered Crook to dismount forty percent of his cavalry and use them as infantry. This also may have had some bearing on Crook's decision to divide his forces and concentrate his cavalry with Averell. See Crook to Grant, April 17, 1864, and Stanton to Grant, April 18, 1864, both in Simon, *Papers of Ulysses S. Grant,* 10:321n.

6. Hayes to Lucy Webb Hayes, various letters, R. B. Hayes Papers, Rutherford B. Hayes Library. Besides the personal correspondence, Lucy Hayes's visits are discussed in Williams, *Hayes of the Twenty-third,* throughout; Hayes's attitude toward Crook is mentioned in Williams, 223. Crook's attitude toward children is in Nickerson, "Major General George Crook," 32.

7. Pond, *Shenandoah Valley,* 11–12.

8. Hayes to Sophia Birchard Hayes, May 1, 1864, and Hayes to Birchard, April 20, 1864, both in R. B. Hayes Papers. Hayes was born more than two months after his father died, and Birchard, a wealthy banker, assumed the paternal role as well as provided financial security for the family.

9. Crook to Melvin, May 23, 1864, *OR,* ser. 1, vol. 37, pt. 1: 10.

10. Hayes, Diary, May 6, 1864, Rutherford B. Hayes Library.

11. Pond, *Shenandoah Valley,* 12; Williams, *Hayes of the Twenty-third,* 174–75; Crook to Melvin, May 23, 1864, *OR,* ser. 1, vol. 37, pt. 1: 10–11.

12. Crook to Melvin, May 23, 1864, *OR,* ser. 1, vol. 37, pt. 1: 11.

13. Hayes to Birchard, May 19, 1864, R. B. Hayes Papers.

14. Schmitt, *General George Crook,* 115; Pond, *Shenandoah Valley,* 12–13; Crook to Melvin, May 23, 1864, *OR,* ser. 1, vol. 37, pt. 1: 11.

15. Schmitt, *General George Crook,* 115–16; Pond, *Shenandoah Valley,* 13; Crook to Melvin, May 23, 1864, *OR,* ser. 1, vol. 37, pt. 1: 12; Capt. Daniel W. Glassie, First Kentucky Battery, to Capt. J. R. McMullin, Chief of Artillery, May 20, 1864, ibid., 39.

16. Pond, *Shenandoah Valley,* 10, 13; Hayes to Sardis Birchard, May 19, 1864, R. B. Hayes Papers.

17. Pond, *Shenandoah Valley,* 22–23; Hunter's orders in Halleck to Hunter, *OR,* ser. 1, vol. 37, pt. 1: 543.

18. Schmitt, *General George Crook,* 116; Eby, *A Virginia Yankee,* 231–32.

19. Crook to Commanding General, Department of West Virginia (i.e., Hunter), May 31, 1864, *OR,* ser. 1, vol. 37, pt. 1: 561; Crook to Lt. Col. Charles G. Halpine, AAG, July 7, 1864, ibid., 120; Hayes to Birchard, May 19, 1864, R. B. Hayes Papers.

20. Schmitt, *General George Crook,* 116; Pond, *Shenandoah Valley,* 27–28; Imboden, "Battle of New Market," 486.

21. Crook quoted in Eby, *A Virginia Yankee,* 250–51; Conway, "Talks with General J. A. Early": 251.

22. Hunter to AG, USA, August 8, 1864, *OR,* ser. 1, vol. 37, pt. 1: 97; Crook to Halpine, July 7, 1864, ibid., 120; Pond, *Shenandoah Valley,* 28–30; Eby, *A Virginia Yankee,* 252–54; Schmitt, *General George Crook,* 116–17; Williams, *Hayes of the Twenty-third,* 202–3. Williams (194, n. 1) states Hunter intended to burn Washington College as well, but was dissuaded by his officers. Strother (in Eby, *A Virginia Yankee,* 256) hints at it, but does not say definitely.

23. Crook to Halpine, July 7, 1864, *OR,* ser. 1, vol. 37, pt. 1: 120–21; Schmitt, *General George Crook,* 117–18; Eby, *A Virginia Yankee,* 264–66; Pond, *Shenandoah Valley,* 33–37; Osborne, *Jubal,* 257–58.

24. Schmitt, *General George Crook,* 118.

25. Crook to Halpine, July 7, 1864, *OR,* ser. 1, vol. 37, pt. 1: 121; Strother diary entry quoted in Eby, *A Virginia Yankee,* 269.

26. Schmitt, *General George Crook,* 119.

27. Early, "Early's March," 492–93, 492n; Lee to Jefferson Davis, June 26, 1864, *OR,* ser. 1, vol. 37, pt. 1: 767; Alvord, "Early's Attack," 3.

28. The move on Washington is described in Vandiver, *Jubal's Raid;* Pond, *Shenandoah Valley;* Grant, *Memoirs;* Early, "Early's March," and Alvord, "Early's Attack."

29. Grant to Halleck, June 12, 1864, quoted in Pond, *Shenandoah Valley,* 71–72.

30. Wright, various reports, *OR,* ser. 1, vol. 37, pt. 1: 265–69; Crook to C. A. Whittier, AAG, October 12, 1864, ibid., 287; Pond, *Shenandoah Valley,* 85–86; Schmitt, *General George Crook,* 122, 122 n. 10. Crook wrote a letter of acceptance of his appointment as brevet major general of volunteers, and signed his oath of office on July 21, 1864. In keeping with the wartime situation, the oath form stated that he had not "yielded a voluntary SUPPORT to any PRETENDED GOVERNMENT, AUTHORITY, POWER or CONSTITUTION WITHIN the United States, HOSTILE or INIMICAL thereto," meaning, specifically, the Confederate Government. (Crook to Thomas, July 21, 1865, ACP—Crook; Oath of Office, July 21, 1864, ibid.).

31. Crook to Hunter, July 27, 1864, *OR,* ser. 1, vol. 37, pt. 1: 286; Osborne, *Jubal,* 300–01; Schmitt, *General George Crook,* 123–24.

32. Schmitt, *General George Crook,* 123; Hayes to Lucy Hayes, July 26, 1864, R. B. Hayes Papers.

33. Hunter to Halpine, July 30, 1864, Halpine Papers, HP 130. This item is reproduced by permission of The Huntington Library, San Marino, California.

CHAPTER 5: SHERIDAN TAKES COMMAND

1. Sheridan, *Personal Memoirs,* 1:463–64; Grant, *Memoirs,* 615.

2. Grant, *Memoirs,* 614; Sheridan, *Personal Memoirs,* 1:459–60.

3. Grant to Hunter, August 5, 1864, reprinted in Sheridan, *Personal Memoirs,* 1:464–65. These instructions were prepared for General Hunter, who originally was to continue command of the department while Sheridan took charge of troops in the field. Hunter, however, asked to be entirely relieved and so the orders, together with total responsibility for West Virginia and the Shenandoah, were transferred to Sheridan.

4. Ibid., 1:466; Stackpole, *Sheridan in the Shenandoah,* 149; Osborne, *Jubal,* 317; War Department, Adjutant General's office, General Orders No. 248, August 30, 1864, *OR,* ser. 1, vol. 43, pt. 1: 962. The VIII Corps was formally designated "Army of Western Virginia" on August 8, 1864 (Headquarters, Middle Military Division, General Orders No. 2, August 8, 1864, ibid., pt. 1: 726). The term *division* could mean either of two things. A *geographical* division, such as the Middle Military Division, consolidated several regional departments under a single command. A *tactical* division was a fighting unit composed of several brigades that, when combined with other tactical divisions, formed part of an army corps. Normally a geographical division had jurisdiction over whatever units were within its boundaries, and might contain any number of tactical divisions, corps, or complete armies.

5. Sheridan, *Personal Memoirs,* 1:498–500; Merritt, "Sheridan in the Shenandoah Valley," 501. A very good summary of Sheridan's operations appears in Time-Life's *Shenandoah 1864,* 77–80.

6. Halleck to Sheridan, August 26, 1864, and A. F. Hayden, endorsement to ibid., August 26, 1864—both in *OR,* ser. 1, vol. 43, pt. 1: 917.

7. Crook to Col. C. Kingsbury, Jr., AAG, Middle Military Division, October 16, 1864, ibid., pt. 1: 360–61; Pond, *Shenandoah Valley,* 144–46; Merritt, "Sheridan in the Shenandoah Valley," 506; Stackpole, *Sheridan in the Shenandoah,* 174–75; Williams, *Hayes of the Twenty-third,* 240–41.

8. Sheridan, *Personal Memoirs,* 2:2–6.

9. Ibid., 2:9–14; Stackpole, *Sheridan in the Shenandoah,* 187–90; Merritt, "Sheridan in the Shenandoah Valley," 506–7. Written some twenty years later, Sheridan's memoir (2:11) says the movement began at 3 A.M.; all other sources say 2 A.M.

10. Merritt, "Sheridan in the Shenandoah Valley," 507; Early, "Winchester, Fisher's Hill, and Cedar Creek," 523; Schmitt, *General George Crook,* 125–26.

11. Schmitt, *General George Crook,* 127–28.

12. Sheridan, *Personal Memoirs,* 2:24. Sheridan does not say who advised him to bring in Crook.

13. Schmitt, *General George Crook,* 126.

14. Crook to Kingsbury, October 17, 1864, *OR,* ser. 1, vol. 43, pt. 1: 361; Sheridan, *Personal Memoirs,* 2:24–25, 27; Early, "Winchester, Fisher's Hill, and Cedar Creek," 253–24.

15. Sheridan, *Personal Memoirs*, 2:28–29.

16. Schmitt, *General George Crook*, 127; Sheridan to Bvt. Maj. Gen. John A. Rawlins, chief of staff, February 3, 1866, *OR*, ser. 1, vol. 43, pt. 1: 47. In this report of the Shenandoah Campaign, written in New Orleans in early 1866, Sheridan said:

> I had from early in the morning become apprised that I would have to engage Early's entire army, instead of two divisions, and determined to attack with the Sixth and Nineteenth Corps, holding Crook's command as a turning column to use only when the crisis of the battle occurred, and that I would put him in on my left and still get the Valley pike. . . . [I placed Crook] directly in rear of the line of battle; as the reports, however, that the enemy were attempting to turn my right kept continually increasing, I was obliged to put him in on that flank, instead of on the left as originally intended. He was directed to act as a turning column, to find the left of the enemy's line, strike it in flank or rear, break it up, and that I would order a left half wheel of the line of battle to support him.

17. Pond, *Shenandoah Valley*, 170, 173–76; Merritt, "Sheridan in the Shenandoah Valley," 510; Sheridan, *Personal Memoirs*, 2:34–36.

18. Schmitt, *General George Crook*, 129.

19. Ibid., 130–31; Union officer quoted in Pond, *Shenandoah Valley*, 177; ibid., 176–77; Sheridan, *Personal Memoirs*, 2:37–38; Stackpole, *Sheridan in the Shenandoah*, 251; Crook to Kingsbury, October 18, 1864, *OR*, ser. 1, vol. 43, pt. 1: 363–64.

20. Schmitt, *General George Crook*, 131–32; Stackpole, *Sheridan in the Shenandoah*, 250–51.

21. Pond, *Shenandoah Valley*, 178–79; Merritt, "Sheridan in the Shenandoah Valley," 510–11; Sheridan, *Personal Memoirs*, 2:45–46.

22. Sheridan, *Personal Memoirs*, 2:35; Merritt, "Sheridan in the Shenandoah Valley," 510, Schmitt, *General George Crook*, 129, 129n–30n; "I learned too late": ibid., 141; Williams, *Hayes of the Twenty-third*, 280; Hayes to Birchard, September 26, 1864, R. B. Hayes Papers; Knight, *Following the Indian Wars*, 43–44.

23. Hayes, Diary, May 24, 1866.

24. Merritt, "Sheridan in the Shenandoah Valley," 512; Sheridan, *Personal Memoirs*, 2:55–56; Pond, *Shenandoah Valley*, 194–97.

25. Crook's losses in Pond, *Shenandoah Valley*, 180; ibid., 220–21; Schmitt, *General George Crook*, 132–33; Sheridan, *Personal Memoirs*, 2:56–62; Merritt, "Sheridan in the Shenandoah Valley," 513–15; Williams, *Hayes of the Twenty-third*, 287–90.

26. Early, "Winchester, Fisher's Hill, and Cedar Creek," 526.

27. Schmitt, *General George Crook*, 133. Williams (*Hayes of the Twenty-third*, 292–93 n. 4) discusses this incident at length, noting that Crook was sparse on details, including the time and place of capture. During the Civil War, the officer of the day personally handled duties that in the modern army would be undertaken by assistants. This

means that he could be anywhere, and that he might have contact with very few people while on night duty. Williams also notes that if the OD was captured after Crook had retired for the night, his absence would not necessarily have been noticed until morning.

28. Schmitt, *General George Crook,* 133; Pond, *Shenandoah Valley,* 224–25; Williams, *Hayes of the Twenty-third,* 302–3; Merritt, "Sheridan in the Shenandoah Valley," 516–17.

29. Pond, *Shenandoah Valley,* 233–34; Early, "Winchester, Fisher's Hill, and Cedar Creek," 528–29.

30. Sheridan, *Personal Memoirs,* 2:68–83; Williams, *Hayes of the Twenty-third,* 304; Pond, *Shenandoah Valley,* 235–37; Schmitt, *General George Crook,* 133–34.

31. Schmitt, *General George Crook,* 134.

32. Ibid., 134.

33. Merritt, "Sheridan in the Shenandoah Valley," 520.

34. Crook to J. C. Kelton, AAG, October 2, 1864, R. B. Hayes Papers.

35. Hayes to Lucy Hayes, December 9, 1864, ibid.

CHAPTER 6: THE CLOSING BATTLES

1. Schmitt, *General George Crook,* 155; Williamson, *Mosby's Rangers,* 301. Quotes specifically concerning Mosby and Blazer are from Williamson.

2. Williams, *Hayes of the Twenty-third,* 317.

3. Invitation "Compliments of the Staff of Maj. Gen'l. Crook, For Friday Evening, Feb. 17, 1865, At the Revere House, Cumberland, Md.", Henry J. Johnson Papers, Rutherford B. Hayes Library (Crook Collection, microfilm edition); Warner, *Generals in Blue,* 103. Crook's attitude toward women is discussed in Nickerson, "Major General George Crook," 31. Schmitt (*General George Crook,* 306) discounts newspaper stories that appeared after Crook's death stating that Mary Dailey had nursed him back to health when he was wounded. He points out that Crook was wounded only once during the Civil War, more than two years earlier and before he would have had an opportunity to meet her. The "wound" was a superficial hit from a spent bullet at Lewisburg, and was more painful than serious.

4. The information on the McNeills comes from Boyd B. Stutler, "The Capture of Generals Crook and Kelley," the most complete account of the incident. The version published by Schmitt (*General George Crook,* 303) does not mention Captain John McNeill's death, stating instead that he led the expedition that captured Crook and that Jesse was part of it. The grudge against General Kelley was not mentioned at all. John McNeill's capture and death were noted by General Sheridan, who called him "the most daring and dangerous of all the bushwhackers in this section of the country." (Sheridan to Grant, October 7, 1864, *OR,* ser. 1, vol. 43, pt. 1: 30–31). In army reports reprinted in the *Official Records* (ser. 1, vol. 46, pt. 1), Major Robert P. Kennedy, assistant adjutant general of the U.S. Army (writing to Sheridan, February 23, 1865,

470), and Confederate General Robert E. Lee (to Secretary of War John C. Brecken-ridge, February 24, 1865, 471–72) state that the Confederates were led by "Lieutenant McNeill," indicating Jesse. Pond (*Shenandoah Valley,* 151) names Jesse as leader of the company at the time of Crook's capture, and Sheridan (*Personal Memoirs,* 2:107) states unequivocally that Jesse McNeill was responsible for Crook's capture.

5. Schmitt, *General George Crook,* 135; Stutler, "Capture of Generals Crook and Kelley," 24.

6. Kennedy to Sheridan, February 21, 1865, *OR,* ser. 1, vol. 46, pt. 1: 469; Lee to Breckenridge, February 24, 1865, ibid., 471–72; Schmitt, *General George Crook,* 135; Hayes to Grant, February 21, 1865, R. B. Hayes Papers. Crook (Schmitt, 135) claimed the men wore Confederate uniforms and represented themselves as Sheridan's scouts. Other sources maintain they wore at least enough of the federal uniform to pass themselves as regular Union soldiers. Union estimates of the number of Confederates range from fifty (see Hayes to Grant letter) to a hundred (see Kennedy to Sheridan letter). The figure of thirty in the text is from Lee, and is used as the official Confederate source.

7. Lee to Breckenridge, February 24, 1865, *OR,* ser. 1, vol. 46, pt. 1: 472; Kennedy to Sheridan, February 21, 1865, ibid., 470; Schmitt, *General George Crook,* 136, 304; Stutler, "Capture of Generals Crook and Kelley," 24; Hayes to Grant, February 21, 1865, and to Lucy Hayes, February 21, 1865, both in R. B. Hayes Papers.

8. Kennedy to Sheridan, February 21, 1865, *OR,* ser. 1, vol. 46, pt. 1: 470; E. W. Whitaker to Capt. L. Siebert, AAG, February 23, 1865, ibid., 471; Hayes to Grant, February 21, 1865, R. B. Hayes Papers; Schmitt, *General George Crook,* 304, Stutler, "Capture of Generals Crook and Kelley," 24.

9. Schmitt, "An Interview with General Jubal A. Early in 1889": 559–60. This article, hereafter cited as "Interview," consists of diary entries by Lt. Lyman W. V. Kennon, General Crook's aide, who interviewed General Early on March 20–22, 1889. Kennon visited Early in Lynchburg while doing a study of the Shenandoah Campaign.

10. Capt. Jed. Hotchkiss, Diary, February 24, 1865, *OR,* ser. 1, vol. 46, pt. 1: 515.

11. "The greatest joke of the war," Hayes to Birchard, February 7, 1864, and "a very mortifying thing," Hayes to Lucy Hayes, February 21, 1865—both in R. B. Hayes Papers; Schmitt, *General George Crook,* 135. Crook was not alone in his low regard for pickets and sentries. In a totally unrelated incident during Hunter's Raid, Strother complained, "I never saw such damnable ignorance and carelessness. The greater part of the sentries did not know where the headquarters of their regiments were. This want of system in this respect is common to our army." (Quoted in Eby, *A Virginia Yankee,* 263).

12. Hayes to Birchard, March 24, 1865, R. B. Hayes Papers; Williams, *Hayes of the Twenty-third,* 319–20; Schmitt, *General George Crook,* 304. Grant apparently did not deem the squabble with Stanton important and did not mention it in his memoirs.

13. Williams, *Hayes of the Twenty-third,* 320; Hancock to AG, USA, February 18, 1867, *OR,* ser. 1, vol. 1, pt. 1: 525; Schmitt, *General George Crook,* 304–5; Grant to

Stanton, March 21, 1865, in Grant, *Personal Memoirs,* 1082; Hayes to Lucy Hayes, March 21, 1865, and Hayes to Birchard, March 24, 1865—both in R. B. Hayes Papers.

14. Grant, *Personal Memoirs,* 687–88.

15. Sheridan, *Personal Memoirs,* 2:134–38; Schmitt, *General George Crook,* 136.

16. Sheridan, *Personal Memoirs,* 2:135ff.; Crook to Bvt. Brig. Gen. J. W. Forsyth, chief of staff, Cavalry, April 18, 1865, *OR,* ser. 1, vol. 46, pt. 1: 1141–42; Schmitt, *General George Crook,* 136–37.

17. Davis, *To Appomattox,* 174, 203; Schmitt, *General George Crook,* 137–39; Sheridan, *Personal Memoirs,* 2:166, 174ff.; Grant, *Personal Memoirs,* 723; Crook to Forsyth, April 18, 1865, *OR,* ser. 1, vol. 46, pt. 1: 1142; Davies to Maj. H. C. Weir, AAG, Second Division, April 14, 1865, ibid., 1145.

18. Sheridan, *Personal Memoirs,* 2:188. Mackenzie's life and career are discussed in Robinson, *Bad Hand.* General Grant's comment is in Grant, *Personal Memoirs,* 772.

19. Sheridan, *Personal Memoirs,* 2:189–90. Custer's brevet rank as major general was for service in the Volunteers. His active rank in the Regulars at this time was captain. At the time of his death, he was a lieutenant colonel. See Utley, *Cavalier in Buckskin,* 30.

20. Ibid., 2:191–94; Davis, *To Appomattox,* 374–76; Robinson, *Bad Hand,* 37–38; Crook to Forsyth, April 18, 1865, *OR,* ser. 1, vol. 46, pt. 1: 1142–43.

21. Crook to Hayes, April 12, 1865, R. B. Hayes Papers, Crook Collection.

22. Schmitt, *General George Crook,* 140–41, 141 n. 6. The controversy over Sherman's terms to Johnston is discussed in Lewis, *Sherman: Fighting Prophet,* 539ff.

23. Crook to Hayes, April 23, 1865, R. B. Hayes Papers, Crook Collection.

24. Hedren to the author, April 15, 2000.

25. Schmitt, "Interview," 559.

26. Schmitt, *General George Crook,* 141, 141 n. 7.

27. Ibid., 141; Crook to Thomas, June 21, 1865, ACP—Crook; Utley, *Frontier Regulars,* 13, 20–21. Utley (page 21) points out that following an overall reform of the system in 1869–70, officers were required to wear the uniform and insignia of actual rank, rather than brevet, and be addressed by actual rank in official communications. Nevertheless, the courtesy continued.

28. Hayes, Diary, May 24, 1866.

29. Utley, *Frontier Regulars,* 11; Schmitt, *General George Crook,* 141; Sheridan to Stanton, May 2, 1866, Miscellaneous Papers, Rutherford B. Hayes Library, Crook Collection; Crook to Thomas, October 6, 1866, and Chauncey McKeever, AAG, MilDivMo, to Sen. A. S. Paddock, May 29, 1896, both in ACP—Crook.

30. Schmitt, *General George Crook,* 303, 305–6.

CHAPTER 7: "I GOT INTERESTED. . . ."

1. Schmitt, *General George Crook,* 142 n. 1; Reade, "Chronicle of the Twenty-Third Regiment of Infantry": 421–22. An infantry regiment designated Twenty-third

previously existed from 1812 to 1815, when it was amalgamated with four other units to form the Second Infantry. See Reade, ibid., 421.

2. Nickerson, "Major General George Crook," 1, 3; Schmitt, *General George Crook,* 141–42; 155.

3. Nickerson, "Major General George Crook," 1–2, Schuyler Papers, WS 58.

4. Crook to Hayes, January 4, 1872, R. B. Hayes Papers, Crook Collection.

5. Nickerson, "Major General George Crook," 4; Schmitt, *General George Crook,* 142.

6. Nickerson, "Major General George Crook," 4, Schuyler Papers, WS 58.

7. Ibid., 4–6.

8. Bancroft, *Works,* 30:531 n. 21.

9. Report of General Halleck, MilDivPac, September 22, 1868, in *Report of the Secretary of War—1869,* 66.

10. Bancroft, *Works,* 30:518–22; Schmitt, *General George Crook,* 142–43, 143 n. 5; Ruby and Brown, *Indians of the Pacific Northwest,* 207–8. Whites generally used the term *Snakes* to designate Paiutes and other Shoshonean peoples during the 1860s and 1870s.

11. Schmitt, *General George Crook,* 143.

12. Bancroft, *Works,* 30:531; King, *Major-General George Crook,* 9–10; Ruby and Brown, *Indians of the Pacific Northwest,* 208; Dunlay, *Wolves for the Blue Soldiers,* 45–46; Crook quoted in Schmitt, *General George Crook,* 144.

13. Dunlay, *Wolves for the Blue Soldiers,* 46; Thrapp, *Al Sieber,* 88–89, n. 3; *Owyhee Avalanche,* August 3, 1867.

14. Schmitt, *General George Crook,* 144; Bancroft, *Works,* 30:532; Nickerson, "Major General George Crook," 9–10, Schuyler Papers, WS 58. Ruby and Brown, *Indians of the Pacific Northwest,* 209.

15. Bancroft, *Works,* 30:533; Ruby and Brown, *Indians of the Pacific Northwest,* 209; Schmitt, *General George Crook,* 145–48; Knight, *Following the Indian Wars,* 34.

16. Schmitt, *General George Crook,* 148–49, 149 n. 18. Camp C. F. Smith, Oregon, was abandoned on March 15, 1869, and should not be confused with Fort C. F. Smith, Montana, which figured in the Red Cloud War that was occurring simultaneously with Crook's campaigns in Idaho and Oregon.

17. Ibid., 149–51.

18. Bancroft, *Works,* 30:535–36; Ruby and Brown, *Indians of the Pacific Northwest,* 209.

19. Bancroft, *Works,* 30:537–38; Schmitt, *General George Crook,* 143 n. 3.

20. Bancroft, *Works,* 30: 534–36; Ruby and Brown, *Indians of the Pacific Northwest,* 209.

21. *Owyhee Avalanche,* July 27, 1867.

22. Knight, *Following the Indian Wars,* 31–32, 43–44; Robinson, *A Good Year to Die,* 57.

23. Bancroft, *Works,* 30:536–37; Schmitt, *General George Crook,* 152–53. Camp Harney was originally designated Camp Steele, but the name was changed twenty-eight days after its establishment.

24. *Owyhee Avalanche,* August 17, 1867; Knight, *Following the Indians Wars,* 47–48. During this period, John Wasson sold the *Avalanche* to W. J. Hill and H. W. Millard, apparently without consulting his brother. Nevertheless, Joe Wasson continued to send dispatches to the paper.

25. Parnell, "Operations against Hostile Indians": 483; Wasson quoted in *Owyhee Avalanche,* September 21, 1867.

26. *Owyhee Avalanche,* September 21, 1867; Dunlay, *Wolves for the Blue Soldiers,* 46; Knight, *Following the Indian Wars,* 48ff.; Parnell, "Operations against Hostile Indians": 484–85; Reade, "Chronicle of the Twenty-third Regiment of Infantry," 422–23.

27. Bancroft, *Works,* 30:539–41; Schmitt, *General George Crook,* 153–54, 155 n. 3; *Owyhee Avalanche,* November 2, 1867; Parnell, "Operations against Hostile Indians": 629.

28. *Owyhee Avalanche,* November 2, 1867.

29. Ibid.; Bancroft, *Works,* 30:541–44, 544 n. 29; Schmitt, *General George Crook,* 154–55, 155 n. 3.

30. *Owyhee Avalanche,* November 2, 1867.

31. Bancroft, *Works,* 30:544.

32. *Owyhee Avalanche,* November 9, 1867. *Piute* was the standard spelling of the nineteenth century.

33. Ibid.; Bancroft, *Works,* 30:548; Schmitt, *General George Crook,* 156–58; Reade, "Chronicle of the Twenty-third Regiment of Infantry": 423.

34. Schmitt, *General George Crook,* 158–59; Parnell, "Operations against Hostile Indians": 633–34; Bancroft, *Works,* 30:548–49; Nickerson, "Major General George Crook," 10–13, Schuyler Papers, WS 58.

35. Bancroft, *Works,* 30:549; Nickerson, "Major General George Crook," 13.

36. Report of General Halleck, MilDivPac, September 22, 1868, in *Report of the Secretary of War—1869.*

37. Letters found in ACP—Crook: Haight to Johnson, November 27, 1868; George Williams, William M. Stewart, and H. W. Corbett to Johnson, November 19, 1868; Scott to Williams and Corbett, November 17, 1868; Gibbs to Johnson, November 17, 1868; Hayes to Johnson, December 28, 1868; Boreman to Johnson, January 4, 1869.

38. Crook to Hayes, October 31, 1869, and January 16, 1870; Hayes to Crook, December 15, 1869; various letters—all in R. B. Hayes Papers, Crook Collection. In the January 16 letter, Crook advised Hayes that Mary was "anxious" about the portrait, which had not arrived. There is no record of whether they received it.

39. Hutton, *Phil Sheridan,* 115.

40. The disputes between the War and Interior Departments, and between the two houses of Congress are discussed in Priest, *Uncle Sam's Stepchildren,* Chapter 2.

41. Ibid., 28ff., 43–44; Welsh, "The Indian Question": 262–63.

CHAPTER 8: ARIZONA: "A SHARP ACTIVE CAMPAIGN"

1. Schmitt, *General George Crook,* 159–60, 160 n. 1; King, *Major-General George Crook,* 10; Utley, *Frontier Regulars,* 34, 192; Warner, *Generals in Blue,* 501–2.

2. Cochise's life is discussed in Sweeney, *Cochise, Chiricahua Apache Chief.*

3. Whitman to Col. J. G. C. Lee, USA, May 17, 1871, Board of Indian Commissioners, *Report,* 31–33; Testimony of C. B. Briesly, acting assistant surgeon, USA, September 16, 1871, ibid., 33–34; Bancroft, *Works,* 17:558–59; Sweeney, *Cochise,* 317; Wooster, *The Military and United States Indian Policy,* 147–48; Thrapp, *Conquest of Apacheria,* 80ff.; Worcester, *Apaches, Eagles of the Southwest,* 115. The soldiers in the Southwest generally used the Spanish word *rancheria* in reference to an Apache camp.

4. Sweeney, *Cochise,* 317; Schmitt, *General George Crook,* 160; Utley, *Frontier Regulars,* 192–93.

5. Townsend to Belknap, May 1, 1871, ACP—Crook.

6. Townsend to Crook, May 2, 1871, ibid.; Schmitt, *General George Crook,* 160–63; Department of Arizona General Orders No. 12, June 4, 1871, official copy in Bourke Diary, vol. 1.

7. Bourke, *On the Border,* 108; Thrapp, *Conquest of Apacheria,* 95, 95 n. 3; Haley, *Apaches,* 265–66. Neither Thrapp nor Haley attempted to explain Crook's feelings toward Whitman, although Haley (282–83 n. 14) speculates there might have been a personal reason that has not been recorded. Normally, Crook did not hound any officer unless he perceived that the officer had somehow crossed him.

8. Haley, *Apaches,* 266.

9. Bourke, *On the Border,* 108–9; Worcester, *Apaches, Eagles of the Southwest,* 123–24.

10. Department of Arizona General Orders No. 18, September 1, 1873. Official copy in Bourke Diary, vol. 1.

11. Porter, *Paper Medicine Man,* 12–13; King, "Needed: A Re-evaluation": 224–25.

12. Bourke's life is discussed in Porter, *Paper Medicine Man,* and his relationship with Crook in his own work, *On the Border with Crook.*

13. Bourke, *On the Border,* 112–13.

14. Crook to AG, USA, September 4, 1871, 1: 1, George Crook Letter Books, The Rutherford B. Hayes Library (microfilm edition); Schmitt, *General George Crook,* 164; Worcester, *Apaches, Eagles of the Southwest,* 143.

15. Schmitt, *General George Crook,* 164–65.

16. Crook to AG, USA, September 4, 1871, 1:1–2, George Crook Letter Books, The Rutherford B. Hayes Library (microfilm edition); Bourke, "General George Crook in the Indian Country," 656; Dunlay, *Wolves for the Blue Soldiers,* 166–67; Ball, *In the Days of Victorio,* 80.

17. Crook, "The Apache Problem," 263; Schmitt, *General George Crook,* 166; Sieber's life is covered in Thrapp, *Al Sieber, Chief of Scouts.*

18. Crook to AG, USA, September 4, 1871, 1:1–4, George Crook Letter Books,The Rutherford B. Hayes Library. Crook generally used the common nineteenth century spelling "Cocheis" although he sometimes used the more modern "Cochise."

19. Sweeney, *Cochise,* 316–17. During this period Apaches soundly defeated a detachment of Third Cavalry under Lt. Howard Bass Cushing near the Whetstone Mountains on May 5, 1871. Many believe Cochise was responsible, but Sweeney and historians Eve Ball and Dan L.Thrapp contend that the Apaches were, in fact, led by Juh. See Sweeney, *Cochise,* 313–14, and Thrapp, *Juh,* 6–7.

20. Crook to AG, USA, September 4, 1871, 1:3–4, George Crook Letter Books. Crook to AG, USA, September 28, 1871, 1:8, ibid.; Schmitt, *General George Crook,* 166–67; Bourke, *On the Border,* 144ff., and "General George Crook in the Indian Country," 655; Haley, *Apaches,* 268.

21. Crook to AG, USA, September 4, 1871, 1:4, George Crook Letter Books.

22. Worcester, *Apaches, Eagles of the Southwest,* 141; Utley, *Frontier Regulars,* 193; Schmitt, *General George Crook,* 167 n. 10.

23. "that spawn of hell": Bourke, Diary, 1:91; "These Indians have been at war": Crook to AG, USA, September 19, 1871, 1:5, George Crook Letter Books; Board of Indian Commissioners, *Report,* 28–29; Bancroft, *Works,* 17:562; Utley, *Frontier Regulars,* 193; Crook to Hayes, October 14, 1871, R. B. Hayes Papers, Crook Collection; Schmitt, *General George Crook,* 167–68.

24. Board of Indian Commissioners, *Report,* 28.

25. "my official duties": ibid., 29; Bancroft, *Works,* 17:562–63; Priest, *Uncle Sam's Stepchildren,* 46; Thrapp, *Conquest of Apacheria,* 103; Welsh, "The Indian Question," 262–63; "could not come of mortal parents": Schmitt, *General George Crook,* 168; "too much money in this Indian business": Crook to Hayes, November 28, 1871, R. B. Hayes Papers, Crook Collection. Ironically, Parker himself was a full-blooded Seneca Indian.

26. Worcester, *Apaches, Eagles of the Southwest,* 133–34.

27. Crook to AG, USA, September 28, 1871, 1:8, George Crook Letter Books.

28. Crook to AAG, MilDivPac, December 7, 1871, 1:10, ibid.; Bancroft, *Works,* 17:563; Thrapp, *Conquest of Apacheria,* 119.

29. Bourke, *On the Border,* 151; Thrapp, *Conquest of Apacheria,* 106.

30. Crook to AAG, MilDivPac, December 7, 1871, 1:10, George Crook Letter Books; Crook to AAG, MilDivPac, September 18, 1872, 1:12, ibid.; Schmitt, *General George Crook,* 173–74; Thrapp, *Al Sieber,* 90ff.; Bancroft, *Works,* 17:560 n. 14; Bourke, *On the Border,* 166–67; Worcester, *Apaches, Eagles of the Southwest,* 146. Crook's autobiography (Schmitt, 174) indicates the Wickenburg Massacre occurred in late August or early September. Other sources, however, place it in November, as does Crook's letter of September 18, 1872.The letter book for the summer and fall of 1871 contains no mention of it.

31. Thrapp, *Conquest of Apacheria,* 106; Bourke, *On the Border,* 167.

32. Thrapp, *Conquest of Apacheria,* 107; Crook to AAG, MilDivPac, September 18, 1872, 1:12, George Crook Letter Books.

33. Schmitt, *General George Crook,* 169–70. Howard discusses his background in his memoirs, *My Life and Experiences among Our Hostile Indians.*

34. Howard, *My Life and Experiences,* 152.

35. Ibid., 149, 151–52; Crook quoted in Schmitt, *General George Crook,* 170; charges against Whitman quoted in Thrapp, *Conquest of Apacheria,* 107–9; Knight, *Following the Indian Wars,* 168. Howard and Whitman were born only a dozen miles from each other. Howard's wife and Whitman's first wife were related. See Thrapp, ibid., 109–110.

36. Howard, *My Life and Experiences,* 157ff.; Thrapp, *Conquest of Apacheria,* 110; all quotes from Schmitt, *General George Crook,* 169–72.

37. Schmitt, *General George Crook,* 173. Howard said nothing about the quarrel in *My Life and Experiences,* although he did mention it in his report. See Schmitt, ibid., 173 n. 17.

38. Bancroft, *Works,* 27:563–64; Thrapp, *Conquest of Apacheria,* 111.

CHAPTER 9: THE GRAND OFFENSIVE

1. Crook to Hayes, October 14, 1871, R. B. Hayes Papers, Crook Collection; Howard, *My Life and Experiences,* 151; Bourke, *On the Border,* 202; "Crook's blood-hounds": "King to 'Dear Mother,'" October 12, 1874, King Papers, Archives Division, State Historical Society of Wisconsin, Madison; Knight, *Life and Manners,* 139. King's life and career are discussed in Russell, *Campaigning with King.* The Huntington Library preserves an extensive collection of Crook-Schuyler correspondence in which Crook, for some reason, always addressed him as "Scuyler" deleting the *h.*

2. Schmitt, *General George Crook,* 306; Summerhayes, *Vanished Arizona,* 63.

3. Crook to AAG, MilDivPac, September 21, 1872, 1:18, George Crook Letter Books.

4. Crook, "The Apache Problem": 261–62.

5. "uneasy and suspicious": Crook to AAG, MilDivPac, September 18, 1872, 1:12–14, George Crook Letter Books; Bourke, *On the Border,* 167–70; Thrapp, *Al Sieber,* 97–99; Schmitt, *General George Crook,* 174.

6. Crook to AAG, MilDivPac, September 18, 1872, 1:12–14, George Crook Letter Books; Crook to AAG, MilDivPac, December 13, 1872, 1:19–20, ibid.; Bourke, *On the Border,* 170; Thrapp, *Al Sieber,* 100–103; Worcester, *Apaches, Eagles of the Southwest,* 147–48.

7. Crook to AAG, MilDivPac, December 13, 1872, 1:20, George Crook Letter Books; "the military was to see": Schmitt, *General George Crook,* 174–75; Thrapp, *Al Sieber,* 105, and *Conquest of Apacheria,* 119–20. In the nineteenth century, *Hualapai* was generally spelled *Hualpai* leaving out the second *a.* The nineteenth-century spelling is used in reference to the military post.

8. Bourke, *On the Border,* 182.

9. Bourke, Diary, 1:1.

10. Ibid., 1:11. During the first few years, the Bourke Diary does not contain all the phenomenal detail that ultimately would characterize it. The first volume includes the period from November 20, 1872, to April 5, 1873. Later volumes would be so extensive that each one covers only a few weeks.

11. Crook to AAG, MilDivPac, December 13, 1872, 1:20, George Crook Letter Books.

12. Schmitt, *General George Crook,* 175.

13. Ibid., 175; Sweeney, *Cochise,* 346ff.; Crook to AAG, MilDivPac, December 13, 1877, 1:21–22, George Crook Letter Books. Bourke, far less opinionated than Crook, observed that General Howard had met with Cochise and negotiated the truce "at great personal discomfort and no little personal risk." (*On the Border,* 235).

14. Bourke, Diary, 1:23–25; Schmitt, *General George Crook,* 175; Crook to AAG, MilDivPac, December 13, 1872, 1:20–21, George Crook Letter Books. Bourke took a much more positive view of Eskiminzin, calling him "an excellent soldier, wily as a cat, and a born general" (Bourke, "General Crook in the Indian Country": 655).

15. Sweeney, *Cochise,* 376–77; Bourke, Diary, 1:25; Crook to AAG, MilDivPac, February 11, 1873, 1:25–26, George Crook Letter Books. In his autobiography (Schmitt, 176–77), Crook claimed that he had already concluded his great offensive and was preparing to move against Cochise when Howard concluded the truce. In fact, the truce had been in effect for about a month when Crook began the offensive. See Thrapp, *Conquest of Apacheria,* 144–45.

16. Crook to AAG, MilDivPac, January 24, 1873, 1:23, George Crook Letter Books; Thrapp, *Conquest of Apacheria,* 145–46; Bourke, Diary, 1:183.

17. Bourke, *On the Border,* 234–35.

18. Bourke, Diary, 1:177–83.

19. Crook to AAG, MilDivPac, February 11, 1873, 1:26–27, George Crook Letter Books; Crook to Pesqueira, February 9, 1873, 1:25, ibid.

20. Bancroft, *Works,* 17:564; Thrapp, *Conquest of Apacheria,* 122ff.; Bourke, *On the Border,* 203.

21. All quotes from Bourke, Diary, 1:75ff.; Bourke, *On the Border,* 185–88; Thrapp, *Conquest of Apacheria,* 124ff. Thrapp's account of this fight is reprinted verbatim from Bourke's diary. There is some conflict in the number of hostile casualties. Thrapp said seventy-six were killed altogether, estimating that fifty-seven were warriors and the balance were women and children (129–30). Two of the wounded prisoners died before reaching internment at Camp McDowell. One warrior apparently survived, hidden beneath a slab of rock under a pile of dead, and managed to escape after the soldiers withdrew.

22. Thrapp, *Conquest of Apacheria,* 130–31. The fight was largely forgotten until 1907, when the site was rediscovered by a cowboy named Jeff Adams. Adams found

the cave full of bones because the dead had not been buried after the fight. As the story once again captured public attention, it came to be known as the Skeleton Cave Massacre. See Thrapp, ibid., 130 n. 16, and Schmitt, *General George Crook,* 176 n. 7.

23. Nickerson, "Major General George Crook," 16–17, Schuyler Papers, WS 58; Thrapp, *Conquest of Apacheria,* 133–34.

24. Schmitt, *General George Crook,* 177–78; Thrapp, *Conquest of Apacheria,* 135–37. Neither Thrapp nor I have been able to locate an official report of this fight, and Crook's account in Schmitt has been used. Crook, however, assumed that the entire summit was surrounded by an escarpment and the men jumped to their deaths, but Thrapp, who climbed the mountain, noted the slope and brush below.

25. Crook to AAG, MilDivPac, April 12, 1873, 1:28, George Crook Letter Books. Even after Cochise's death, Crook could never bring himself to accept that Howard had succeeded in achieving peace with the Chiricahua leader.

26. Crook and Cha-lipun quoted in Schmitt, *General George Crook,* 179. Bourke gives Cha-lipun's surrender as April 6, but April 7 is the generally accepted date. See *On the Border,* 212.

27. Bourke, *On the Border,* 212–13; Reade, "Chronicle of the Twenty-third Regiment of Infantry," 424; Dunlay, *Wolves for the Blue Soldiers,* 168.

28. Headquarters, Department of Arizona, General Orders, No. 12, April 7, 1873. Printed copy in Bourke, Diary, 1:186.

29. Headquarters, Department of Arizona, General Orders, No. 13, April 8, 1873. Printed copy of orders in Bourke, 1:188.

30. Crook to AAG, MilDivPac, Annual Report, September 22, 1873, 1:39–40, George Crook Letter Books; Bourke, *On the Border,* 216–17; Schmitt, *General George Crook,* 183; Crook to Schuyler, July 24, 1873, Schuyler Papers, WS 15.

31. Belknap, Directive, October 29, 1873, and Crook to AG, USA, November 9, 1873, both in ACP—Crook; Schmitt, *General George Crook,* 183 n. 14.

32. Hutton, *Phil Sheridan,* 126; Wooster, *Nelson A. Miles and the Twilight of the Frontier Army,* 77, 127; Pohanka, *Nelson A. Miles,* 148.

33. Newton Booth, governor of California, to Grant, January 12, 1874, ACP—Crook.

34. Undated, unattributed newspaper clipping, Bourke Diary, 1:187; Schmitt, *General George Crook,* 181; Thrapp, *Conquest of Apacheria,* 142, 154–55; Crook to Schuyler, September 15, 1873, Schuyler Papers, WS 18.

35. Thrapp, *Al Sieber,* 121–25; ibid., *Conquest of Apacheria,* 155.

36. Crook to Schuyler, July 13, 1874, Schuyler Papers, WS 21; Nickerson, "Major General George Crook," 14–15, Schuyler Papers, WS 58; Utley, *Frontier Regulars,* 45–46; Schmitt, *General George Crook,* 181; Thrapp, *Conquest of Apacheria,* 157–58.

37. Crook to Schuyler, June 23, 1874, quoted in Thrapp, *Conquest of Apacheria,* 160. Thrapp's book was published in 1967. Thirty years later, when I obtained copies of

the Crook-Schuyler correspondence from the Huntington Library, I could not locate this letter, nor could I consult with Thrapp, who died in 1994.

38. Thrapp, *Conquest of Apacheria,* 160–61; Bourke, *On the Border,* 220; Schmitt, *General George Crook,* 181–82.

39. Bourke, *On the Border,* 216–17: Schmitt, *General George Crook,* 183–85; Bancroft, *Works,* 17:565–68.

40. Nickerson, "Major General George Crook," 17, Schuyler Papers, WS 58.

41. Crook to AAG, MilDivPac, July 7, 1873, 1:32, George Crook Letter Books; Bancroft, *Works,* 17:565.

42. Nickerson, "Major General George Crook," 15.

CHAPTER 10: THE GREAT SIOUX WAR

1. The Fort Laramie Treaty and the events leading to the Great Sioux War of 1876–77 are covered in Edward Lazarus, *Black Hills White Justice;* Charles M. Robinson III, *A Good Year to Die;* and John S. Gray, *Centennial Campaign.* Most of the following material is drawn from these works. The Lakota view of the Black Hills is discussed in the same works and in Utley, *The Lance and the Shield,* 115.

2. Utley, *The Lance and the Shield,* 118–20; Robinson, *A Good Year to Die,* 33–36; Gray, *Centennial Campaign,* 17ff.; William D. Whipple, AG, USA, to Sheridan, March 17, 1875, RG 393, Special File, Military Division of the Missouri, "Citizens Expeditions" to the Black Hills; various unattributed newspapers clippings, in Bourke, Diary, vol. 2.

3. Schmitt, *General George Crook,* 187; Hutton, *Phil Sheridan,* 273–76; Maj. George D. Ruggles, AAG, Platte to Crook, September 16, 1875, 1:370, George Crook Letter Books; Bourke, Diary, 29:10.

4. Bancroft, *Works,* 25:221; Sheridan to Crook, undated [September 1875], and Sheridan to Schofield, September 7, 1875—both in Sheridan Papers; Ruggles to Crook, September 16, 1875, 1:370–71, George Crook Letter Books. The Department of the Platte included Iowa, Nebraska, Wyoming, Utah and, after 1875, southern Idaho.

5. Schmitt, *General George Crook,* 188–89; Gray, *Centennial Campaign,* 2; Lazarus, *Black Hills White Justice,* 79; Crook, Proclamation, July 29, 1875, copy courtesy of Paul L. Hedren; Crook to AAG, MilDivMo, August 16, 1875. 1:368–69, George Crook Letter Books.

6. Crook to AAG, MilDivMo, September 15, 1875, 1:375, George Crook Letter Books. This letter is sometimes cited as Crook's annual report. Actually it appears to have been a cover letter for the annual report, which was prepared by Ruggles (Ruggles to Crook, September 16, 1875, 1:369–73, ibid.) and forwarded to Chicago. Having commanded the Platte for less than five months, Crook did not feel competent to prepare an annual report, and left that chore to Ruggles.

7. Robinson, *A Good Year to Die,* 37–40; Gray, *Centennial Campaign,* 21; Lazarus, *Black Hills White Justice,* 79–82. Delano quoted in Bancroft, *Works,* 25:776–77.

8. Crook to AAG, MilDivMo, December 22, 1875, 1:375, George Crook Letter Books; Gray, *Centennial Campaign,* 25–27, 31; Robinson, *A Good Year to Die,* 40ff.; Lazarus, *Black Hills White Justice,* 79; Hutton, *Phil Sheridan,* 300–1; Hedren, *Fort Laramie in 1876,* 52; "Gen. Crook is of the opinion": Sheridan to Sherman, January 3, 1876, Sheridan Papers; "Of all the wars": Crawford, *Exploits of Ben Arnold,* 240.

9. Robinson, *A Good Year to Die,* 51ff.; Hutton, *Phil Sheridan,* 301.

10. Robinson, *A Good Year to Die,* 57–58; Bourke, Diary, 3:1–2, 38–39; Bourke, *On the Border,* 254.

11. Bourke, Diary, 3:1–2. Over the years, Bourke substantially modified his position, blaming white avarice for many of the problems. In *On the Border with Crook,* written in 1890, he viewed the same war in an entirely different light, commenting:

> Much of our trouble with these tribes could have been averted, had we shown what would appear to them as a spirit of justice and fair dealing in this negotiation. It is hard to make the average savage comprehend why it is that as soon as his reservation is found to amount to anything he must leave and give up to the white man. Why should not Indians be permitted to hold mining or any other kind of land? The whites could mine on shares or on a royalty, and the Indians would soon become workers in the bowels of the earth. . . . The policy of the American people has been to vagabondize the Indian, and throttle every ambition he may have for his own elevation" (244).

See also Porter, *Paper Medicine Man,* 65–67.

12. Bourke, Diary, 3:4–6; "as sweet a lot of cutthroats": ibid., 3:38; Bourke, *On the Border,* 255; Robinson, *A Good Year to Die,* 59–61, 63, 152; Crawford, *Exploits of Ben Arnold,* 215; "could speak perfect Sioux": ibid., 241. Grouard's story is told in De Barthe, *The Life and Adventures of Frank Grouard,* which discusses the hiring of scouts on pp. 177–81. Grouard styled himself "chief of scouts," but that position generally was held by the army officer who supervised the scouts, in this case Major Stanton. Grouard's actual position was "chief scout," which was the senior civilian scout, a sort of foreman for the others.

13. Crook to Custer, February 27, 1876, George Crook Papers, (A24), University of Oregon; Robinson, *A Good Year to Die,* 58; Bourke, *On the Border,* 283.

14. Bourke, Diary, 3:18.

15. Ibid., 3:14; "We are outsiders": Crawford, *Exploits of Ben Arnold,* 233; Robinson, *A Good Year to Die,* 58, 61.

16. Crook to AAG, USA, May 7, 1876, Subreport 6A, Report of the Secretary of War, 1876, 503; Robinson, *A Good Year to Die,* 62; Bourke, *On the Border,* 270. In his autobiography, Crook implies that he was in complete command of the expedition, barely acknowledging Reynolds other than to blame him for the failure of the subsequent fight. See Schmitt, *General George Crook,* 190–91.

17. Mills, *My Story,* 407; De Barthe, *Frank Grouard,* 485.

18. Bourke, *On the Border,* 257–59, and Diary, 3:27ff.; Schmitt, *General George Crook,* 191; Robinson, *A Good Year to Die,* 66–69.

19. Mangum, "Battle on the Powder River": 17; Bourke, *On the Border,* 259ff.; Robinson, *A Good Year to Die,* 70–71.

20. Mangum, "Battle on the Powder River": 17–18; Bourke, *On the Border,* 270–72; Robinson, *A Good Year to Die,* 71–75.

21. The Powder River fight is covered in many works, including Mangum, "Battle on the Powder River"; Bourke, *On the Border;* Robinson, *A Good Year to Die;* and Gray, *Centennial Campaign.*

22. Nickerson, "Major General George Crook," 21, Schuyler Papers, WS 58; Crook to AAG, USA, May 7, 1876, Subreport 6A, Report of the Secretary of War, 1876, 503.

23. Utley, *The Lance and the Shield,* 122–24, 132–33; Robinson, *A Good Year to Die,* 70–71, 85–87; Lt. George Ruhlen to Terry, April 19, 1876, with endorsements, RG 393, Special File, Military Division of the Missouri, Sioux War, 1876–77, hereafter referred to as "Special File—Sioux". A large number of clippings concerning the fight, taken from both eastern and western newspapers, are pasted in Bourke, Diary, vols. 11–13.

24. Bourke, *On the Border,* 285; Robinson, *A Good Year to Die,* 117; Schmitt, *General George Crook,* 192–93; Mangum, *Battle of the Rosebud,* 9–10.

25. Nickerson, "Major General George Crook," 22, Schuyler Papers, WS 58; "Crook's Chagrin," *Cheyenne Daily Leader,* April 5, 1876; "Partial Failure of Its Object," *New York Tribune,* April 7, 1876; Vaughn, *With Crook at the Rosebud,* 8.

26. The movements of the Indians and of the Montana and Dakota columns are described in Robinson, *A Good Year to Die,* and Gray, *Centennial Campaign.* The size of the Indian camp and number of inhabitants is from Utley, *The Lance and the Shield,* 135.

27. Schmitt, *General George Crook,* 193; Mangum, *Battle of the Rosebud,* 23–24; Robinson, *A Good Year to Die,* 117–18; Bourke, *On the Border,* 284–85; Crook to Sheridan, May 29, 1876, Special File—Sioux.

28. Robinson, *A Good Year to Die,* 119.

29. *Omaha Herald,* May 19, 1876.

30. Bourke, *On the Border,* 285–87; Robinson, *A Good Year to Die,* 118–19; Hutton, *Phil Sheridan,* 312–13.

31. Bourke, *On the Border,* 289–91, 299–300; Robinson, *A Good Year to Die,* 120–24; Mangum, *Battle of the Rosebud,* 25; Knight, *Following the Indian Wars,* 159ff.; Mills, *My Story,* 397–98. Bourke puts the discovery of Calamity Jane at Goose Creek camp in the foothills of the Bighorns. Mills's account is used because it is more detailed; apparently he had been given responsibility for looking after her.

32. Capron, Diary, 9, 18–19, 21–23; Bourke, *On the Border,* 293, and Diary, 4:346; Robinson, *A Good Year to Die,* 124ff.; Finerty, *War-Path and Bivouac,* 88–90, 92–96. Years later, Arnold claimed he could "make out nothing of what [the Crow] said. If

it had been daytime I could have talked with him in the Chinook sign language." See Crawford, *Exploits of Ben Arnold,* 242–43.

33. Bourke, *On the Border,* 296.

34. The position of Crazy Horse as an individual, and the office of war chief itself, were exaggerated in the minds of whites, who applied their own interpretation of leadership to Plains Indians, and used it to justify army reverses. Although some autocratic chiefs, like Ouray of the Utes, and Washakie of the Shoshones, were able to impose their wills over their people to the point of virtual dictatorship, in most cases a chief's authority was based on individual prestige and force of personality. Even in battle no warrior was legally or morally bound to obey a chief if he believed his own interests were not served. Lt. W. Philo Clark, Second Cavalry, probably understood better than most the true situation, in a summary of the war prepared for Crook:

> Great prominence has been given Crazy Horse and Sitting Bull in this war; the good fighting strategy and subsequent muster by retreats being attributed to them, whereas they are really not entitled to more credit or censure than many others so far as plans and orders were concerned, but they headed two of the worst bands on the plains, and were the two fiercest leaders the Sioux nation has produced for years. Clark to AG, Platte, September 14, 1877, Special File—Sioux.

See also Utley, *The Lance and the Shield,* 161–62.

35. The stated reason for the move to Goose Creek is found in Bourke, *On the Border,* 297. The correspondents, however, indicated in their dispatches that there were other reasons. Robert Strahorn bluntly stated that Goose Creek had been Crook's intended destination from the start, but that the command had gotten lost and so wasted time camped on the Tongue. See Gray, *Centennial Campaign,* 116.

36. Capron, Diary, 25–28; Bourke, *On the Border,* 297–303; Robinson, *A Good Year to Die,* 130, 132–33; Gray, *Centennial Campaign,* 115–17; Crook to AAG, MilDivMo, June 20, 1876, Special File—Sioux, copy in 1:380, George Crook Letter Books.

37. Robinson, *A Good Year to Die,* 164.

38. Ibid., 130, 132–35; Capron, Diary, 26–29; Nickerson, "Major General George Crook," 22–24; Bourke, *On the Border,* 298ff.; Finerty, *War-Path and Bivouac,* 100–102, 105; Mangum, *Battle of the Rosebud,* 42–45; Hebard, *Washakie,* 183–84.

39. Capron, Diary, 28; Robinson, *A Good Year to Die,* 136–37; Bourke, *On the Border,* 305–6; Finerty, *War-Path and Bivouac,* 105, 117; Mills, *My Story,* 398. Various sources disagreed on the time the march began, but all place it between 5 and 6 A.M. Very likely it took at least an hour to get the entire column underway, and the chroniclers of the march simply noted the times that they and/or their units began moving.

40. King, "Address by General Charles King," 410. At this time, King was with Carr and the Fifth Cavalry in Nebraska, but would join the expedition the following month.

CHAPTER 11: ROSEBUD GEORGE

1. Capron, Diary, 30–31; Bourke, *On the Border,* 307–10; Robinson, *A Good Year to Die,* 138–39; Utley, *The Lance and the Shield,* 162. Much of the material in *On the Border with Crook* for this period is taken directly from the Bourke Diary. It should be noted, however, that the diary itself, for the two-month period of July 28 through September 28, 1876, was reconstructed from memory, the original having been lost about 1877–78.

2. The Battle of the Rosebud is described in Vaughn, *With Crook at the Rosebud;* Mangum, *Battle of the Rosebud;* Robinson, *A Good Year to Die,* 140ff.; Gray, *Centennial Campaign,* 121ff.,; Mills, *My Story,* 400ff.; De Barthe, *Frank Grouard,* 223ff.; and Bourke, *On the Border,* 311ff., among others. Quote from Bourke, ibid., 311.

3. Crook to AAG, MilDivMo, June 20, 1876, Special File—Sioux, copy in 1:381, George Crook Letter Books; Nickerson, "Major General George Crook," 25–26, Schuyler Papers, WS 58. Mills, *My Story,* 405; Schmitt, *General George Crook,* 194–95. Crook's autobiography ends with the Rosebud fight. The balance of the narrative was researched and written by Martin Schmitt. The deployment of the various units is discussed in Capron, Diary, 32–33; Vaughn, *With Crook at the Rosebud,* 90–91; and the various action reports, which are included in Special File—Sioux, and reprinted in Vaughn, ibid., 213ff.

4. Mills, *My Story,* 403–4; De Barthe, *Frank Grouard,* 241.

5. Bourke, Diary, 5:421; Robinson, *A Good Year to Die,* 147–49; De Barthe, *Frank Grouard,* 242; "realized for the first time": Mills, *My Story,* 405; Vaughn, *With Crook at the Rosebud,* 66; Crook to AAG, MilDivMo, June 20, 1876, Special File—Sioux, copy in 1:381, George Crook Letter Books, and reprinted in Vaughn, *With Crook at the Rosebud,* 214–17; Hutton, *Phil Sheridan,* 314. Capron's diary (33) lists one officer and twenty men wounded, and nine soldiers killed; and one government Indian killed and eight wounded, which is close to Crook's figures. He may have used the official tally.

6. Bourke, *On the Border,* 317–18; Robinson, *A Good Year to Die,* 149–50; Crawford, *Exploits of Ben Arnold,* 261; Utley, *The Lance and the Shield,* 143; Finerty, *War-Path and Bivouac,* 151; Knight, *Following the Indian Wars,* 193. A group of young warriors located the grave and plundered the bodies almost immediately after the soldiers departed.

7. Bourke, Diary, 5:431–34.

8. Robinson, *A Good Year to Die,* 108, 163–64; Hutton, *Phil Sheridan,* 314; Capt. E. W. Smith, AAAG, Department of Dakota, to Custer, June 22, 1876, Special File—Sioux. Mangum (*Battle of the Rosebud,* 96–97) points with some justice to the difficulties that Crook would have had in attempting to communicate directly with Terry, and notes that he did follow procedure by sending a report to Sheridan. Nevertheless, Terry dispatched couriers directly to Crook following the Custer fight, and these couriers eventually did get through, even though Crook already had been officially

notified by Sheridan. Despite the various difficulties in communication, one cannot help but feel, as historian John Carroll noted in his introduction to *The Court Martial of Frederick W. Benteen*, (i–ii), that Crook at least should have made some attempt get a message to Terry. There is no question that Custer was the author of his own destruction; nevertheless, Crook's lackadaisical attitude toward a coordinated effort with Terry, and his failure to provide for an extended period in the field must be factored into the situation.

9. Bourke, Diary, 5:437–40; and *On the Border*, 328.

10. Robinson, *A Good Year to Die*, 222, 227.

11. Carr to Mary Carr, July 3, 1876, Carr Papers.

12. Merritt to AG, MilDivMo, July 15, 1876, Special File—Sioux. The War Bonnet Creek fight is discussed in many works, including Hedren, *First Scalp for Custer*; King, *Campaigning with Crook*, 26ff.; Cody, *Life of the Hon. William F. Cody*, 341–47; and Robinson, *A Good Year to Die*, 228–33.

13. Bourke, *On the Border*, 329ff.; Robinson, *A Good Year to Die*, 220–22; Hebard, *Washakie*, 194–96; Sibley to AAG, Big Horn and Yellowstone Expedition, July 12, 1876, Special File—Sioux; Capron, Diary, 51; Crawford, *Exploits of Ben Arnold*, 257–58.

14. Robinson, *A Good Year to Die*, 226.

15. Crook to Sheridan, July 26, 1876, Special File—Sioux.

16. Davenport in *New York Herald*, July 6, 1876, reprinted in Green, *Battles and Skirmishes*, 26ff.; *New York Herald*, June 27, 1876; Crook to Sheridan, July 27, 1876, Special File—Sioux; Bourke, Diary, 5:621; Knight, *Following the Indian Wars*, 243–44; Mangum, *Battle of the Rosebud*, 91–93.

17. Crook to AAG, MilDivMo, September 25, 1876, Special File—Sioux, copy in 1:383, George Crook Letter Books; Gray, *Centennial Campaign*, 212–13; Capron, Diary, 66; King, *Campaigning with Crook*, 54.

18. King, *Campaigning with Crook*, 57–58. The orders were those recorded by King for the Fifth Cavalry, but were essentially the same for every unit.

19. Crook to AAG, MilDivMo, September 25, 1876, Special File—Sioux, copy in 1:384, George Crook Letter Books; King, *Campaigning with Crook*, 73–75, 79; Bourke, *On the Border with Crook*, 352–56.

20. King to Rufus King, August 18, 1876, King Collection, Archives Division, State Historical Society of Wisconsin, Madison.

21. Finerty, *War-Path and Bivouac*, 255–56.

22. Schuyler to George Washington Schuyler, November 1, 1876, Schuyler Papers, WS 87.

23. Bourke, *On the Border*, 357–59.

24. Crook to AAG, MilDivMo, September 25, 1876, Special File—Sioux, copy in 1:384, George Crook Letter Book; Robinson, *A Good Year to Die*, 241–42.

25. Finerty, *War-Path and Bivouac*, 275–76.

26. Capron, Diary, 102; Greene, *Slim Buttes*, 37–38.

27. Bourke, *On the Border,* 367–68; Carr to Mary Carr, September 8, 1876, Carr Papers; Greene, *Slim Buttes,* 42; "water and tightened belts": Schuyler to George Washington Schuyler, November 1, 1876, Schuyler Papers, WS 87.

28. Schuyler to George Washington Schuyler, November 1, 1876, Schuyler Papers, WS 87.

29. Greene, *Slim Buttes,* 46–48; Mills to Lt. George F. Chase, battalion adjutant, Third Cavalry, September 8, 1876, reprinted in Mills, *My Story,* 428; Utley, *The Lance and the Shield,* 166.

30. Bourke, *On the Border,* 368; Greene, *Slim Buttes,* 66–68.

31. "ought to be hung": Carr to Mary Carr, September 8, 1876; "brought to trial": Carr to Mary Carr, September 25, 1876—both in Carr Papers.

32. Letter by "Mac," September 17, 1876, in *Ellis County Star,* October 12, 1876, reprinted in Dobak, "Yellow-Leg Journalists," 105.

33. King, *Campaigning with Crook,* 158–59.

34. Bourke, Diary, 9:868; King, "Address by General Charles King," 419; Finerty, *War-Path and Bivouac,* 280–81.

35. Schuyler to George Washington Schuyler, November 1, 1876, Schuyler Papers, WS 87. Charley White, a crony of Buffalo Bill Cody, had joined the expedition with Cody earlier in the summer. Cody accompanied Merritt and the Fifth Cavalry to join Crook's march, but departed after Crook linked up with Terry. The official reason was theatrical commitments in the East, but in fact, Cody was disgusted with Terry's inept leadership (see Greene, *Slim Buttes,* 29–30). White remained with Crook until his death at Slim Buttes. The nickname "Buffalo Chips" was bestowed by Sheridan, "Chips" being a sanitized version of the stronger epithet Sheridan supposedly used.

36. Bourke, Diary, 9:871 ff., and *On the Border,* 371; Robinson, *A Good Year to Die,* 251–53, 262–63; Greene, *Slim Buttes,* 69; Schuyler to George Washington Schuyler, November 1, 1876, Schuyler Papers, WS 87; King to "Dear Mother," November 12, 1876, King Collection.

37. Schuyler to George Washington Schuyler, November 1, 1876, Schuyler Papers, WS 87.

38. Robinson, *A Good Year to Die,* 263–64.

CHAPTER 12: A BLOODY CAMPAIGN OF ATTRITION

1. Athearn, *William Tecumseh Sherman,* 311; Robinson, *Bad Hand,* 198–201; Buecker, *Fort Robinson,* 65.

2. Mackenzie's mental instability is a recurring theme in Robinson, *Bad Hand.*

3. Gray, *Centennial Campaign,* 259–61; Robinson, *A Good Year to Die,* 261; Lazarus, *Black Hills White Justice,* 89–91.

4. Hedren, *Fort Laramie in 1876,* 170–72; Buecker, *Fort Robinson,* 85–89; Robinson, *A Good Year to Die,* 264–66; and *Bad Hand,* 202–206; Gray, *Centennial Campaign,*

264–66; Grinnell, *Two Great Scouts,* 249–55; "The other bands": Crook to AAG, MilDivMo, October 30, 1876, Special File—Sioux.

5. Sheridan, endorsement of Crook to AAG, MilDivMo, October 30, 1876, Special File—Sioux, copy in Sheridan Papers.

6. Crook to Sheridan, October 24, 1876, Special File—Sioux; Bourke, *On the Border,* 387–88; Robinson, *A Good Year to Die,* 266–67.

7. *New York Herald,* October 2, 1876; Kime, *Powder River Expedition,* 65 n. 42. Crook's officers also reacted to Davenport's accusations. Bourke, who of course would have numbered among the "familiars and toadies," compared Davenport to "a whipped cur" (Diary, 5:621). In the 1890 Harper and Brothers edition of *Campaigning with Crook* (154–55), King described a correspondent identified as "Mr. D——," who was "wofully [*sic*] green, a desperate coward." Davenport threatened a libel suit, and Harper withdrew the book. Upon investigating, King admitted the allegation of cowardice was unfounded hearsay, and a new edition, also dated 1890, contained an apology. The latter edition was reprinted in 1964 by the University of Oklahoma Press. Don Russell's introduction to the Oklahoma edition (xvii–xix) discusses the Davenport squabble, and King's apology appears on pages 145–46. Davenport got in his own licks, calling King's writings "trashy and ephemeral stuff" (Russell, *Campaigning with King,* 102). Davenport's dispatch on the Slim Buttes fight did prompt three officers, Lts. John Bubb, Emmet Crawford, and Frederick Schwatka, to call him a "Munchausen Reporter" (*Army and Navy Journal,* November 11, 1876), but they were responding to his criticism of Capt. Anson Mills, and did not mention his comments on Crook.

8. *New York Times,* October 11, 1876, reprinted in *Army and Navy Journal,* October 21, 1876.

9. Ibid. Crazy Horse was present at the Rosebud, but there is no evidence of any one chief assuming leadership during the fight (See Robinson, *A Good Year to Die,* 151–52).

10. Sherman to Sheridan, November 10, 1876, Special File—Sioux.

11. Robinson, *A Good Year to Die,* 282–84; Bourke, Diary, 14:1367–74; Grinnell, *Two Great Scouts,* 261–62.

12. Robinson, *A Good Year to Die,* 284–85; "best equipped and best officered": Bourke, Diary, 14:1374–80; Hedren, *Fort Laramie in 1876,* 171; Kime, *Powder River Expedition Journals,* 62, 69–70, n. 51; Bourke, "Mackenzie's Last Fight," 4. Cantonment Reno was renamed Fort McKinney in August 1877. The Powder River site was abandoned in June 1879, and the post relocated forty miles northwest near present-day Buffalo, Wyoming.

13. Robinson, *A Good Year to Die,* 283. The Dodge diaries of the Powder River Expedition, which are in the Everett D. Graff Collection of the Newberry Library in Chicago, were edited and annotated by Wayne R. Kime and published as *The Powder River Expedition Journals of Colonel Richard Irving Dodge,* by the University of Oklahoma Press.

14. Kime, *Powder River Expedition Journals,* 64–66.

15. Ibid., 72–74; Bourke, "Mackenzie's Last Fight," 9–11; quotes from Grinnell, *Two Great Scouts,* 262–63.

16. Kime, *Powder River Expedition Journals,* 75–76.

17. Ibid., 75–76, 75 n. 62. Dodge finally solved the problem by appealing to Capt. Otis Pollock, post commander, who closed Adair down.

18. Ibid., 78, 78 n. 67; Bourke, Diary, 14:1403–6; Crook to Sheridan, November 21, 1876, in Bourke, ibid., 14:1406; Bourke, "Mackenzie's Last Fight," 13.

19. Kime, *Powder River Expedition Journals,* 81–83; Crook to AAG, MilDivMo, January 8, 1877, Special File—Sioux. The Crazy Woman is sometimes called the Red Fork of the Powder River.

20. Kime, *Powder River Expedition Journals,* 84–85. Kime (84 n. 80) quotes John S. Collins, post trader at Fort Laramie, who remarked that a "good angel" seemed to look after Crook in some of his more foolhardy exploits.

21. Ibid., 85ff.; Robinson, *A Good Year to Die,* 299–300. Dull Knife was the name by which this Cheyenne chief was called among the Lakotas. To his own people, he was Morning Star. Dull Knife is used here because it is the more familiar name. After the fight, the surviving Cheyennes sought refuge with Crazy Horse who, because of his own strained resources, gave them only minimal assistance before asking them to move on. This ended the century-old alliance between the two nations. The Cheyennes then followed Crook's trail, scavenging what they could at the abandoned army campsites. See Robinson, ibid., 304–5.

22. Carr to Grace D. Carr, November 26, 1876. Carr Papers.

23. Quoted in Bourke, "Mackenzie's Last Fight," 44.

24. Ibid., 44; Robinson, *Bad Hand,* 221–22; Kime, *Powder River Expedition Journals,* 98. One trooper was buried on the battlefield, and five at the Crazy Woman camp. McKinney's body was sent to his family in Memphis, Tennessee.

25. Crook to AAG, MilDivMo, January 8, 1877, Special File—Sioux; Kime, *Powder River Expedition Journals,* 103–7, 135–36, 157; Robinson, *A Good Year to Die,* 305–6.

26. Robinson, *Bad Hand,* 232. The election and ensuing controversy are discussed in Hoogenboom, *Rutherford B. Hayes,* Chapters 16 and 17. Grant's term officially ended on March 4, which was Sunday. A strict observer of the Sabbath, Hayes scheduled the formal inauguration for Monday, and privately took the oath on Saturday night. See Hoogenboom, 294–95. Normally, Crook's personal letters addressed Hayes by his last name. After he became president, however, Crook leaned more toward addressing him as "General."

27. Schmitt, *General George Crook,* 192–93 n. 8; Mangum, *Battle of the Rosebud,* 9–10; Hedren, *Fort Laramie in 1876,* 215–17.

28. Miles is the subject of several works, not the least of which are two autobiographies, *Personal Recollections and Observations of General Nelson A. Miles* and *Serving the Republic: Memoirs of the Civil and Military Life of Nelson A. Miles, Lieutenant-General,*

United States Army. Among the recent biographies are *Nelson A. Miles: A Documentary Biography of His Military Career 1861–1903* edited by Brian Pohanka, and Robert Wooster's *Nelson A. Miles and the Twilight of the Frontier Army.* Miles's activities in the Great Sioux War are covered by Jerome A. Greene in *Yellowstone Command: Colonel Nelson A. Miles and the Great Sioux War 1876–1877.*

29. Quoted in Athearn, *William Tecumseh Sherman*, 314.

30. Robinson, *A Good Year to Die*, 323–24.

31. Crook to AAG, MilDivMo, January 8, 1877; Sherman to Sheridan, February 2, 1877, both in Special File—Sioux.

32. Sheridan to Sherman, February 9, 1877, Sheridan Papers.

33. Buecker, *Fort Robinson*, 90–92.

34. Robinson, *A Good Year to Die*, 326–31; Crook to AAG, MilDivMo, August 1, 1877, 1:408–9, George Crook Letter Books; *Chicago Tribune*, February 11, 1877; Bourke, Diary, 19:1885–88.

35. Bourke, Diary, 19:1879. The term "loafer" was used to describe Indians who had long since abandoned their old ways, and hung around the military posts and agencies looking for handouts.

36. Ibid., 19:1905–8; Buecker, *Fort Robinson*, 93–94.

37. Schubert, *Outpost of the Sioux Wars*, 16; Robinson, *A Good Year to Die*, 332.

38. Buecker, *Fort Robinson*, 98–100; Schmitt, *General George Crook*, 217; Crook to AAG, MilDivMo, August 1, 1877, 1:409, George Crook Letter Books.

39. Schmitt, *General George Crook*, 217–19; Schubert, *Outpost of the Sioux Wars*, 16–17; Buecker, *Fort Robinson*, 104ff.; Robinson, *A Good Year to Die*, 337–39; William Garnett's account appears in Clark, *The Killing of Chief Crazy Horse*, 93–94, and He Dog's account in the same book, 65–66.

40. Initially, it was thought that the Nez Perces would head south into Crook's jurisdiction, and he sent a battalion of cavalry and a battalion of Indian scouts to intercept them. The Nez Perces, however, turned north, remaining in General Howard's jurisdiction, and the impact of their movements on Crook's department was negligible. See Crook to AAG, MilDivMo, September 13, 1878, 1:417, George Crook Letter Books.

41. Schmitt, *General George Crook*, 219–21; Crook to AAG, MilDivMo, December 6, 1877, 1:411, George Crook Letter Books; quote from Crook to AG, USA, December 13, 1877, 1:412, ibid.; Robinson, *A Good Year to Die*, 339–40.

CHAPTER 13: "IT IS AN OUTRAGE"

1. Marchman, *Story of a President*, 23.

2. Ruby and Brown, *Indians of the Pacific Northwest*, 249–50; Schmitt, *General George Crook*, 221; *Army and Navy Journal*, June 29, 1878. The background for the Bannock outbreak is discussed in detail in Brimlow, *The Bannock Indian War of 1878*. Some government documents erroneously refer to the Camas Prairie as the "Kansas Prairie."

3. Ruby and Brown, *Indians of the Pacific Northwest*, 249; Brimlow, *Bannock Indian War*, 61 ff.; Crook to AAG, MilDivMo, September 23, 1878, 1:417, The George Crook Letter Books.

4. Crook to AG, MilDivMo, April 3, 1878, 1:413, George Crook Letter Books; Brimlow, *Bannock Indian War*, 65–66; Hutton, *Phil Sheridan*, 121.

5. *Army and Navy Journal*, June 29, 1878.

6. Ibid.; Ruby and Brown, *Indians of the Pacific Northwest*, 249–50; Brimlow, *Bannock Indian War*, 65–68; Schmitt, *General George Crook*, 221–22. Due to a typo, Schmitt gives the date of Crook's visit as April 1879.

7. Crook to AAG, MilDivMo, September 23, 1878, 1:418, George Crook Letter Books.

8. *Army Navy Journal*, July 29, 1878.

9. Crook to AAG, MilDivMo, July 17, 1878, 1:415, George Crook Letter Books; Schmitt, *General George Crook*, 222; Brimlow, *Bannock Indian War*, 98.

10. Bourke, Diary, 23:34–35; Crook to Hayes, June 16, 1878; Crook to Hayes (second telegram), June 16, 1878; Headquarters, Department of the Platte, General Orders No. 8, July 17, 1878, copies in Bourke Diary, 23:35–37.

11. Hebard, *Washakie*, 253–54; Dunlay, *Wolves for the Blues Soldiers*, 114. On May 21, 1887, President Grover Cleveland created a military reservation of 1,405 acres around the post that was maintained until March 30, 1909, when both the fort and reservation were turned over to the Department of the Interior. The fort was formally abandoned the same day, although some officers remained on post to close out accounts until April 7.

12. A couple of generations earlier, the Cheyennes as a people had split into two distinct national groups, Northern and Southern. Although they maintained contact with each other, the latter group had become essentially a southern plains people who were well acclimated to the Territory, but their Northern cousins found it unendurable. The only work devoted exclusively to the outbreak is Mari Sandoz's well-written but somewhat romanticized and fictionalized account, *Cheyenne Autumn*.

13. Grinnell, *Fighting Cheyennes*, 398 ff.; Schmitt, *General George Crook*, 223; Buecker, *Fort Robinson*, 129; Crook to AAG, MilDivMo, January 22, 1879, 1:422, George Crook Letter Books. Grinnell and Sandoz downplay the Cheyenne depredations in Kansas, indicating that whatever raiding took place was prompted by necessity, and that killings were largely in self-defense. There is a substantial amount of evidence, however, that much of the pillage was wanton. Buecker suggests that the Cheyennes were randomly striking back at the white culture that had caused so much of their suffering.

14. Crook to Webb C. Hayes, September 14, 1878, Webb C. Hayes Papers, Rutherford B. Hayes Library, Crook Collection.

15. Quotes from Crook to AAG, MilDivMo, January 22, 1879, 1:421–22, George Crook Letter Books, ibid.; Schmitt, *General George Crook*, 223–24; Grinnell, *Fighting*

Cheyennes, 414–17; Schubert, *Outpost of the Sioux Wars,* 19–20; Buecker, *Fort Robinson,* 134–35; Sandoz, *Cheyenne Autumn,* 118–19.

16. Crook to AAG, MilDivMo, January 22, 1879, 1:422, George Crook Letter Books; R. Williams, AAG, Platte to Commanding Officer, Camp Robinson, December 20, 1878, copy in Bourke, Diary, 27:192; Wessells to AAG, Platte, December 24, 1878, ibid., 193; Crook to AAG, MilDivMo, December 20, 1878, ibid., 191–92; Wessells to AAG, Platte, December 26, 1878, ibid., 194–95; Crook to MilDivMo, December 24, 1878, ibid., 193–94; Grinnell, *Fighting Cheyennes,* 418; Buecker, *Fort Robinson,* 136–37.

17. Williams to Wessells, December 30, 1878, copy in Bourke, Diary, 27:197; Wessells to AAG, Platte, January 3, 1879, ibid., 197; Wessells to AAG, Platte, January 5, 1879, ibid., 198–99; Buecker, *Fort Robinson,* 139–40.

18. Crook to AAG, MilDivMo, September 27, 1879 (annual report), 1:433, George Crook Letter Books.

19. Crook to Sheridan, January 6, 1879, copy in Bourke, Diary, 27:199.

20. Grinnell, *Fighting Cheyennes,* 420–21; Buecker, *Fort Robinson,* 123; Crook to AAG, MilDivMo, January 22, 1879, 1:423, George Crook Letter Books; Sheridan to Crook, January 7, 1879, copy in Bourke, Diary, 27:200–201; Wessells to Crook, January 10, 1879, ibid, 201; Wessells to Crook, January 11, 1879, ibid., 202; Wessells to Crook, January 12, 1879, ibid., 203; Crook to Wessells, January 14, 1879, ibid., 205.

21. *Chicago Times,* January 17, 1879; Schuyler to Crook, February 1, 1879, copy in Bourke, Diary, 27:208–9; Crook to Sheridan, January 18, 1878 [*sic*], ibid., 210.

22. Grinnell, *Fighting Cheyennes,* 412–13; Wooster, *Nelson A. Miles and the Twilight of the Frontier Army,* 127; Miles, *Personal Recollections,* 1:306.

23. Buecker, *Fort Robinson,* 147; Grinnell, *Fighting Cheyennes,* 426–27.

24. Sheridan to Sherman, January 22, 1879, Sheridan Papers.

25. Ibid.

26. Sandoz, *Cheyenne Autumn,* 240.

27. Crook to AAG, MilDivMo, September 27, 1879 (annual report), 1:434–35, George Crook Letter Books.

28. Schmitt, *General George Crook,* 226–27; Williams to AAG, MilDivMo, October 4, 1879, RG 393, Special File, Military Division of the Missouri, White River Utes, 1879, hereafter cited as "Special File—Utes"; Williams to Commanding Officer, Fort Fred Steele, Wyoming, September 16, 1879, ibid.

29. Schmitt, *General George Crook,* 226–27; Williams to Crook, September 30, 1879; Williams to Crook, October 1, 1879; Crook to Sheridan, October 3, 1879; Williams to AAG, MilDivMo, October 4, 1879; Williams to Sheridan, October 8, 1879; Crook to Sheridan, October 10, 1879, Crook to Sheridan, October 10, 1879 (second telegram), all in Special File—Utes. An eyewitness account of the Thornburgh expedition and fight at Milk River was written by Capt. J. S. Payne, Fifth Cavalry, entitled "Incidents of the Recent Campaign Against the Utes," in *The United Service* magazine.

30. Schmitt, *General George Crook,* 227–28; Crook to Sheridan, October 16, 1879, Special File—Utes.

31. Crook to Tibbles, June 19, 1879, *New York Tribune,* October 10, 1879, copy also in Bourke, Diary, 29:26–37.

32. Tibbles to The Editor of the Tribune, October 4, 1879, *New York Tribune,* October 10, 1879.

33. Crook to AAG, MilDivMo, October 25, 1879; Crook to AAG, MilDivMo, October 29, 1879, both in Special File—Utes.

34. Schmitt, *General George Crook,* 228–30.

CHAPTER 14: THE PONCA AFFAIR

1. Porter, *Paper Medicine Man,* 316 n. 19.

2. Ibid., 66

3. Bourke, *On the Border,* 437.

4. Although the Great Sioux Reservation was established in Dakota Territory and did not extend into Nebraska, the line separating Nebraska and Dakota was not clearly established. This led to confusion as to the exact location of various Indian agencies and reservation lands until 1874, when the boundary was surveyed. The survey placed most of the Ponca lands on the Nebraska side. See Buecker, *Fort Robinson,* 22–23.

5. Mathes, "Helen Hunt Jackson and the Campaign for Ponca Restitution, 1880–1881," 26–27; Howard, *The Ponca Tribe,* 33–36; Hoogenboom, *Rutherford B. Hayes,* 450–52; Clark, "Ponca Publicity," 495–95; Mardock, *Reformers and the American Indian,* 169; Tibbles, *Standing Bear and the Ponca Chiefs,* 16.

6. Tibbles's life is discussed in Kay Graber's introduction to Tibbles, *Standing Bear and the Ponca Chiefs,* xii, and in his autobiography, *Buckskin and Blanket Days.*

7. Bourke, Diary, 25:75–77; Tibbles, *Standing Bear and the Ponca Chiefs,* 28–32.

8. Letter from E. H. E. Jameson, Baptist Church, et. al., to Schurz, March 31, 1879, reprinted in Tibbles, *Standing Bear and the Ponca Chiefs,* 28.

9. Tibbles, *Buckskin and Blanket Days,* 193–96.

10. Ibid., 194, and *Standing Bear and the Ponca Chiefs,* 141–42; King, "A Better Way," 244–45.

11. Tibbles, *Standing Bear and the Ponca Chiefs,* 32–33; Bourke, *On the Border,* 427.

12. Mardock, *Reformers and the Indian,* 173; Lazarus, *Black Hills White Justice,* 89. The concentration policy and the involvement of the humanitarians are discussed in Priest, *Uncle Sam's Stepchildren,* Chapter 1.

13. King, "A Better Way," 247; Tibbles, *Buckskin and Blanket Days,* 199–200, and *Standing Bear and the Ponca Chiefs,* 34–36. The petition and replies by General Crook as defendant on behalf of the government are reprinted in *Standing Bear and the Ponca Chiefs,* 36–45.

14. Hayt to Schurz, April 10, 1879, reprinted in Tibbles, *Standing Bear and the Ponca Chiefs,* 46–49.

15. Tibbles, ibid., 49–52.

16. Ibid., 44–45; King, "A Better Way," 248.

17. Tibbles, *Buckskin and Blanket Days,* 201–2.

18. Tibbles, *Standing Bear and the Ponca Chiefs,* 108–11.

19. Mardock, *Reformers and the American Indian,* 174; Schurz to Helen Hunt Jackson, January 17, 1880, in Bancroft, *Speeches, Correspondence and Political Papers,* 3:496–99.

20. Mathes, *Helen Hunt Jackson,* 21; Jackson to William Hayes Ward, January 27, 1880, in Mathes, *Indian Reform Letters,* 89. Besides Tibbles, Standing Bear was accompanied by the daughter of an Omaha chief, Susette La Flesche, also known as Bright Eyes, whom the widowed Tibbles married in 1881.

21. Schurz to Edward Atkinson, November 28, 1879, in Bancroft, *Speeches, Correspondence and Political Papers,* 3:481–82; Jackson to Henry Wadsworth Longfellow, March 2, 1881, in Mathes, *Indian Reform Letters,* 186; Priest, *Uncle Sam's Stepchildren,* 77–78; Welsh, "The Indian Question," 263–64. Helen Hunt Jackson was less concerned with Indian citizenship and suffrage than she was with the seemingly endless carving up of Indian lands and opening them for settlement. Initially, she staunchly supported Schurz. She turned against him with much misgiving and only after becoming convinced that he had lied to her concerning his views of the situation (see Mathes, "Helen Hunt Jackson and the Campaign for Ponca Restitution, 1880–1881"). Schurz expressed his position in detail in an article entitled "Present Aspects of the Indian Problem," in the July 1881 issue of *North American Review.*

22. Jackson to Longfellow, March 2, 1881, in Mathes, *Indian Reform Letters,* 186–87; Crook to Tibbles, June 19, 1879, copy in Bourke Diary, 29:30–31, and published in *New York Tribune,* October 10, 1879.

23. *Salt Lake Tribune,* August 10, 1880.

24. Schmitt, *General George Crook,* 235; Bourke, Diary, 35:678 ff.

25. Bourke, Diary, 35:695–97, 709. The Biblical quotation is Psalm 19:1.

26. Ibid., 35:711.

27. Ibid., 35:715, 734–35.

28. Mardock, *Reformers and the American Indian,* 174; Priest, *Uncle Sam's Stepchildren,* 78–79; Clark, "Ponca Publicity," 510–13; Hoogenboom, *Rutherford B. Hayes,* 453; Schmitt, *General George Crook,* 234; AG, USA to Crook, December 10, 1880, ACP—Crook; Crook, invitation acceptance, December 15, 1880, R. B. Hayes Papers, Crook Collection; Hayes, memorandum, December 18, 1880, U.S. Senate, *Message of the President,* Senate Executive Document No. 30, 5 (hereafter cited as SED 30).

29. Jackson to Dawes, December 10, 1880, in Mathes, *Indian Reform Letters,* 148–49.

30. Transcripts of the meetings with the Poncas of the Territory and Nebraska are in SED 30, 13 ff., and in Bourke, Diary, 38:933 ff. As Crook's aides-de-camp, Bourke

and Capt. C. S. Roberts, Seventeenth Infantry, were assigned secretarial and clerical duties. See also *Niobrara* (Nebraska) *Pioneer,* January 14, 1881, and King, "A Better Way," 253.

31. Report of Special Commission to the Poncas, January 25, 1881, SED 30, 5–6; Hayes to the Senate and House of Representatives, February 1, 1881, ibid., 4, reprinted in Richardson, *Messages and Papers,* 6:4584–86

32. Minority Report, SED 30, 6–13.

33. King, "A Better Way," 253–54; Hayes to the Senate and House of Representatives, February 1, 1881, SED 30, 4, reprinted in Richardson, *Messages and Papers,* 6:4584–86; Schmitt, *General George Crook,* 235; Howard, *The Ponca Tribe,* 37–38: Hoogenboom, *Rutherford B. Hayes,* 453–54.

34. King, "A Better Way," 254.

CHAPTER 15: ARIZONA: "JUSTICE TO ALL—
INDIANS AS WELL AS WHITE MEN"

1. Russell, *Campaigning with King,* 94–97; King, *Campaigning with Crook* (1964 Oklahoma edition), xix. Unlike many of Crook's relationships, the friendship with King persisted until Crook's death on March 21, 1890. A few weeks later, on April 2, King presented a paper, "Major General George Crook, United States Army," to the Wisconsin Commandery, Military Order of the Loyal Legion of the United States. The paper was later published separately. King continued to correspond about his service under Crook well into the 1920s. Paul L. Hedren, who edited *Campaigning with King* for publication following Don Russell's death in 1986, speculates that King may have wanted to write a biography of Crook, possibly with the general's encouragement (Hedren to the author, April 15, 2000; King Papers, various letters).

2. Schmitt, *General George Crook,* 237; quote from Oliver Crook, ibid., 238 n. 14; Crook to Schuyler, January 18, 1880, Schuyler Papers, The Huntington Library.

3. Crook to Schuyler, March 11, 1880, Schuyler Papers, WS 29.

4. Schmitt, *General George Crook,* 237–38.

5. Sacket to Crook, March 18, 1880, Schuyler Papers, Huntington Library.

6. Schmitt, *General George Crook,* 239; Crook to Schuyler, April 18, 1880, Schuyler Papers; quoted in Crook to Schuyler, April 28, 1880, Schuyler Papers, WS 32.

7. Schmitt, *General George Crook,* 239; Crook to Schuyler, April 18, 1880; Crook to Schuyler, April 30, 1880; Crook to Schuyler, July 25, 1880; Sheridan to Crook, July 27, 1880; Crook to Schuyler, August 8, 1880—all in Schuyler Papers.

8. Crook to Schuyler, December 6, 1880, Schuyler Papers, WS 38.

9. Schmitt, *General George Crook,* 240; Crook to Schuyler, March 20, 1881, Schuyler Papers; Crook to Schuyler, December 31, 1881, Schuyler Papers, WS 41.

10. Schmitt, *General George Crook,* 240.

11. Crook to Hayes, July 10, 1881, R. B. Hayes Papers, Crook Collection.

12. Delegates of the Territories of Arizona, Dakota, Idaho, Montana, New Mexico, Washington and Wyoming, Petition to the President, undated (received by the Department of War February 17, 1882); Sen. A. Sanders, Nebraska, to Arthur, January 16, 1882; various letters. All are in ACP—Crook.

13. Crook to Webb Hayes, December 14, 1881, and January 17, 1882, Webb C. Hayes Papers, Crook Collection.

14. "To his Excellency The President of the U.S.," March 29, 1882, ACP—Crook.

15. Walker to Maj. J. P. Martin, AG, Platte, March 21, 1882; Charges and Specifications Preferred Against Brigadier General George Crook, U.S. Army, Commanding Department of the Platte, April 22, 1882, with endorsements, all in ACP—Crook.

16. Thrapp, *Conquest of Apacheria,* 165–66, 231; Schmitt, *General George Crook,* 241–42; Athearn, *William Tecumseh Sherman,* 340; Bourke, *On the Border,* 437–38. Some writers, including Bourke, have maintained that the concentration at San Carlos was designed, at least in part, to accommodate corrupt contractors and agents. See Thrapp, ibid., 256–57.

17. The Victorio War is described by Thrapp, *Conquest of Apacheria;* Ball, *In the Days of Victorio;* Wellman, *Death in the Desert,* and other works.

18. Carter, *From Yorktown to Santiago,* 210ff.; Dunlay, *Wolves for the Blue Soldiers,* 170–74; Thrapp, *Conquest of Apacheria,* 217ff., and *General Crook and the Sierra Madre Adventure,* 17ff.; Ball, *Indeh,* 52–55. The military records of the Cibicu fight are contained in RG 94, Letters Received by the Office of the Adjutant General (Main Series) 1881–1889, File 4327 AGO 1881. The site is sometimes spelled "Cibicue."

19. Thrapp, *Conquest of Apacheria,* 231, 250, and *General Crook and the Sierra Madre Adventure,* 29ff.; Bourke, *On the Border With Crook,* 433; Schmitt, *General George Crook,* 243.

20. Crook, *Annual Report, 1883,* 2; Crook to AAG, MilDivPac, September 6, 1882, 1:68, George Crook Letter Books. Crook's letter books are arranged according to command rather than chronologically, so that the letters for the two tenures in Arizona are together, as are those for his two tenures in the Platte, even though he alternated between the two departments. The date of assuming command is in Crook, *Annual Report, 1883,* 1. Thrapp (*Conquest of Apacheria,* 256) puts the date at September 3.

21. Crook to AAG, MilDivPac, September 28, 1882, 1:69–70, George Crook Letter Books; Crook to U.S. District Attorney J. W. Zabriskie, October 8, 1882, ibid., 73–74.

22. Headquarters, Department of Arizona, General Orders No. 43, October 5, 1882, reprinted in Crook, *Annual Report, 1883,* 18.

23. Thrapp, *Conquest of Apacheria,* 257–58, and *General Crook and the Sierra Madre Campaign,* 122.

24. *Tucson Star,* October 24, 1882, reprinted in Bourke, *On the Border,* 438–40. Another aspect of the allegations of malfeasance was mentioned by Lt. Charles P. Elliott, Fourth Cavalry, who became provost at San Carlos in 1884. He contended that part of the reason for corruption on the part of the agents was to augment their

inadequate government salaries. See Elliott, "An Indian Reservation under General George Crook," 96.

25. Haley, *Apaches*, 356; Worcester, *Apaches, Eagles of the Southwest*, 264; Crook, *Annual Report, 1885*, 4; "The Government": Davis, *Truth about Geronimo*, 42–43; "Mr. Wilcox has to contend": Crook to Teller, February 23, 1883, 1:81–82, George Crook Letter Books; "against the villains who fatten": quoted in Bourke, *On the Border*, 445. Teller was the former senator from Colorado who had been involved in the Ponca case.

26. Crook to AAG, MilDivPac, September 6, 1882, 1:68, George Crook Letter Books; Crook, *Annual Report, 1883*, 2–3; Bourke, *On the Border*, 445–46; Worcester, *Apaches, Eagles of the Southwest*, 262–63; Davis, *Truth about Geronimo*, 31–32. Bourke states that 1,128 at San Carlos were capable of bearing arms, but that figure does not include Fort Apache. The combined figure of 1,400 is from Davis, ibid., 40.

27. Crook, *Annual Report*, 1883, 3; Thrapp, *General Crook and the Sierra Madre Adventure*, 108; Worcester, *Apaches, Eagles of the Southwest*, 264–65; Davis, *Truth about Geronimo*, 36–37; Davis, *Truth about Geronimo*, 38–39; "The Mexicans": Crook to AAG, MilDivPac, September 28, 1882, 1:69, George Crook Letter Books; Sieber quoted in Thrapp, *Al Sieber*, 262. Crook was discreet about the spy companies, mentioning them in one sentence of a four-page letter to divisional headquarters in 1883, and alluding to them in an annual report and in his *Resume of Operations against Apache Indians, 1882 to 1886*. See Crook to AAG, MilDivPac, March 28, 1883, 1:94, George Crook Letter Books; Crook, *Annual Report, 1885*, 14; and *Resume of Operations*, 4–5.

28. Crook, *Annual Report, 1883*, 4; Thrapp, *General Crook and the Sierra Madre Adventure*, 112–14; all quotes from Crook to AAG, MilDivPac, March 7, 1883, 1:83–87, George Crook Letter Books.

29. Simmons, *Massacre on the Lordsburg Road*, 88ff; Crook, *Annual Report, 1883*, 4–5; Robinson, *Bad Hand*, 309–10; Crook to AAG, MilDivPac, March 26, 1883, 1:89, George Crook Letter Books.

30. J. C. Kelton, AAG, MilDivPac, to Commanding General, Department of Arizona, March 31, 1883, reprinted in Crook, *Annual Report, 1883*, 23.

31. Crook to Major General Commanding Mexican Troops, Hermosillo, Sonora, March 28, 1883, 1:93, George Crook Letter Books.

32. Crook, *Annual Report*, 5; Thrapp, *General Crook and the Sierra Madre Adventure*, 119–21; Davis, *Truth about Geronimo*, 58–59; Bourke, *An Apache Campaign*, 14–16; transcript of interview in Bourke, Diary, 65:20–31. Jason Betzinez, a member of the Chiricahua band in Mexico, claimed that Peaches was a willing participant in Chato's raids, but grew homesick when the party reach Arizona. Far from escaping, he left the party publicly and with the good wishes of the others. See Betzinez, *I Fought With Geronimo*, 116–18.

33. The Mexican rank of *general de división* (major general) was more common than its U.S. counterpart, because the Mexican National Army of the nineteenth

century often was substantially larger than the U.S. Army. In addition to the conventional roles of defense and Indian pacification, the National Army had clearly defined political and internal security responsibilities, which required large units to be posted throughout Mexico. For that reason, a single Mexican state could have as many as three major generals handling various political, military, and security duties, while the United States might have only three major generals in a continental command structure that included every state and territory.

34. Quote from Crook to AAG, MilDivPac, July 23, 1883, reprinted in Crook, *Annual Report, 1883*, 25–26 (the letter also appears in 1:104ff., George Crook Letter Books; Thrapp, *General Crook and the Sierra Madre Adventure*, 123–25; Robinson, *Bad Hand*, 310; Bourke, *An Apache Campaign*, 12–13, 15–17, and Diary, 66:1–17.

35. "recognize that a literal construction": Crook to AG, USA, March 30, 1883, 1:98, George Crook Letter Books; "*no* military movements must be made": Sherman to Crook, April 28, 1883, 1:99, ibid.; "It is my intention": Crook to AG, USA, April 30, 1883, 1:99–100, ibid.; Thrapp, *General Crook and the Sierra Madre Adventure*, 126–27.

36. Quotes from Crook to AAG, MilDivPac, July 23, 1883, in Crook, *Annual Report, 1883*, 26–27; Thrapp, *General Crook and the Sierra Madre Adventure*, 128, 131–32, 137.

37. All quotes from Crook to AAG, MilDivPac, July 23, 1883, in Crook, *Annual Report, 1883*, 27–28; Bourke, *An Apache Campaign*, 44ff.; "Crook's Diary As Kept by a Member of His Command," May 9–11, 1883, undated, unattributed newspaper clipping pasted in Bourke, Diary, 70:77.

38. Bourke, *An Apache Campaign*, 71–72, 75–76; all quotes from "Crook's Diary As Kept by a Member of His Command," May 24, 1883, undated, unattributed newspaper clipping pasted in Bourke, Diary, 70:78.

39. Crook to AAG, MilDivPac, July 23, 1883, Crook, *Annual Report, 1883*, 28–30; Bourke, *An Apache Campaign*, 77–79; Randall in *El Paso Times*, June 12, 1883, clipping pasted in Bourke, Diary, 70:51.

40. "Crook's Diary As Kept by a Member of His Command," May 24, 1883, undated, unattributed newspaper clipping pasted in Bourke, Diary, 70:78. On November 22, 1883, Crawford reported that Ka-e-te-na brought in a white boy, but witnesses, including Judge J. M. Wright of Silver City, confirmed that he was not Charley McComas. "The boy supposed to have been Charley McComas they all say was never seen after the fight in the Sierra Madres & I believe what they tell is true," Crawford wrote. Shortly before his death in 1955, Sam Haozous, who was a boy in 1883, told Angie Debo that when the scouts attacked, they killed an old woman whose son, in a rage, smashed Charley McComas's head with a rock. Haozous said his mother and aunt found Charley, injured but alive, the following day and, fearing reprisal from the troops if they took him to Crook's camp, left him to die in the brush. Jason Betzinez, who was out with Geronimo at the time, said he heard essentially the same story at Carlisle Indian School from Chihuahua's daughter, Ramona, who claimed to

have witnessed the beating. The story, however, conflicts with an account given to Eve Ball in 1960 by Haozous's daughter, Ruey Darrow, who cited a family traditional story that when Crook's scouts attacked, the fleeing Apaches found Charley unconscious and dying of a wound from a stray bullet. Because he was beyond aid, they left him behind. Juh's last surviving son, Asa Daklugie, told Ball he understood Charley was killed earlier, on the return trip from New Mexico, when Chato's camp was attacked by the Mexicans. In his definitive study of the McComas affair, Marc Simmons points out that Charley's body was never found, but there are no confirmed reports that he was alive after the fight with Crook's scouts. So whether he died or lived to reach adulthood is a matter of pure speculation. See Crawford to Crook, November 22, 1883, Crook Collection, Miscellaneous Letters, R. B. Hayes Papers; Debo, *Geronimo,* 189–90; Betzinez, *I Fought with Geronimo,* 118–20; Ball, *Indeh,* 51; Simmons, *Massacre on the Lordsburg Road,* 180ff.

41. *Boston Globe,* May 27, 1883. Brig. Gen. E. R. S. Canby was murdered by Modoc Indians during a peace parley on March 10, 1873. He was the only U.S. general to die in the Indian Wars. Custer was a general by brevet only, and had the active rank of lieutenant colonel at the time of his death.

42. *Chicago Times,* undated clipping in Bourke, Diary, 72:99–102; "was ushered in to have a talk with General Crook," ibid., 67:76; all other quotes from Crook to AAG, MilDivPac, July 23, 1883, Crook, *Annual Report, 1883,* 30–31; Thrapp, *General Crook and the Sierra Madre Adventure,* 155–58; Thrapp, *Conquest of Apacheria,* 290–91. Juh died accidentally near Casas Grandes in September 1883. One version says he was drunk and fatally injured in a fall, and the other holds that he suffered a heart attack on the bank of the Casas Grandes River and fell into the water. See Thrapp, *Juh, An Incredible Indian,* 35–36.

43. Clippings of news stories recounting receptions, and dinners, and interviews with Crook appear in Bourke, Diary, vol. 70.

44. Undated, unattributed newspaper clipping in Bourke, Diary, 70:78.

45. Heth to Crook, June 14, 1883; Sigel to Crook, June 18, 1883, both in Crook Collection—Oregon.

46. Crook to Topete, June 13, 1883, 1:100, George Crook Letter Books.

47. Crook to AAG, MilDivPac, July 23, 1883, Crook, *Annual Report, 1883,* 32.

48. Crook, *Annual Report, 1885,* 4–7; Schmitt, *General George Crook,* 248–51; Thrapp, *Conquest of Apacheria,* 293ff. Bancroft (*Works,* 17:571–71 n. 29) remarked on "a theory that in the campaign of 1883 Gen. Crook, through placing too much confidence in his scouts, found himself really in the power of the Chiricahuas, and was obliged to accept Geronimo's terms. I have not attached much importance to this theory, though the events of 1885–6 tend somewhat to give it plausibility."

49. Porter, *Paper Medicine Man,* 201–2.

50. Athearn, *William Tecumseh Sherman,* 341–42; Hutton, *Phil Sheridan,* 346–49.

CHAPTER 16: GERONIMO

1. Crook, *Annual Report, 1884,* 1; Thrapp, *Conquest of Apacheria,* 293–94.

2. Elliott, "An Indian Reservation under General George Crook," 96; Crook, *Annual Report, 1885,* 12, 14.

3. *Army and Navy Journal,* June 21, 1884.

4. Elliott, "An Indian Reservation under General George Crook," 96; Crook to Welsh, July 16, 1884, 1:158, George Crook Letter Books.

5. Crook, *Annual Report, 1884,* 1–2.

6. Schmitt, *General George Crook,* 251–52; "that either I be sustained": Crook, *Annual Report, 1885,* 8; Crook to AAG, MilDivPac, January 20, 1885, with endorsement, copy in ibid., 20–22; "and talking to Indians": Crawford to Crook, January 18, 1885, ibid., 23–24.

7. Chauncey McKeever, AAG, USA, to Crook, February 14, 1865, copy in Crook, *Annual Report, 1885,* 25.

8. "for the behavior of any of the Indians": Crook to AG, USA, February 19, 1885, copy in Crook, *Annual Report, 1885,* 9; "If General Crook's authority": Pope, endorsement, February 24, 1885, ibid., 10; "better to place new people in charge": ibid., 11; Headquarters, Department of Arizona, General Orders No. 7, February 27, 1885, ibid., 28–29.

9. Bancroft, *Works,* 17:572; Davis, *Truth about Geronimo,* 142, 146; Thrapp, *Conquest of Apacheria,* 310–11; Crook, *Annual Report,* 13; Debo, *Geronimo,* 233–34.

10. Porter, *Paper Medicine Man,* 204, 207–8.

11. Geronimo's life is discussed by Angie Debo in *Geronimo: The Man, His Time, His Place.*

12. Bancroft, *Works,* 17:572; Debo, *Geronimo,* 233–35; Davis, *Truth about Geronimo,* 146; Crook, *Annual Report, 1885,* 13–14.

13. Davis, *Truth about Geronimo,* 143ff.; Davis to Pierce, May 15, 1885, copy in Crook, *Annual Report, 1886,* 13. A band of thirteen women and children had been captured by the Mexicans while en route to Arizona, and Crook was negotiating with the Chihuahua government for their return. (Crook to Governor of Chihuahua, April 29, 1885, 1:185, George Crook Letter Books.

14. "It's nothing but a tizwin drunk": Davis, *Truth about Geronimo,* 148; Crook, *Annual Report, 1886,* 1.

15. Crook, *Annual Report, 1885,* 1; "The vigor of the pursuit": ibid., *Annual Report, 1886,* 2–3; Crook to Col. Egan, Clifton, Arizona, May 28, 1885, 1:198, George Crook Letter; Books, Thrapp, *Conquest of Apacheria,* 311ff.

16. Crook to Sheridan, March 29, 1886, reprinted in Crook, *Resume of Operations,* 10; ibid., *Annual Report, 1886,* 4–6. The action reports of the various field commands are found in the appendices to the *Annual Report,* beginning on page 13.

17. Crook, *Annual Report, 1886,* 6; Thrapp, *Conquest of Apacheria,* 334–39; Crook to AG, MilDivPac, January 11, 1886, copy in Crook, *Annual Report, 1886,* 21–24; Hutton, *Phil Sheridan,* 364–66; Wellman, *Death in the Desert,* 243–47. Wellman calls the leader "Ulzana." Most other sources say "Josanie," including Crook (*Annual Report, 1886,* 7).

18. Crook to Torres, January 11, 1886, 1:245–46, George Crook Letter Books; Maus to Roberts, January 21, 1886, reprinted in Crook, *Annual Report, 1886,* 54–58; Thrapp, *Conquest of Apacheria,* 340–42. Tom Horn later became a stock detective, and was hanged in Cheyenne, Wyoming, in 1903, on a dubious charge of murder.

19. Wooster, *Nelson Miles and the Twilight of the Frontier Army,* 141–43.

20. Porter, *Paper Medicine Man,* 209.

21. Bourke, *On the Border,* 479; Crook to Sheridan, March 29, 1886, reprinted in Crook, *Resume of Operations,* 10; "though tired of the constant hounding": Crook, ibid., 9.

22. Bourke, *On the Border,* 476; "Record of a Conference Held March 25th and 27th, 1886, at Cañon de Los Embudos (Cañon of Funnels), Twenty Miles S.S.E. of San Bernardino, Spanish Mexico, between General Crook and the Hostile Chiricahua Chiefs, First Day," copy in Crook, *Annual Report, 1886,* 72–76, hereinafter cited as "Record of Conference."

23. Bourke, *On the Border,* 477–78; Crook to Sheridan, March 26, 1886, reprinted in Davis, *Truth about Geronimo,* 198, and in Crook, *Resume of Operations,* 10.

24. "Record of Conference, Second Day," copy in Crook, *Annual Report, 1886,* 76–79; Bourke, *On the Border,* 478–79; Crook to Sheridan, March 27, 1886, reprinted in Davis, *Truth about Geronimo,* 199.

25. Hutton, *Phil Sheridan,* 368.

26. Sheridan to Crook, March 31, 1886, reprinted in Crook, *Resume of Operations,* 12.

27. "four or five Chiricahua mules, already saddled": Bourke, *On the Border,* 480–81; "filled with fiery mescal": Crook, *Resume of Operations,* 11; Crook to Sheridan, April 4, 1886, ibid., 17–18; Thrapp, *Conquest of Apacheria,* 346–47. Thrapp speculates that Tribollet might have been in league with the Tucson Ring to sabotage the peace.

28. Smith, *View from Officers' Row,* 169; Hutton, *Phil Sheridan,* 366; Sheridan to Crook, March 31, 1886, first draft in Sheridan Papers, final draft reprinted in Crook, *Resume of Operations,* 12.

29. Crook to Sheridan, March 31, 1886, reprinted in Crook, *Resume of Operations,* 13.

30. Sheridan to Crook, March 31, 1886, reprinted in Crook, *Resume of Operations,* 13; "a thousand men could not have surrounded them": Crook to Sheridan, March 31, 1886, ibid., 14; Sheridan to Crook, April 1, 1886, ibid., 15; "I believe that the plan": Crook to Sheridan, April 1, 1886, ibid., 16.

31. Hutton, *Phil Sheridan,* 367; Thrapp, *Conquest of Apacheria,* 349.

32. Porter, *Paper Medicine Man,* 209–10.

33. "under the terms directed by the President": Sheridan to Crook, April 3, 1886, reprinted in Crook, *Resume of Operations,* 17; "The present terms not having been agreed to here": Sheridan to Crook, April 5, 1886, ibid., 19; Crook to Sheridan, April 4, 1885, ibid., 18; Crook to Sheridan, April 7, 1886, ibid., 19.

34. Wooster, *Nelson A. Miles and the Twilight of the Frontier Army,* 145ff; Hutton, *Phil Sheridan,* 367–68.

35. Wooster, *Nelson A. Miles and the Twilight of the Frontier Army,* 148–50; Hutton, *Phil Sheridan,* 368.

36. Wooster, *Nelson A. Miles and the Twilight of the Frontier Army,* 159–60; Bancroft, *Works,* 17:573. On the same page, Bancroft referred to Geronimo's escape as a "misfortune, or blunder." Crook took exception, writing Bancroft that the choice of words "does not correctly state facts, and as I feel sure you would not intentionally do me injustice, I take the liberty of enclosing my official report of operations against the Apache Indians during the period of my last command in Arizona, which contains an accurate and succinct narration of events connected with the Indian troubles of the period." Upon reading the reports, he suggested Bancroft "will kindly make such correction as I feel I am entitled to ask from a writer of such prominence." Bancroft's reply, if any, was not located. (Crook to Bancroft, October 25, 1889, 2:33, George Crook Letter Books.

37. Ball, *Indeh,* 111.

CHAPTER 17: DIVISION COMMANDER

1. Crook, Diary, April 12–27, 1886.

2. Ibid., various entries, October–December 1886.

3. Ibid., December 18, 1886.

4. Ibid., May 23–24, 1886; June 17, 1887; August 27, 1887.

5. Ibid., various entries, October 1885–February 1886; January 6, 1887; April 3, 1888; November 29, 1888.

6. Bourke, *On the Border,* 359–60.

7. Schmitt, *General George Crook,* 196.

8. Kennon, Diary, entry for August 7, 1886, pasted on back board of diary.

9. Schmitt, *General George Crook,* 196; Mangum, *Battle of the Rosebud,* 92–94. Mangum lists errors committed in both the conduct of the Great Sioux War and the Rosebud fight itself to demonstrate that there was enough blame to go around.

10. Carroll, *Court Martial of Frederick W. Benteen,* i–ii; ibid., Exhibit A, 72.

11. Ibid., ii; letter in Kansas City *Times,* January 3, 1887, reprinted in Carroll, iii–vi.

12. Ibid., vi, 4–5.

13. Ibid., Exhibit A, 72–73.

14. Ibid., Exhibit A, 75–77; ibid., 18, 50–51

15. Ibid., 70; Crook, endorsement to proceedings, March 11, 1887, ibid., 71; Sheridan, endorsement to proceedings, April 9, 1887, ibid., 71; Cleveland, endorsement to proceedings, April 20, 1887, ibid., 72.

16. Schmitt, *General George Crook,* 268.

17. Ibid., 267.

18. Crook, "The Apache Problem," 267.

19. J. C. Kelton, AAG, USA, to Crook, March 8, 1887, miscellaneous letters, Rutherford B. Hayes Library, Crook Collection.

20. Crook to AG, USA, March 16, 1887, copy in Kennon, Diary, 62–63.

21. Schmitt, *General George Crook,* 267; Crook, *Resume of Operations against Apache Indians, 1882 to 1886;* "would prefer": Cleveland to Gen. R. C. Drum, acting secretary of war, August 23, 1886, reprinted in Welsh, *Apache Prisoners,* 24; Miles to Gen. Francis C. Barlow, January 18, 1888, Miles Papers.

22. Crook, *Letter from General Crook on Giving the Ballot to the Indians,* quoted in Schmitt, *Major General George Crook,* 269–70.

23. Frederick O. Prince, chairman, et. al. to Crook, February 3, 1887, Crook Correspondence, 1872–1890, Crook-Kennon Papers.

24. Schmitt, *General George Crook,* 268–71; Kennon, Diary, 17–18; Crook, Diary, February 23–28, 1887.

25. Reported in *Boston Post,* February 28, 1887, reprinted in Schmitt, *General George Crook,* 271.

26. Crook, Diary, March 1–3, 1887; Schmitt, *General George Crook,* 272 n. 7.

27. Schmitt, *General George Crook,* 272.

28. Kennon, Diary, 50–51.

29. Ibid., 78–79, 82–83.

30. Welsh, "The Indian Question," 265; Prucha, *The Great Father,* 209. Very good analyses of the Dawes Act are found in Paula Marks, *In a Barren Land,* 217–18, and Edward Lazarus, *Black Hills White Justice,* 106–9. Little, if any, thought has been given to another possible motivation—that in terminating communal ownership of tribal land, the government might have been attempting to destroy a great unifying force among the members of a particular tribe, thereby reducing the potential for uprising. Some years later, President Theodore Roosevelt hinted at the possibility, when he called the Dawes Act a "mighty pulverizing engine to break up the tribal mass." The British government implemented a similar program in Scotland following the Jacobite Rising of 1745. To break the power of the great Highland clans, traditionally the source of rebellion, Parliament abolished the system of communal clan land holdings by giving title to the chiefs alone, thus making them part of the British establishment.

31. Wooster, *Nelson A. Miles and the Twilight of the Frontier Army,* 166–68.

32. Miles to Cameron, April 11, 1888, Miles Papers.

33. Crook Oath of Office, May 1, 1888, ACP—Crook.

34. Crook, Diary, May 6–10, 1888. The dinner at the Calumet Club was hosted by Marshall Field and other prominent Chicago citizens. Besides Sheridan, the guests included former Secretary of War Lincoln. Although Crook estimated the combined wealth of the twenty-three guests at $40,000,000, he commented, "A nicer set of modest gentlemen it has never been my fortune to meet." Ibid., May 9, 1888.

35. Hutton, *Phil Sheridan,* 371–72.

36. Kennon, Diary, 131ff.; "I am glad you are getting along so well": Crook to Kennon, February 13, 1889; Crook to Kennon, February 22, 1889; Crook to Kennon, March 1, 1889; "to think the matter over": Crook to Kennon, May 4, 1889—all in George Crook Papers, (A24), University of Oregon. Kennon's book apparently never materialized, although he did contribute a chapter on Crook for an anthology about West Virginia in the Civil War, which was published in 1895.

37. Osborne, *Jubal,* 469; Schmitt, "Interview," 551–52. The account published by Schmitt is transcribed from Kennon's diary, 161ff.

38. Schmitt, "Interview," 551.

39. Osborne, *Jubal,* 470.

40. Schmitt, "Interview," 551.

41. Robinson, *Bad Hand,* 326–28.

42. Crook, Diary, week of January 19, 1889; Hoogenboom, *Rutherford B. Hayes,* 507; Crook to Hayes, June 29, 1889, R. B. Hayes Papers, Crook Collection.

43. *Chicago Herald,* reprinted in the *Army and Navy Journal,* February 8, 1890. The term *democrat* is used in its nineteenth century sense, which is to say egalitarian. In politics, Crook nominally was a Republican.

44. Crook to Hayes, April 25, 1888, R. B. Hayes Papers, Crook Collection.

45. Porter, *Paper Medicine Man,* 250–53, 254–55; Bourke, Diary, Vol. 91, n.p., entry for March 28, 1889.

46. Lazarus, *Black Hills White Justice,* 109–12; Schmitt, *General George Crook,* 283ff.; Prucha, *The Great Father,* 214–16; Utley, *The Lance and the Shield,* 276–78; Crook, Diary, August 3, 1889; Crook to Kennon, June 14, 1889, George Crook Papers, (A24), University of Oregon.

CHAPTER 18: THE LAST BATTLE

1. Welsh, *Apache Prisoners,* 5.

2. Porter, *Paper Medicine Man,* 225–28.

3. Welsh, *Apache Prisoners,* 5–6; Worcester, *Apaches, Eagles of the Southwest,* 313.

4. Welsh, *Apache Prisoners,* 16.

5. Porter, *Paper Medicine Man,* 229–32; Worcester, *Apaches, Eagles of the Southwest,* 314. An evaluation of *Ramona,* its impact and its shortcomings, is found in Chapter 5 of Valerie Sherer Mathes's *Helen Hunt Jackson and Her Indian Reform Legacy.*

6. Worcester, *Apaches, Eagles of the Southwest,* 314–15; Schmitt, *General George Crook,* 290–91; quote from Ball, *Indeh,* 138–39.

7. Porter, *Paper Medicine Man,* 254–55. Bourke prepared a lengthy report of the visit to Mount Vernon. Dated July 5, 1889, and submitted to the AG, USA, a copy is pasted onto the pages of vol. 93 of his diary.

8. Worcester, *Apaches, Eagles of the Southwest,* 315; Schmitt, *General George Crook,* 289–92. Crook's hunting trip was cut short when a soldier's rifle accidentally discharged, fatally wounding another soldier.

9. Schmitt, *General George Crook,* 292, Worcester, *Apaches, Eagles of the Southwest,* 314, 316; Wooster, *Nelson A. Miles and the Twilight of the Frontier Army,* 173.

10. Crook, Diary, December 25–26, 1889.

11. Crook to Secretary of War (i.e., Proctor), January 6, 1890 2:35, George Crook Letter Books; Schmitt, *General George Crook,* 292; Worcester, *Apaches, Eagles of the Southwest,* 316; Crook, Diary, December 28–30, 1889. The former Confederate governor of North Carolina, Zebulon Vance was a popular orator who used his talent to champion oppressed people. His most famous lecture, "The Scattered Nation," attacked anti-Semitism by citing Jewish culture and tradition among the foundations of Western civilization.

12. Schmitt, *General George Crook,* 293–94, 294 n. 12; Notes of an Interview between *Major General George Crook, U.S. Army,* and *Chato, Ka-e-te-na, Noche* and other *Chiricahua Apaches; Mount Vernon Barracks, Alabama, January 2, 1890,* 2: 39ff., George Crook Letter Books.

13. Schmitt, *General George Crook,* 293; Notes of an Interview between *Major General George Crook, U.S. Army,* and *Chato, Ka-e-te-na, Noche* and other *Chiricahua Apaches; Mount Vernon Barracks, Alabama, January 2, 1890,* 2: 40, George Crook Letter Books. This transcript of the meeting refers to Naiche by the usual "Natchez," not to be confused with Noche, who was another Chiricahua.

14. Notes of an Interview between *Major General George Crook, U.S. Army,* and *Chato, Ka-e-te-na, Noche* and other *Chiricahua Apaches; Mount Vernon Barracks, Alabama, January 2, 1890,* 2: 41ff., George Crook Letter Books. The Indians who visited Washington remarked on the irony of their being given government peace medals, then being shipped to internment.

15. Ibid., 48.

16. Crook, Diary, January 4, 1890; Osborne, *Jubal,* 469.

17. Crook to Secretary of War, January 6, 1890, 2: 35–39, George Crook Letter Books. The death rate is discussed in Worcester, *Apaches, Eagles of the Southwest,* 313–16, and Porter, *Paper Medicine Man,* 256. Tuberculosis, popularly called consumption, was only dimly understood in the late nineteenth century, and few considered the possibility of contagion.

18. Worcester, *Apaches, Eagles of the Southwest,* 317; Richardson, *Messages and Papers,* 8:5495.

19. Wooster, *Nelson Miles,* 157–58, 173; Worcester, *Apaches, Eagles of the Southwest,* 317; Crook to Kennon, February 5, 1890, George Crook Papers, (A24), University of Oregon.

20. Schmitt, *General George Crook,* 294–95; Porter, *Paper Medicine Man,* 261; "anything to beat me": Crook to Kennon, March 7, 1890, Crook-Kennon Papers.

21. Schmitt, *General George Crook,* 296; Crook to Kennon, January 12, 1890, January 31, 1890, and February 3, 1890—all in George Crook Papers, (A24), University of Oregon.

22. Schmitt, *General George Crook,* 295.

23. Crook to Kennon, February 5, 1890, George Crook Papers, (A24), University of Oregon.

24. "have trumped up a lot of charges": Crook to Kennon, March 3, 1890, Crook-Kennon Papers; "could be a very important witness": Crook to Kennon, February 3, 1890, George Crook Papers, (A24), University of Oregon; Porter, *Paper Medicine Man,* 236–37.

25. McClellan to Surgeon General, USA, March 21, 1890, ACP-Crook; Nickerson, "Major General George Crook," 35.

26. McClellan to Surgeon General, USA, March 21, 1890, ACP—Crook.

27. Bourke, *On the Border,* 487.

28. Ibid., 489–91; Hoogenboom, *Rutherford B. Hayes,* 513.

29. Wooster, *Nelson A. Miles and the Twilight of the Frontier Army,* 174–75; Pohanka, *Nelson A. Miles,* 185. Basically a humanitarian despite all his quirks and flaws, Miles changed his position on sending the Apaches to Fort Sill in response to a congressional plan to scatter them among military posts throughout the country in hopes that they would disappear as a people. See Worcester, *Apaches, Eagles of the Southwest,* 321.

30. King, *Major-General George Crook,* 20.

31. 51st Congress, 1st Session, S. 3257, March 25, 1890, ACP—Crook; 51st Congress, 1st Session, House of Representatives, Report No. 2596, June 27, 1890, ibid.; Schmitt, *General George Crook,* 306.

32. The anecdote about Taylor and the lieutenant is in Eisenhower, *So Far from God,* 35–36; the story of Crook and the correspondent appears in Hedren, *Fort Laramie in 1876,* 172–73.

33. Bourke, *On the Border,* 486.

34. Ibid., 487.

BIBLIOGRAPHY

—m—

GOVERNMENT DOCUMENTS AND PUBLICATIONS

Abbot, Henry L. *Report of Lieut. Henry L. Abbot, Corps of Topographical Engineers upon Explorations for a Railroad Route, From the Sacramento Valley to the Columbia River, Made by Lieut. R. S.Williamson, Corps of Topographical Engineers, Assisted by Lieut. Henry L. Abbot, Corps of Topographical Engineers.* Thirty-third Congress, Second Session, Senate Executive Document No. 78.Vol. 6.Washington, D.C.: Beverley Tucker, Printer, 1857.

Crook, George. *Annual Report of Brigadier General George Crook, U.S.Army. Commanding Department of Arizona. 1883.* N.d., n.p.

———. *Annual Report of Brigadier General George Crook, U.S. Army. Commanding Department of Arizona. 1884.* N.d., n.p.

———. *Annual Report of Brigadier General George Crook, U.S. Army. Commanding Department of Arizona. 1885.* N.d., n.p.

———. *Annual Report of Brigadier General George Crook, U.S. Army. Commanding Department of Arizona. 1886.* N.d., n.p.

Howard, James H. *The Ponca Tribe.* Smithsonian Institution Bureau of American Ethnology Bulletin 195. 1965. Reprint, Lincoln: University of Nebraska Press, 1995.

Richardson, James D., comp. *A Compilation of the Messages and Papers of the Presidents.* 11 volumes with supplements.Washington: Bureau of National Literature and Art, 1910-1929.

United States Board of Indian Commissioners. *Peace with the Apaches of New Mexico and Arizona. Report of Vincent Colyer, Member of the Board of Indian Commissioners. 1871.* 1872. Reprint, Tucson: Territorial Press, 1964.

United States Department of War. *Report of the Secretary of War, with Accompanying Papers Abridged.* Washington: Government Printing Office, 1869.

————. *Report of the Secretary of War: Being Part of the Message and Documents Communicated to the Two Houses of Congress at the Beginning of the Second Session of the Forty-fourth Congress.* Washington: Government Printing Office, 1876.

————. Office of the Adjutant General.

——. RG 94 2229 ACP 1882. Letters Received by the Appointment, Commission, and Personal Branch, Adjutant General's Office, 1871-1894. Crook, George. National Archives Microfiche Publication M1935 Fiche ACP 000017. Washington: National Archives, n.d.

——. RG 94, Letters Received by the Office of the Adjutant General (Main Series) 1881-1889, File 4327, AGO, 1881. National Archives Microfilm Publications 689. Rolls 36-39. Washington: National Archives, n.d.

——. RG 393. Division and Department of the Pacific, 1848-66. Letters Sent, vol. 4, January 1849-July 1865. National Archives. Washington, D.C.

——. RG 393. Department of the Pacific, 1854-1858, Letters Received. National Archives. Washington, D.C.

——. RG 393. Special File. Military Division of the Missouri. National Archives Microfilm Publication 1495. Washington: National Archives, n.d. As follows:

Roll 2. "Citizens Expeditions" to the Black Hills.

Rolls 2-4. Sioux War, 1876-77.

Roll 7. White River Utes, 1879.

————. *The War of the Rebellion: A Compilation of the Official Records of the Union and Confederate Armies.* 130 vols. Washington, D.C.: Government Printing Office, 1881–1898.

United States Senate. *Message from the President of the United States, Transmitting a Report of the Commission Appointed December 18, 1880, to Ascertain the Fact[s] in Regard to the Removal of the Ponca Indians.* Forty-sixth Congress, Third Session, Senate Executive Document No. 30. Washington, D.C.: Government Printing Office, 1881.

MANUSCRIPT SOURCES

Bourke, John Gregory. Diary. United States Military Academy Library, West Point, N.Y.

Capron, Thaddeus. Diary. American Heritage Center. University of Wyoming, Laramie. MS 1694.

Carr, Eugene A. Papers. United States Army Military History Institute. Carlisle Barracks, Pa.

Crook, George. Cadet Expense Book. George Crook and Lyman W. V. Kennon Papers. United States Army Military History Institute. Carlisle Barracks, Pa.

————. Collection. Microfilm edition. Rutherford B. Hayes Library, Rutherford B. Hayes Presidential Center, Fremont, Ohio.

————. Diary. George Crook and Lyman W. V. Kennon Papers. United States Army Military History Institute. Carlisle Barracks, Pa.

————. Letter Books. 2 vols. George Crook Collection. Microfilm edition. Rutherford B. Hayes Library, Rutherford B. Hayes Presidential Center, Fremont, Ohio.

————. Papers, (A24), University of Oregon. Eugene, Ore.

————, and Lyman W. V. Kennon. Papers. United States Army Military History Institute. Carlisle Barracks, Pa.

Dodge, Richard Irving. Diary of the Powder River Campaign, 1876–1877. Everett D. Graff Collection, Newberry Library, Chicago, Ill. MS 1110.

Halpine, Charles Graham. Papers. Henry E. Huntington Library and Art Gallery, San Marino, Calif.

Hayes, Rutherford Birchard. Diary. Rutherford B. Hayes Library, Rutherford B. Hayes Presidential Center, Fremont, Ohio.

Hayes, R. B. Papers. Rutherford B. Hayes Library, Rutherford B. Hayes Presidential Center, Fremont, Ohio.

Hayes, Webb C. Papers. George Crook Collection. Microfilm edition. Rutherford B. Hayes Library, Rutherford B. Hayes Presidential Center, Fremont, Ohio.

Johnson, Henry J. Papers. George Crook Collection. Microfilm edition. Rutherford B. Hayes Library, Rutherford B. Hayes Presidential Center, Fremont, Ohio.

Kautz, August Valentine. Papers. United States Army Military History Institute. Carlisle Barracks, Pa.

Kennon, Lyman W. V., Diary. George Crook and Lyman W. V. Kennon Papers. United States Army Military History Institute. Carlisle Barracks, Pa.

King, Rufus, and Charles King. Collection. State Historical Society of Wisconsin. Madison.

Miles, Nelson Appleton. Papers. United States Army Military History Institute. Carlisle Barracks, Pa.

Nickerson, Azor Howitt. "Major General George Crook and the Indians." Typescript. Walter Scribner Schuyler Papers. Henry E. Huntington Library and Art Gallery, San Marino, Calif.

Schuyler, Walter Scribner. Papers. Henry E. Huntington Library and Art Gallery, San Marino, Calif.

Sheridan. Philip Henry. Papers. Library of Congress. Washington, D.C.

BOOKS

Primary Sources

Andrew, Abram Piatt, III. *Some Civil War Letters of A. Piatt Andrew, III.* Gloucester, Mass.: Privately printed, 1925.

Ball, Eve, with Nora Henn and Lynda A. Sanchez. *Indeh: An Apache Odyssey.* 1980. Reprint. Norman: University of Oklahoma Press, 1988.

Bancroft, Frederic, ed. *Speeches, Correspondence and Political Papers of Carl Schurz.* 6 vols. New York: G. P. Putnam's Sons, 1913.

Betzinez, Jason, with Wilbur Sturtevant Nye. *I Fought with Geronimo.* 1959. Reprint, Lincoln: University of Nebraska Press, 1987.

Bourke, John Gregory. *An Apache Campaign in the Sierra Madre: An Account of the Expedition in Pursuit of the Hostile Chiricahua Apaches in the Spring of 1883.* 1886. Reprint. Lincoln: University of Nebraska Press, 1987.

————. *On the Border with Crook.* 1891. Reprint, Alexandria, Va.: Time-Life Books, 1980.

Carroll, John M., ed. *The Court Martial of Frederick W. Benteen, Major, 9th Cavalry; or Did General Crook Railroad Benteen?* N.p., n.d. (Bryan, Tex.: 1981).

Clark, Robert A. ed. *The Killing of Chief Crazy Horse: Three Eyewitness Views by the Indian, Chief He Dog, the Indian-White, William Garnett, the White Doctor, Valentine McGillycuddy.* 1976. Reprint, Lincoln: Unversity of Nebraska Press, 1988.

Cody, William F. *The Life of the Hon. William F. Cody Known as Buffalo Bill the Famous Hunter, Scout and Guide.* 1879. Reprint, Alexandria, Va.: Time-Life Books, 1982.

Crawford, Lewis F. *The Exploits of Ben Arnold, Indian Fighter, Gold Miner, Cowboy, Hunter, and Army Scout.* Originally published as *Rekindling Camp Fires.* 1926. Reprint, Norman: University of Oklahoma Press, 1999.

Crook, George. *Resume of Operations against Apache Indians, 1882 to 1886.* Omaha: n.p., 1886 (actually 1887).

Davis, Britton. *The Truth about Geronimo.* 1929. Reprint. Lincoln: University of Nebraska Press, 1976.

Eby, Cecil D., Jr., ed. *A Virginia Yankee in the Civil War: The Diaries of David Hunter Strother.* Chapel Hill: University of North Carolina Press, 1961.

Finerty, John F. *War-Path and Bivouac: The Big Horn and Yellowstone Expedition.* 1955. Reprint. Lincoln: University of Nebraska Press, 1966.

Frazer, Robert W., ed. *Mansfield on the Condition of the Western Forts, 1853–54.* Norman: University of Oklahoma Press, 1963.

Grant, Ulysses S. *Memoirs and Selected Letters: Personal Memoirs of U. S. Grant; Selected Letters, 1839–1865.* New York: Literary Classics of the United States, Inc., 1990.

Greeley, Horace. *An Overland Journey, From New York to San Francisco, in the Summer of 1859.* New York: C. M. Saxton, Braker & Co.

Greene, Jerome A., comp. *Battles and Skirmishes of the Great Sioux War, 1876–1877: The Military View.* Norman: University of Oklahoma Press, 1993.

Howard, Oliver Otis. *My Life and Experiences among Our Hostile Indians.* 1907. Reprint, New York: Da Capo Press, Inc., 1972.

Johnson, Robert Underwood, and Clarence Clough Buel, eds. *Battles and Leaders of the Civil War.* 4 vols. 1887–88. Reprint, New York: Thomas Yoseloff, Inc., 1956.

Kime, Wayne R., ed. *The Powder River Expedition Journals of Colonel Richard Irving Dodge.* Norman: University of Oklahoma Press, 1997.

King, Charles. *Campaigning with Crook.* With an Introduction by Don Russell. Norman: University of Oklahoma Press, 1964.

————. *Campaigning with Crook and Stories of Army Life.* New York: Harper & Brothers, 1890.

Mathes, Valerie Sherer, ed. *The Indian Reform Letters of Helen Hunt Jackson, 1879–1885.* Norman: University of Oklahoma Press, 1998.

McClellan, George B. *McClellan's Own Story: The War for the Union, the Soldiers Who Fought It; the Civilians Who Directed It and His Relations to It and to Them.* New York: Charles L. Webster & Company, 1887.

————. *Report on the Organization and Campaigns of the Army of the Potomac: To Which Is Added an Account of the Campaign in Western Virginia, with Plans of Battle-Fields.* 1864. Reprint, Freeport, N.Y.: Books for Libraries Press, 1970.

Miles, Nelson Appleton. *Personal Recollections and Observations of General Nelson A. Miles.* 1896. Reprint, 2 vols. Lincoln: University of Nebraska Press, 1992.

————. *Serving the Republic: Memoirs of the Civil and Military Life of Nelson A. Miles, Lieutenant-General, United States Army.* New York: Harper & Brothers, 1911.

Mills, Anson. *My Story.* 2d ed. Washington: Press of Byron S. Adams, 1921.

Schmitt, Martin F., ed. *Major General George Crook: His Autobiography.* Norman: University of Oklahoma Press, 1946. Reprint, 1986.

Scott, Hugh Lenox. *Some Memories of a Soldier.* New York: Century Co., 1928.

Sheridan, Philip Henry. *Personal Memoirs of P. H. Sheridan.* 2 vols. New York: Charles L. Webster & Company, 1888.

Simon, John Y., ed. *The Papers of Ulysses S. Grant.* Vol. 10. Carbondale: Southern Illinois University Press, 1982.

Summerhayes, Martha. *Vanished Arizona: Recollections of the Army Life of a New England Woman.* 2d. ed. 1911. Reprint, Lincoln: University of Nebraska Press, 1979.

Tibbles, Thomas Henry. *Buckskin and Blanket Days: Memoirs of a Friend of the Indians.* 1957. Reprint. Lincoln: University of Nebraska Press, 1973.

————. *Standing Bear and the Ponca Chiefs.* Originally published as *The Ponca Chief.* 1880. Reprint, Lincoln: University of Nebraska Press, 1995.

Welsh, Herbert. *The Apache Prisoners in Fort Marion, St. Augustine, Florida.* Philadelphia: Office of the Indian Rights Association, 1887.

Williamson, James. J. *Mosby's Rangers: A Record of the Operations of the Forty-Third Battalion Virginia Cavalry, From Its Organization to the Surrender.* 1896. Reprint, Alexandria, Va.: Time-Life Books, 1982.

BOOKS

Secondary Sources

Athearn, Robert G. *William Tecumseh Sherman and the Settlement of the West.* Norman: University of Oklahoma Press, 1956.

Ball, Eve. *In the Days of Victorio: Recollections of a Warm Springs Apache.* Tucson: University of Arizona Press, 1970. Reprinted 1994.

Bancroft, Hubert Howe. *The Works of Hubert Howe Bancroft.* 39 vols. San Francisco: A. L. Bancroft & Company and The History Company, 1883—91.

Boorstin, Daniel J. *The Discoverers.* New York: Random House, 1983.

Brimlow, George Francis. *The Bannock Indian War of 1878.* Caldwell, Idaho: Caxton Printers, Ltd., 1938.

Buecker, Thomas R. *Fort Robinson and the American West 1874–1899.* Lincoln: Nebraska State Historical Society, 1999.

Carter, W. H. *From Yorktown to Santiago With the Sixth Cavalry.* 1900. Reprint, Austin: State House Press, 1989.

Cullum, George W. *Notes of the Biographical Register of Officers and Graduates of the U.S. Military Academy at West Point from 1802 to 1867, Revised Edition, with a Supplement Containing a Register of Graduates to January 1, 1879.* 3 vols. New York: James Miller, Publisher, 1879.

Davis, Burke. *To Appomattox: Nine April Days, 1865.* New York: Rinehart & Company, Inc., 1959.

De Barthe, Joe. *The Life and Adventures of Frank Grouard, Chief of Scouts, U.S.A.* 1894. Reprint. Alexandria, Va.: Time-Life Books, 1982.

Debo, Angie. *Geronimo: The Man, His Time, His Place.* Norman: University of Oklahoma Press, 1976.

Downey, Fairfax. *The Indian Fighting Army.* 1941. Reprint, Fort Collins, Colo.: Old Army Press, 1971.

Dunlay, Thomas W. *Wolves for the Blue Soldiers: Indian Scouts and Auxiliaries with the United States Army, 1860–90.* Lincoln: University of Nebraska Press, 1982. Reprinted 1987.

Eisenhower, John S. D. *So Far from God: The U.S. War with Mexico 1846–1848.* New York: Random House, 1989.

Garrison, Webb. *Civil War Curiosities: Strange Stories, Oddities, Events, and Coincidences.* Nashville: Rutledge Hill Press, 1994.

Gray, John S. *Centennial Campaign: The Sioux War of 1876.* 1976. Reprint, Norman: University of Oklahoma Press, 1988.

Greene, Jerome A. *Slim Buttes, 1876: An Episode of the Great Sioux War.* 1982. Reprint, Norman: University of Oklahoma Press, 1990.

———. *Yellowstone Command: Colonel Nelson A. Miles and the Great Sioux War, 1876–1877.* Lincoln: University of Nebraska Press, 1991.

Grinnell, George Bird. *The Fighting Cheyennes.* 1915. Reprint, Norman: University of Oklahoma Press, 1983.

———. *Two Great Scouts and Their Pawnee Battalion: The Experiences of Frank J. North and Luther H. North, Pioneers in the Great West, 1856–1882, and Their Defence of the Building of the Union Pacific Railroad.* 1928. Reprint, Lincoln: University of Nebraska Press, 1973.

Haley, James L. *Apaches: A History and Culture Portrait.* 1981. Reprint, Norman: University of Oklahoma Press, 1997.

Hebard, Grace Raymond. *Washakie, Chief of the Shoshones.* 1930. Reprint, Lincoln: University of Nebraska Press, 1995.

Hedren, Paul L. *First Scalp for Custer: The Skirmish at Warbonnet Creek, Nebraska, July 17, 1876.* 1980. Reprint, Lincoln: University of Nebraska Press, 1987.

———. *Fort Laramie in 1876: Chronicle of a Frontier Post at War.* Lincoln: University of Nebraska Press, 1988.

Hoogenboom, Ari. *Rutherford B. Hayes, Warrior and President.* Lawrence, Kans.: University Press of Kansas, 1995.

Hutton, Paul Andrew. *Phil Sheridan and His Army.* Lincoln: University of Nebraska Press, 1985.

Jackson, Helen Hunt. *A Century of Dishonor: A Sketch of the United States Government's Dealings with Some of the Indian Tribes.* 1885. Reprint, Norman: University of Oklahoma Press, 1995.

King, Charles. *Major-General George Crook, United States Army. A Paper Read before the Commandery of Wisconsin, Military Order of the Loyal Legion of the Untied States, April 2, 1890.* War Paper No. 6. Commandery of the State of Wisconsin, Military Order of the Loyal Legion of the United States. Milwaukee: Burdick, Armitage & Allen, Printers, 1890

Knight, Oliver. *Following the Indian Wars: The Story of the Newspaper Correspondents among the Indian Campaigners.* Norman: University of Oklahoma Press, 1960. Reprint, 1993.

———. *Life and Manners in the Frontier Army.* Norman: University of Oklahoma Press, 1987. Reprint, 1993.

Lazarus, Edward. *Black Hills White Justice: The Sioux Nation Versus the United States, 1775 to the Present.* New York: HarperCollins, 1991.

Lewis, Lloyd. *Sherman: Fighting Prophet.* New York: Harcourt, Brace and Company, 1932.

Mangum, Neil C. *Battle of the Rosebud: Prelude to the Little Bighorn.* El Segundo, Calif.: Upton & Sons: 1996.

Marchman, Watt P. *The Story of a President: Rutherford B. Hayes and Spiegel Grove.* Rev. ed. Fremont, Ohio: Rutherford B. Hayes Presidential Center, 1988.

Mardock, Robert Winston. *The Reformers and the American Indian.* Columbia, Mo.: University of Missouri Press, 1971.

Marks, Paula Mitchell. *In a Barren Land: American Indian Dispossession and Survival.* New York: William Morrow and Company, Inc., 1998.

Mathes, Valerie Sherer. *Helen Hunt Jackson and Her Indian Reform Legacy.* 1990. Reprint, Norman: University of Oklahoma Press, 1997.

McPherson, James M. *Battle Cry of Freedom: The Civil War Era.* Oxford History of the United States. New York: Oxford University Press, 1988.

Millett, Allen R. *The General: Robert L. Bullard and Officership in the United States Army 1881–1925*. Westport, Conn.: Greenwood Press, 1975.

Osborne, Charles C. *Jubal: The Life and Times of General Jubal A. Early, CSA, Defender of the Lost Cause*. Chapel Hill, N.C.: Algonquin Books of Chapel Hill, 1992.

Palfry, Francis Winthrop. *The Antietam and Fredericksburg*. Campaigns of the Civil War. New York: Charles Scribner's Sons, 1882.

Pohanka, Brian C., ed. *Nelson A. Miles: A Documentary Biography of His Military Career, 1861–1903*. Glendale, Calif.: Arthur H. Clark Company, 1985.

Pond, G. E. *The Shenandoah Valley in 1864*. Campaigns of the Civil War. New York: Charles Scribner's Sons, 1883

Porter, Joseph. *Paper Medicine Man: John Gregory Bourke and His American West*. Norman, University of Oklahoma Press, 1986. Reprinted 1989.

Prucha, Francis Paul. *The Great Father: The United States Government and the American Indians*. Abridged ed. Lincoln: University of Nebraska Press, 1991.

Priest, Loring Benson. *Uncle Sam's Stepchildren: The Reformation of United States Indian Policy, 1865–1887*. 1942. Reprint, New York: Octagon Books, 1972.

Robinson, Charles M., III. *Bad Hand: A Biography of General Ranald S. Mackenzie*. Austin: State House Press, 1993.

————. *A Good Year to Die: The Story of the Great Sioux War*. New York: Random House, 1995.

————. *Shark of the Confederacy: The Story of the CSS* Alabama. Annapolis: Naval Institute Press, 1995.

Ruby, Robert H., and John A. Brown. *Indians of the Pacific Northwest: A History*. Norman: University of Oklahoma Press, 1981. Reprinted 1988.

Russell, Don. *Campaigning with King: Charles King, Chronicler of the Old Army*. Edited by Paul L. Hedren. Lincoln: University of Nebraska Press, 1991.

Sandoz, Mari. *Cheyenne Autumn*. 1953. Reprint, Lincoln: University of Nebraska Press, 1992.

Schubert, Frank N. *Outpost of the Sioux Wars: A History of Fort Robinson*. Originally published as *Buffalo Soldiers, Braves, and the Brass: The Story of Fort Robinson, Nebraska*. 1993. Reprint, Lincoln: University of Nebraska Press, 1995.

Schwartz, E. A. *The Rogue River Indian War and Its Aftermath, 1850–1980*. Norman: University of Oklahoma Press, 1997.

Simmons, Marc. *Massacre on the Lordsburg Road: A Tragedy of the Apache Wars*. College Station: Texas A&M University Press, 1997.

Smith, Sherry L. *The View from Officers' Row: Army Perceptions of Western Indians*. Tucson: University of Arizona Press, 1990.

Stackpole, Edward J. *From Cedar Mountain to Antietam August–September, 1862: Cedar Mountain—Second Manassas—Chantilly—Harpers Ferry—South Mountain—Antietam*. Harrisburg, Penn.: Stackpole Company, 1959.

————. *Sheridan in the Shenandoah: Jubal Early's Nemesis.* Harrisburg, Penn.: Stackpole Company, 1961.

Strobridge, William F. *Regulars in the Redwoods: The U.S. Army in Northern California, 1852–1861.* Spokane, Wash.: Arthur H. Clark Company, 1994.

Sweeney, Edwin R. *Cochise, Chiricahua Apache Chief.* Norman: University of Oklahoma Press, 1991.

Time-Life Books, Editors of. *Chickamauga.* Voices of the Civil War. Alexandria, Va.: Time- Life Books, 1997.

————. *Shenandoah 1862.* Voices of the Civil War. Alexandria, Va.: Time-Life Books, 1997.

————. *Shenandoah 1864.* Voices of the Civil War. Alexandria, Va.: Time-Life Books, 1998.

Thrapp, Dan L. *Al Sieber, Chief of Scouts.* Norman: University of Oklahoma Press, 1964. Reprinted 1995.

————*The Conquest of Apacheria.* Norman: University of Oklahoma Press, 1967.

————. *General Crook and the Sierra Madre Adventure.* Norman: University of Oklahoma Press, 1972.

————. *Juh, an Incredible Indian.* 2d ed. El Paso: Texas Western Press, 1992

Utley, Robert M. *Cavalier in Buckskin: George Armstrong Custer and the Western Military Frontier.* Norman: University of Oklahoma Press, 1988.

————. *Frontier Regulars: The United States Army and the Indian, 1866–1891.* 1973. Reprint, Lincoln: University of Nebraska Press, 1984.

————. *Frontiersmen in Blue: The United States Army and the Indian, 1848–1865.* 1967. Reprint, Lincoln: University of Nebraska Press, 1981.

————. *The Lance and the Shield: The Life and Times of Sitting Bull.* New York: Henry Holt and Company, 1993.

Vanderpot, Rein, and Teresita Majewski. *The Forgotten Soldiers: Historical and Archaeological Investigations of the Apache Scouts at Fort Huachuca, Arizona.* Tucson: Statistical Research, Inc., 1998.

Vandiver, Frank E. *Jubal's Raid: General Early's Famous Attack on Washington in 1864.* 1960. Reprint, Lincoln: University of Nebraska Press, 1992.

Vaughn, J. W. *With Crook at the Rosebud.* 1956. Reprint, Lincoln: University of Nebraska Press, 1988.

Wallace, Andrew. *Gen. August V. Kautz and the Southwestern Frontier.* Tucson: Privately printed, 1967. Galleys in the August Valentine Kautz Papers, United States Army Military History Instititute. Carlisle Barracks, Pa.

Warner, Ezra J. *Generals in Blue: Lives of the Union Commanders.* Baton Rouge: Louisiana State University Press, 1964.

Wellman, Paul I. *Death in the Desert: The Fifty Years' War for the Great Southwest.* 1935. Reprint. Lincoln: University of Nebraska Press, 1987.

Williams, T. Harry. *Hayes of the Twenty-third: The Civil War Volunteer Officer.* 1965. Reprint, Lincoln: University of Nebraska Press, 1994.

Worcester, Donald E. *The Apaches, Eagles of the Southwest.* Norman: University of Oklahoma Press, 1979.

Wooster, Robert. *The Military and United States Indian Policy, 1865–1903.* 1988. Reprint, Lincoln: University of Nebraska Press, 1995.

————. *Nelson Miles and the Twilight of the Frontier Army.* Lincoln: University of Nebraska Press, 1993.

ARTICLES

Primary

Abbot, Henry L. "Reminiscences of the Oregon War of 1855." *Journal of the Military Service Institution of the United States,* vol. 40, no. 162 (November-December 1909): 436–42.

Alvord, Henry E. "Early's Attack upon Washington, July, 1864." Military Order of the Loyal Legion of the United States, Commandry of the District of Columbia. War Papers 26. Read at the Stated Meeting of April 7, 1897.

Bourke, John Gregory. "General Crook in the Indian Country." *The Century Magazine,* vol. 41, no. 5 (March 1891): 643–60.

————. "Mackenzie's Last Fight with the Cheyennes: A Winter Campaign in Wyoming and Montana." 1890. Reprint, New York: Argonaut Press Ltd., 1966.

Conway, William B. "Talks with General J.A. Early." *Southern Historical Society Papers.* Vol. 30 (1902): 250–55.

Cox, Jacob D. "The Battle of Antietam." In Johnson and Buel, *Battles and Leaders of the Civil War* 2:630–60.

————. "Forcing Fox's Gap and Turner's Gap." In Johnson and Buel, *Battles and Leaders of the Civil War* 2:583–90.

————. "West Virginia Operations under Fremont." In Johnson and Buel, *Battles and Leaders of the Civil War* 2:278–81.

Crook, George. "The Apache Problem." *Journal of the Military Service Institution of the Untied States,* no. 7 (September 1886):257–69.

Early, Jubal A. "Early's March to Washington in 1864." In Johnson and Buel, *Battles and Leaders of the Civil War* 4:492–99.

————. "Winchester, Fisher's Hill, and Cedar Creek." In Johnson and Buel, *Battles and Leaders of the Civil War* 4:522–30.

Elliott, Charles P. "An Indian Reservation under General George Crook." *Military Affairs* 12 (Summer 1948): 91–102.

Imboden, John D. "The Battle of New Market, Va., May 15th, 1864." In Johnson and Buel, *Battles and Leaders of the Civil War* 4:480–86.

King, Charles. "Address by General Charles King, Given before the Order of the Indian Wars, Feb. 26, 1921." Reprinted in Mills, Anson. *My Story.* 2d ed. Washington: Press of Byron S. Adams, 1921: 409–27.

Merritt, Wesley. "Sheridan in the Shenandoah Valley." In Johnson and Buel, *Battles and Leaders of the Civil War* 4:500–21.

Parnell, W. R. "Operations against Hostile Indians with General George Crook, 1867–'68." In *The United Service,* vol. 1 (New Series), no. 5 (May 1889): 482–98; vol. 1 (New Series), no. 6 (June 1889): 628–35.

Payne, J. S. "Incidents of the Recent Campaign against the Utes." In *The United Service,* vol. 2, no. 1 (January 1880): 114–29.

Pettit, James S. "Apache Campaign Notes—'86." *Journal of the Military Service Institution of the United States,* vol. 7 (1886): 331–38.

Reade, Philip. "Chronicle of the Twenty-third Regiment of Infantry, U.S.A." *Journal of the Military Service Institution of the United States,* vol. 35, no. 132 (November–December 1904): 419–27.

Robbins, Harvey. "Journal of Rogue River War, 1855." *Oregon Historical Quarterly,* vol. 34, no. 4 (December 1933): 345–58.

Schmitt, Martin F, ed. "An Interview with General Jubal A. Early in 1889." *Journal of Southern History,* vol. 11, no. 4 (Nov. 1945): 547–63.

Schurz, Carl. "Present Aspects of the Indian Problem." *North American Review,* vol. 133, no. 296 (July 1881): 1–24.

Welsh, Herbert. "The Indian Question Past and Present." *New England Magazine,* New Series 3 (October 1890): 257–66.

Secondary

Clark, Robert Carlton. "Military History of Oregon, 1849–59." *Oregon Historical Quarterly,* vol. 36, no. 1 (March 1935): 14–59.

Clark, Stanley. "Ponca Publicity." *The Mississippi Valley Historical Review,* vol. 29, no. 4 (March 1943): 495–516.

Dobak, William A. "Yellow-Leg Journalists: Enlisted Men as Newspaper Reporters in the Sioux Campaign, 1876." *Journal of the West* (January 1974): 86–112.

King, James T. "'A Better Way': General George Crook and the Ponca Indians." *Nebraska History* 50 (Fall 1969): 239–256.

———. "Needed: A Re-evaluation of General George Crook." *Nebraska History* 45 (September 1964): 223–35.

Mangum, Neil C. "The Battle on the Powder River." *Yellowstone Corral of Westerners Hoofbeats,* vol. 13, no. 1 (Spring-Summer 1983): 16–18; no. 2 (Fall-Winter 1983): 4–6.

Mathes, Valerie Sherer. "Helen Hunt Jackson and the Campaign for Ponca Restitution, 1880–1881." *South Dakota History,* vol. 17, no 1 (Spring 1987): 23–41.

Stutler, Boyd B. "The Capture of Generals Crook and Kelley." *Civil War Times,* vol. 2,
    no. 6 (Oct. 1960): 24.

NEWSPAPERS AND PERIODICALS

Army and Navy Journal.
Boston Globe.
Cheyenne Daily Leader.
Chicago Times.
New York Tribune.
Niobrara (Nebraska) *Pioneer.*
Omaha Herald.
Salt Lake Tribune.
Silver City (Idaho) *Owyhee Avalanche.*

INDEX

Index